PARALLAX VISIONS

ASIA-PACIFIC:

CULTURE, POLITICS, AND SOCIETY

Editors:

Rey Chow,

H. D. Harootunian,

and

Masao Miyoshi

PARALLAX VISIONS

MAKING SENSE OF AMERICAN–EAST ASIAN RELATIONS

AT THE END OF THE CENTURY

Bruce Cumings

DUKE UNIVERSITY PRESS   *Durham & London 1999*

Acknowledgments

Some of the chapters in this book were first published elsewhere, although all have since been expanded and revised. Chapter 1 appeared in Masao Miyoshi and H. D. Harootunian, *Japan in the World* (Durham: Duke University Press, 1993), pp. 79–111; I am grateful to Harry Harootunian, Peter Katzenstein, James Kurth, Masao Miyoshi, and Immanuel Wallerstein for their helpful comments. Chapter 2 has been published only in Japanese, in the journal *Bungei Shunju*, "Symposium on the Meaning of War" (Tokyo, October 1996). Chapter 3 is unpublished, although it was first prepared for the Annual Meeting of the American Political Science Association, Chicago, August 1995, and was presented as a lecture at Stanford University in January 1997; I am grateful to Atul Kohli, Lisa Anderson, and Mark Peattie for their comments on it. An early version of chapter 4 appeared in Korean in the journal *Ch'angjak kwa Pip'yong* (Seoul, spring 1995), but is unpublished in English. Chapter 5 is a revision of my essay in Raju G. C. Thomas, ed., *The Nuclear Non-Proliferation Regime* (New York: Macmillan, 1997), pp. 207–41. An abridged version of chapter 6 came out in *The National Interest*, no. 43 (spring 1996), pp. 28–41. Chapter 7 appeared first in *The Bulletin of Concerned Asian Scholars* vol. 29, no. 1 (Jan–March 1997), pp. 6–26. Chapter eight is unpublished, although some sections appeared in my "Japan and Northeast Asia into the Twenty-first Century," in Peter J. Katzenstein and Takashi Shiraishi, eds., *Network Power: Japan and Asia* (Ithaca, N.Y.: Cornell University Press, 1997), pp. 136–68. I would like to thank J. Reynolds Smith, Miriam Angress, and Jean Brady of Duke University Press for their fine work on this book, and Cynthia Bertelsen for her superb work on the index.

INTRODUCTION

> *Parallax:* Apparent displacement, or difference in the apparent position, of an object, caused by actual change (or difference) of position of the point of observation.—*Oxford English Dictionary*

In the past decade sharp reversals have occurred in American thinking about Japan, Korea, and China—as Japan's economic prowess seemed to fade, as North Korea and the United States moved toward a new war only to discover a new relationship, as South Korea moved from brutal dictatorship to a budding democratic society, and as China increasingly replaced Japan as a perceived menace to American interests.

If these reversals seem clear, it is by no means clear that they represent the reality of shifting power relations. Rather, they seem to mark shifting points along a line of observation as Americans watched their own fortunes rise through a prolonged recovery in the U.S. economy and in the world competitiveness of U.S. firms, and as a young president sought to make his country a beacon of both market economics and liberal democracy as his justification for a surprisingly vigorous foreign economic strategy. In this book, I hope to link the shifting vicissitudes of international relations and political economy to the often incommensurable ways in which our thinking about that subject changes over time: I want to explain the reversals of meaning that trail along behind or advance ahead of the reversals of fortune. Each chapter of the book takes up an important problem—for example, the recent tensions between the United States and China or North Korea, or the way in which American specialists on East Asia have gone about their work—and seeks to move away from contemporary commentary toward a theoretical and historically informed understanding of the problem. The theory that I am most interested in for this book, however, is quite close to home: American liberalism.

In *The Birth of Tragedy*, Friedrich Nietzsche wrote, "When after a forceful attempt to gaze on the sun we turn away blinded, we see dark spots before our eyes, as a cure."[1] One of the leading American interpreters of Japan in the past decade has been James Fallows. He is also an exemplar of the liberal view of Japan. Without too much oversimplification, this view can be summarized as follows: Modern Japan (we can also substitute South Korea or China) is a successful market-driven democracy and a responsible member of international society—unless it is not. The simultaneous illogic and truth of this sentence calls up the mirrored gaze of the American liberal, a sort of partially occluded bifocal optic in which the clear, acute lens on the top locates something familiar in America's "near abroad" (which is to say, the whole world), whereupon the mirror lens on the bottom declares it to be liberal and therefore Good. Or, the clear lens locates something unfamiliar and the mirrored lens declares it illiberal and therefore Bad. With the demise of the Soviet bloc the liberal lens cleared dramatically; democracy and the market were everywhere—except in 1990s East Asia.

Fallows's recent book *Looking at the Sun* is a continuous series of back-and-forth glances between the Japanese (or East Asian) sun and the American spots on his eyes. He begins one chapter of his book with a story about finding an English translation of Friedrich List's *The Natural System of Political Economy* in a bookshop near Hitotsubashi University. He said it had taken him five years to find an English version of List's thought, and upon doing so he exhales his version of "Eureka": *"Friedrich List!!!"* He goes on to argue that List, not Adam Smith, was Japan's economic guru.[2]

Now compare Japan scholar E. H. Norman, who began a passage in his 1941 book *Origins of the Modern Japanese State* about Prussian influence on post-Restoration Japan by saying "it is a commonplace that Ito modelled the Japanese constitution [and much else] very closely upon the Prussian."[3] Or compare Karl Marx, who in a little-known 1857 essay, "Bastiat and Carey," noted that the only original American economist was Henry Carey, a follower of Friedrich List, who saw the United States as a late developing industrial power needing strong protection of its market and its nascent industries and who thought Harvard economists were hopelessly Smithian.[4] Since Carey's *Principles of Social Science* was widely read in Japan in the 1880s, perhaps Fallows ought also to exclaim "Henry Carey!!!" In a mere few sentences we have uncovered not a truth about civilizational "difference," but a circular argument that ignores capitalist similarity and the influences of temporal stages and international competition on industrial policy.

Fallows has many intelligent and useful things to say in this book, but he mistakes Japan's Western learning from the continent and from the Anglo-American realm for essential political, economic, and cultural difference.

Like many other analysts who conceive of places called "Japan" and "Korea" as separate and distinct from the American hegemonic realm, he gets the context of action and decision wrong, as I think will be clear before this book ends. Fallows has dark spots before his eyes, but he is by no means alone in this regard. A lack of historical knowledge and sensibility about American strategy since 1945 is quite common in the literature of American relations with East Asia.

A more formidable and in many ways more reprehensible account is that of Samuel Huntington, who conjures up a "clash of civilizations," in which a declining Atlanticist civilization embracing Western Europe and the United States meets a rising East Asia, which Huntington finds useful to divide into two: China and Japan, he says, represent separate and distinct non-Western civilizations.[5] This bifurcation would not occur to East Asian specialists, but it serves Huntington's purposes. Perhaps he expects Japan and China eventually to come to blows again, thinking that might be in the American interest. Or perhaps he just wishes to keep American troops out of East Asian battles, which they have not been able to win since 1945. Mainly, I think, he wants to replace George Kennan's containment doctrine with a new paradigm. Kennan's 1940s *realpolitik*, as we will see, obscured a similar preference for Western civilization and a corresponding disdain for all other cultures; Huntington's civilizational discourse masks a new *realpolitik* for the twenty-first century in which the West, as he conceives it (mostly through the lenses of 1950s modernization theory), will husband its remaining strength for a coming global confrontation—one in which it may or may not choose to fight.

Fallows and Huntington articulate what it is they do not like about East Asia, but they do not explore their own country and its responsibility for the world we all live in. To understand American interactions with East Asia requires first of all to know oneself, and to know one's native land. We need to grind our lenses, not our axes, so that we can retrieve the unseen and the unknown from the recent past. Only after that, the reconnoitering of the foreign. And then after that, a stance that displaces both the native and the foreign for purposes of observation. Nietzsche (such a fully Western, European man) put this point best:

> Let us be on guard against the dangerous old conceptual fiction that posited a "pure, will-less, painless, timeless knowing subject"; let us guard against the snares of such contradictory concepts as "pure reason," "absolute spirituality," "knowledge in itself": these always demand that we should think of an eye that is completely unthinkable, an eye turned in no particular direction, in which the active and interpreting forces,

through which alone seeing becomes seeing *something*, are supposed to be lacking; these always demand of the eye an absurdity and a nonsense. There is *only* a perspective seeing, *only* a perspective "knowing"; and the *more* affects we allow to speak about one thing, the *more* eyes, different eyes, we can use to observe one thing, the more complete will our "concept" of this thing, our "objectivity," be.[6]

Two works that successfully achieve this sort of perspective are Masao Miyoshi's *Off Center* and Roland Barthes's *Empire of Signs*.[7] Miyoshi, who made his scholarly reputation as a literary critic of Elizabethan novels and now writes about Japan (and the United States) with a rare insight born of rare experience, adopted a stance placing the scholar neither in his native country nor on the ground he studies but in a place "off center." This yielded a parallax view and a depth of perception essential to new knowledge about anything. Barthes used Japan not as a mirror to reflect back to the West what is good and true here and sadly lacking there (i.e., the eastward-gazing function of "enlightenment" since the eighteenth century), but as a system of difference to develop a radical critique of the West and its assumptions. Barthes applied an optic that offers another parallax view, a salutary reflection, to question ourselves. As he said, Japan afforded him "a situation of writing . . . in which a certain disturbance of the person occurs, a subversion of earlier readings, a shock of meaning." He continued, "Someday we must write the history of our own obscurity—manifest the density of our narcissism."[8]

In this book I have made a conscious attempt to take nothing for granted but to step back and cast sidelong glances at East Asia and the United States as a means toward understanding, toward getting at truth, and toward speaking truth to power. In many American accounts of U.S.–East Asian relations, so much about the American side is assumed, unspoken, implicit, taken for granted. Historians and other analysts of East Asia often suppose that their native country is transparent, known, a thing understood. For many years, however, I have thought that my country is difficult to understand. A deep, abiding, and often unexamined "consensus" is so rooted in the United States that it is not a matter for conscious reflection (i.e., it is a species of Gramscian hegemony), and therefore Americans conceive of themselves as people without ideology. A people that thinks its goals are self-evident and universal also has trouble grasping that it is bound by its own history and particularity. Benedict Anderson wrote that "no nation imagines itself coterminous with mankind," which suggests that the imagined community of the nation is finite in this sense.[9] But the minute he says it, it occurs that the United States might be the exception to that rule. In chapter 4, therefore, I will explore the American side of liberalism and democracy for many pages— before getting to East Asia.

Theodore White once wrote that practicing "Pekingology" was like watching two great whales do battle beneath the ocean; occasionally they surface and spout a bit, which is your only evidence about what the trouble might be. But American politics, too, is often like "Chinese" politics: you need to do some "Washingtonology," read newspapers carefully, watch the rise and fall of key figures, look for power struggles.[10] Yet to say these things runs deeply against the American grain. It violates our conceptions of politics, of history, of human action. It conjures up conspiracy theory.[11] A people with a built-in ahistoricity is ill accustomed to retrospective digging, to lifting up rugs, to searching for subterranean forces and tendencies. It is only among radicals of the Left and Right that one finds a passion for excavation, for first causes; a Nietzschean "predestination for the labyrinth" is alien to the American soul.

If the United States strikes a native as opaque and elusive, it is remarkably so for the peoples of East Asia. In late 1997 the South Korean press, for example, was full of shock at the peremptory way in which the International Monetary Fund, supported by the highest American officials, presumed to rewrite the rules of Korean political economy. This was followed by much outraged commentary about American perfidy in breaking a trust with an old friend, in dissolving the "blood alliance" (hyŏlt'ong) that had existed since 1950. Meanwhile, the average well-educated American knows next to nothing about Korea and couldn't care less if its economy is in trouble (they are more likely to applaud). Earlier in the same year, Chinese leaders were equally outraged to find themselves targeted by a Senate investigation as archconspirators in the 1996 U.S. presidential election campaign; but even the senator who made these charges, Fred Thompson of Tennessee, could not interest the broader public in his months-long inquiry. So it just died—a result that probably amazed Beijing as much as Thompson's original charges.

I will also argue in this volume that East Asia and the United States—utterly different civilizations to Huntington—share much in common and that there is much similarity in their modern experience (in part because so much of that experience has been generated by a strong American presence in the region). If we take Japan and the United States, for example, we find that both nations look at the world with a bifurcated stare, yielding in both nations a dialectic of "to the world" or "away from the world." In *The Liberal Tradition in America*, Louis Hartz identified this as the primary pattern in America's relationship to the world: the United States sets out to transform the world in the American image; this is followed by a predictable failure and a retreat into some form of isolation.[12] His is the best explanation we have of the curious welling up of 1990s-style isolationism amid a globe-ranging hypercapitalism. Hartz and Tocqueville understood that this was not a back-and-forth orientation to the geographic external world but an oscillation about the European world: the center of civilization, Americans ran toward

Europe (Anglophilia, Atlanticism, and "Europe First") or away from it (Anglophobia, the New Order for the Ages,[13] the frontier, and "Asia First"). For the leaders of American foreign policy since roughly the War of 1812, the Atlanticist gaze did not avert, spots did not grow on the eyes; instead, the gaze was soothing (if shaded by the British Navy), like watching a setting sun sink into the horizon on a lazy August evening (it is an old world; we are the new; patience is our virtue).

Curiously, Japan has a similar optic and a similar pattern of involvement and disengagement with the external world. Perhaps this is because island Japan and "island" America gather comfortably in the shelter of great oceans, with eyes and ears fixed on imagined threats and distant thunder, while the domestic order remains unperturbed and imperturbable (save for a civil war from time to time). Or perhaps it is because both the United States *and* Japan announce to the twentieth century a New Order for the Ages. Like the United States, Japan also had a choice between worlds: the dialectic was "to the West" or "to Asia"; liberal reformer Fukuzawa Yukichi coined Japan's version of "Europe first" (*datsu-a*, or "away from Asia") and has thereby warmed the cockles of liberal hearts ever since. And, of course, Japan has never lacked for "Asia firsters": nationalist Ishihara Shintaro, coauthor of the 1989 potboiler *The Japan That Can Say No*, got together recently with Malaysian Prime Minister Mahathir Mohamed to write *The Asia That Can Say No* amid much hyperbole about Japan's dangerously deepening economic position in East and Southeast Asia. Even more curious, both nations have preferred a West-first to an Asia-first orientation except for two disastrous expeditions (plunges into China at the Marco Polo Bridge in 1937 and the Yalu River in 1950), with each choice morally valenced by the liberal mainstream as "internationalism vs. nationalism."

For both the United States and Japan, this choice was between a new world (modernity as industrialism defined it) and an old world (civilization as Europe or China defined it). Japan's choice was much more acute, however, because it posed a completely unknown Western modernity against the long-standing authenticity of the sinic world order. Japan's "East" was China, just as America's "West" was England. Both are derivative civilizations and they know it (both embody certain elements of a barbarian periphery).[14] But the American remove from Europe was into a perceived wilderness, whereas the Japanese choice for Asia was a walk back into the woods toward a deeply known and revered civilization. European and American modernity was the sun upon which Japan could not gaze for long without seeing spots; China was the agreeable and familiar setting sun that one could contemplate with relative equanimity, even when it was the very red sun of Mao Zedong: after all, the sun reddens as it sets. (Only the Sun King of Korea discomfited Japan, owing to the mad fear that Kim Il Sung's North Korea was a risen sun whose people did "Japan" one better than the Japanese.)

Japan's nineteenth-century choice (Korea's and China's, too) was *not* between a Western international system and no system but between a Western system predicated on the sovereign equality of nations but seeking to subordinate Japan, Korea, and China and an East Asian international system of centuries' longevity predicated on the sovereign hierarchies of the Middle Kingdom but affording nearly complete autonomy to Japan and Korea. It is amazing to see how even the experts on late-nineteenth-century East Asia take the Western theory as the norm and cannot get it through their heads that there *was* an international system (and therefore a norm) in East Asia, that it had lasted for centuries, and that China, Japan, and Korea knew each other, cross-fertilized each other, and traded with each other, whereas in the mid-nineteenth century it was the Western system that was utterly new, deeply threatening, and entirely untried and unproved in East Asia.

After transcending the unequal treaties and the threat of direct subordination, Good Japan looked to find itself mirrored and admired in the hegemonic lens, a wish met by the British imperial looking glass of the early part of this century, as we will see, and by the American looking glass in the 1920s ("Taisho democracy"), and again from 1945 to 1970 (modernization theory). Since trade conflict began in the early 1970s, double vision has afflicted both Japan and the United States, but this is still merely double vision, a long and remediable stage before blindness. Oddly enough, Bad Japan also wants to see its reflection in the hegemonic lens—a dead giveaway that even the baddest of Japanese cannot avoid the measure of the hegemonic eye (something both John Dower and Akira Iriye have argued, in very different ways).

Today Americans also get sunspots in their eyes. Japan is assumed to have but one form of political economy, a state-driven mercantilism in contrast to American market capitalism, a form that seems to have spent itself in the speculative fervor of the "bubble economy"—only to migrate to China, which quickly replaced the Japan threat in the American mind. One would never know that the United States was more mercantilist than free trade oriented until the postwar period, and, as Mike Davis has shown in his *City of Quartz*, it was precisely the central state that provided the organization and the funds for the industrialization of southern California and much of the American West and Southwest.[15] Throughout this book I will therefore try to avoid distinctions between a putative "market-driven" capitalism and a "state-driven" capitalism; much of the existing analysis in this vein either chases its own tail or reinvents the wheel from decade to decade.

I will also make use of a world-system perspective, which can do for American self-knowledge what the study of America's role in the world did for a great historian, William Appleman Williams: "Williams discovering America, almost like Columbus," in Warren Susman's brilliant observation.[16] Williams reading America from the outside in, to put it another way. Global theory can help us locate what is similar about the United States and what is exceptional. Historians often take Louis Hartz's *Liberal Tradition* to be the grand text of American exceptionalism, but I think that gets things exactly upside down: like Huntington, Hartz was a *European* exceptionalist, that is, a devotee of what neo-conservatives exalt as "the West." European civilization is the only one they really care about. But Hartz also knew his country of birth very well. He had the idea that the New World was not Europe: to him the United States was a fragment and an implant that had only a partial understanding of the European project. A Lockean liberalism never fully known and understood—now there's an idea that can help us explain the genealogy of American relations with the rest of the world and the people who write about that subject, with their atheoretical empiricism, their (often unconscious) affinity for making the interpretations of American diplomats into their own, and their peculiarly American lack of connection with what European intellectuals think about. For example, a European intellectual named Marx, who wrote that America in 1857 was

> a country where bourgeois society did not develop on the foundation of the feudal system, but developed rather from itself; where this society appears not as the surviving result of a centuries-old movement, but rather as the starting-point of a new movement; where the state, in contrast to all earlier national formations, was from the beginning subordinate to bourgeois society, to its production, and never could make the pretence of being an end-in-itself; where, finally, bourgeois society itself, linking up the productive forces of an old world with the enormous natural terrain of a new one, has developed to hitherto unheard-of dimensions . . . and where, finally, even the antitheses of bourgeois society itself appear only as vanishing moments.[17]

Here we find the kernel of Hartz's idea that the United States was not so much "exceptional" as fully bourgeois: the most advanced capitalist society, spinning out its telos in a vacuum called North America in a time called the future. Fredric Jameson is correct to say that Marx understood the world market as "the ultimate horizon of capitalism," with the United States occupying that vista since the mid–nineteenth century (Commodore Perry "discovering" Japan in 1853, and so on).[18] It still occupies that horizon in the 1990s.

1

ARCHAEOLOGY, DESCENT, EMERGENCE:

AMERICAN MYTHOLOGY AND EAST ASIAN REALITY

This is how one pictures the angel of history. His face is turned toward the past. Where we perceive a chain of events, he sees one single catastrophe which keeps piling wreckage upon wreckage and hurls it in front of his feet. The angel would like to stay, awaken the dead, and make whole what has been smashed. But a storm is blowing from Paradise; it has got caught in his wings with such violence that the angel can no longer close them. This storm irresistibly propels him into the future to which his back is turned, while the pile of debris before him grows skyward. This storm is what we call progress.—Walter Benjamin

In the most general sense of progressive thought, the Enlightenment has always aimed at liberating men from fear and establishing their sovereignty. Yet the fully enlightened earth radiates disaster triumphant.—Max Horkheimer and Theodor W. Adorno

The breakdown of [the Enlightenment] project provided the historical background against which the predicaments of our own culture can become intelligible.—Alasdair MacIntyre

It is simply not true that capitalism as a historical system has represented progress over the various historical systems that it destroyed and transformed. Even as I write this, I feel the tremor that accompanies the sense of blasphemy.—Immanuel Wallerstein

How does it happen that serious people continue to believe in progress, in the face of massive evidence that might have been expected to refute the idea of progress once and for all?—Christopher Lasch

Setting aside an apocalyptic awakening of the neighboring San Andreas Fault, it is all too easy to envision Los Angeles reproducing itself endlessly across the desert with the assistance of pilfered water, cheap immigrant labor, Asian capital, and desperate homebuyers willing to trade lifetimes on the freeway in exchange for $500,000 "dream homes" in the middle of Death Valley.

Is this the world-historic victory of Capitalism that everyone is talking about? —Mike Davis

It is one thing for Walter Benjamin in 1940 to fear a storm blowing in from Paradise as the Nazis marched through Europe.[1] And it is one thing for Max Horkheimer and Theodor W. Adorno, aware by 1944 of the ultimate catastrophe of Nazi power, to conjure an Enlightenment project gone mad.[2] But it is quite another thing for American intellectuals, from neo-Marxists to petit bourgeois populists to Benedictine Catholics, to author influential books arguing (in shorthand) that (1) national development is destructive whether accomplished by capitalists or socialists, and we are both relatively and absolutely worse off than before the modern epoch (Wallerstein);[3] (2) South Boston offers more hope for our salvation than Cambridge (Lasch);[4] (3) the Pacific Rim paradise called Los Angeles, city of the American future, where Horkheimer and Adorno wrote their book in 1944, is a 1990s techno-cultural nightmare (Davis);[5] or (4) the new dark ages are upon us, and thus we await another St. Benedict (MacIntyre).[6]

We seem to be in the midst of a fundamental paradigm shift—propelled by economic decline, moral collapse, and the rumored death of Marxism—away from "progress." All one has to do to dispel this depressing intellectual scene, however, is cross the Pacific—to Shanghai, where construction cranes sprout like bamboo shoots, and growth speeds along at an annual double-digit clip, or to Tokyo, where the fabric of morality, national development, and urban civility are all intact, even if the 1990s appear to have dealt Japan a bad hand (the "bubble economy" has burst, but no one knows whether this is a fundamental problem or a passing one). In China and Japan, the trains run on time, kids think drugs are what you buy in a drug store, and Mom kisses Dad as he goes off to work. And if Marx is dead, no one seems to have noticed.

Had Walter Benjamin not been blocked in his attempt to escape the Nazis through Spain, he might have been carted up and down the United States as "the last European" (the fate he feared 1940s America held in store for him). At that time, the United States was certain of its morality, its urban civility, and its belief in eternal progress: it was springtime for the American Century. Not for Americans an angel of history who cannot distinguish progress from a heap of debris. Lasch's lower-middle-class populists were safely submerged in a self-confident New Deal liberalism—they were MacIntyre's good Catholics, "left behind" by secular progressivism and "modernization" or condemned to a populist lunatic fringe by social scientists in Cambridge. Instead of Davis's "city of quartz," Los Angeles was the city of dreams, just sniffing a new phenomenon called smog in the mid-1940s. (The only wonder is that Horkheimer and Adorno could have been so irredeemably pessimistic in the Los Angeles of that halcyon period.)

The epigraphs I selected to begin this chapter—and our brief tour of Shanghai and Tokyo—raise questions: Is this paradigm shift or provincialism? Are we witness to fin de siècle angst or declining industrial sectors? Does our time herald a new morality or merely the autumn of the American Century? Methodologically, if intellectuals no longer believe in progress, how can we think? How can we purge our minds of a "progress" that was the *point d'honneur* of Western civilization and that held much of postwar academe in its thrall (here, I refer to the proponents of modernization theory, the end of ideology, "New" Leftism, and rational-choice theory)?

Let us assume merely for the purpose of argument that Wallerstein's blasphemy is correct: the modern system is capitalist, its theory is progress, and that theory is wrong. Without the notion of progress and its corollary "opiate" (Wallerstein's term) of rationality, universalism, and a resulting "truth" known to modern man,[7] how are we to understand our world? If we accept Wallerstein's viewpoint, we must understand the Enlightenment, the French Revolution—even the Industrial Revolution—as mere moments in the rise and decline of the capitalist world system, or as a mere discourse (not his point) no more or less compelling than the Confucian doctrine that the golden age lay in the past, or the Buddhist belief that humans should not disturb the universe but live ascetically within it. Indeed, Wallerstein's third volume in his *Modern World-System* is essentially an historiographical polemic that seeks to deconstruct all the great modern moments save one, the sixteenth-century "big bang" in which the world system itself was created.[8]

The discourse of progress is inseparable from an industrial mode of production, which is its justification, its verification, and, from Wallerstein's point of view, its structural base. If we assume he is also correct here, we must search for a method that does not reflect an epistemology of empiricist rationality, progress, and universalism, yet that is also capable of understanding the mechanisms of industrial capitalism (which the Confucian or Buddhist worldview cannot).

My position is that an archaeology of the present and a genealogy of the past can provide us with a way of doing so: that is, I follow Nietzsche and Foucault for the purposes of *method* while taking no position on the implications of their thought for human morality for how we live.[9] Through an archaeology of the present we can *excavate* the debris gathering at the feet of the angel of history and poke around through the shards of lost worlds and lost worldviews, available to us moderns only as fragments.[10] (I hesitate to admit that this metaphor occurred to me when I was eating a Japanese breakfast that looked like the effluvia left on the beach when the tide ran out: a dead fish, some seaweed, and a few clams.) Through a genealogy of *descent*, we can avoid an epistemology of progress that so often defines the discipline of history. Finally, through a conception of *emergence*, we can hope to define those turning points when rumblings in the "nondiscursive" (power) detonate changes in the "discursive" (knowledge).[11] I will first seek to explicate a method that accounts for the discourse of U.S.-Japan relations and then examine the relations themselves.

GARY AND P'OHANG

To make the archaeological metaphor more vivid, we might imagine a Martian reconnoitering our world in the aftermath of a world-historical disaster that eliminated humanity but not human chattels: a terrible hailstorm of asteroids that darkened and cooled the planet for some years, like the one that some think eliminated the dinosaurs; or perhaps the effects of a yawning ozone hole; or simply a neutron-bomb holocaust. Our Martian would find all the people gone. Unable to read the books in the libraries, he would inspect sites of modern civilization in the way archaeologists excavate a site of antiquity.

Wandering today as if we were that Martian, we can witness the human wreckage and rust-belt debris of an old steel town like Gary, Indiana, existing in global simultaneity with the "vibrant dynamism" (to sample the progressive view) of P'ohang, steel city for the industrialization of the Republic of Korea. Paean to American decline and Korean advance?

On the Monongahela River near Pittsburgh is the great Homestead Steel Mill, site of a strike central to American labor history. It is now a museum—that institution we designate to be the repository of our archaeological finds. Paean to American decline?

In the 1940s, Pittsburgh was a symbol of American industrial prowess, as well as a headquarters of pollution. In the 1990s, Pittsburgh has neither steel nor pollution but has burgeoning service industries and is considered by yuppie trendsetters to be one of the "most livable cities in America." Paean to American progress?

In the 1920s, Gary had its own measure of tourism, its own admirable "lifestyle," its own avant-garde architecture, and a considerable measure of culture. "It had a settled air of community," to cite one source: thirteen movie theaters; eighteen hundred hotel rooms, making it the convention capital of Indiana; thirteen hundred retail stores; an opulent, bourgeois WASP West Side; a stable, working-class East Side; and two new, identical art-deco houses of city and county government sitting side by side.[12] Today, its empty, gutted, or shuttered theaters, hotels, shop fronts, and bourgeois homes, and its shattered human beings, surround the still functioning art-deco buildings of state. In the documentary film *Roger and Me,* the residents of Flint resent being placed three hundredth among three hundred American cities: "Haven't they been to Gary?" exclaims one Flintite. Paean to American decline?

Surveying the industrial archipelago of the 1990s, our archaeology would locate the most efficient integrated steel complex in the world in the bustling city of P'ohang. Paean to Korean progress? P'ohang Steel was installed by Japanese technicians using Japanese technology. It is a paean to Japan's investments in (Belgian-discovered) basic oxygen-steel technology in the 1950s, after the American Air Force had renovated Japan's steel industry by bombing it to bits.

If we observe P'ohang in the 1920s, we find a sleepy port city of a few thousand people and no industry subsisting in a Japanese colony by exporting some rice. In 1950, P'ohang barely existed, having been blasted to smithereens as it changed hands several times between Korean People's Army forces straining to punch through the "Pusan Perimeter" and American forces using "high-tech" firepower to throw them back. Paean to Korean decline?

The North Korean siege was broken when General Douglas MacArthur landed at Inch'ŏn. Shortly afterward, his forces were in Wŏnsan, where they came upon the up-to-date, technologically sophisticated Wŏnsan Oil Refinery, a Soviet-Korean joint company. Paean to Soviet technical prowess? Not quite: close inspection revealed this to have been a refinery installed in the 1930s by the Japanese. Paean to Japanese technical prowess? Not quite: the Japanese had used American oil company "blueprints and consultations," a reflection of American dominance in the world oil regime of the 1930s.[13]

The town of Ŭnsan was the point at which Sino-Korean forces roared out of the mountains in 1950 and turned MacArthur's Inch'ŏn victory into a stark defeat. Moving forward to 1987, we find the North Koreans inviting Japanese firms to help them upgrade their mining technology at this same Ŭnsan, which was the site of mining operations by Japan's Chosen Mining Company. These mines were the centerpiece of Korea's most valuable mineral export in the late 1930s: gold, dug from mines that were the technological leader in East Asia. Paean to Japanese progress?

Descending into the mines, we would discover not Japanese but American machinery—and not just that, but a firm owned by Americans for four decades until just before Pearl Harbor (the Oriental Consolidated Mining Company), long after the establishment of Manchukuo and the presumed closing of "the open door." If we were to investigate the investors who owned this mining concession, we would find a group of right-wing Republicans, associated with Herbert Hoover in the 1920s, who also controlled the Homestake Gold Mine in Nevada, the Cerro de Pasco copper mines in Peru, and the Insular Lumber Company in the Philippines—all renowned symbols of American imperialism or untender mercies for labor.[14]

Our archaeology would determine that upwards of fifty thousand Koreans were directly dependent on gold-mining companies for their livelihood in the

1930s and that Americans trained "a small army of efficient native miners." Korean mine labor was considered the best in the Orient and certainly among the cheapest in the world: the miners earned sixty sen per day, about thirty-five Mexican centavos. (Yes, Dr. Archaeologist, the mine used Mexican dollars as currency in this period [as did many foreign enterprises in China] along with guards on horseback wearing Pancho Villa bandoliers to guard the loot.)

The Japanese allowed American expansionists to profit from Korean gold mines because they needed American technology. Japan occupied "an intermediate position" in mining: it was an imperial power that had mines, but it required advanced technology it did not have to exploit them.[15] In other words, Japan was still "semiperipheral" in mineral extraction at mid-century.

If we continue backward in time to 1900 and move across the Japanese industrial archipelago, we find that Japanese textile firms, the leading sector in Japan's first phase of industrialization, for decades bought their machines from the renowned Pratt Brothers of England. In about 1930, they came up with their own "high-tech" equipment and quickly became the most efficient textile producer in the world (as well as England's primary bête noire of industrial dumping, market stealing, and general commercial miscreance). A few years later the obsolescent Pratt machines were serving Korea's first textile conglomerate, courtesy of "technology transfer" and Korea's labor-cost advantage.[16]

Going further back in time, to the 1880s and Japan's first wave of industrialization, we find fish canneries in Hokkaido; the pioneer Kashima Cotton Mill; the huge Kobe Paper Factory; the first cigarette company; tanning and leather firms; the Osaka Watch Company; the Tokyo Electric Company, with its own brand of lightbulbs; even tasty Kirin Beer. Every last one was based on American technological start-ups or American expertise. And we would find that Japan's favorite economist in the 1880s was an American, the protectionist Henry Carey.[17]

Moving to Seoul a few years later, we would happen upon the Seoul Electric Light Company, the Seoul Electric Car Company, the Seoul "Fresh Spring" Water Company—all American firms. Korean imports from the United States included Standard Oil Company kerosene, Richmond Gem cigarettes, California fruit and wine, Eagle Brand milk, Armour's canned meats, Crosse & Blackwell canned foods, flour, mining machinery, railway goods, cotton, and clothing. Meanwhile, the Japanese were upsetting the Rockefellers by copying their trademark kerosene cans and putting them on the Korean market at a cheaper price.[18]

What is the point of this tour through time and space? Our archaeologist would have uncovered in little-known, far-off Korea, and in Japan proper, the modern world system and the limits of a Japan-centered regional political economy: Japan depended on American and/or British technology, and it was a subimperial power, that is, semiperipheral vis-à-vis the United States but a "core" power vis-à-vis Korea and China. It was a dependency of both the regime of technology and the system of states. Using the world as our "unit of analysis," our archaeology has placed us in the anarchic march of "progress" (ca. 1880, 1900, 1950, and 2000) and led us to an epistemology that makes it impossible to comprehend our world, whether then or now, *except* as a global system with endlessly shifting points of production.

Sooner or later, our archaeologist would conclude that the industrial archipelago he had uncovered illustrated little more than the uneven development—the simultaneous creation and destruction—of industrial capitalism. The contemporary discourses of Gary and P'ohang are mutually incommensurable, and it would be inconceivable to most American pundits today that Japan's industrial march was founded in part on the thought of an American protectionist.

Genealogy, Descent, Emergence

Archaeology is useful, but it is not sufficient for our task. We also need genealogy. The former is static: it takes a photograph of Gary and P'ohang at one flash-frozen point. The latter is dynamic, but it does not necessarily imply development. Through a genealogy of the past, we can understand not a "progress," but a *descent*, perhaps from that fluorescent point in 1920s Gary or from the Los Angeles of the 1940s to the Los Angeles of today. But doesn't genealogy also imply *ascent?* From P'ohang in 1920 to P'ohang today? From Shanghai in 1880 to Shanghai today?

Genealogy does not imply ascent; it implies *emergence:* P'ohang emergent adds a new word to the industrial vocabulary (and in 1989, a new professorship to M.I.T.: the P'ohang Steel Chair). Japan (or China) emergent bids fair to be the dominant economy of the next century (or at least experts said so, ca. 1995). But will this mean progress, from the American vantage point? Is it really Japan or China that the intellectuals surreptitiously complain about, as "progress" migrates to "the East"?

Archaeology and genealogy give us a method to excavate history and to observe descent and emergence. They give us a way to link discourse with reality or, to put it another way, to link the superstructure of thought with the world system or industrial structure. I will use this method to seek an analysis that connects knowledge with power and that is not reductionist, that is, an analysis that operates at both ends of Althusser's problematic, which Stuart Hall has described as "the necessity—and difficulty—of holding on to 'both ends of the chain' at once: the relative autonomy of a region (e.g., ideology) and its 'determination in the last instance' . . . by the economic."[19] I will attempt a move to what Foucault called "the nondiscursive," the realm where power shapes and unifies discursive practice.[20] I will seek the nondiscursive in industrial structure and a specifiable world system of industrial competition.

Using this method, I will argue in this first chapter that however close it may be to hegemonic emergence (and I don't think it is very close), Japan for this entire century has been a subordinate partner in either bilateral American hegemony or trilateral American-British hegemony. The exception is the six months between Pearl Harbor and the Battle of Midway, or, if you wish more latitude for Japanese agency, the four years from the summer of 1941 to the summer of 1945.

To my knowledge, no one has ever argued this position before,[21] not because it isn't correct but for reasons that lie deep within the discourse of industrial competition. Steadily thriving within the hegemonic net for ninety years, Japan nonetheless "emerges" in the Western mind at three critical and incommensurable points: at the turn of the century, when it was a British wunderkind (but a "yellow peril" to the Germans and the Russians); in the world depression of the 1930s, when it was an industrial monster to the British (but a wunderkind to the Germans and the Italians); and in the 1980s, when it was a wunderkind to American internationalists (but a monster to American protectionists). Here is our metaphor for the twentieth century: Japan as number two. I will stop the argument in the late 1940s, by which time the essentials of the postwar hegemonic system were in place, and then return at the end of the book to argue that Japan still moves within the system today.[22]

MENU OF QUOTATIONS

Walter Benjamin said his greatest ambition was to compose a book made up entirely of quotations. Mine is more modest: to compose one section of a chapter entirely of quotations.

> Whatsoever of morality and of intelligence; what of patience, perseverance, faithfulness, of method, insight, ingenuity, energy; in a word, whatsoever of Strength the man had in him will lie written in the Work he does. . . . Produce! Were it but the pitifullest infinitesimal fraction of a Product, produce it, in God's name![23]

> The most of us work in this country.[24]

> They are Asiatics, it is true, and therefore deficient in that principle of development which is the leading characteristic of those ingenious and

persevering European races . . . but amidst Asiatics the Japanese stand supreme.[25]

It was part of the Commodore's deliberately formed plan, in all his intercourse with these orientals, to consider carefully before he announced his resolution to do any act, but, having announced it, he soon taught them to know that he would do precisely what he said he would.[26]

[Japan] has proved to be the most formidable ground for the development of the *bacillus capitalistic.* It is not yet thirty years since Japan emerged from its "grand revolution" . . . [but] the *bacillus capitalistic* found here the most desirable conditions for its growth . . . especially plenty of extremely cheap labor. [In the not distant future] the *bacillus capitalistic* will be killed by the *phagocitus socialisticus.*[27]

In one large hall of [Tokyo Commercial] School . . . a number of bays, or recesses, are labeled with the names of the principal mercantile centers of the world, and in each of these a number of students . . . taking the parts, respectively, of bankers, importers, exporters, brokers, insurance agents and shipping agents, carry on active, simulated international trade in strict accordance with the business usages of the places at which they are supposed to be dealing.[28]

I shall turn Japanese for they at least can think, and be reticent! [Witness] their organization, their strategy, their virile qualities, their devotion and self-control. Above all, their national capacity for self-reliance, self-sacrifice, and their silence![29]

Witness the magnificent spectacle of Japan today; the State above the individual; common good above personal good; sacrifice of self and devotion to the community.[30]

[The Japanese] shame our administrative capacity . . . shame our inventiveness . . . shame our leadership.[31]

The wily Jap [is] determined to stop at nothing in his efforts to bamboozle shoppers in this country [and is] STEALING OUR MARKETS! [*sic*][32]

To the poltroonery of American liberalism one cannot imagine a better antithesis than the exquisite temperance and the sublime abnegation of the Japanese. Dear, gentle, elegant, heroic Japanese! Be welcomed at our side. We will conquer.[33]

The Japanese are, to the highest degree, both aggressive and unaggressive, both militaristic and aesthetic, both insolent and polite, rigid and adaptable, submissive and resentful of being pushed around, loyal and treacherous, brave and timid, conservative and hospitable to new ways.[34]

Our economic frontier now embraces the trade potentialities of Asia itself; for with the gradual rotation of the epicenter of world trade back to the Far East whence it started many centuries ago, the next thousand years will find the main problem the raising of the sub-normal standards of life of its more than a billion people.[35]

Japan has dealt more successfully with more of the basic problems of post-industrial society than any other country.[36]

[The Japanese state elite has] the security, the ability, and an ethos that enable it to concentrate on what is good for the nation as a whole.[37]

I am really very troubled when I think through the consequences of the rise of Japanese power.[38]

[Japan has] these really fundamental weaknesses—energy, food, and military security . . . it is an extraordinarily weak country.[39]

The most *crucial* factor determining Japan's socio-political reality . . . is the near *absence* of any idea that there can be truths, rules, principles or morals that always apply, no matter what the circumstances (emphasis added).[40]

I believe that the Japanese are individuals. . . . I have met quite a few who want to be taken for distinct persons.[41]

[Japan is an example of] state corporate capitalism, as opposed to entrepreneurial capitalism . . . what we used to call fascism.[42]

Japan does not aspire to replace America as the world's leader; it will be content to stay number two.[43]

[The Japanese are] creatures of an ageless, amoral, manipulative and controlling culture . . . suited only to this race, in this place.[44]

At a superficial level, my quotations are useful for demonstrating that contemporaneous debate on Japan operates within limits, or within a discourse, that has been around since Japan first began industrializing. More than that, this discourse applies equally well to any "late" industrializer, whether Germany in the late nineteenth century or Korea and China in the late twentieth century. (In the American mind, Korea and China are increasingly linked with Japan as a "threat.") The quotations allow us to place both Ezra Vogel (Japan as model) and Karel van Wolferen (Japan as threat) within a century-long discourse. They allow us to construct an either/or dyad of interpretation, a dualism common to historical interpretation (for example, Gibbon, rise and decline; Toynbee, challenge and response; Fairbank, Western challenge and Eastern response). The inscriptions also enable us to recognize a *moral valence* attached to each dyad: Model is good; threat is bad. Diligence is good; purloining is bad. Democracy is good; "state corporate capitalism" is bad. The chrysanthemum definitely beats the sword.

Yet our quotations generate a dyad of incommensurable judgment: Are the Japanese a threat or a model? Are they aesthetes or militarists—the chrysanthemum or the sword? Are they innovative, or do they copy? Are they inventors or purloiners? Is Japan the exception in East Asia or the rule? (The Webbs and most others thought Japan the exception at the turn of the century, but would they say so today, in the face of Korean and Chinese industrial prowess?) Is Japan's political economy unique, or does it replicate earlier industrial experience? Is the Japanese state an authoritarian menace or an enlightened pilot (the "benevolent bureaucracy of the future socialist state," according to Beatrice Webb)?[45] Is the Japanese polity sui generis (as per the nativist *kokutai* doctrine in 1938 and as Ishihara Shintaro says in *The Japan That Can Say No*),[46] or is it the enlightened if imbedded state of welfare postindustrialism (as Ezra Vogel had it)? Is Japan autonomous or dependent? Do we face today MacArthur's "rotation of the epicenter" of world trade back to East Asia, or did the superpowers merely spend themselves into decline in the four decades of the cold war, enabling the rise of their former enemies, Japan and Germany? Will Japan be the hegemonic power of the twenty-first century, or was all that talk rendered obsolete when large firms and banks went belly up in 1997 amid a prolonged crisis of governance, thus putting all the blather about the Pacific Rim and the "dawning Pacific century" in the shade?

Who's to say?

Benjamin liked to quote other people because he thought that "the transmissibility of the past had been replaced by its citability."[47] In place of the authority of tradition, we find a tendency to "settle down in the present," complacently, and accept its random evidence and its incommensurability.[48] The quotations may also be taken as metaphors for Japan observed over more than a century and for the attempt to give these observations human meaning in the here and now. But the more important point is the *correspondences* (or rather, the incommensurability, the lack of correspondence to any consistent interpretation of Japan other than that it has spent this century becoming an industrial power).

Benjamin's metaphor for the historian is thus "the pearl diver," searching for the effluvia of the past to bring up to the surface and to place alongside other effluvia, all in the simultaneity with which we moderns experience the past. He says, "Quotations in my works are like robbers by the roadside who make an armed attack and relieve an idler of his convictions."[49] Quotations have the meaning for us that they would for an antique collector, an archaeologist, or a pearl diver: valuable effluvia, but ripped from context; fragments of a lost past, but nonetheless precious. The mind reads them and says to itself, you can't have it both ways, or *plus ça change, plus c'est la même chose*. The quotations and dyads are incommensurable, but why? What structures the discourse? What places the boundary of these antinomies? And the moral valence?

MANIFEST DENSITY: E + D + EM = A

Barthes's optic, we will remember, gave us a parallax view to question ourselves: "Someday we must write the history of our own obscurity—manifest the density of our narcissism." Our quotations, almost all of them Western, "manifest the density of our narcissism." They do not exist in thin air, however, but have an origin, a cause, and a historical meaning. In *The Genealogy of Morals*, Nietzsche wrote that he ceased looking for the origin of morality behind the world, but rather *in* the world; he found that "the cause of the origin of a thing and its eventual utility, its actual employment and place in a system of purposes, lie worlds apart; whatever exists, having somehow come into being, is again and again reinterpreted to new ends."[50]

"Japan" or "China" are endlessly reinterpreted, but not because of their "progress." The "evolution" of something, Nietzsche says, is "by no means its *progressus* toward a goal" (77); words like "progress" and "purpose" are only signs that some master has imposed upon history a meaning. What we know as history is always "a fresh interpretation . . . through which any previous 'meaning' and 'purpose' are necessarily obscured and even obliterated" (77). History is thus "a continuous sign-chain of ever new interpretations" (77).

Thus our quotations function as a sign chain, a genealogy of moral valence: China or Japan "stand still" or do what they always have since joining the race with the West; but "Japan" and "China" metamorphose with the ups and downs of Western perception.

Foucault took up Nietzsche's argument in a famous essay, "Nietzsche, Genealogy, History."[51] Genealogy "opposes itself to the search for 'origins'" (142); for historians origins means "that which was already there" (142), as if it did not require a human being to determine "what was there" but can simply be "found." The site of historical truth, of true "origin," he says (and here he draws on Benjamin[52]), "lies at a place of inevitable loss . . . the site of a fleeting articulation that discourse has obscured and finally lost" (143). The genealogical method "excavat[es] the depths," "allow[s] time for these elements to escape from a labyrinth where no truth had ever detained them." And so history "is the concrete body of a development, with its moments of intensity, its lapses, its extended periods of feverish agitation, its fainting spells; and only a metaphysician would seek its soul in the distant ideality of the origin" (145). In other words, my quotations are a discourse with humanly applied limitations and oscillations; their "history" is in the "feverish agitation" and "fainting spells" with which the West greets notable Chinese or Japanese success, or new-found power.

Foucault goes on to say that *herkunft,* one German word for origin, is closer to "stock" or "descent." An examination of descent "permits the discovery, under the unique aspect of a trait or a concept, of the myriad events through which they were formed" (145–46). The duty of genealogy is not to demonstrate that the past actively exists in the present, through a predetermined form or through some necessary causality; the past is not an evolution and it does not map the destiny of a people: "On the contrary, to follow the complex course of descent is *to maintain passing events in their proper dispersion*" (146; emphasis added). History is not a determined or meaningful heritage, "a possession that grows and solidifies"; "it is [instead] an unstable assembly of faults, fissures, and heterogeneous layers that threaten the fragile inheritor from within and from underneath" (146). The "fragile inheritors" of the Enlightenment tradition, as we have seen, now find themselves threatened from within, from underneath . . . and from the East.

Nietzsche also deployed the word "emergence" (*entstehung*), "the principle and the singular law of an apparition" (146). Descent does not mean uninterrupted continuity, and emergence does not mean "the final term of a historical development," even if both may appear as a culmination of trends. "Culminations" are "merely the current episodes in a series of subjugations" (146), and so "Emergence is thus the entry of forces; it is their eruption, *the leap from the wings to the center stage* . . . emergence designates a place of confrontation" (148–49; emphasis added). An emergence is not a decision, a treaty, a war, but "the reversal of a relationship of forces, the usurpation of power, the appropriation of a vocabulary turned against those who had once used it" (149). And thus his conclusion: "The body [or history, or the descent] is molded by a great many distinct regimes" (149).

In other words "emergence" indicates not just a reversal, but a prior moment of apprehension, when things not heretofore salient suddenly become so and thereby prepare the ground for a revaluation. This is a very Nietzschean formulation on Foucault's part, but Nietzsche added to the phenomenon a sense of alarm and a dimension of the unconscious: "an unrecognized motivation serving an unacknowledged purpose," in MacIntyre's apt phrase.[53] Much of the alarmist American discourse on Japan and China is precisely that, alarm coming from unrecognized motivations, serving unacknowledged purposes.

We may now formulate an equation to make the positivist heart go pitter-patter: let E stand for excavation, D for descent, Em for emergence and A for archaeology, thus: $E + D + Em = A$, our archaeology (or history) of the present, a critical method for doing history that seeks something more than the usual "let the facts speak for themselves" empiricism, something more than mere "pearl diving," and something other than history as "progressus toward a goal."

This conception seeks to examine a descent, that is, "passing events" *in their proper dispersion*, assuming an excavation, an emergence, a body with a great many distinct regimes—that is, a discernible genealogy. It is consistent with Nietzsche's and Benjamin's idea of the past as an accumulation of fragments, shards of a former reality, appearing in new and changed forms, rising up before us in moments of danger, not to mention Nietzsche's conception of all history as the history of the present. It is associated with excavation, unearthing, uncovering, as is the science of archaeology, but it also examines emergence as an appearance (or apparition), as a qualitative change in the incremental movement or "progressus" of what we usually call history—the leap from the wings to center stage in episodes of emergence and recession.

JAPAN EMERGENT

In the past decade, Japan and China have flashed up at a moment of feverish agitation,[54] but not for the first time. More than 130 years ago Marx noted that Americans, unable to conceive of contradictions in economic relations in the world market as integral to the workings of capitalism, saw such contradictions "as soon as they appear on the world market as *English* relations," that is, as British capital's distortion of the natural order of things.[55] Today the disturber of the natural order of things is Japan, and if not Japan, then China. But let us stick with Japan for a while. Over the past hundred years, Western conjurings of "Japan" have expressed the problems of world competition for markets and of industrial decline in acute fashion. Historically, when industrial structure is a problem, Japan becomes a problem—although our industrialists would have it the other way round.

In spite of the sharp reversals in Western discourse about Japan, for most of our century Japan has been caught in the nets of several global regimes, but especially the *regime of technology* and the *system of states.* Japan was not simply in alliance with England from 1902 to 1922, but was content to "prosper in the collective informal empire" of the British and the Americans throughout the first quarter of the century and to feed off a British-American technological regime without making any significant technological innovations until the late 1920s—and then only in textiles, an industry already in incipient decline in England and America.

Pratt Machines long underpinned the developing Japanese textile industry, as we have seen. General Electric was dominant in the delivery of electricity, and by the 1890s Standard Oil had placed Japan, Korea, and China well within the world oil regime, which was increasingly dominated by American firms. Standard's comparative advantage was financial and technical, but also resided in innovative marketing schemes: monopoly on a world scale, combined with creative ways to sell "oil for the lamps of China."[56] The joint British-American technical condominium was perhaps best symbolized by the British-American Tobacco Company, a subsidiary of the Duke tobacco interests in North Carolina, which got Japan and China hooked on something else, a cigarette habit so deep that nonsmoking sections can hardly be found anywhere in either country in the 1990s.[57]

Even the spearhead for Japan's penetration of Manchuria, the South Manchurian Railway Company, got its reputation for advanced and efficient service by importing thousands of the latest American locomotives and railway cars, not to mention tons of American steel railway ties, all known for decades as the best in the world.[58] (Today it is South Korea that imports General Motors locomotives, for local assembly and finishing.) Japan has striven and usually thrived within this network of dependency since the turn of the last century, yet almost always "Japan" is treated in the West as an independent (and as often as not, mysterious) entity, to be loved or reviled.

Japan's industrialization has proceeded through three phases, the last of which is now dominant. The first phase began in the 1880s with textiles being the leading sector; the textile phase lasted through Japan's rise to world power, an ascent marked by foreign aggression in every decade after the 1880s (aggression that was errant counterpoint to the roseate imagery of Japanese success, but par for the course among the industrial nations). In the mid-1930s Japan began the second, heavy phase, based on steel, chemicals, automobiles, and (before 1945) armaments; this phase was dominant until the mid-1970s. The third phase, of course, emphasized high-technology "knowledge" industries such as electronics, communications, and silicon-chip microprocessors.[59]

Within Japan, each phase, in good product-cycle fashion, has been marked by strong state protection for nascent industries, creative adaptation of foreign technologies, and the deployment of comparative advantages deriving from cheap labor costs, technological and organizational innovation, or "late-ness" in world time. Then there would be a bursting forth into the world market that always struck foreign observers as abrupt and unexpected, thus inspiring both fear and loathing and awe and admiration. Far from disturbing "the natural order of things," for a century Japan has followed the natural trajectory laid out by leading capitalist ideologues, especially classic notions of the product cycle. In so doing, however, Japan has gotten itself into a lot of trouble.

A Janus-faced, startled surprise greeted Japan's first clear moment of "emer-gence," its defeat of Russia in 1905. At the turn of the century, Japan mate-rialized like a Rorschach inkblot onto which Americans and Europeans pro-jected their own hopes and fears. For Westerners accustomed to think in racial terms, Japanese success was inexplicable because they were "yellow" and not white (although they soon became honorary whites). Meanwhile, missionaries began referring to "the untiring industry" of the Japanese: "All night long the sleepless sounds of labor are rampant and furious. This habit of ceaseless occupation extends to the very highest classes."[60]

Westerners usually explained all this through a combination of Japanese sweating of labor and shameless copying of foreign models, not knowing that in saying so they simply mimicked British myths of the 1880s about another late developer, Germany. The French were also not very sanguine about Japan, worrying about "the competition of yellow labor"; even if at present (1905) "Nippon labor does not seem to be the cause of the depreciation of salaries" in the West, it would be so "if Japan, victorious over Russia and master of the Celestial Empire, organized Chinese labor."[61]

British socialists projected their fond hopes and sharp morals onto the Japanese. Beatrice Webb, perhaps with her husband, Sydney, not the most discerning of Fabians in foreign lands, wrote in 1904 that Japan was a "rising star of human self-control and enlightenment." On her trip to the Orient in 1911 she found the Chinese to be "a horrid race," the Koreans also "a horrid race" (for Sydney, these were "lowly vertebrates" who "show us, indeed, what homo sapiens can be if he does not evolve"). Beatrice liked the "inno-vating collectivism" of Japan and its "enlightened professional elite" with its "uncanny" purposefulness and open-mindedness. Here was the "benevolent bureaucracy of the future socialist state."[62] H. G. Wells, it may be remem-bered, called his elite "samurai" in *A Modern Utopia* (1905), and in the 1930s the Webbs were to liken Stalin's cadres to "the samurai vocation for leadership."[63]

Why were British writers of all stripes lauding Japan in the first decade of the twentieth century? The answer is simple: British decline and German and Japanese advance. Germany was a nearby threat, but Japan was the British ally after 1902. After two great waves of industrialization lasting a century and a half, England found itself beset by newly risen industrial powers and by an obsolescent industrial base. A period of fervent soul-searching therefore marked most debate, with the watchword being efficiency: "Give us efficiency or we die." Alfred Stead entitled his 1906 book *Great Japan: A Study of National Efficiency*. British pundits wished to discover models of efficiency and productivity and looked to a "Japan" that, it was thought, "afforded lessons from which the British might learn to solve their internal problems."[64] Here was the reason for all the silly Japanophilia of the period, when the real problems for Britain were two: declining industries and the threat of Germany.

Germany was an example of a country pulling itself up in the space of a few decades through a program of "national economy" from agriculture to industry, through hard toil, help from the state, protectionism, diligence, wicked copying, "purloined" technology, and "an alert progressiveness, contrasted with the conservative stupor of ourselves [the British]."[65] That is, Germany was for England what Japan and China are for our industrialists today: a combination of miracle and cheap tricks.

The image of Japan in the West can turn on a dime. During World War I, Japan was the scheming jackal, enjoying a war boom and tripled exports; but in the 1920s, when it entered a period of economic stagnation and pursued free trade policies, it was lauded for its liberal institutions. The period of Taisho democracy was for modernization theorists the progressive culmination of the Meiji success story (marred later by the aberration of the decade of militarism, 1936–1945).[66] Whether the 1920s were the exception to or the rule of Japanese development, we might at least note that the benign image corresponds to a very benign Japan, undercutting no one's exports and markets and acquiescing in the 1920s international system that defined America, England, and Japan in a perfect trilateral formula: 5:5:3 (in numbers of naval ships in the Pacific, but it can stand for everything else).

By the mid-1930s, with the world in depression, protective tariffs everywhere, and Japan embarking on heavy industrialization, "Japan" was again a problem. For liberal internationalists like Henry Stimson, the lament was that Japan, "with a tradition of original friendliness toward the U.S.," should have gone off the free trade regimen and onto such a bender in Manchuria, destroying the "open door."[67] For Guenther Stein, who in 1935 wrote a prescient book with the ironic (for then) title, *Made in Japan*, the country was a model of industrial efficiency that, were it not for tariff walls, "might become the largest exporter in the world—and in a very short time." Stein rightly saw in the heavy industrialization spurt of the mid-1930s "the beginning of a new epoch in the industrialization of the world"; Japan's problem was that it had upset the balance of the world system, "and this is the real reason why other countries complain about her."[68] Within Japan, however, its sharp departures of policy in the mid-1930s were justified, as they had been since 1868, by the requisites of harsh competition in a world that others dominated: "The chief object of [our] planned economy is successful competition in world markets through a complete industrialization of the country. . . . In the execution of the standardization of national life, which is quite economic in nature, some limitation may be placed upon the laissez-faire policy, but this is a world-wide tendency . . . [it] is not to be taken as the harbinger of a fascist regime."[69] Also announced at the time was the first Datsun motorcar, symbol of the "dawning new age," appearing in a Japanese auto market "which has long been dominated by Fords, Chevrolets, and other American cars."[70]

With Japan's attack at Pearl Harbor, of course, its increasingly tough image of the late 1930s turned into one born of pure racism. As *Life* said in December 1941, "The whole cartoon aspect of the Jap changed overnight. Before that sudden Sunday the Jap was an oily little man, amiable but untrustworthy, more funny than dangerous." *Time*'s issue of the same day (December 22) featured Admiral Yamamoto Isoroku on the cover, his face polished in the hue of a moldering lemon, and gave readers instructions on how to tell "Japs" from "Chinamen." By 1943, most of the characteristics that the Fabians had admired were being used to explain why the Japanese were aggressors: the strong group life, the all-powerful state, and "mindless" subordination to authority.[71]

The shifting and incommensurable imagery of Japan in the first half of the century derived from sharp industrial competition in the world system, a conflict that routinely overlooked Japan's continuing technological inferiority to England and America. But that system is also a system of states, not just markets. How did Japan fit in there?

JAPAN AS NUMBER TWO

The primary and "normal" mechanism that corresponds to the hierarchies of the capitalist system of states is *hegemony*, a term that encompasses empire, colonialism, "neocolonialism," and what is sometimes called informal empire, but goes beyond all these terms as well. In its economic aspects, hegemony means the simultaneous *and temporary* "productive, commercial and financial pre-eminence of one core power over other core powers"; the critical element is "productive advantage," which conditions the other two (commerce and finance). Military advantage, which *realpolitik* conventionally assumes to be crucial to hegemony, merely "locks in" the existing sinews of hegemonic power. The hegemonic power favors openness in trade, decolonization or informal empire, and liberalism everywhere—sometimes even in the home market.[72]

Our archaeology has already uncovered in the depths of the "nondiscursive" a regime of technology (the productivist aspect of American-British hegemony) in prewar Japanese industry, moving temporally and geographically according to what is commonly known as a product cycle (American rolling stock in Manchuria, American-blueprinted refineries in Wŏnsan, basic oxygen furnaces in P'ohang).[73] Now we will excavate "Japan as number two" in the discourse of international politics: states arrayed in a hierarchy of power, sometimes known as the balance of power, and states as both autonomous and penetrated, their structures the outcome of both domestic and international forces.[74] Here too, the discursive gives way to the nondiscursive, the deep structure of a world system in which Japan has been an important, but almost always subordinate part.

An archaeology of Japan in the twentieth century world system unearths the following timelines:

A. 1900–1922: Japan in British-American hegemony

B. 1922–1941: Japan in American-British hegemony

C. 1941–1945: Japan as regional hegemon in East Asia

D. 1945–1970: Japan in American hegemony

E. 1970–1990s: Japan in American-European hegemony

Here we highlight another aspect of this structure: three of the periods (A, B, and E) are trilateral partnerships, and none are colonial or necessarily imperial. A bilateral regime is predictable in the temporary phase of comprehensive hegemony (1945–1970 for the United States), a trilateral regime in the rising and falling phases of transitional hegemonies. Period C is the exception that proves the rule.

Rather than elaborate this pattern in the nondiscursive of power relations (for which, see chapter 8), let us just sample the discursive, found readily in the oeuvre of the dean of diplomatic histories of East Asia, Akira Iriye, whose books dominate the field. Because Iriye has dwelt at one end of Althusser's "chain," the realm of culture, ideas, and imagery in international relations,[75] and perhaps because of his understated style, few recognize just how deeply revisionist his work is. Iriye has consistently argued through his career that:

1. Japanese imperialism (conventionally dated from the Sino-Japanese War and the seizure of Taiwan in 1895) was subordinate to British imperialism and coterminous with a similar American thrust toward formal empire in the 1890s, and no different in kind from the British or American variety.[76]

2. Japan pursued a "cooperative" policy of integration with the world system

(not his terms) at all times in the twentieth century, except from the critical turning point of July 1941 and the resulting war.[77]

3. Japan got the empire the British and Americans wanted it to have, and only sought to organize an exclusive regional sphere when the other powers did the same, after the collapse of the world system in the 1930s (and even then their attempt was half-hearted, and even then the development program was "orthodoxly Western").[78]

4. Japan's presumed neomercantilist political economy of protection at home and export to the free trade realm abroad, with corresponding trade surpluses, has been less important over the past ninety years than an open market at home and a cooperative policy abroad.

Japan first "emerged," of course, with its "opening" by Commodore Matthew Perry and the subsequent Meiji Restoration (which some Japanese scholars are increasingly coming to interpret as an outcome of world market forces) and when England was the hegemonic power facing growing competition from the United States.[79] Both powers followed a "cooperative" policy toward Japan, however, or what we would call a "trilateral" policy.

The "hooking" of Japan into the hegemonic system was most obvious diplomatically in the Anglo-Japanese Alliance of 1902,[80] something also connected to the building of railroads in Korea and China, which Americans (particularly the E. H. Harriman Trust) pursued as assiduously as did British interests.[81] But if that alliance "locked in" Japan for the British, it probably was less important historically than the growing American presence in the technological and energy regime in Japan, and the arrival of an opportunistic ploy by the rising hegemon: an "open door" policy abroad, combined with the ongoing development of a protected national market at home (and in America's near reaches, known as the Monroe Doctrine).

William Appleman Williams was the discerning historian who discovered in John Hay's "open door notes" of 1900 a metaphor for American expansion, and who grasped that this new form of hegemony had its inception in East Asia.[82] Michael Hunt has detailed an "Open Door constituency" in American export industries like cotton and cotton textiles, oil, tobacco, and railroad equipment; even though residual anti-English sensitivities ruled out a formal alliance with England, American leaders like Hay and Roosevelt continued to see an identity of interests with Great Britain (as they had since the War of 1812). Meanwhile, Japan was the chosen junior partner of both; Roosevelt "looked to Japan as an advanced country and regional power uniquely qualified to instruct backward China" (and thus captured American policy thereafter toward Japan's colonial and continental dependencies).[83]

Iriye thinks that the Russo-Japanese War turned Japan into an "imperialist" power, which he seems to define in the narrow terms of forcible subordination of other nations. Yet he immediately notes, correctly, that as long as the direction of Japanese imperialism was toward Korea and Manchuria, it had the blessing of Americans (not to mention the British), especially Theodore Roosevelt, accompanied by the usual retinue of cheerleading American scholars.[84]

Roosevelt's successor, Taft, was less enamored of Japan than of China (Taft visited Japan in 1905 and decided that "a Jap is first of all a Jap and would be glad to aggrandize himself at the expense of anybody").[85] He was also enamored of "dollar diplomacy" and a sphere of influence in Manchuria. Taft's secretary of state, Frank Knox, and the classic American expansionist Willard Straight (a long-time advisor to Harriman) developed a "grandiose vision," in Charles Neu's words, for an "economic, scientific, and impartial administration of Manchuria" (in Knox's words), a joint supervision of the great powers, especially England and the United States and especially over the railways. The goal of the plan was to create "an immense commercial neutral zone"—that is, an open door—from which all the powers would benefit.[86]

Taft thus inaugurated a pattern that has lasted until the present, in which American diplomacy occasionally flirts with a "China-first" policy (the foreign policies of Franklin Roosevelt, Richard Nixon, and Jimmy Carter are good examples), only to be called back to the hard reality that Japan, with an advanced industrial base, is the more important power in East Asia. Taft learned that fact by 1910, when his plans to develop Manchurian railways under British-American auspices lay in ruins.[87] Neu notes that Taft's plan did not proceed out of hostility to Japan; he "admired Japan's achievements and had approved of her absorption of Korea." But just to underline the importance of these events, in 1909 U.S. Navy planners had decided on Pearl Harbor as the chief American base in the Pacific, and in 1910, the Taft administration's General Board "began systematic consideration of war with Japan and by March 1911 had worked out a detailed Orange Plan."[88] (It seemed a bit early to send this chill up the American-Japanese spine.)

Shortly after World War I ended, in 1922 to be overly exact, America came to be the major partner in the trilateral hegemony in Northeast Asia. This was the period when American banks became dominant in the world economy,[89] the Anglo-Japanese alliance had become tattered, and the United States became more important than England in Japanese diplomacy. The Washington Conference was the occasion for this transfer of the baton, a "locking in" with the critical element of global military reach, the American Navy.

Bill Williams found an American informal empire beginning in the 1890s and maturing under Wilson and Harding, with both resisting radical change in the East Asian status quo (in spite of the very different rhetoric employed by each). The instrumentality of American-dominated consortia (to which others have paid far more attention than they deserve) appeared to Williams as a device to constrain simultaneously Bolsheviks, Asian nationalists, and old imperialists.[90] Iriye really doesn't disagree, he just uses a different discourse to find the emergence in the same period of what he calls a new, cooperative international order.[91] The Washington naval system was explicitly trilateral, in that the United States and England kept their naval superiority, while the United States, England, and Japan all cooperated to keep China a subordinate actor in the East Asian system—amid much American rhetoric about preserving China's (barely observable) national integrity.[92]

Japan accommodated to these trends with a low-posture diplomacy throughout the 1920s. Meanwhile, it girded its loins at home for trade competition, inaugurating tendencies in its political economy that remain prominent today. Here was an early version of what is now termed "export-led development." Both Johnson and Fletcher date the origins of Japan's national industrial strategy and "administrative guidance" from the mid- to late 1920s; both the Americans and the British were most receptive to Japan's late-arriving strategies of political economy.[93] (It has only been in 1939–1945 and the 1980s–1990s that this strategy has been perceived as a problem for the United States.)

The Export Association Law of 1925 was an important turning point, stimulating industrial reorganization, cartels, and various state subsidies to exporters; Japan was careful to direct these exports to the noncolonial semiperiphery, not to the colonies—even less to the core markets—of America and England.[94] The 1920s also inaugurated a period of import-substitution industrialization[95] that went hand in hand with the exporting program, even if it was more pronounced in the 1930s when Japan accomplished its heavy-industrial spurt and began its virtuoso mastery of the industrial product cycle.

The result of all this was that in the midst of the world depression and shrunken world trade Japan's total exports more than doubled between 1932 and 1937 and "appeared to flood world markets." Cotton yarn, woven goods, toys, iron, and steel led the advance. Yet Japan registered a trade surplus only in 1935, when its exports were but 3 percent of the world total, compared to the United States' 10 percent. Despite that, Japan's trade partners got obsessed about its exporting. The American economist Miriam Farley explained this by saying that Japan had merely "picked the wrong century in which to industrialize"—not a bad observation. By 1936, every major nation had curtailed the influx of Japanese exports, yet Japanese business groups still "tried to induce Americans to invest in Manchuria" even in the late 1930s. Meanwhile, American textile concerns "lobbied for restraints on exports to the U.S. despite a massive trade surplus with Japan."[96] So it goes.

On the critical 1941–1945 period, Iriye notes that until the Japanese military's "turn south" in mid-1941 (a decision deeply conditioned by Soviet power), Japan was still dependent on the United States, which he terms (in a nice summary of the change that came in the early 1920s) "the key to postwar international relations . . . its capital, technology, and commodities sustained the world economic system throughout the 1920s . . . as the financial, business, and political center of the world."[97] The United States invoked the outer limits of its hegemonic power by embargoing oil to Japan, which came as a tremendous psychological shock to Japan and made its leaders assume that the only alternative was war.

Pearl Harbor was an event (a sign) that rendered everything that went before it since 1868 in a different hue, the hue of a moldering lemon, for *Time*'s cover picture of Yamamoto: Behold, the aggressor. If from a longer historical viewpoint it was a sudden reversal, it also revalued history instantly: now it seemed that everything presaged and foretold Japan's Pearl Harbor aggression. Today the "reemergence" of Japan, and of course Germany, however much they may have changed in fifty years, again enters a discourse of antinomies: the discourse of eternal mistrust, relating to Pearl Harbor and the crimes of the Nazis. A. M. Rosenthal contributes all he can to this discourse from his perch on the *New York Times* editorial page, deploying it now against Germany, now China, and now Japan: in late 1990, he conjured the "nightmare" that "the Japanese Army will soon again become a political force"; the rightists in Japan "dream, ever, of a new militarism, a new empire . . . would you say it could never happen again?"[98]

One would never know that Japan's restoration was America's project for twenty-five years after the war ended; that as early as 1942 a small cadre of internationalists in the American State Department and in Japan began moving on remarkably parallel lines to reintegrate Japan into the postwar American hegemonic regime;[99] that by 1947 George Kennan had elaborated plans for Japan's industrial revival; and that these plans called for a modified restoration of Japan's former colonial position in northeast Asia.[100]

Stated succinctly, Japan in the postwar period has been an engine of the world economy, an American-defined "economic animal," shorn of its prewar military and political clout. This happened coterminous with the emergence of the cold war and deepened as Japan benefited from America's wars to lock in an Asian hinterland in Korea and Vietnam. In this era, which ran from Truman's administration through Johnson's, Japan was a dutiful American partner, and America was tickled pink at Japan's economic success. As the

American capacity unilaterally to manage the global system declined in the 1960s, however, a new duality afflicted the U.S.-Japan relationship: Japan should do well, yes . . . but not so well that it hurt American interests. (The symbol and pivot of this reversal was Richard Nixon's "New Economic Policy" in 1971, announced on V-J Day.) American thinking about Japan remains firmly within that duality today, symbolized by the inability of elites to do more than oscillate between free trade and protectionism, between admiration for Japan's success and alarm at its prowess, or between satisfaction at the bursting of Japan's "bubble economy" and alarm at China's rapid growth, whereupon all the negative tropes migrate westward toward Shanghai.

CONCLUSION

Behind the bipolar boundaries forged between 1947 and 1950 and the economic pump priming of two catastrophic wars, the East Asian industrial economies have exercised a powerful gravity on the world system, even if Japan, Korea, and Taiwan remain within the hegemonic boundaries of the postwar settlement. In the 1980s, Japan became for the United States what the United States became for England in the 1920s: the apparent center of world financial and technical prowess, but one that was still unwilling to "share burdens" in the policing of the world. History will tell us whether American global leadership continues well into the twenty-first century or whether the baton will pass to Japan or Germany or, less provocatively, to the Pacific Rim or the European Community. If it is the last, it will be an ironic tribute to Japanese and German prowess and to the shortsightedness of American strategy circa 1947. Predicated on being "number one" for the ages, it may eventually make America the junior partner in a new trilateral condominium: America as number two.

Yet Japan and Germany are nations with an uncertain relationship to the Enlightenment project. Nazi Germany's barbarous crimes sowed doubts about the very idea of progress in an entire generation of intellectuals. This doubt was brought to its apotheosis in 1944, with Horkheimer and Adorno's declaration that the Enlightenment "is the line both of destruction and of civilization," an enlightened earth-radiating disaster.[101] Militarist Japan was guilty of lesser crimes—mere garden-variety aggression and mass slaughter by twentieth-century standards. Yet many observers still assume Japan to be somehow outside the hallowed liberal realm. *Industrialization without Enlightenment* might well be the subtitle of Karel Van Wolferen's *Enigma of Japanese Power*. Japan is closed and inscrutable, run by a mysterious "system." Its people do not recognize or believe in (Western) abstract universals. They do not privilege individualism.

Here is the problem: If Japan or China or Germany prove to be the nations most fitted to the rivalries of the twenty-first century, the Enlightenment project does not explain it. If the rotation of the epicenter places France, England, and America in the shade, what happened to the French Revolution? The British Industrial Revolution? The American *novus ordo seclorum*? What happened to progress?

We verge on "paradigm shift" because an industrial leap from the wings to center stage induces "a certain disturbance of the person, a subversion of earlier readings, a shock of meaning," and Barthes's truth comes home to us. Someday, indeed, we must write the history of our own obscurity.

2

East Wind, Rain   Red Wind   Black Rain

The United States–Japan War,

Beginning and End

There is, upon the whole, nothing more important in life than to find out the right point of view from which things should be looked at and judged of, and then to keep to that point.—Clausewitz, *On War*

There was a desert wind blowing that night. It was one of those hot dry Santa Anas that come down through the mountain passes and curl your hair and make your nerves jump and your skin itch. On nights like that every booze party ends in a fight. Meek little wives feel the edge of the carving knife and study their husbands' necks. —Raymond Chandler, *Red Wind*

Pearl Harbor and Nagasaki were the alpha and the omega of a four-year period of estrangement—a brief, temporary anomaly in the decades of good relations and partnership that have marked U.S.-Japan relations throughout the twentieth century, regardless of the shifting Western interpretations that we just examined. Yet the names of both places resonate ominously down to the present as symbols of a war that began badly and ended well for the United States, and that began well and ended badly for Japan. Or do we still disagree about the moral valence to be attached to these real and imagined beginnings and endings?

There is a famous book about this estrangement titled *The Winds of War*. I never could understand what the title meant because the author, Herman Wouk, says nothing—or nothing interesting—about the winds that marked the war between Japan and the United States: the East Wind that began it at Pearl Harbor; the Red Wind that destroyed Tokyo and other cities in early 1945; and the Black Wind that incinerated Hiroshima and Nagasaki, ending the war and precipitating the age of nuclear terror. Wouk's *winds* metaphor is a way to *avoid* addressing untoward aspects of what Americans call "the good war." I will address precisely those aspects of this war that upset and confound this label—from the right point of view.

Japan is known for its seasonal typhoons, but continental America experiences fierce winds in at least three varieties: the typhoons along the Atlantic coast (called hurricanes), the wind whirlpools of the Midwest (called tornadoes), and the desert sciroccos that blow from the Sierra Nevada range into the Los Angeles basin. The red scirocco winds are the least well-known of these, but when the scorching tempests of the desert roar through the passes and down the valleys, they suck the life out of the sprawling city that the Angelenos watered and watered until the desert basin greened and they could call it home.

The great body of water—the Pacific Ocean—that marks the edge of Los Angeles and the sun-washed days that stretch endlessly, made early pioneers think they had found a Mediterranean paradise—until the red winds came and burned their huts down. But California had another paradox waiting for the American nomads: Were they an Atlantic people or a Pacific people? Were they England's offspring, internationalists tutored in the nineteenth-century sway of Pax Britannica, or were they expansionists, moving away from Europe? Were they "protected by two great oceans" (not to mention the British Navy) and therefore able to incubate an exceptional polity, or were they the human-all-too-human residue of a Europe all too often at war with itself? Were they the offspring of northern European civilization, or were they founding a new world (a *novus ordo seclorum*)?

Japan is washed, nurtured, and protected by that same ocean, which separates it from mainland Asia. Its archaic sobriquet, "the land of the rising sun," reflects a perspective available only to those on the mainland.[1] One of the favorite conceits of Japan's leaders in this century has been the virtue of this putative distance from the trials and tribulations of mainland Asia. The only nation in the world to have made an artform out of eating raw fish, Japan draws sustenance in every possible way from the ubiquitous, surrounding, and ever present waters of the Pacific.

So we have two Pacific peoples, washed by the same vast ocean, each claiming a kind of exceptionalism from the rest of the world,[2] a critical distance, and (as we saw in the introduction) a schizophrenic orientation to a center of civilization. For most writers, however, it is not the similarities but the manifold differences between the two peoples that quickly become apparent: for example, Japan is an ethnically homogeneous nation; the United States, a melting pot. But judging by Los Angeles at any point before 1941, America was ethnically pure as well. No other city was ruled for so long into the twentieth century by a cohesive white Anglo-Saxon protestant majority.

It was World War II that industrialized Los Angeles and brought millions of minorities into the city, but WASP political control was not broken until the late 1960s. What was true for southern California was largely true for the rest of the country: "the national interest" was the wholly owned preserve of a WASP upper class in the first two-thirds of this century. It is usually foreigners who point this out to Americans, however. For example, British writer Godfrey Hodgson has remarked that the "Eastern Establishment" is "fondest of scoffing at the very idea that it exists." He goes on to say, "To an extent that is quite astonishing to Europeans, who are brought up to think of the U.S. as a great populist democracy with a strong anti-aristocratic bias, the foreign policy of the U.S. as a great world power over the whole seventy years from 1898 to 1968 was a family affair."[3] Of course, this took a different form on the Pacific coast, where WASP elites associated themselves with legends about conquerors and cowboys, the frontier and the free market (a mythology that Ronald Reagan embodied).

At any rate, we see again that many presumably permanent differences between the United States and Japan are artifacts of recent history—post-1941 at a minimum, perhaps post-1960s (when the civil rights movement, in particular, brought rights that had long been enjoyed by the white majority to African Americans, Asian Americans, and other minorities, thus disrupting a previously uniform WASP hegemony).

WHAT IS WAR?

Like so many other important words in our vocabulary, *war* has become a fungible term. We hear about the "trade war" over the Lexus and Infiniti sedans, or Patrick Buchanan's "culture war" and the war in Bosnia that often consists of random mayhem (for example, seventy-one young, middle-class people being killed by a mortar shell crashing into outdoor cafes and coffee shops in one terrible incident in May 1995).

In the Western tradition, Thucydides was the first to examine the nature of war. Perhaps the most famous line from *The Peloponnesian War* is this: "War is a stern teacher." This comes not from a consideration of war in general, however, but from his analysis of the civil war in Corcyra: "War is a stern teacher. So revolutions broke out in city after city. . . . What used to be described as a thoughtless act of aggression was now regarded as the courage one would expect to find in a party member; to think of the future and wait was merely another way of saying one was a coward; any idea of moderation was just an attempt to disguise one's unmanly character."[4] Corcyra was a civil war like the Korean or Vietnam wars. It is far more common to find in Thucydides' work the distant origin of *realpolitik* theory—of power politics between nation-states—as if the realism of our time was also the realism of his time. Or one can simply read Thucydides' analysis of the abandoned nature of the war in Corcyra to apply to wars in general. But of course it does not. At many times and places before the twentieth century, in East and West, war was a rule-governed, even chivalrous activity engaged in by professional soldiers, with elaborate codes, oaths, and norms that abstracted it from the daily life of noncombatants. It goes without saying that no one needs to tell this to students of Japanese history. Both East and West produced something we might call "civilized warfare."[5] Clausewitz's *On War* drove home the difference between premodern and modern war. War as he understood it was indeed the product of a "civilization," of a "culture." War of a certain kind is the product of a civilization and a culture that is indistinguishable from the modern, industrial epoch that dawned just as "modern war" came into being. And this is uncivilized warfare, driven by a determined race for national power. It was above all Napoleon who pioneered modern warfare, with all the people and all the nation aroused and mobilized for the fight. In the words of Anatol Rapaport, "Napoleon taught one great lesson: the universal currency of politics is power, and power resides in the ability to wreak physical destruction. Clausewitz embodied this lesson in unifying a philosophy of politics with a philosophy of war."[6] It is with Clausewitz that we can begin to understand the nature of modern war in general and World Wars I and II specifically. "War," in his famous definition, "is an act of violence intended to compel our opponent to fulfill our will."[7] This statement leads logically to the idea that the goal of war is "complete victory." Thus, "moderation in war is an absurdity."[8]

It would be a distinct understatement to say that *On War* is a text that is destined constantly to be misread—especially by those military professionals who seem over and over to focus only on this statement. A full reading of Clausewitz's text leads to a quite different conclusion, namely, that war is a fully *political* human activity in which a rational intelligence marries the means of warfare to the ends of policy. How this is done involves logic, strategy, and cunning but also an intuitive knowledge of the battlefield and the totality—the "organic whole"—of war and politics that can come only to one fully experienced in both. War is not something left to the generals or to the politicians; it is the province of the statesman or, in Clausewitz's time, the sovereign king or his executive minister of state.[9]

For Clausewitz, the politics of war do *not* dictate the use of every means at one's disposal or the absolute obliteration of the enemy; like everything else about war, the conclusion of the victory is also political. "The result in war is never absolute," he wrote; if war were mere force, "the moment it is called forth by policy it would step into the place of policy."[10] But this idea is "radically false," he continues, since war "is not an extreme thing which expends itself at one single discharge; it is the operation of powers" (118–19). War is "a wonderful trinity," he writes in a key passage: it is composed of the hatreds and animosities that brought it about (which he locates in "blind instinct") and the play of probability and chance ("which make it a free activity of the soul"); last but most important, war is a subordinate element of politics and in that sense "belongs purely to . . . reason" (121). War is therefore not to be left to the generals or the specialists in the use of force. War moves toward its goal, which is the surrender of the enemy. But that, too, is a politically governed activity. "Unconditional surrender" rarely occurs and "is not a condition necessary to peace. . . . the idea of a complete defeat of the enemy would be a mere imaginative flight" (124–29).

The Napoleonic Wars coincided with the first industrial revolution, which began the ceaseless technological innovation that has prevailed ever since and that has given to modern capitalism's cycles of creation and destruction (Joseph Schumpeter's terms)[11] a kinetic velocity. The technologies of the second industrial revolution (which led to the development of submarines, warplanes, the machine gun, and poison gas) combined with Napoleonic national mobilization to give us the irrational slaughters of World War I—a war known to the cunning of history as "the war to end all wars."

From Clausewitz's viewpoint (the necessity for war to be commanded by a rational political intelligence; war as "politics by other means") World War I is inexplicable. No "correlates-of-war" research project (such as those of Quincy Wright)[12] and no "rational-actor" analysis has ever satisfactorily explained the outbreak of the war in 1914 on the heels of the assassination of Archduke Ferdinand at Sarajevo; the mobilization for war was born of the automaticity of military-bureaucratic planning (e.g., Germany's "Schlieffen Plan") and of preexisting blueprints for state mobilization (e.g., those of Russia), both of which were independent of human intelligence. And then the war bogged down to a merciless slaughter in the trenches; it became a cataclysmic human waste from which no one profited and to which no rational laws of warfare applied. Bernard Brodie was correct to say that World War I vitiated all of Clausewitz's dicta about war being governed by politics—that is, by an intelligent rationale.[13]

World War I did ring down the curtain on one phase of modern war, however, and that was the eighteenth- and nineteenth-century practice of wars of aggression for "reasons of state"—war as the commonplace exercise of the power of great nations. War had been understood as "a *normal and perpetual state of affairs*"[14] (indeed, this was a key aspect of the Old World that Americans sought to escape). But no more: the dominant discourse of the interwar period was peace, international cooperation, and the attempt to codify and outlaw warlike behavior. Aggression across national boundaries was now something "Bismarckian," something to be placed in and of the past. The Kellogg-Briand Pact of 1928 sought to outlaw war except for self-defense; it is but one example of a deep and intense interwar effort at what we now call "peace studies," which began with the so-called "inquiry" into the causes and consequences of World War I, and in which John Maynard Keynes first manifested his distinguished intelligence. The League of Nations, of course, was the embodiment of the Wilsonian idea of a world under law (even if the U.S. Senate broke President Wilson's heart by refusing to join).

These laudable efforts toward a world under the rule of law rather than the law of the jungle did not occur in a vacuum, of course, but in a world still carved up by several imperial powers and still under the hegemonic hand of Pax Britannica. After World War I, however, that hand was faltering and palsied, and the putative new hegemon—the United States—was involved in another episode of withdrawal from world affairs. England's inability to hold the system together, and America's unwillingness to do so, mark one critical explanation of the coming of World War II.[15]

The United States was probably the leading productive force in the world by 1900, and by the early 1920s, American banks had displaced British and European capital in the world economy. American mass production, symbolized by the assembly lines of the Ford Motor Company, was the envy of the world. In October 1929, the Wall Street crash detonated a world depression, which was followed within a few years by a complete collapse of the world economy and any hope of international cooperation. An immobilized world system that refused to function was the essential backdrop to the idiosyncratic national solutions embarked upon by all the great powers. "The snapping of the golden thread brought a world revolution," was Polanyi's metaphor for the effects of the collapse of the gold standard in 1933, which was itself a metaphor for the absence of a hegemonic hand.[16]

The United States was lucky to get only a New Deal; the nations of Europe, and soon Japan and its colonial holdings, got a New Order. Polanyi's great insight was to understand that each nation "withdrew" from the world system in terms of the complex of social, economic, and political forces at home—and, I might add, the *space* available to it in the globe's imperial geography. For Germany and Japan, this was a combustible mix, made more so by their respective "lateness" in world time as industrial and imperial powers. Napoleon's national mobilization for war became, in the 1930s, a series of national mobilizations for industrial production—including Stalin's massive, pitiless, but ultimately successful achievement of socialist industrialization "in one country" from 1928 to 1941. Meanwhile, Japan and Germany, with a similar if less visible brutality, had begun to industrialize themselves out of the world depression by 1935. Their growth rates advanced rapidly thereafter. In my view, the "domestic mix" in Japan and Germany was different: Germany got a virulent fascism and Japan got a virulent militarism, but militarism is still not fascism. Others may disagree. It is more important for this chapter to ask what these 1930s structural conditions meant for Japan's place in the world and the coming of the Pacific War.[17]

The force field driving Japan and the United States toward confrontation was the absence of a clear hegemon (or the existence of a contested hegemony) in vast reaches of the Pacific Ocean, as well as the relative indeterminacy of northeast Asia in the imperial geography. Japan's vigorous industrialization in the 1880s and after occurred in one of the few remaining "breathing spaces" in a world occupied by European imperialism—as E. H. Norman was among the first to argue.[18] Its expansion into Korea required clearing the Russian presence from the Korean Peninsula (in the 1904–1905 war), but Japan was the Anglo-American favorite in this rivalry. This preference was driven by England's standing in the European balance of power and the new American position in the Philippines. In a sense, Japan got the empire that the United States and England wanted it to have, or at least had few qualms about—witness Theodore Roosevelt's Nobel Prize for brokering the peace between Tokyo and Moscow at Portsmouth, after Japan had established its "protectorate" in Korea. The United States never again challenged Japan's control of Korea until the Cairo Declaration in 1943.

Korea, and subsequently Manchuria, were "frontiers" for Japanese acquisition and development in part because no other great power claimed them after 1905. Japanese leaders likened their settlement to the settling and development of the American West (they even spoke of a "covered-wagon movement" to try to get Japanese to migrate to Manchuria). This attempt to strike a note of similarity to the American experience is less far-fetched than it seems when we adopt the perspective of the 1930s. At that time, the Atlanticist internationalism of Roosevelt was overshadowed by forces that came to be known as "isolationist."

Isolationism was always a bad term; American nationalism might be a better term. American nationalism in the 1930s meant high tariffs and a self-contained political economy based on the vast national market—still not fully developed—combined with a unilateralist foreign policy directed toward Central America and East Asia. "Isolationists" did have a foreign policy: it was to expand into regions "open" to their interests. They tended to support Roosevelt's Latin American policies but tried to avoid regions of British empire building.[19]

In an important analysis, Gareth Stedman Jones finds the characteristic nonterritoriality of American imperialism abroad (except in the Philippines) to be "founded on an unprecedented territorialism 'at home.'" He describes the opening of the American West as "one vast process of territorial seizure and occupation."[20] After the closing of the frontier, it was East Asia that held expansionist attention; the march toward East Asia was an extension of the Westward march to the frontier—"a straight line of march drawn by its length almost to a circle," as Richard Drinnon put it.[21] The American empire pushed toward the setting sun, toward "those distant regions where the Far West becomes the Far East," in John Hay's phrase.[22] Walter LaFeber found the same expansionist thrust westward; he linked Frederick Jackson Turner's frontier theses with the imperialism of the 1890s and Woodrow Wilson's "new frontiers" in "the Far Pacific."[23] The distinction, however, is that expansionists preferred unilateral American sway in the Pacific, whereas internationalists favored cooperation with imperial Britain.

As we saw in the previous chapter, until the world depression, Japan fit rather well within Anglo-American hegemony (the "internationalism" of that era), at a time when American expansionism was relatively dormant. Japan more or less got the empire the British and Americans wanted it to have, and only sought to organize an exclusive regional sphere when several other countries did the same—after the collapse of the world economy in the 1930s.

I have now briefly assessed "the nature of the whole" in which the Pacific War occurred, to use the phrase Clausewitz uttered immediately after he posed the question What is war?[24] I think I have done it from Clausewitz's "right point of view"—even if this is not the American or Japanese point of view. The nature of the whole was this: a globe divided by colonialism and imperialism, with a world system under the hegemonic hand of England and its upcoming junior partner, the United States. This was the organic whole that animated the war plans of Japan's decision makers in the months after war began in Europe.

Perhaps we are ready to address that war now. But we must ask another question: not simply "what is war," but is there such a thing as war for a righteous cause? That is, something called "just war"? The central text for answering this question in contemporary American discourse is Michael Walzer's *Just and Unjust Wars*. "A just war is one that it is morally urgent to win," he writes.

> Critical values are at stake: political independence, communal liberty, human life. Other means failing (an important qualification), wars to defend these values are justified. . . .
> We need to seek the legitimate ends of war, the goals that can be rightly aimed at. These will also be the limits of a just war. Once they are won, or once they are within political reach, the fighting should stop.[25]

Just-war doctrine, beginning with St. Augustine, has always recognized the right of self-defense as the first principle justifying the use of force. Many analysts take this to be self-evident, as if we always know self-defense when we see it. But of course we don't, and so the interwar period saw endless efforts to define aggression, since aggression must exist before we can think about justified resistance. This idea is intrinsic to Walzer's entire conception of just war. He adds to Augustine's dictum the idea of a rule-giving international community that is capable of defining aggression and self-defense, and he believes he thereby derives "a powerful theory" of just war.[26]

At a time when the breakdown of the world economy went hand in hand with the breakdown of collective security, what international community was there to define aggression in the late 1930s? When North Korea invaded South Korea in 1950, why was the international community known as the United Nations able to define as aggression military action occurring within well-recognized Korean national territory, when no Korean was a member of that community and no Korean assisted the United States in drawing a line at the thirty-eighth parallel? The second objection highlights the illogic of Walzer's understanding of the Korean War as a just war;[27] however, the first does not necessarily undermine his interpretation of World War II as just. In the absence of a legitimate international body, we can still determine that Hitler's invasion of Poland was aggression, which gave the Poles the right to use force in self-defense. It was indeed Bismarckian; had Hitler been Bismarck, it might not have been more than that. But given the uniqueness of Nazi crimes, namely, the attempt to destroy entire peoples just because they *were* certain peoples (above all European Jewry)—a holocaust gratuitous and incidental to any conceivable war aim—it was something more. It was a "good war"—because people of good will thought it was "morally urgent" to defeat Hitlerism. Hitler offended the "right point of view" of the common man, of humanity, and rightly so.[28] What about Japan?

JAPAN AT WAR: ATROCITY? GENOCIDE? HOLOCAUST?

It is no accident that both the Eastern and Western philosophical traditions dwell upon what things are called: naming and the rectification of names as a central aspect of thinking, judging, and remembering. By naming, we locate or recall something in our memory, rescue it from oblivion, retain it and keep it for thought. The opposite of memory is forgetting. In a passage that had a deep influence on Freud, Nietzsche wrote that forgetting is no mere result of inertia: "It is rather an active and in the strictest sense positive faculty of repression." The human animal needs to be forgetful, he says, for forgetfulness is "like a doorkeeper, a preserver of psychic order, repose and etiquette. . . . there could be no present without forgetfulness."[29] And of great relevance to our discussion is this, again from Nietzsche: " 'I have done that,' says my memory. 'I cannot have done that,' says my pride, and remains inexorable. Eventually—memory yields."[30] In these ideas we find the virtue and the necessity of examining the many melancholy questions still existing from the Pacific War—from a history that has been buried for too long and that all too many people would like to keep buried.

Japan's moral nadir in the Pacific War is the infamous bacteriological and medical experiments carried out on prisoners of war and political dissidents in China by Unit 731.[31] What do we call this? It constitutes an atrocity but not genocide (because of the small scale). That should be of little comfort to anyone, since Unit 731's activities caused universal revulsion when they were revealed. The sordid history of the *ianfu*, or "comfort women," had the atrocious scale of genocide but might better call forth a new term, "femicide." Added to the atrocity of sexual slavery is the scale, the race, and the gender of the majority of the victims, that is, Korean women (somewhere between 100,000 and 200,000). This was the worst of atrocities perpetrated on the Korean people, but it was part and parcel of a larger if lesser atrocity, namely, the mobilization for forced labor and forced soldiery of millions of Koreans in the Pacific War.[32] (The forced relocation of 120,000 Americans of Japanese descent is an analogue to Japan's mobilization policy, the key differences today being the U.S. government's clear expression of regret in 1988 and its compensation for the victims, in contrast to the still halting attempts to do something similar in Japan.)

The Nanjing Massacre was an atrocity of extraordinary scale, with upwards of three hundred thousand victims. Although done by rampaging troops at a particular extremity, it was nevertheless part of a general Japanese strategy of conducting annihilation campaigns throughout northeast and north China from 1931 on; this was motivated primarily by anticommunism and racism. Perhaps twenty million Chinese and Koreans died as a result, making this despicable strategy one of the great crimes of the twentieth century. It was genocidal. Although claims were made that it had some relationship to the goals of war, it really had none but the rape, pillage, and murder of innocent people. With regard to Japan's crimes, it seems that we can agree upon atrocity and genocide—but not holocaust—as appropriate descriptions of the worst of Japanese behavior. Let me now turn to the American side.

John Dower argues that Hiroshima and Nagasaki constituted "nuclear genocide," and Richard Minear, in a fascinating and provocative essay, likens these acts to the destruction of European Jewry.[33] Earlier, I suggested that Hitler's final solution was unique in World War II because it had no possible relationship to the war effort and was aimed at the elimination of an entire people, that is, at genocide. Genocide can also occur in the absence of rudimentary concern about taking innocent lives in large numbers.

Hiroshima, I would argue, was not genocide. It was an atrocity on a large scale and therefore a war crime. American leaders conceived of Hiroshima as a means toward ending suffering rather than prolonging it—that is the best that can be said for their intent, and it does not override the atrocious nature of the act for reasons given below. But it was not genocide. Nagasaki is different: If it was gratuitous at best (atomic annihilation as an afterthought), it was therefore genocidal at worst (because it served no clear war purpose). Its large scale and its lack of rudimentary concern for innocent life places it alongside the red winds of March 1945: genocidal. Before thinking more about the end of this war, however, we should also examine the beginning.

EAST WIND, RAIN

"On the morning of December 7, 1941"—can one write those words yet again?—with the opening shot coming at 7:57 A.M., two waves of Japanese bombers, 250 planes in all, destroyed large portions of the American Pacific Fleet at Pearl Harbor (conveniently huddled together to "prevent sabotage") and hit nine airfields elsewhere in the American territory called Hawaii. Nine hours later more Japanese aircraft hit Clark Field in the Philippines, where General Douglas MacArthur and his staff inexplicably still had various aircraft gathered together (again, to prevent sabotage), including two squadrons of valuable B-17D bombers. Total American casualties in the Pearl Harbor raid were 2,335 navy, army, and Marine personnel dead, and 1,143 wounded. The Americans lost eight battleships, three light cruisers, three destroyers, and four auxiliary craft. Total civilians killed: 68.[34] The stunning (if Pyrrhic) success of Japan's strategic operation is frequently noted, but few note the precision with which the attack separated soldier and civilian. A counterforce attack directed exclusively at military targets, it had a soldier-to-civilian kill ratio of about thirty-four to one.

What would Clausewitz say of the rationale and conduct of the Pearl Harbor assault? He would say that it fulfilled the goals of his chapter titled "Boldness"—"the noblest of virtues" in a soldier and the essential "right of citizenship" in war.[35] Japan was clearly weaker than the United States, directing attention to the advantages of surprise; furthermore its position in the Pacific was a wasting asset as the European war continued to develop, bringing ever closer the prospect that the United States would enter the war against Japan's allies. The move to the offensive, Clausewitz wrote, "is always commanded when the future holds out a better prospect, not to ourselves, but to the adversary."[36] The martial virtues of courage and aggressive initiative must always be restrained by those of foresight and prudence, however.[37] Here is revealed the attack's ultimate foolhardiness—that it served only to waken "a sleeping giant and fill him with terrible resolve" (in the words of the man who planned it, Fleet Admiral Yamamoto Isoroku).

According to Seisaburo Sato, Saburo Ienaga, and Akira Iriye, it was oil that made the difference in Japan's singularly autonomous foreign-policy decision in July 1941 to "move south," which culminated in the attack on Pearl Harbor.[38] A new book offers much evidence that this conflict over mineral resources went well beyond oil to many strategic raw materials: still, it was these materials that were the Japanese target and the lever that brought the United States into the war.[39] In other words, the best Japanese and American historians agree that the attack occurred, as many Japanese leaders continue to argue, in the context of an Asia that was still divided up by Western imperial powers. But that does not justify the attack, and Sato, Ienaga, and Iriye make that clear. There is little evidence that the Western powers were averse to an imperial Japan that played second fiddle to England or America as a kind of junior partner. The tightening American embargoes in 1939–1941 were designed to get Japan back into that comfortable framework. These measures did not make of the aggressive actions of Japan's militarists a morally defensible use of force—a "just war." It was aggression, but it was no more than that.

To refute another rationale for Pearl Harbor that was offered at the time—and sometimes, even today—Japan did not "liberate" East Asians from Western imperialism. Korea, Japan's first victim, had many followers of Japanese modernism before 1910 but hardly any thereafter. The same was true of China after the infamous Twenty-One Demands. To be a Korean or Chinese nationalist was to be anti-Japanese. The Pacific War was not short but very long (1931–1945) and involved a vastly deepened oppression of Korea and China. So "the right point of view" here is: another unjust war.

Still, in the Clausewitzian sense, Pearl Harbor was mere garden-variety aggression; it differed little from numerous other military adventures and therefore does not qualify as a special sort of war crime. Given the precise targeting and the conduct of the attack, it was certainly not atrocious. Japan's crime, as had been the case so often in the modern era, was to be a latecomer, and one that used anachronistic methods—in this case, Bismarckian methods—in an Anglo-American world where the preservation of peace and collective security had become the watchwords (at least until Japan in 1931, Italy in 1936, and Germany in 1938 proved the words to be hollow). The most important point is this: Pearl Harbor did not provide sufficient justification for any act of revenge that went beyond compelling the aggressor to surrender. If war crimes came later in "the good war" (and I will argue that they did), there can be no claim of moral equivalency between those crimes and Japanese aggression in 1941.

These points should be obvious to the honest historian, even if they are denied from time to time by American apologists and Japanese politicians long associated with the right wing of the Liberal Democratic Party (LDP). What is not obvious, and what Japan did not understand at the time, is what I have called "the American way of going to war."[40] A nation of superior strength will often find it to its advantage to let the weaker side strike first. The reasons can be gleaned from Clausewitz's discussion of "the superiority of the defense over the attack," but also in Mao Zedong's dictum, related by Chou Enlai, that "we control others by letting them have the initiative."[41] The United States was still sitting out World War II in December 1941, more than two years after Hitler invaded Poland and quickly went on to unify Europe under his control (thus transforming the balance of power in the world).

About ten days before Pearl Harbor, Secretary of War Henry Stimson entered in his diary a famous and much-argued statement—that he had met with President Roosevelt to discuss the evidence of impending hostilities with Japan, and the question was "how we should maneuver them [the Japanese] into the position of firing the first shot without allowing too much danger to ourselves." The preeminent American historian in the 1930s, Charles Beard, quoted this in his book about Pearl Harbor.[42] Beard also quoted another statement by Forrest Davis and Ernest Lindley:

> The question perplexing high officials was how, in the absence of a direct Japanese attack on the American flag, to summon the nation, divided as it then was on questions of foreign policy, to the strong action which they believed essential. . . . It was commonly supposed that the Japanese were too smart to solve this problem for the President by a direct assault on the American flag. (418)

Beard also cited Stimson's testimony before Congress in 1946 in which he said that it is dangerous to "wait until [the enemy] gets the jump on you by taking the initiative" (519); nonetheless, Stimson continued,

> in letting the Japanese fire the first shot, we realized that in order to have the full support of the American people it was desirable to make sure that the Japanese be the ones to do this so that there should remain no doubt in anyone's mind as to who were the aggressors.
>
> It is axiomatic that the best defense is offense. It is always dangerous to wait and let the enemy make the first move. . . . On the other hand, I realized that the situation could be made more clean cut from the point

of view of public opinion if a further warning [to the Japanese] were given. (526–27)

It is not my purpose here to argue that Stimson and Roosevelt "maneuvered" America (or Japan) into the war but merely to cite this analysis and to note that most American wars have begun when "the other guy" fired the first shot. The strategy of passive defense is not necessarily innocent of considerations of power, as any psychoanalyst knows. But what is interesting in the 1990s is to see how many Japanese analysts are now coming to understand this point as part of the "total field" of the Pearl Harbor attack and thus to question not only the end but also the beginning of the U.S.-Japan war.

The U.S.-Japan war was short. As most historians now understand, the die for Japan's defeat was cast in the Pacific at Midway (July 1942) and on land after Guadalcanal (December 1942). *How* the war would end (if not when) was visible within six months to a year after Pearl Harbor: Japan was going to lose. So the point of moral leadership was not to use every element of power at hand to bring about surrender. Precisely this aspect of the U.S.-Japan war— a contest of unequals—raises another element of justice in warfare.

Friedrich Nietzsche, a great student of power, said this: "Equality before the enemy: the first presupposition of an *honest* duel. Where one feels contempt, one *cannot* wage war; where one commands, where one sees something beneath oneself, one has no business waging war."[43] Jean Bethke Elshtain finds in Nietzsche's teaching a "refusal to bring all one's power to bear" and thus an argument against revenge.[44] As Hannah Arendt understood, this was also Christ's radical teaching—"freedom from vengeance, which encloses both doer and sufferer in the relentless automatism of the action process."[45] The renunciation of power, of course, is a principle that is also enshrined in Japan's *bushido* tradition.[46] But here we are talking about American responsibility for *jus in bello,* that is, for the *conduct* of a "good war." As Walzer argues over and over, "war is always judged twice," first by its ends and second by its means; good wars can be fought unjustly and bad wars can be fought justly.[47] Being a victim of aggression does not absolve the victim of responsibility for civilized warfare. When we think through this aspect of the just-war tradition, we can begin to understand the wartime consequences of American racism toward the Japanese people, and of Japanese racism toward Koreans and Chinese.

RED WIND

Fire and water are essential life forces, or so some ancients taught us; others spoke of earth, wind, and fire. Water is smooth, supple, slippery—a flow that in its natural state exemplifies the archaic ideal of the golden mean. It upsets nature and humanity only at the extremes of draught and deluge. Fire is always volatile, always extreme, always ready to flare. It knows no balance or neutrality except before its victims, which it annihilates with a perfect equanimity. Even its smallest quantities can awaken a holocaust: periodically, the errant match tossed into the chaparral ignites fires all over southern California. That is why the fire's trace—its spark—has no linguistic counterpart in water: surely it is not the water's trace—the "drop"—which in its scant volume still has beauty and can still save a life.

Wind shares with fire the qualities of volatility, extremity, lack of balance, and neutrality. The human being consumed by fire or wind experiences an original innocence before nature's power. In the spring of 1947, my family and I survived an Indiana tornado that destroyed our home. I can still remember the delight I felt as a three-year-old when my father first told me about the power of a tornado to flatten a building or throw a car sixty feet through the air. I was even more delighted on the day when he told me we were experiencing "tornado weather." The sun came and went all day, punctuated by brief rain showers. The radio reported tornadoes in our area. What a thrill!

Suddenly, shards of lightning struck the ground, and deep thunder rolled above us; the sky turned black in the middle of the day, and a distant, constant roaring grew louder and louder, closer and closer. My father ran to herd us into the basement, but he could not overcome a powerful vacuum holding the door shut. Now the sound was like a freight train bearing down upon us. We all jumped under my parents' double bed just as the central pillar of the tornado ripped through the house. Now my mental state was one of complete vertigo, helplessness, and terror: shock.

Seconds later the air was miraculously still, and we emerged from beneath the bed and shook off plaster dust from our legs. Only one wall of the house was still standing. The roof had blown off, and a large tree had fallen in our living room. Another one had crushed our car. My father's eyeglasses lay undisturbed on a bedside table. None of us were hurt or even scratched. But I never again wished to hear about the power of tornadoes (though both my sons ask me to lull them to sleep with this same story).

One point to this experience is that one who has not lived through either a natural or a man-made inferno cannot possibly understand the stark, unmediated terror with which the human being experiences tornadoes of wind or fire. And therefore no one—including Robert Oppenheimer himself—could imagine what an atomic explosion would really be like.[48] Survivors of Hiroshima and Nagasaki are in many cases mute testimony to this fact in their inability to tell us what really happened.

Baptisms come by fire and water, but according to time-honored mythology, humans are tried and judged only by fire. Los Angeles has always had too much of the capricious elements, fire and wind, and not enough of the propitiating other, water. And so the city sits poised on catastrophe, violating the Confucian middle way, that is, the composed balance that regulates life. The Los Angeles basin's survivors—those best adapted to its nature—are the fireplants: the dense chaparral that covers the ground and warms up in the sun, heating to the point that it reaches an infernal equinox, whereupon it germinates. This is the evil genius of the chaparral: Los Angeles needs it for watershed, to hold back the overflow; but it's so combustible that fire consumes it, spreads it, and then brings along in its absent wake the flood, too. (This was another bad joke the American frontier had waiting for the nomads who peopled it.)

The late comedian John Belushi starred in a film titled *1941*, a farce about the Japanese bombing Los Angeles based on a minor panic that ensued in the city shortly after Pearl Harbor. Let us imagine this city in the midst of a prolonged heat wave—no rain for weeks, the lawns and the hillsides parched and dead, the dense and ubiquitous chaparral at its most combustible, and the red wind howling through the mountain passes from the desert. Suddenly 334 bombers appear in the distance, their motors droning in unison, their bellies full of bombs, the bombs full of jellied gasoline, phosphorous, magnesium, and napalm. The bombers come in low, at six thousand feet, conscious of the prevailing winds and the turbulence of the Los Angeles basin. Suddenly, the entire city is put to the torch. The atmospheric conditions are such that the incendiaries create wild firestorms—fire hurricanes—that course back and forth across the city.

> The wind had whipped hundreds of small fires into great walls of flame, which began leaping streets, firebreaks, and canals at dizzying speed.[49]
>
> Under the wind and the gigantic breath of fire, immense incandescent vortices rose in a number of places, swirling, flattening, sucking whole blocks of houses into their maelstrom of fire.[50]
>
> The conflagration . . . was rapaciously expansive, a pillar of fire that was pushed over by the surface winds to touch the ground and gain new fury from the oxygen and combustibles it seized.[51]

Temperatures as high as eighteen hundred degrees fahrenheit send Angelenos running toward the river basins, but they are dry. So they then flock to the coast for relief, but the Pacific is salt to their wounds.

> A woman spent the night knee-deep in the bay, holding onto a piling with her three-year-old son clinging to her back; by morning several

of the people around her were dead of burns, shock, fatigue and hypo-thermia. Thousands submerged themselves in stagnant, foul-smelling canals with their mouths just above the surface, but many died from smoke inhalation, anoxia, or carbon monoxide poisoning, or were boiled to death when the fire storm heated the water.[52]

It was, of course, Tokyo that experienced the *akakaze* (red wind) on 9–10 March 1945, not Los Angeles. Sixty-five other cities would be razed be-fore the war ended, but none with the hurricane and tornado force of Air Force commander General Curtis LeMay's pyromania on that night. Sixteen square miles of a densely populated, modern city burned, leaving at least eighty-four thousand dead and a like or greater number injured—often cru-elly and horribly so.[53] What would the American people have felt then—or today—if it had been Los Angeles? Would they be forgiving? Would they offer to a Japanese version of LeMay the American equivalent of the medal LeMay received in Tokyo on 6 December 1964, the First Class of the Rising Sun?[54] Would they call this man-made inferno a war crime?

In a recent book on war and morality, Robert L. Holmes examines Augus-tinian just-war theory (finding it much less clear than have others) and goes on to argue that given the horrible destructiveness of modern technology, no modern war can be just because innocents will always be sacrificed.[55] In somewhat similar fashion Anatole Rapaport suggests that Clausewitz's con-ception of total war (growing out of Napoleon's innovations) must be dif-ferent from the total war conceptions of mid-twentieth-century strategists. If the first conception involves the mobilization of all national capacities, the second conjures up exterminism and therefore all discussion of "just wars" becomes moot.

Rapaport shows how the exterminism acquiesced to by all the powers in World War II became the reigning doctrine during the long years of the Soviet-American "balance of terror": "It is doubtful whether Clausewitz ever envisaged 'civilized war' as a slaughter of civilian populations. Even in his 'absolute war' he saw slaughter confined to the battlefield. . . . The modern advocates of 'total war,' e.g. the Nazis and some partisans of 'total victory' in the United States, explicitly included (and now include) civilian populations as military targets. For example, the U.S. Air Force ROTC manual, *Funda-mentals of Aerospace Weapons Systems*, defines a 'military target' as fol-lows: 'Any person, thing, idea, entity, or location selected for destruction, inactivation, or rendering non-usable with weapons which will reduce or destroy the will or ability of the enemy to resist.' "[56] The embodiment of such thinking on the American side in World War II was LeMay, the architect of the firebombing of Japanese cities. LeMay was the winner of many medals and awards, but with his dull wit, his utter absence of reflective mind, his crude racism,[57] and his mindless devotion to the use of every weapon at his disposal, he was a classic representative of Clausewitz's "blind instinct" and Hannah Arendt's "banality of evil." To put it simply, LeMay's *akakaze* was an atrocity, a war crime.

BLACK RAIN: HIROSHIMA AND NAGASAKI

At 8:15 A.M. on 6 August 1945, the American B-29 Superfortress *Enola Gay* swooped down over Hiroshima and released a uranium-235 bomb weighing eight thousand pounds, which burst over the city at a height of 580 meters. Within one millionth of a second, the billowing fireball reached several million degrees centigrade. "Thereafter, with the movement of the shock front, or wave, a tremendous pressure rapidly builds up, and the fireball now consists of two concentric regions—an inner hot region and an outer region of somewhat lower temperature. For some time the fireball continues to expand, but the shock spreads more rapidly. With the spread of the shock front, the temperature of the air surrounding the fireball rises and becomes luminous."[58] Whereas LeMay had to concentrate large numbers of incendiaries to create a firestorm, the atomic bomb at Hiroshima caused an immense volume of superheated air to spiral upward—a cataclysmic "black wind" that funneled evaporated human and material substance into a terrible void at the center, then hurled it skyward, sucking cold air in from all directions behind and below it. This fresh oxygen fueled the firestorm that blew for hours in the city with velocities of eighteen meters per second. The fireball of a conventional incendiary bomb would burn or blow away wooden houses within forty meters of the epicenter. The Hiroshima bomb, deploying a force equivalent to 12.5 kilotons of TNT, did the same thing at a radius of two kilometers, destroying a total of about thirteen square kilometers. Starting from about 11 A.M., a violent whirlwind blew northward through the city from the epicenter, only calming down by the late afternoon.

Meanwhile, amid the firestorms, about an hour after the blast, an ominous, highly radioactive "black rain" began to fall on the northern and western neighborhoods of Hiroshima.[59] It was composed of minute particles of the evaporated city—carbonized wood, flesh, and bone. The dreadful drops fell for another five hours, leading not a few to assume that the heavens wept for the dead of Hiroshima. Those who were far enough away to survive the blast now witnessed a march of the walking dead as silent people with no faces filed by, trying to escape to the hills (there might be another bomb) or find water. "Great sheets of skin had peeled away from their tissues to hang down like rags on a scarecrow."[60] This single uranium-235 bomb killed eighty thousand people, followed by another hundred thousand in succeeding months and years.

Three days later, at 11:00 A.M. on 9 August, the B-29 nicknamed *Bock's Car* appeared over Nagasaki with a bombardier named Kermit Beahan sitting in the Plexiglas nose of the plane. It was his twenty-seventh birthday. He released a plutonium-239 bomb called the Fat Man over the city. Attached to a parachute, it weighed nine thousand pounds and took forty seconds to fall one and a half miles to its point of detonation, five hundred meters above a Catholic cathedral. Equivalent to twenty-two kilotons of TNT, this bomb nearly doubled the force of the first atomic bomb. But it created a smaller firestorm because the direction of the blast was through the valley to the north of Nagasaki, where there was a lower density of population and housing. About twenty minutes after the explosion, more black rain fell on the Nishiyama neighborhood, east of the epicenter.[61]

At the Junshin School that morning, a nun led a group of girls in chanting psalms honoring twenty-six Catholic martyrs who had died centuries earlier. The girls all perished in the Nagasaki firestorm. This inspired Nagai Takashi to write

Virgins like lilies white
Disappeared burning red

In the flames of the holocaust
Chanting psalms
To the Lord.[62]

About thirty thousand people died in the first minutes after the blast, and forty-four thousand more perished later of wounds, burns, or radiation poisoning.

It has now become commonplace to argue that a kind of mindless reflex prevailed in the use of the atomic bombs against Hiroshima and Nagasaki. In this view, they are but the culmination of an unthinking, inexorable policy of strategic bombing begun by Hitler's Luftwaffe over London, adopted by London and Washington to punish German cities, and reaching a penultimate climax in the firestorms of Dresden and Tokyo.[63] They also are a consequence of the automaticity with which nuclear physicists, once embarked on the Manhattan Project and immersed in the technicalities of the bomb, continued their work never stopping to inquire whether the bomb ought to be used on human beings. The physicists thought it would be used against Germany, itself engaged in an atom-bomb project. Most (if not all) then went along with the decision to drop it on Japanese cities instead. (Recent new information has shown that military planners preferred Japan as a target because if the bomb was a dud, capturing it would not help the Japanese with a nuclear program as it might well do for Germany.)

However, on the fiftieth anniversary of its use, in 1995, the atomic bomb grated against the common American desire to remember and commemorate the Good War, detonating an explosion of controversy. To most people and to many historians, the burden of history is first and foremost to be a custodian of "the facts," and once the facts have been "found," to let the facts "speak for themselves." That this is an epistemologically naive notion does not stop people—including historians—from believing it.[64] Knowing what we know now, Hiroshima and perhaps especially Nagasaki cannot be looked at from the innocent perspective of the facts. Historians such as Barton J. Bernstein who have studied Truman's atomic decisions with all the benefits of time, hindsight, and declassified papers are not "revisionists" or postmodern relativists. They are empirical historians. The problem is that the facts they keep finding reveal that these devilish bombs were not necessary to get a quick Japanese surrender. Or they tell us that hundreds of thousands of innocent civilians perished to save tens of thousands of invading combatants, something that does not find a justification in just-war (or good-war) doctrine.

Of course, there is still much controversy among the historians of these decisions (see, for instance, the spring 1995 issue of the respected scholarly journal *Diplomatic History*). But the consensus, as given by a moderate and mainstream historian (J. Samuel Walker), is that the official story of Truman's decision to use the atomic bomb—that it was done to save American lives (an argument presented to the public in the first instance by none other than Henry Stimson in a famous *Harper's* article in 1947)—is wrong. "The United States did not drop the bomb to save hundreds of thousands of American lives," Walker writes. He points out that according to military estimates from the time, the number of lives that might be lost in the invasion of Japan that was set to commence with the island of Kyushu in November 1945 was around twenty-five thousand—not the half million to one million that Stimson and Truman later claimed. Nor, he says, did the bombs end the war: "The scholarly consensus holds that the war would have ended within a relatively short time without the atomic attacks and that an invasion of the Japanese islands was an unlikely possibility."[65]

The consensus also extends to the second bomb, the plutonium device detonated over Nagasaki. Martin Sherwin's 1975 book *A World Destroyed: The Atomic Bomb and the Grand Alliance* contained evidence leading the reader to conclude that the Nagasaki bomb was gratuitous at best and genocidal at worst.[66] Although Nagasaki does not draw the attention that Hiroshima does, it is fair to say that most historians now agree with Sherwin.[67] There is a doubly and triply unsettling element about Nagasaki, however, and that is the city's location and history. This is the port city through which

"Dutch learning," which began Japan's modernization and Westernization, first came. During the Tokugawa isolation, from 1600 to 1868, it was home to various heterodoxies that were less tolerated in other places in Japan. It was home also to many Christians, Nagasaki being the one shining success in a nation otherwise impervious to missionary proselytizing. Imagine all this going up in the swirling black wind of August 9 from a bomb gratuitous to the war effort or any other clear purpose exploded above the red domes of the Catholic cathedral at Urakami, long claimed to be the most splendid church in East Asia—it really is too much to contemplate.

Evidence continues to accumulate as to Emperor Hirohito's growing involvement in the war effort as time passed and his crucial role not in bringing about a surrender but in delaying it. "He intervened frequently and directly in ongoing combat operations as well as in planning," Herbert Bix writes in a deeply researched and cogent article. Bix notes that beginning in February 1945, the emperor continuously rejected recommendations that the war be brought to a halt, and his "warmindedness" helped to create the suicidal military mentality that made Okinawa such a bloody "last battle."[68] Claiming upwards of 300,000 lives, at least 150,000 of them civilians, Okinawa to Americans was a premonition of the carnage (American and Japanese) that awaited the invasion of Japan proper; it provided still more reasons for ending the war with atomic decisiveness. Politics on both sides of the Pacific also shaped the crucial issue of Hirohito's position after surrender. Americans who argued for a surrender that enabled the continuation of the imperial dynasty had to bow before wartime passions that had linked Hirohito with Hitler. Japanese who pushed for negotiations had to reckon with an Allied demand for unconditional surrender that might bring the spectacle of the emperor hauled before a war-crimes tribunal. Yet the verdict of Bix's essay is that in spite of all this, the atomic bombs were unnecessary to achieve a Japanese surrender before the invasion of Kyushu.[69]

Stimson figures even more centrally in the remaining unresolved big question about these decisions, namely, whether Truman rushed to use the bombs on Japanese cities not to end World War II but to start the cold war—that is, to staunch the rapid influx of the Soviet Red Army into northeast Asia (and ultimately Japan) in early August 1945 and to intimidate Stalin and thus gain more compliant Soviet behavior at the diplomatic table. This argument has been put forward most vigorously by Gar Alperovitz in his 1965 book *Atomic Diplomacy* and in a subsequent book published in 1995.[70] Stimson and his diary have always been the centerpieces of Alperovitz's evidence. He quotes Stimson as saying, in April 1945, that the bomb "had such a bearing on our present foreign relations and . . . such an important effect upon all my thinking."[71]

In Stimson's words in April 1945, and in his many similar statements, we see the effect that atomic weapons had on the top executive. (Roosevelt was dead, Truman was inexperienced, and so Stimson functioned as Clausewitz's rational agent of the state, aware of the total field of foreign relations.) News of the successful development of the atomic bomb had a great effect on President Roosevelt, too. As Clausewitz would have predicted, Roosevelt instantly understood the political uses of the bomb. Never letting control of the bomb "slip from his grasp" and hearkening to Churchill's judgment that the bomb "would be a terrific factor in the postwar world giving an absolute control to whatever country possessed the secret," by mid-1943 Roosevelt came to see atomic weaponry as integral to all his diplomacy and the shaping of the postwar world.[72]

The American political system disperses power into three branches of government, into a federated national system of states, and into the give-and-take of a raucous democratic politics. In this system, the president has an ultimate power that is at the same time both fettered (by the congressional war-making power, for example) and temporary (gone with the next election). He is above all *alone*—with his great but fleeting power, his insecurity of office, and his singular responsibility for decisions no one else wishes, or has the authority to make. From the perspective of the lonely president, the atomic bomb is irresistible. Symbolically, this magical destructive power holds sway above all the daily flux of politics, bureaucratic infighting, and intramilitary rivalry. It is the one thing that he and he alone controls, a tangible symbol of his singular power compared to that of anyone else. Another top American executive, John J. McCloy, not only backed the new master weapon, the hydrogen bomb, in January 1950 but said the United States "should also build the oxygen bomb" if it existed. Such was the intoxication brought to the executive branch by these new weapons of mass destruction.

President Truman lodged control of atomic power with the Atomic Energy Commission, which kept the fissionable cores of the bombs out of the hands of the American military. Other presidents did likewise in the early years of the cold war. Over and over we can find evidence of the "atomic envy" of the President that other high officials possessed, particularly those in the Air Force so used to delivering the affirmation of raw power, alone and from on high. I do not have the space to extend this argument, but it is here, in Sherwin's researches and in a theory of the executive in the American system, that we can understand why the bomb, once readied, was used: not just to intimidate the Russians, but to intimidate everyone from recalcitrant Republican congressmen to isolationists in the broad body politic to Hirohito to Stalin to Churchill to the "total field" in which the American president has held sway since 1941, namely, the world. (It requires a certain

Clausewitzian definition of knowledge and power to grasp the meaning of this point, I think.)

The true reflection of the American mood about the Good War more than fifty years later is not the growing consensus among historians but the growing unwillingness of a much broader public to confront unpalatable facts. This unwillingness is pandered to by certain writers and publishers. We might call this "the David McCullough strategy"—something increasingly useful in the current milieu of American public opinion. That strategy is to write history apart from the historians and thus to reconstitute a public history that is indistinguishable from the official story. McCullough, of course, is the author of the Pulitzer Prize–winning and best-selling biography *Truman.* He revives the Truman-Stimson rationale that the bomb saved American lives (250,000 of them in his rendering) and does not trifle with archival material to the contrary.[73] His stratagem is to extrude the historians and their documents. That turned out to be the strategy of the Smithsonian Institution as well.

On 30 January 1995, the secretary of the Smithsonian Institution, I. Michael Heyman, decided simply to delete the historians' commentary that had been prepared for the Space Museum's exhibit *The Last Act: The Atomic Bomb and the End of World War II*—commonly known as "the *Enola Gay* exhibit." Accompanying a display of the airplane was a complex narrative of the decision to drop the bomb by several of the American historians most qualified to write it. After a firestorm of protest over this text from Congress and the American Legion, among others, the Smithsonian—our national repository of historical artifacts—caved in under political pressure and dumped the historians in the nearest dustbin—a sure sign of a growing pathology in the body politic.

Why did the Smithsonian do this? I don't know the full answer, but part of it was to avoid making American veterans of World War II feel bad. The head of the American Legion, who was born around 1960, led the charge against the historians' interpretation. When I debated him about the *Enola Gay* exhibit at the Harold Washington Public Library in Chicago, he argued that veterans have the right to commemorate their victory by sharing their collective memories without historians spoiling things with a lot of nitpicking. When I asked what there is to commemorate about a B-29 named *Enola Gay* and why the museum does not instead commemorate the real heroism of the "last battle" in Okinawa, he replied that he agreed with me. For his part, Secretary Heyman explicitly justified his January decision by saying that the exhibit should be a commemoration, not an exploration, of the decision to drop the bomb.[74]

Every veteran has a right to his hard-won memories just as every historian has a duty to inform the people, and there is no way to square that inevitable circle and make everyone happy. We honor and value the soldier because he risks everything for his country's victory—his livelihood, his family, his life, and above all his future (since young men fight wars). But it is the job of the historian—not that of the soldier—to instruct us about the past. Veterans who were scheduled to take part in the invasion of Japan have every right to be happy that the atomic bombs saved their necks; they have no right to tell historians who know better that this justifies Truman's decision.[75] People who have not thought about crucial just-war questions of proportionality, or the difference between the soldier's solemn oath and the innocence of a woman or child, have no right to tell us that saving twenty-five thousand combatants by killing several hundred thousand civilians is justified.

American newspapers do not cover Japan in any detail, but they never fail to report another war-related revision of secondary-school textbooks or another reactionary belch by an LDP right-winger with full commentary about how the Japanese have not come to terms with their record in World War II.[76] I think it is true that Japan's postwar leaders—in contrast to any number of Japan's writers, scholars, religious figures, political activists, and common people—have not properly atoned for the millions of atrocities from the Pacific War that are correctly laid at Japan's door.[77] But American journalists rarely examine their own high-school textbooks. Yet according to several recent surveys, nearly all of these textbooks "sustain myths and questionable interpretations" about the atomic bombings of the two Japanese cities.[78]

THE ATOMIC BOMB AND MORALITY IN WAR

On 9 August 1945, Samuel McCrea Cavert, the head of the Federal Council of the Church of Christ, wrote to Truman condemning the "indiscriminate" killing at Hiroshima. Two days later Truman responded, "Nobody is more disturbed over the use of the Atomic bombs than I am but I was greatly disturbed over the unwarranted attack by the Japanese on Pearl Harbor and their murder of our prisoners of war. The only language they seem to understand is the one we have been using to bombard them. When you have to deal with a beast you have to treat him as a beast. It is most regrettable but nevertheless true."[79] Here is the reasoning: Japanese naval and air units attacked our naval and air outposts, and some of their soldiers killed our captured soldiers. Therefore the Japanese are beasts. To deal with beasts you must become a beast, however regrettable. Now compare the words of Kaiser Wilhelm II in World War I, quoted by Judge Radhabinod Pal of India in his famous dissent at the Tokyo War Crimes Trial: "My soul is torn, but everything must be put to fire and sword; men, women, and children and old men must be slaughtered and not a tree or a house be left standing. With these methods of terrorism, which are alone capable of affecting a people as degenerate as the French, the war will be over in two months, whereas if I admit considerations of humanity it will be prolonged for years." Such thinking makes it painfully apparent that even Truman could not rise above the racism inherent in American attitudes toward Imperial Japan, which made no distinction between fanatical militarists and the Japanese people, or between combatants and innocent civilians. Bernstein comments cogently, "Which group—American leaders or ordinary citizens—was more willing to kill the Japanese in vast numbers, including non-combatants? Is not the process of trying to reach an answer, as well as the answer itself, profoundly troubling?" Truman himself came to a belated recognition on 10 August that atomic warfare was morally distinct from conventional bombing. According to Vice President Henry Wallace, Truman told the cabinet that "the thought of wiping out another 100,000 people was too horrible. He didn't like the idea of 'killing all those kids.' "[80]

To say that Tojo or Hitler or Stalin would have used the bomb had it been available to them is no doubt true, but those who use this argument (and it was a stock rationale during the cold-war balance of terror) do not seem to understand that they thereby place American leaders on a plane with monsters of the twentieth century. It is just another stupidity, bereft of clear thinking. Furthermore this was not the red wind (an extreme atrocity by fire, but scarcely unknown to warfare on a lesser scale) but the atomic black wind, something uniquely new, carrying ever since "a dimension of totality, a sense of ultimate annihilation—of cities, nations, the world."[81] In other words, here was the dawn of exterminism.

Some argue that the killing of innocents in warfare is "merely foreseen and [therefore] not intended."[82] Innocents will be killed in wars, just as they will in automobile crashes on interstate highways. For Walzer, the test in wartime is intent *to kill innocents*, when the proper course for soldiers ought to be intent *to save civilian lives*, even at the risk of soldiers' lives.[83] Truman and his advisors clearly "foresaw" the killing of innocents, thus prompting two intentions: General Marshall's, that a clear military target be designated to save innocent lives, as contrasted with everybody else, who made no distinction between combatant and civilian in choosing a city-busting strategy, intended to incinerate large numbers of innocents. Marshall's recommendation is the only one which meets this moral test; Truman is worse than the rest because he makes no distinction among "Japanese beasts" between leader and led.

By not exercising his moral faculty and instead giving in to the passions of war, Truman is morally culpable of wrongdoing. We have said that war is judged twice; most will say that Truman's ends were noble in bringing a quick end to a just war, but his means were ignoble. Walzer, however, finds American leaders guilty of "a double crime": arguing that the war could have been concluded before Hiroshima, he writes that "to press the war further . . . is to re-commit the crime of aggression. In the summer of 1945, the victorious Americans owed the Japanese people an experiment in negotiation. To use the atomic bomb, to kill and terrorize civilians, without even attempting such an experiment, was a double crime."[84] Many will disagree, but few can justify Truman's methods as *jus in bello*; instead, they have prejudiced the course of modern history ever since. Joseph Schumpeter, the great Austrian economist who had visited Japan in the early 1930s, provided the best epitaph for Hiroshima and Nagasaki when he wrote in his diary shortly after the bombs were dropped, "It is a stupid bestiality or a bestial stupidity."[85]

Now consider a different epitaph for Truman: World science placed ultimate power in the palm of his hand, and he chose not to use it. China's greatness as a towering influence on all of East Asian history is based on many things, but one of them is the ancient Confucian idea that the best leadership is *moral* and *by example*. Imagine Truman telling the Japanese on 6 August 1945 that

1. The United States possesses the most decisive, terrible, and diabolical weapon the world has ever known.
2. We understand that the Japanese people are different from the warmongers who recklessly attacked Pearl Harbor and started this war.
3. Therefore, to address the militarists in Tokyo in the only language they understand, we are going to drop this weapon on an island in Tokyo Bay two hours from now, before they can move American POWs into the area.
4. If they still refuse to surrender, one week later we will follow it up with another demonstration, this time on a major military installation.
5. Meanwhile, we will continue to roll more such bombs off our assembly lines and establish a full naval and air blockade of the Japanese islands until that point in November 1945 when we will have marshaled the greatest invasion force in world history.

This would have been an exercise in *moral* judgment and leadership, but it also has to do with *power*. Had Truman undertaken this essential *renunciation* of the vast power that American science had put in his hands, nothing he ever did in the rest of his life—and no historian, no generation of historians, no history buff, no "revisionist"—could ever have taken that moral moment away from him or from his nation. As Clausewitz said, ultimately politics governs the use of force, and this moral act, which would also have been a deeply political act, would have been a cornerstone in postwar American global power.

The possibility of a noncombat demonstration of the bomb's effects was discussed twice in high-level deliberations, on 31 May and 11 June 1945. The idea was rejected because the bomb might be a dud and because the Japanese might move Allied POWs into an announced demonstration point. The first objection is nulled, however, because of new information, released in 1995, that Japan was a target precisely *because* a dud would be no help to their nonexistent bomb project (in contrast to Germany). The second objection is invalid because the demonstration could have been either unannounced (the shock effect of an unannounced demonstration would probably have been greater) or announced an hour or so before detonation. There was also a brief discussion of using the bomb only on combatants. On 29 May General George C. Marshall urged upon Stimson the use of the bomb "against straight military objectives such as a large naval station," since less "opprobrium" would descend upon the American leadership for killing innocent civilians.[86] This recommendation, unknown until after Marshall died, would also have met the test of moral leadership.

In the same way that atomic weapons enhance the singular power of the executive, so does his or her responsibility for exemplary moral conduct. The executive cannot escape being the ultimate moral example for the nation. Among the many expectations placed on an ultimate leader, this, perhaps, is the greatest. But it is also a great resource and element of his or her power. People can tolerate all sorts of all-too-human behavior from their fellow men and women, but they cannot tolerate it in their chief of state. It is this power that Truman had in his hand in August 1945 but chose not to exercise. The result was to end a good war in a bad way, a way that increasingly makes commemoration of that victory difficult for Americans.

Perhaps, though, we ought not to expect in our elected leaders more moral intelligence, or a lesser tendency toward expediency and rationalization, than in the best minds that America produces. Robert Oppenheimer, however bright his intellect and however brilliant his leadership of the Manhattan Project, was a man crippled by the itch for power and fame. And this, in turn, deprived him of the opportunity to set a moral example. Oppenheimer tried many times to grasp that mantle, beginning with the (probably apocryphal) story that when he witnessed the Trinity test at Alamagordo, the words of the *Bhagavad Gita* came to him: "I am death, the destroyer of worlds." In a similar vein, he later remarked that "the physicists have known sin." These ideas cannot have been deeply felt, however, for almost a decade after Hiroshima we find him in the following colloquy with Paul Nitze (with Dean Acheson, Dean Rusk, and other luminaries present): Nitze remarked upon the warmth and nobility of the Japanese people "even in Hiroshima," and Oppenheimer responded, "Oh, especially in those towns . . . they were fantastic." Nitze went on, "There was a kind of feeling: 'My goodness, we survived this; we had . . .'" And Oppenheimer supplied the conclusion: "We had it coming."[87]

CONCLUSION: U.S.-JAPAN SIMILARITY AS WITNESSED BY KOREA

If the symbolic alpha and omega of the U.S.-Japan war was "East Wind, Rain," and "Black Rain," the place to look for American-Japanese resemblance, for the similarity we began with, is Korea, where again came the Red Wind. For both countries, Korea is a displaced nation, an afterthought, a sideshow: Japanese leaders appear to be genuine when they apologize for war crimes in China, but they reserve for Korea a stunning indifference and insensitivity. Americans are no less indifferent to Korean sensibilities and probably more uninformed about Korean history. For Japan in the Pacific War, one alpha might be Ambassador (and Admiral) Nomura Kichisaburo handing a message to Cordell Hull on 6 December 1941, and the omega, Foreign Minister Shige-mitsu signing the surrender documents aboard the U.S.S. *Missouri* in Tokyo Bay on 2 September 1945. Both limped to their task, the result of a terrorist bombing in Shanghai on 29 April 1932—to which Nomura also lost his right eye. Gordon Prange, ever the empiricist historian determined to get things exactly right to the last detail, blames this act on "a Chinese terrorist."[88] It was, in fact, Korean Kim Ku who organized this attack. Kim was an anti-colonial nationalist who killed his first Japanese colonizer in the aftermath of the Japanese-orchestrated assassination of Queen Min in 1896.

This is merely one anecdote to show how a lack of knowledge about Korean history undermines our understanding of modern Japanese and American history; there are many, many others. For example, the scholarly debate over the decision to drop the atomic bomb continues to be too narrow in its primary focus on Japan and the USSR. Decision makers were concerned not only with those countries but with China, Korea, Indochina, and a host of other places in the region. The Alamagordo explosion not only short-circuited a negotiated peace with Japan, it affected Korea as well. It was possible at Potsdam, in my view, to have negotiated an agreement between Washington and Moscow either to neutralize Korea or to mount a joint American-Soviet occupation. Instead, the successful atom-bomb test emboldened Truman to abjure diplomacy and seek to minimize Soviet involvement in the postwar settlement in northeast Asia.

Korea was divided precisely at the time that Japan's first serious peace initiative was issued by Foreign Minister Tōgō Shigenori on 10 August 1945. Around midnight that evening, John J. McCloy, Dean Rusk, and Charles Bonesteel drew a fateful line at the thirty-eighth parallel that still bisects the ancient unity of the Korean nation even today. When MacArthur issued General Order Number One for the Japanese surrender in the Pacific on 15 August, the full breadth of American thinking for Asia became evident to the world. Korea was divided at the thirty-eighth parallel and Vietnam at the sixteenth, while Nationalist China was given responsibility for the surrender in mainland China, which it could not possibly implement from its exile and rump position in Chungking.

The reasoning for this expansive decision was, first, American worry not just about the onrushing Soviet Red Army but about communist and nationalist revolution throughout Asia, and second, an Anglo-American desire unilaterally to occupy those colonial territories still available to them, especially southern Korea and Vietnam. Seoul and Saigon were both targets of rapid movement by American and British forces, with the American occupation of Korea pushed forward as quickly as possible and the British entering Saigon to hold it for the French. In this history, we come to understand an overlooked or at least underemphasized reason for Japan's surrender, namely, the implicit Japanese, American, and British assumption that communism was a worse prospect than whatever issues continued to divide Tokyo, Washington, and London. By the end of August, Japanese commanders in Seoul were exchanging numerous messages with American forces on Okinawa, urging them to occupy Korea as rapidly as possible lest "communists" take advantage of the power vacuum. An instant camaraderie between Americans and Japanese led the Americans to reinstate the full government-general apparatus in Seoul, including its Japanese personnel, until Washington overruled the use of high Japanese officials. But the colonial state structure endured and became the administrative basis of the Republic of Korea.[89]

More broadly, we can ask what might have happened had the Red Army fought its way into Japan in conjunction with an American invasion. A divided Japan would have resulted, much like divided Germany. Today "South Japan" would probably be an "Asian tiger," and "North Japan" would be ruled by a hereditary Confucian/communist dynasty. Quite possibly, another war would have raged across Japan's territory. In other words, Japan would be Korea, and with a certain historic justice. Instead, Japan got a very hard defeat that was followed instantly by a soft peace, while divided Korea continues to suffer a historic injustice.

The sorry American record in Korea after 1945 and especially in the Korean War, when fully known, cannot be an example to anyone. Like the Japanese before them, Americans saw Koreans as a dehumanized "other"—an inferior race where the highest Korean ultimately counted less than the lowest American. Even today, it is rare to find an American who knows or cares much about Korea, in spite of the millions of American soldiers who have served there in the past fifty years. Least of all would anyone expect American leaders to reflect upon, let alone apologize for, the war crimes that Americans committed there. Yet

1. The U.S. Air Force reduced every North Korean city to rubble by incendiary bombing that involved the use of oceans of napalm (which even Churchill criticized), killing hundreds of thousands of innocent civilians (the overall civilian-to-soldier kill ratio for World War II was 40 percent; in Korea, it was 70 percent).
2. In May and June 1953 the U.S. Air Force demolished huge dams in North Korea, flooding many square miles of farm territory and thus denying food to the enemy—something that had been planned for Japan but was not done on the grounds that it was against the laws of warfare.
3. Through Operation Hudson Harbor in the fall of 1951, the U.S. Air Force terrorized North Korea by dropping dummy atomic bombs from B-29s in tests to see whether the bomb could be used in battlefield conditions.
4. General Ridgway requested permission to use chemical weapons against North Korean and Chinese forces in the winter of 1950–1951, only to be turned down by MacArthur.
5. Both MacArthur (December 1950) and Ridgway (May 1951) asked Washington for permission to use more than twenty atomic bombs against North Korea and China.
6. Truman denied those requests, but sent the atomic cores of the bombs (for the first time) to the northeast Asian theater, to assemble and ready atomic bombs for possible use against North Korea and China; he issued operational orders to do so in April 1951, should major new Chinese forces join the fighting, but the order was never carried out because MacArthur was relieved a few days later.[90]

This is the same conflict that is now called "the forgotten war" in the United States, and as Nietzsche would say, it is no accident that it has this name: as with Hiroshima, forgetting is a necessity for psychic order and moral repose.

Japan's record in Korea over the first half of the century is still considerably worse than the American record in the second half. For example, many years after the events, it came to be known that at least ten thousand Koreans, mostly conscripted laborers, perished at Hiroshima and Nagasaki. Yet in the Hiroshima Peace Park, even today, no Korean is buried among the many Japanese victims. It is a shame that Japan as a matter of high state policy cannot truly reflect and show remorse for its sorry record in Korea. Nobel Prize winner Oe Kenzaburo had this to say: "In the history of our modernization in general but, in particular, in the war of aggression that was its peak, we lost the right to be a part of Asia and have continued to live without recovering that right. Without that rehabilitation we shall never be able to eradicate the ambivalence in our attitude toward our neighbors, the feeling that our relationships aren't real."[91]

In this chapter, I have tried to derive moral and political lessons from World War II, but I have also, in passing, given substance to the judgments that I first read twenty years ago in the work of historian Saburo Ienaga. Ienaga achieved a certain fame (or notoriety) by fighting the "textbook issue" over a thirty-year period all the way to Japan's supreme court. He was the first Japanese historian in my experience to write about the Rape of Nanking, the "kill-all, burn-all, loot-all" campaigns in China, the sexual slavery of the *ianfu*, Unit 731's germ warfare, and the vicious subordination of Korea and Koreans that Japanese leaders have practiced or supported through much of this century. What's more, he did it all twenty-five years ago, long before these events became sufficiently well-known to cause controversy.[92] Let me briefly summarize his judgments:

1. On Pearl Harbor: Japan's militarists "charged recklessly into an unwinnable war and continued to the point of national destruction."
2. On the militarists' domestic political repression: "A healthy political and social consciousness cannot develop in a society where the exchange of vital facts and ideas is fettered."
3. On what I earlier called "the American way of going to war": "By allowing Japan to strike the first blow, even the [American] isolationists were swept up by the patriotic clamor for war and victory," and this fascinating statement: "Talking about 'international morality' and allowing others always to get the jump on us will give Japan the short end of the stick."

As for the atomic bombs, Ienaga begins with the firebombing of Tokyo in March 1945. He sees no difference between that episode and Hiroshima: both are examples of the slaughter of innocents from the air that all the allies participated in. He then cites H. M. S. Blackett, the Nobel Prize physicist, who said that the United States should have carried out a demonstration of the bomb's effects. He concludes by agreeing with Radhabinod Pal of the Tokyo War Crimes Tribunal, who said that both the firebombing and the atomic bombing were war crimes and atrocities—that is, "indiscriminate murder."[93]

Ienaga has the one virtue we must always demand of the historian and that we so rarely get: independence. The historian's domain is not power, but the model of the human being trying to weigh the best evidence and come to the best conclusion regardless of where the chips may fall. That historian's product may not be truth, but a claim to truth—a construction of what happened or what might be a good account of what happened. Still, there is no better example for the rest of us on how to be democratic citizens. Fredric Jameson writes, "The past always is assumed: we are not free to have no attitude toward it. It cannot be changed; but we always lend the changeless facts a meaning in terms of the lives we lead and even the forgetting of them."[94]

EPILOGUE

At 8:15 A.M. on 6 August 1945, two Korean laborers, Yu Chun-sŭng and Shin T'ae-ryông, arrived at Hiroshima Station. Yu looked at his watch just as a hot, blinding flash enveloped him.

> He ran desperately toward Mt. Futuba behind the station. He kept running while stumbling over the rails and iron fence of the station. . . . He reached the foot of Mt. Futuba, spent the night in a half-ruined farmhouse, and on the following day was carried by a rescue truck to the navy hospital in Kure. He lay with gauze dipped in oil on his burned face, and after a few days maggots hatched on the burns. . . .
> Around 1950 he started to vomit blood and have bloody stools. . . .

In 1972, Yu was living with his four family members in a tiny *ondol* room next to the kitchen of a farmer's thatched-roof hut. Born in Chôngûp in 1917, he was drafted in 1944 to labor in a naval engineering operation. A few years after Hiroshima Yu's wife bore a child, Dong Su. The lower half of his body never developed. Another child had the same small lower body but a head that was twice as big as that of a normal baby. He died after three months. Yu had some success as a greengrocer, but around 1968 he again fell ill. By 1972, when he was but fifty-five, he could not move from his tiny hovel. He was "thin as a ghost" and had a "wax-white face."

> He suffered attacks at intervals of about one minute, and when he did, his limbs and entire body writhed, and he gnashed his teeth, which he closed to endure the pain.

Yu died a few months later. As Dong Su reached puberty, he tried to commit suicide three times. After his father passed away, he went insane and refused to eat, dying within a year.[95]

On a hot, sultry morning, 9 August 1945, one Father Ishikawa, a Korean Catholic priest aged thirty-six, was ministering to patients in the Urakami Hospital in Nagasaki, where he was chaplain. Soon would come the day of the Ascension of the Virgin Mary, and his flock wanted to confess their sins in advance of the grand festival planned for 15 August. Around eleven o'clock, as he returned to his room to get a book that he needed, "a sudden white flash filled the corridor with light." This was followed by "a great roar," which flung him through the air, where he struck his head on a concrete post. Somehow he made it back to the chapel, where nurses found him lying on the floor. They roused him, and in spite of his head wounds, he administered last rites to the walking dead who soon appeared at the doorstep of the hospital. He later returned to Korea, where he became a Catholic bishop and lived into the late 1970s.[96]

3

COLONIAL FORMATIONS AND DEFORMATIONS:

KOREA, TAIWAN, AND VIETNAM

The changes that have come about in the island within the thirty-three years of Japanese possession speak well for Japan's greatness as a colonizing people. What Japan has done for Formosa is the exact counterpart of what the U.S. has done in the Philippine Islands, in Cuba, and in Porto Rico [*sic*]. Both nations have instituted much needed legal reforms, have cleaned up the filthy cities, have built highways and railways, and have reorganized all their institutions of life in harmony with scientific principles.—Harold and Alice Foght

You ask why Taiwanese like Japan but Koreans do not. . . . One reason may be . . . the better Japanese colonial rule in Taiwan, but I think a more basic reason is the different personality of the Taiwanese: they would be easier for anyone to govern—no long tradition of nationalism, and so much politer than Koreans.—Kishi Nobosuke

The colonial system was founded more or less on the fact that the state administration had merely superimposed the French trading and currency principles on the traditional farming and cultivation methods of the [Indochina] colonies without significantly modifying the latter. The political role of the colonial administration was largely confined to enforcing the hegemony of metropolitan monopolies against foreign intervention and indigenous competition and to financing the construction of basic economic infrastructure designed to establish a favorable climate for expanded metropolitan trade and investment.—Martin Murray

A debate has emerged about the sources of economic growth in South Korea and Taiwan: Did it all begin around 1960, when both had minuscule per capita incomes but somehow launched themselves onto a trajectory of export-led growth, or do the origins of growth go back further, into the legacies of Japan's colonial rule?[1] This debate also bears on the export-led plans of a different former colony, at a very different time: Vietnam in the 1990s.

First we need to know what a "colonial legacy" is, and why colonial history is still such a neuralgic point in East Asia today. I consider a colony to have been one way of organizing territorial space in the modern world system, one that obliterated political sovereignty and oriented the colonial economy toward monopoly controls and monopoly profits (even if done differently by the various imperial powers). A *legacy* is something that appears to be a follow-on to the different historical experiences of colonialism. Legacy is a term that can be good, bad, or neutral: the legacy of a rich family might be seen as good, an alumni legacy to an entering freshman class bad, and a railroad running from Hanoi to Saigon neutral, good, or bad depending on one's point of view. As it happens, the comparative "points of view" afforded by our three cases are very different, offering much food for thought about nationalism, resistance, development, and modernity. I will examine colonial legacies for their utility in explaining the postwar growth of Taiwan, Korea, and—in a curious way—Japan itself; and the virtual opposite in Vietnam, namely, the thirty years of war and revolution that was the prime postcolonial "legacy" of the French.

The nationalist point of view is that there is no such thing as a good colonial legacy, and therefore the contribution of imperialism to growth was zero, really minus-zero: for example, Korean historiography (South and North) sees anything good or useful deriving from Japanese colonialism as incidental to the ruthless pursuit of Japanese interests; even if a railroad from Pusan to Sinŭiju is useful, a railroad built by Koreans, for Koreans, would have been better. (The rail system, for example, would not have connected Pusan and Sinŭiju on a diagonal southeast to northwest trajectory linking Japanese shipping through the port of Pusan with the raw materials of Manchuria.) Furthermore, absent the Japanese, a native railway system would still have been built. Koreans assume that Japan aborted their drive for modernity rather than merely distorting it.

The Taiwanese, on the other hand, have tended to look upon their colonial experience with Japan as a reasonably tolerable and efficacious interlude between ineffectual Ch'ing dynasty rule and rapacious Chinese Nationalist rule. A political scientist's sojourn in Taiwan as late as 1970 found nostalgia for the Japanese era at every turn.[2] (Example: "Taiwan under the pigs is hell" as compared to its prewar state.) Japan held Taiwan longer than any of its colonies—from 1895 to 1945. Did it do something here that it did not do in Korea? Or did it do the same thing, with a very different native response?

The French took a long time to colonize Vietnam (from 1856 to 1885) and then held on to it until 1945. There followed a thirty-years' war. At the end of that war, in 1975, Vietnam was one of the most impoverished nations in the world. Meanwhile, South Korea, North Korea, and Taiwan were all mid-1970s success stories (in 1975, per capita GNP in South and North Korea was about the same, and Taiwan's was higher than either). Vietnamese planners soon found that Soviet-style development schemes that emphasized heavy industry were unsuitable in a country that was still primarily agrarian. They compared their low starting point in the late 1970s with that of North Korea in 1945 and China in 1949.[3] Today, Vietnamese planners look to South Korea and Taiwan as models of export-led development. Did this different outcome have anything to do with the nature of French colonialism, as contrasted with Japanese colonialism? Or did the thirty-years' war bequeath a backward economy?

I will argue in this chapter that the differing colonial experiences of these nations did make a big difference (if by no means the only difference) in their postwar development. It is a complex argument, however, because Taiwan and Korea experienced the same type of colonialism with very different results; because each of these nations had different precolonial experiences; and because South Korea and Taiwan got all the benefits of postcolonial American hegemony, while Vietnam and North Korea got all the drawbacks of being the objects of postcolonial American hegemony. Primarily, though, I want to make the case that the "East Asian model" of capitalism, so widely discussed these days, has deep historical roots and cannot be understood merely as an outcome of salutary policy packages that encouraged "export-led development." It is in many ways, as I will argue briefly at the end of this chapter and at greater length elsewhere,[4] an East Asian adaptation of the nineteenth-century European (continental) conception of the state and its relation to the national industrial economy in a world system of dog-eat-dog competition.

THE MODERN AND THE COLONIAL

At the onset of colonial rule, Taiwan and Vietnam were backward by almost any measure of modern or industrial development. Vietnam was purely agrarian; Taiwan had a minispurt of development in 1885–1891, followed by a four-year slowdown and then absorption by Japan.[5] Korea, however, had begun to "modernize" on the usual indices in the 1880s; the results were mixed by 1905, when Japan began its Protectorate, but certainly Korea had progressed farther than Taiwan or Vietnam. Angus Hamilton found Korea in 1904 to be "a land of exceptional beauty,"[6] with Seoul being much superior to Beijing: "The streets [of Seoul] are magnificent, spacious, clean, admirably made and well drained. The narrow, dirty lanes have been widened; gutters have been covered, and roadways broadened. . . . Seoul is within measurable distance of becoming the highest, most interesting, and cleanest city in the East" (13). There was for Hamilton "no question of the superiority" of Korean living conditions, both urban and rural, to those in China (if not Japan). Seoul was the first city in East Asia to have electricity, trolley cars, and water, telephone, and telegraph systems all at the same time. Most of these systems were installed and run by Americans, as we have seen. The Seoul Electric Light Company, the Seoul Electric Car Company, and the Seoul "Fresh Spring" Water Company were all American firms. Schools of every description—law, engineering, medicine—abounded in Seoul. Hamilton noted that King Kojong wanted personally to supervise all public business; he was, Hamilton thought, a progressive monarch who had chosen well from the models put before him by the West and Japan. The period since the opening of the country had afforded Koreans countless opportunities "to select for themselves such institutions as may be calculated to promote their own welfare" (13).

This is powerful evidence supporting the Korean claim that their route to modernity was not facilitated but was instead derailed and hijacked by Japan. Still, note the indices that the American Hamilton chooses to highlight: electricity, telephones, trolleys, schools, cleanliness, and consumption of American exports. If we find that Japan brought similar facilities to Seoul and Taipei, do we place them on the ledger of colonialism or modernization? The Korean answer is colonialism, and the Japanese and Taiwanese answer is modernization.

Timothy Mitchell has a better answer to this question, which is to address "the place of colonialism in the critique of modernity": "Colonising refers not simply to the establishing of a European presence but also to the spread of a political order that inscribes in the social world a new conception of space, new forms of personhood, and a new means of manufacturing the experience of the real."[7] Following Michel Foucault, Mitchell examines British colonialism in Egypt as a matter of a "restrictive, exterior power" giving way to the "internal, productive power" demanded by modernity, a disciplining that produces "the organized power of armies, schools, and factories" and above all the modern individual—"constructed as an isolated, disciplined, receptive, and industrious political subject" (xi).

There is much more to be said here, but if we put things this way, with a conception of Foucauldian power and Foucauldian modernity, then there is no fundamental distinction between second-phase (i.e., late-nineteenth-century) colonialism and the modern industrial project itself. Thus—at this level of abstraction—there is no basic distinction between Japanese colonialism, American hegemony, and South Korean, North Korean, or Taiwanese modernization. At the very least, none of these national discourses of modernity can tell you what's wrong with the precise timing of the factory punch clock or the railway timetable or the police officer's neighborhood beat; they differ only over the auspices of their introduction and their effects on national sovereignty. Every political entity just mentioned, but above all Japan, put its citizens through a regimen of public education that seemed perfectly designed to develop the industrious political subject. Each inculcated in its citizens the vices of self-surveillance and repression that Mitchell discerned in British Egypt.

The Vietnamese, however, find nothing good to enter on either the colonial or the modernization ledger: the literature of anticolonialism shouts itself hoarse over French exploitation,[8] the French literature almost always takes to task its own colonization project,[9] and the "industrious political subject" never appeared. Indeed, French education was more likely to create the industrious political rebel (e.g., Ho Chi Minh, who studied in Paris in 1921). The French were not "late" colonizers in Indochina; they did not tie colonial development to metropolitan industrialization efforts. Like the Portuguese, who had been in Africa since the sixteenth century, they preferred to spend comparatively little money—just enough to keep the colonial settlers happy; the rice, rubber, and tin flowing; and the natives pacified.

And here we see the undeniable legacy (and the irony) of Japanese colonialism: they were imperialists but also capitalists, colonizers but also modernizers. They were every bit as interested as a Frederick Taylor in establishing an industrial grid and disciplining, training, and surveilling the workforce. Threatened by the modern project in the form of Western imperialism, after 1868 the Japanese internalized it, made it their own, and imposed it on their neighbors. It was a highly disciplined, rational, almost Weberian type of colonialism, but one that was ultimately irrational because it could not last over time without creating its own competitors, thus digging its own grave. (The best symbol of this is the Korean-owned, spanking new textile mill in Manchuria that came onstream just in time to fall into the hands of the Russians in August 1945.)[10] Above all, the Japanese imposed the modern project *on themselves*—late in world time and with all the attendant uprootings, distortions, self-disciplinings and self-negations, fractured outcomes, and moth-toward-a-flame terrors that mark modern Japan's history and still play upon the national psyche (Hiroshima and Nagasaki being the obvious but also ultimate reference points). Modernity was an inorganic growth, and the Japanese in their internal self-colonization have always known it.

JAPAN'S MOST IMPORTANT AND MOST RECALCITRANT COLONY: KOREA

Among Koreans, north and south, the mere mention of the idea that Japan somehow "modernized" Korea calls forth indignant denials, raw emotions, and the imminent sense of mayhem having just been, or about to be, committed. For the foreigner, even the most extensive cataloguing of Japanese atrocities will pale beside the bare mention of anything positive and lasting that might have emerged from the colonial period. I do not wish to argue that Japan "developed" Korea or that postwar South Korea owes its growth to Japan. I wish instead to contrast the different retrospective optics of the people of Korea and Taiwan on Japanese imperialism and to mark the differences between Japanese and French imperialism.

The critical difference between Korea and Taiwan begins with Korea's millennium-long history of continuous, independent existence within well-recognized territorial boundaries, combined with startling ethnic homogeneity and pronounced ethnic, linguistic, and cultural difference from its neighbors (in the case of neighbor Japan, a difference compounded by 250 years of mutual isolation after the wars of the 1590s). Colonial difference ends with the stunningly dissimilar Japanese policy toward Koreans in the harshest days of the Pacific War, when millions were forcibly relocated to Japan, Manchuria, and northern Korea for hard labor in mines and factories— or, in the worst case, for sexual slavery. By contrast, Taiwan, which was never a nation, never had a central state before the 1890s, and put up only marginal resistance to Japan's entry, had but a handful of Taiwanese leave the island for Japan or the empire before 1945 (altogether, they amounted to some thirty thousand citizens, most of whom were not forcibly mobilized).[11] Few Taiwanese even left their native village for Taipei. I see Japan's treatment of Korea in the years 1935–1945 as the reason for Korea's combination of development and underdevelopment and the key to its resulting postwar turmoil and civil strife, but I have written much about this elsewhere and merely highlight it here. The point is that within five years of Japan's defeat, its colonial effort had left the Taiwanese complaining about Chinese Nationalist "pigs,"[12] South Koreans with gnawing respect/hate feelings toward Japan, and a state organized totally as an anti-Japanese entity called North Korea. With that said (and with no illusions that Korean nationalism is hereby appeased), we can highlight important continuities between the pre-war and postwar political economies of Korea, continuities that began in the 1920s. Unlike Taiwan, Korea had an integral role in Japan's "administrative guidance" of the entire northeast Asian regional economy. Korea was a bridge linking the metropole to the hinterland economies; it is from this point that we can date Japan's specific brand of architectonic capitalism that has influenced northeast Asia down to the present.

As we have seen, Japan entered a period of economic stagnation after World War I and generally pursued free trade, political liberalization at home, and less repressive colonial policies in both Korea and Taiwan. When we turn to

Korea in this period, however, we can see the kernel of a subsequent logic—the logic of administrative guidance. In the Government-General's Industrial Commission of 1921, for the first time planners called for supports to Korea's fledgling textile industry and for it to produce not just for the domestic market, but especially for exports to the Asian continent, where lower Korean labor costs would give its goods a price advantage. This was by no means a purely "top-down" Japanese exercise, for Koreans were part of the commission and quickly called for state subsidies and hothouse "protection" for Korean companies. The nurturing of a Korean business class was a necessity if the new policy of "gradualism" (adopted after the independence uprisings of 1 March 1919) was to have any meaning. The convening of the Industrial Commission was in effect the new policy's birthday party, but it was a controversial one (three days before the commission opened, two bombs were lobbed into the Government-General Building).[13] That Japan had much larger ideas in mind, however, is obvious in the proposal for a General Industrial Policy put before the 1921 conference: "Since Korea is a part of the imperial domain, industrial plans for Korea should be in conformity with imperial industrial policy. Such a policy must provide for economic conditions in adjacent areas, based on [Korea's] geographical position amid Japan, China, and the Russian Far East."[14] One of the Japanese delegates explained that Korean industry would be integral to the overall planning being done in Tokyo and would require some protection if it was to accept its proper place in "a single, coexistent, coprosperous Japanese-Korean unit."[15]

Also visible at this early point was the developmental model of using state-sponsored loans at preferential interest rates as a means of shaping industrial development and taking advantage of "product cycle" advantages.[16] This yielded firms whose paid-in capital was often much less than their outstanding debt. Businessmen did not offer shares on a stock market but went to state banks for their capital. Strategic investment decisions were in the hands of state bureaucrats, state banks, and state corporations (such as the Oriental Development Company). This meant that policy could move "swiftly and *sequentially*" in ways that subsequently and indelibly marked South Korean development in the 1960s and 1970s.[17]

The depression delayed full implementation of this model, but by the mid-1930s, this sort of financing had become a standard practice. The key institution at the nexus of the colonial model was the Korean Industrial Bank (Chōsen Shokusan Ginkō), the main source of capital for big Korean firms. By the end of the colonial period, about half of its employees were Korean. Meanwhile, Seoul's Bank of Chōsen played the role of central bank and provisioned capital throughout the imperial realm in northeast China. It had twenty branches in Manchukuo and served as fiscal agent for Japan's Kwan-

Table 1   *Koreans Employed in Industry within Korea, 1923–1943*

Year	Number of Persons	Index of Increase
1932	384,951	100
1936	594,739	154
1940	702,868	183
1943	1,321,713	343

Source: Bruce Cumings, *Origins of the Korean War* (Princeton, N.J.: Princeton University Press, 1981), 1:26.

Note: This table excludes mining and transportation, which employed tens of thousands more workers, and does not count the millions of Koreans laboring outside the country in the 1940s.

tung Army, and it also had an office in New York to vacuum up American loans for colonial expansion. On the side, it trafficked in opium and silver and engaged in textile smuggling. It also participated in the infamous Nishihara Loan, which was designed to buy off Chinese opposition to Japan's Twenty-One Demands—about nineteen of which bit off pieces of Chinese sovereignty. Most important for Korea, however, was the Industrial Bank's role under Ariga Mitsutoyo (1919–1937) in "jump-starting Korea's first industrial and commercial entrepreneurs, men such as Min T'ae-shik, Min Kyu-sik, Pak Hŭng-sik, and Kim Yŏn-su."[18]

By 1936, heavy industry accounted for 28 percent of total industrial production in Korea, quite unlike Taiwan, and more than half a million Koreans were employed in industry—a figure that had tripled by 1945. Industry expanded in Korea at double or triple the rate in Taiwan (see Table 1). By 1943, the ratio of production between Korea's heavy and light industry had become equal. It is not really the case that northern Korea had all the big factories, and the south only light industry; in the middle of the war, the south surpassed the north in machine building, electric machinery, heavy vehicles, mining tools, and the like.[19] Thus, Korea's industrial revolution began in earnest during the last fifteen years of Japanese rule.

Hermann Lautensach, no apologist for colonialism, was much impressed by the rapid development of Korea in the late 1930s. Here was an "obvious, indeed astonishing success," even if the development was "oriented toward the needs of the empire."[20] This, combined with a succession of excellent harvests in 1936–1938, yielded the notion of a "Korean boom," according to Lautensach. With "the rapid development of all of Korea's economic capacity . . . a certain amount of prosperity is beginning to enter even the farmer's huts" (383). He noted that the northeast corner of Korea, long backward, was "experiencing an upswing unlike any other part of Korea," mainly because of its incorporation into Manchukuo trading networks (386–87). There is much more to be said, but given space limitations, I must direct the reader to my previous work on colonialism in Korea and go on to Taiwan and Vietnam.[21] I will merely conclude this brief account with the comment that postwar South Korea, far from being an anticolonial entity, often contained virtual replicas of Japanese forms in industry, state policies toward the economy, education, police, military affairs, the physiognomy of its cities, and its civic culture (such as it was). Newspapers were identical in form, if not in content, to Japan's; South Korean schools were museums of colonial practice until the early 1980s—down to the black uniforms, pressed collars, and peaked hats that every male student wore.

North Korea was an anticolonial entity par excellence, but in its haste to deny everything Japanese, it created mirror-image institutions, beginning with the emperor-like leader principle, the corporate political system, the leader's ubiquitous *chuch'e* ideology, and the establishment of the leader/emperor's birthday as a national holiday. Even some of P'yŏngyang's wretched excesses, such as the botanist-produced orchids and begonias christened Kimilsungia and Kimjongilia, have their counterparts in Japanese practice.[22] Instant experts will never know this, of course; only prolonged experience with postwar Korea yields knowledge of just how far the Japanese got under the Korean skin. Of course, in comparative perspective, this is hardly surprising, and few Koreans could ever match (nor did they want to) the accomplished assimilationism of other colonized peoples the world over—from Angolans in Lisbon to Vietnamese in Paris to Americans at the court of King George. Such evidence only surprises us in the context of postwar Korean nationalism.

JAPAN IN ITS MODEL COLONY, TAIWAN

In the recent literature on the East Asian "newly industrializing countries" (NICS), much has been made of Taiwan's manifold differences from Korea: a less intrusive state, more light industry, few big *chaebŏl*, more small-business and family enterprises, continuous export-led development, more egalitarian distribution, less nationalism, less hatred of the Japanese. Fine. But if this is true, it has been true not since the vaunted Rostovian "takeoff" of the 1960s but since the 1920s or 1930s. Gustav Ranis, among others, has argued that the typically dispersed and rural character of Taiwan's industrialization effort was a key reason for its quick growth: it reduced the high costs of urbanization, helped labor-intensive industries (with low-cost rural labor, etc.), and led to rational economies of scale. This explains the relative smallness of various firms and the relatively less centralized nature of Taiwan's

Table 2 *Taiwan's Exports as a Percentage of Gross Value of Production*

1922	1929	1937
44.7	46.3	49.4

Source: Andrew Grajdanzev, *The Economic Development of Formosa* (Shanghai: Kelly and Walsh, 1941), 153.

capitalism as compared to Korea. But this was also true throughout the colonial period. The Japanese had dispersed Taiwan's transportation network so that it was well connected and articulated with the main ports of Kaohsiung, Keelung, and Hwalien. This existing infrastructure, then, greatly aided "the heavy export of domestic raw material–intensive products in the 1950s and early 1960s" and also facilitated the location of new export processing zones (EPZS).[23]

Much hoopla accompanied the opening of Kaohsiung's free export zone in 1966. However, the industrialization of Kaohsiung had already begun during the colonial period: "In the late nineteenth century Kaohsiung was little more than a sleepy fishing village. By the end of World War I it had sprouted into the second busiest port in Taiwan, handling more than 40 per cent of the island's import and export trade.... As the city steadily grew into one of the foremost industrial centers of the island, it flourished as the site of refineries to process imported petroleum. Because of its oil refineries, port facilities, and numerous factories Kaohsiung was heavily bombed from the air during World War II."[24]

If Taiwan was a fine example of export-led industrialization (ELI) after 1960, it was a fine example of it in the colonial period as well. In fact, Taiwan has had a kind of ELI throughout its industrial history. In 1911–1915, the average annual total of exports was 63 million yen; in 1926–1930, the average was 252 million; this growth in the 1920s was clearly export led (see Table 2). Hyman Kublin calls the increase in exports during the 1920s "literally astounding." But it quickly went higher. From 1935 to 1937, exports were about half of the net national product (NNP) (with imports at 40 percent of NNP); Kublin wrote that "these very high ratios" were not regained until the 1970s.[25] Foodstuffs were the most important export in the mid-1930s; they retained this position in the 1960s and 1970s. Maurice Scott calls Taiwan's exporting in the 1960s and 1970s "a return to normal," with the ratio of imports and exports as a percentage of gross domestic product (GDP) being 38 percent in 1935–1937 and 38 percent again in 1975; this was the fourth highest ratio in the world in the mid-1970s.[26] But it was fourth highest in the 1930s as well—and the figures for both Taiwan and Korea were higher than those for Japan (see Table 3).

Table 3   *Estimated Per Capita Value of Foreign Trade Circa 1939*
(U.S. dollar equivalents)

	Year	Imports	Exports	Total
New Zealand	1939	109	127	236
British Malaya	1939	61	72	133
Australia	1938–39	67	64	131
Taiwan	1937	16	23	39
Korea	1939	15	11	26
Japan (proper)	1939	10	13	23
Philippines	1939	8	10	18
Burma	1938–39	5	12	17
Thailand	1938–39	4	5	9
Indochina	1937	3	4	7
China	1939	.85	.25	1.1

Source: George W. Barclay, *Colonial Development and Population in Taiwan* (Princeton, N.J.: Princeton University Press, 1954), 33.

While *Time* magazine and others were lauding the Taiwan miracle in the late 1960s, the natives were telling a political scientist that their situation had been better in the late 1930s. The only sectors in which per capita production increased between 1939 and 1965 were citrus, cement, electricity, and fish.[27] As for Taiwan's vaunted egalitarian income distribution, land and wealth distribution actually became "more equal" between 1931 and 1950, before the effects of land reform were felt. In complete contrast to Korea, many tenants moved into the owner-tenant category. Susan Greenhalgh found "significant continuity in the distribution of income and wealth" from the middle of the Japanese period into the 1950s.[28] Other sources describe the late 1930s and early 1940s as "Taiwan's period of greatest material progress," when Taiwan became second only to Japan in East Asian industrialization.[29] All this evidence illustrates the extraordinary leg up that Taiwan had, not from the onset of ELI in the early 1960s but from the colonial experience in the 1930s.

Japan also taught its colonies how to export while protecting the domestic market. As in South Korea, Taiwan's market was nearly closed during the first phase of import-substitution industrialization (ISI). The state imposed strict import controls in the spring of 1951, along with a highly pegged exchange rate; high tariffs, tight import licensing systems, and 100 percent deposits paid in advance by importers were prevalent for many goods. These controls yielded effective premiums above the actual cost of imports ranging from 48 percent on wheat flour and 33 percent on cotton yarn to 100 percent on ammonium sulphate, 275 percent on soda ash, and 350 percent on woolen yarn. Meanwhile, state officials rode herd on ISI producers: in 1954 K. Y. Yin, vice chair of the Taiwan Production Board from 1951 to 1954 and later the minister of economic affairs, and well-known for promoting domestic glass, cement, plastics, plywood, and of course textiles, in 1954 ordered some twenty thousand Taiwan lightbulbs smashed in a park in Taipei. Yin then announced that he would liberalize imports if the quality of local lightbulbs did not improve within three months.[30]

Much like Japan's prewar industrial program, Taiwan industrialized on the backs of its peasantry. The colonial state mobilized resources through a complex maze of land taxes, squeezing what Rong-I Wu called "a massive fund for industrialization" out of the countryside, while offering very generous tax policies toward private savings and capital formation. Taiwan did the same thing in the early 1960s when ELI took off, becoming a tax haven for exporters (offering five-year tax holidays and many other incentives).[31]

The financing of industrialization also mimicked Japan and Korea. The leading student of Taiwan's colonial economy placed much emphasis on the state's financing and harnessing of investment for the industrial boom in the mid-1930s: "Bank credit was made available for new investments at low fixed interest rates. Subsidies were granted widely to induce old firms to enter new fields. Corporations were spared the burden of taxes."[32] A specialist on postwar Taiwan's financial system acknowledged that Taiwan "inherited a relatively advanced banking system," especially the rural credit cooperatives, farmers associations, and post office savings deposit systems.[33] In 1949 the Chinese Nationalists' Central Bank of China, established in 1928, was suspended and did not return until 1961; thus, Taiwan's financial system was essentially colonial in origin and not relocated from the mainland. Although Taiwan had no central bank from 1949 to 1961, the largest commercial bank, the Bank of Taiwan, performed central banking functions—issuing currency notes, handling the state's business, and so on. This bank's main mechanism to influence the economy was its control of interest rates on bank deposits and loans, a control that Erik Lundberg calls "more or less complete." With a small bond market and virtually no stock exchange (although one was founded in 1962, it wasn't active until the mid-1980s), most financing came through the state. Big corporations got most of it, especially the state companies inherited from Japanese colonialism. After the switch to ELI, the state financed low rates of interest for exporters.[34]

What about nationalism and resistance to the Japanese in Taiwan? There was hardly any: the Japanese pacified the island within five months, meeting some resistance in the south but almost none in the north. The only recalcitrants thereafter were aborigines in the mountains (who remain recalcitrant today, not to colonialism but to modernity). Even after the March First Movement in Korea and the May Fourth Movement in China, an observant American traveler, Harry A. Franck, noted that some Taiwanese wore Japanese clothes, whereas "I cannot recall ever having seen a Korean in *geta*s and kimono." There was a big "independence question" in Korea, he wrote, but "Independence, if it is ever considered at all in Taiwan, is evidently regarded as hopeless, not even worth thinking about."[35] Hyman Kublin wrote that "it would be misleading even to imply that Taiwan was shaken by this tide of change" after World War I, except for a bit of labor organizing in the late 1920s; thereafter until 1945 "Taiwan was practically devoid of any unrest."[36]

Quiescent Taiwan nonetheless got the same ubiquitous national police system that Korea got, instituted in 1898 by the paradigmatic Gotō Shimpei: the colonizer as rigorous administrator rather than swashbuckling conqueror. This is how Patti Tsurumi described the new police system: "Under Gotō the police became the backbone of regional administration. In addition to regular policing duties, the police supervised the collection of taxes, the enforcement of sanitary measures, and works connected with the salt, camphor and opium monopolies. . . . They superintended road and irrigation improvements, introduced new plant specimens to the farmers, and encouraged education and the development of local industries."[37] Taiwan's Chinese settlers, far from resisting, appreciated Gotō's reforms; even Sun Yat Sen found it difficult to organize on the island. American travelers liked what they saw, too: "Taihoku [Taipei] gives one a queer, almost an uncanny feeling, after months in China; for here all is orderliness in complete contrast to Chinese disorder on the other side of the channel, a Prussian exactness which Prussia never matched. . . . The Nipponese, it is quickly impressed upon such a visitor, hate any suggestion of irregularity as bitterly as the Chinese seem to love it."[38]

Gotō's ubiquitous policing structure was erected on top of the traditional Chinese system for local surveillance, the *paochia*: ten families formed a *chia* and ten *chia* formed a *pao*. The *pao* had one hundred families or about five hundred to six hundred people; at the end of 1938, for example, there were 53,876 *chia* heads and 5,648 *pao* heads (or *paochiang*). Interestingly, all of these leaders were elected by members of the *chia* or *pao*, even if they required approval by province governors and chiefs of districts.[39] The Japanese, of course, made the *paochia* system far more efficient: its functions were every bit as extensive and total as the postwar Chinese Communist and North Korean local *tanwei* (*tanŭi* in Korean) committees. The *paochia* reported births and deaths, recorded and controlled "all movements of persons in and out of its area along with [monitoring] the conduct of the permanent residents,"[40] implemented Japanese health and sanitation regulations, mobilized labor details, disseminated information about crops, seeds, and fertilizer, collected many local taxes, and aided the police in every way. The colonizers liked this hybrid Sino-Japanese system so much that they "kept the regulations in full force throughout the entire span of their rule," and an American in 1954 called this a "most efficient" system of "refined" coercion.[41] More to our point, it was a Japanese fulfillment of the British (and Benthamite) project of omnipresent surveillance that the Anglo-Saxons never quite perfected in Egypt.

All in all, colonial Taiwan was a project that American academics could only applaud in the heyday of modernization theory: "Taiwan . . . developed into one of the most successful colonial programs in the world. . . . The Japanese rationalized . . . Taiwan's agriculture . . . established a strong and efficient government, the first that the island ever had. With a shrewd combination of police force and political guile, they imposed strict public order and penetrated every town and village with a structure of organized control. . . . This was a success that would satisfy most of the countries striving for modernization today."[42]

In many ways, Taiwan continued to be a colony after the mainlander debauch in the late 1940s, with Nationalists monopolizing executive government and political positions and taking over the many state-owned enterprises. The Nationalist political elite took over industrial assets that Japan had controlled; "the economic power of the Taiwanese elite—always much greater during colonialism than Chinese historiography admits—was quickly stripped away."[43] As in the Japanese period, the economy was open to the natives (mostly for small business), but politics was closed. Unlike the Japanese, carpetbagging Chinese bankrupted the carefully regulated economy within a year of "liberation."[44]

The Nationalists were never politically well-organized on the mainland, but they quickly came to appreciate Japanese innovations and added their overbearing centralism to the ubiquitous grassroots structures of the colonial period. As Edwin A. Winckler wrote, even the carefully manipulated local elections that the Kuomintang (KMT) allowed "remained backstopped by the same pervasive police network through which the Japanese had controlled the island," with Nationalist secret security agencies added on "for good measure."[45] Thomas Gold noted that "the economic and political structures that emerged were remarkably similar to the colonial ones": a minority of mainlanders monopolized politics and the state, controlled the means of violence, and used "thorough police repression" to hold on to power.[46]

VIETNAM: COLONIZATION WITHOUT DEVELOPMENT
OR MODERNITY

The French took a long time to colonize Vietnam and to drag it toward even the most exploitative forms of capitalist enterprise. Beginning in 1859, the

French navy took almost a decade to occupy parts of southern Vietnam or Cochinchina; the French seized other outposts, establishing themselves at the mouth of the Mekong River but only moving inland slowly. In the early 1880s, the French invaded central and northern Vietnam (Annam and Tonkin) and finally obliterated Vietnamese independence in 1885. Their colonization of Vietnam, however, was incidental to their desire for a southern point of entry to China.

Once they got control, the French primarily encouraged extractive economic activity, oriented toward exports of agromineral products. The transportation and communications infrastructure developed accordingly, if slowly, shaped by the export trade in rice, rubber, tin, and other commodities; Vietnam's extensive riverine landscape made canal building and dredging much more cost-effective than the road and railway network that the Japanese built in Korea and Taiwan. Large natural resource companies like Michelin monopolized economic activity. The main function of the colonial state was to facilitate the movement of commodities out of Vietnam; the state served the interests of the exporters by building the necessary routes to the sea and organizing a franc bloc and tariffs to protect export-oriented production.[47]

French policies introduced in effect a money economy without much else, tying Mekong Delta rice prices to the world market and thus upsetting the annual peasant "round of time" and drowning marginal subsistence farmers; the result was major unrest in 1940 and 1941, and an unbeatable Vietminh insurgency by the late 1940s.[48] A mere glance at the transportation network discloses French goals (or their absence): quite irrationally, Vietnam's longest rail line and asphalt road ran side by side along the coast, recapitulating existing (and more economical) sailing routes and veering away from the most developed parts of Vietnam to run through miles of empty rural areas until it got to China.[49]

An obsession with cost-effective administration by the relatively small colonial government left Vietnamese villages mostly self-sufficient and autonomous, unlike Japanese penetration to the lowest levels of administration in Korea and Taiwan. The colonizers tended to maintain rural order with periodic punitive military campaigns, unlike Japan's constant presence and surveillance (although the French did mobilize village informants to monitor their neighbors and report miscreants to the authorities). Another way to save money was to buy off collaborators with large land grants, a practice also found in Korea and Vietnam but without subsequent French programs to rationalize land arrangements or develop agriculture scientifically. Instead of a central colonial budget and financial pump priming of industry, the French had local budgets for the three regions of Vietnam and financed them through state monopolies of customs, duties, stamps, salt, alcohol, and opium. The state's revenue extraction was much lower than in Korea or Taiwan, particularly from the multitude of agricultural producers; instead of controlling and reducing the opium trade, as the Japanese did (particularly in Taiwan, where the use of opium was extensive), the French encouraged it. Early on, it was their most lucrative colonial enterprise.[50]

The general French emphasis on monopoly control and coercion without corresponding investment in human capital can best be seen in the constant recourse to corveé for so-called public works projects. The Haiphong-Laokay railway, for example, was completed in 1904–1906 with five separate labor drafts totalling almost thirty thousand laborers,[51] and such practices continued into the 1930s. When they weren't organizing great corveé projects, the French relied on seasonal migration of laborers between the rubber and the tin plantations, yielding a large, uneducated, underemployed, unskilled or semiskilled labor force. Both these forms of labor mobilization were rarely used by the Japanese in Korea and never in Taiwan; massive corvée might describe the forced labor of Koreans in the war years, but in a typically Japanese, highly organized fashion. Ngo Vinh Long estimates that perhaps two hundred thousand Vietnamese out of a total late-1930s population of over twenty million were workers, but large numbers were unskilled seasonal migrants, with forty thousand alone in the rubber industry and another forty-nine thousand in mining.[52]

The one period of real development in Vietnam was the "roaring '20s," when after 1924 the French poured capital into Indochina. Still, the main direction was toward plantation agriculture, above all rubber but also rice, sugar, tea, cotton, and other goods, and to the transportation and communications overhead necessary to move the goods out of the country. Martin Murray writes that by the 1930s "Indochina had become the most immensely exploited of all European colonies in Asia," but extraction was still mostly from primary-product processing; he notes that even in the 1920s boom, the colonial state was not very important, but more like an appendage of metropolitan French interests.[53] In the 1930s, Vietnamese communist and nationalist organizers achieved an extraordinarily rapid and sustained mobilization of peasants for radical activity, something that never occurred in Taiwan; in Korea, radical organizers in the 1930s did well in those counties and border areas away from the purview of the central state, but not elsewhere.

France was full of its *mission civilatrice* after World War I and sought to put its cultural stamp on Vietnam—above all, in an educational system designed to turn out an elite of Vietnamese *assimilados*, not a mass of industry-ready workers.[54] Thus, we find fully Francophile Vietnamese elites like "Emperor" Bao Dai, who retired to a villa outside of Paris, and others who were nonexistent in Taiwan and Korea outside of rank collaborationist circles.

(Perhaps Korea's Prince Yi, vegetating with a Japanese wife in his Akasaka residence after 1910, might be comparable, but no one thought him fit for leadership after 1945; meanwhile by 1947, Dean Acheson and Dean Rusk saw Bao Dai as Vietnam's anticommunist "white hope.") As a rule, the French paid little attention to education (there were more teachers in Vietnam before the French arrived than after they left);[55] the schools could assimilate a thin stratum of the natives but did not foster the industrial and administrative skills that Japanese disciplines produced. In the early 1930s, there were about twenty-eight thousand Vietnamese in elementary schools, but more than three hundred thousand Taiwanese; this at a time when Taiwan had eight million people and Vietnam twenty million.[56]

The 1920s did witness something never seen in Korea, however: local elections, which began in 1921 for village councils (and continued until 1941 when Bao Dai abolished them). These were merely one more way in which the French left (or created) space for traditional autonomy or contemporary resistance at the level where most Vietnamese lived, the rural villages, leaving an enormous gap between city and countryside. Instead of fostering the development and differentiation of Vietnamese society, French colonialism tended to preserve the hierarchy of social relationships in the rural hinterlands, with the state and the trading companies at the top, French businessmen and local agents in the middle, and the mass of the people consigned irrevocably to the bottom.

Quite unlike Taiwan, the French inhibited even "the most meager forms" of small business, much of the middle-level commerce (rice mills and the like) was in Chinese hands, and poor peasant interests tended to vector horizontally rather than vertically given the general absence of prospects for upward mobility.[57] As Jeffrey Paige, Ngo Vinh Long, and others have shown, of course, such a political economy has a tendency to promote peasant revolution—an important point, but one that bears no restatement given the punctuation of Vietnam's thirty-years' war from 1945 to 1975.

French investment of all types dropped off rapidly after the depression began, and by the end of the 1930s the global war had started, a war that eventually loosened the French grip on Vietnam. European settlement (never very high and much smaller than Japanese settlement in Korea and Taiwan) dropped off to nothing; the colonizers stopped building railroads (they had never built many anyway), using existing roads or new ones with motorbus conveyances. Murray speaks of "colonial nonindustrialization" in the 1930s,[58] in complete contrast to the way Japan used its colonies to industrialize itself out of the depression.

A good example of "colonial nonindustrialization," and a startling contrast to Japan in Korea, was the French Imperial Conference of 1934–1935. It was beset with a controversy, in Murray's words, over whether "state-managed control of colonial economic affairs (*étatisme*), state economic planning for a coordinated and 'rational' imperial economy (*dirigisme*), or the doctrines of economic liberalism (*laissez-faire*) provided the most efficient and profitable strategy by which to integrate metropolitan economic affairs with the overseas colonial territories" (207). The French brought forth a plan for the industrialization of Indochina in 1938, including the fostering of chemical, automobile, and textile production, which might have brought its policies close to the combination of *étatisme* and *dirigisme* that the Japanese had pioneered in Korea and Taiwan. But the plan was deemed impractical and the French were debating what else to do when World War II broke across their horizon and borders, placing a premium on the rubber and minerals that France had always extracted from Vietnam (207–208). Meanwhile, Japan had opted for an integral colonial development strategy as early as 1921, as we have seen.

Northeast Asia's Modern/Colonial/Developmental Project

In the past twenty years, American economists have been wont to explain East Asian industrial success as the outcome of successive "big bangs" (Japan in 1949, Taiwan in 1958–1960, Korea in 1961–1963) when policy packages focusing on comparative advantage, correct pricing, devalued currencies, and the like launched export-led miracles. The general tendency is then to develop tables starting with absurdly biased per capita income or exporting base figures (Japan in 1949 and South Korea in 1953 after devastating wars, Taiwan in 1952 after international and civil war plus massive mainlander influx and carpetbagging), and then show the enormous geometric leaps propelled by each country's having accepted the wisdom of neoclassical ideas. Economists thereby accomplish the miracle of empirically based self-fulfilling prophecy.

Simon Kuznets is a Nobel laureate and a major malefactor in all this, but he is also more learned and subtle than many garden-variety developmental economists. In the middle of a highly technical article where he proposes to test all sorts of propositions about Taiwan's economic success, he pauses to note that

> given the expected economic flows among market economies, particularly those in geographical and historical proximity to each other, the fact that some of them experience a rapid rate of growth in total and per capita product makes it easier to explain a similar experience in other countries of the group. Thus Japan's spectacular economic growth from

the early 1950s to the early 1970s is a significant factor in the high growth rates of Japan's trading neighbors, including Taiwan; reciprocally, the high growth rate in Japan's trading neighbors contributes to Japan's growth. In that sense, the growth experience of any single country is a function of the growth of others.[59]

At a later point in his monograph, Kuznets also cites "the growth-stimulating effect" of "the backlog of unexploited production opportunities" provided by "the forward movement of technology and efficiency in other countries not affected by the conditions that retarded progress elsewhere." This effect occurs "even in LDCs [less developed countries]":

> Though a backlog is presumably continuously present in them, even in some less developed countries per capita product may have grown in the past (as in Taiwan under Japanese occupation), a process that may have been interrupted by war preparations and war (again as in Taiwan since the early or middle 1930s). If, as noted above, Taiwan managed, even with Japanese dominance and constraints on domestic industrialization, to attain a growth rate of between 1 and 2 percent per capita per year before war preparations began, the interruption added to the effective backlog of production opportunities. Once the institutional and political conditions had changed, a much higher growth rate could be attained. (53)

This is an interesting example of the reasoning of American economists, particularly their supposition that language—in this case, tortured English prose—is transparent and meaning is self-evident above a certain level of literacy. For example, what does "historical proximity" mean beyond a redundancy for geographical proximity, as Japan, Korea, and Taiwan have not moved any closer since their human settlement a few tens of thousands of years ago? This might, however, signify Kuznets's recognition of a "historical proximity" known as Japanese imperialism, when Tokyo's Birnam Wood did indeed march to the hinterland's Dunsinane. Here we also get to sample the concern of economists for historical accuracy (Taiwan was unaffected by the Pacific War before 1937, somewhat affected after Japan turned south in 1941, and only hurt in the last year of the war—and then not badly).

More important, these statements would seem to render impossible the scientific separating out and measuring of economic growth in Taiwan, Korea, and Japan, and instead underline the influence of the history of economic interaction and the northeast Asian regional economic effort, whether in the 1930s, the 1960s, or the 1990s. But if that is so, in an interdependent world made "global city" by the latest technologies, how do we separate out any large trading nation and its linear history or developmental trajectory from all the rest? How separate out the influence of the trading organizations of those nations, otherwise known as transnational corporations, represented everywhere in northeast Asia? Don't we now require a holistic and dialectical analysis to figure all this out, rather than the linear teleology and parceled-out empiricism of neoclassical economics (pant pant . . .)?

Kuznets, however, has made a good point in spite of his theory. He draws this conclusion to his discussion: "In short, one could attempt to explain the high rate of aggregate growth in the last two to two and a half decades in Taiwan by examining the contributions of the stimulating effects of a wide backlog of unexploited new production opportunities, of the major structural changes in economic and social institutions, and of the effect of high growth rates generated for similar reasons in important neighboring countries and in much of the world at large" (53). Now, if we just extrude "major structural changes in economic and social institutions" from his argument about Taiwan (or South Korea, for that matter) on the grounds that both nations inherited not simply a workable model of rapid industrial growth but the economic, social, and political institutions that went with it, we have an agreement that regional synergy, late industrialization (Kuznets's "backlog"), and inherited institutions drove the industrial growth of Taiwan and Korea from the 1930s to the present, excepting (as Kuznets did) the years when wars raged—and with no obvious need to isolate a particular turning point when someone finally saw the light at the end of the export-led tunnel.

What, then, is the East Asian "developmental model"? Because many people have written about this subject before (myself included), let me just sketch briefly the northeast Asian model of political economy, which we find in Japan and its colonies by the mid-1930s if not earlier, and then successively in postwar Japan, South Korea, and Taiwan (with many mirror-image reflections in North Korea). Since premodern Japan had a very different political system from Korea or China (feudal-style parcelized sovereignty vs. centralized agrarian bureaucracy), and since other postcolonial nations (e.g., the Philippines, Vietnam, Indonesia, Burma, and India) do not demonstrate the characteristics outlined below, it seems reasonable to think that modern and colonially imposed Japan had a good deal to do with this difference. But the main point for this chapter is more modest, namely, that postwar economic successes in northeast Asia have roots going back well before the Rostovian period of "take-off" in the early 1960s. Let's have a sketch of this regional bureaucratic-authoritarian industrializing regime (or BAIR, as I have called it):

1. A *bureaucratic* state, drawing on native Confucian statecraft and civil service, modified by modern Weberian (usually German or French) models; centralized *national capitals* that are administrative, commercial, and transportation-communication nerve centers with populations dwarfing

other cities (Tokyo, Seoul, Taipei, P'yŏngyang); little or no local autonomy (center-appointed officials down to county or lower levels); national administrative and policing systems

2. *Education of the masses* necessary to create the disciplined proletariat, secretariat, and salariate requisite to the BAIR; corresponding de-emphasis on higher education (the university as playground and networking site)

a. Japan: the education system formed after Meiji and continuous down to the present, yielding the highest level of general mass education in the world (in contrast to France's elite system or America's mass system), with a narrow, exam-monitored entry gate to small elite universities

b. Korea and Taiwan: about 70 percent of schoolchildren getting elementary education by the late 1930s (in contrast to 2 percent of Vietnamese in elementary school in the 1930s)

c. Postwar South Korea: elementary schools as museums of colonial models, complete with Japanese uniforms, into the 1980s; narrow gate to small elite universities

d. Postwar North Korea and Taiwan: universal elementary school education, with practices modified by Soviet and Kuomintang influences; narrow gate to small elite universities

3. Effective *surveillance* of those same masses by every means necessary:

a. Prewar Japan: emperor/great leader, authoritarian constitutions, national police, registration of all citizens, meaningless elections, absence of civil and political rights, many secret police and intelligence groups, extremes of torture and thought reform for dissidents, close neighborhood surveillance by police and resident families

Postwar Japan: reformed emperor, democratic constitution (but lingering authoritarian political culture and single-party dominance in 1955–1993), national police (after Occupation reforms), local police, and family neighborhood surveillance

b. South Korea (1945–1992): maximum great leader or general (Rhee, Park, Chun, Roh), authoritarian constitutions, national police, registration of all citizens, meaningless elections, absence of civil and political rights, many secret police and intelligence groups, extremes of torture and thought reform for dissidents, close neighborhood surveillance by police and resident families[60]

c. Taiwan (1947–1989): great leader/emperor (Chiang Kai-shek and Chiang Ching-guo), authoritarian constitutions, national police, registration of all citizens, no elections (martial law regime enforced by mainlanders), absence of civil and political rights, many secret police and intelligence groups, extremes of torture and thought reform for dissidents, close neighborhood surveillance by police and resident families

d. North Korea (1945–1998): great leader/emperor (Kim Il Sung and Kim

Jong Il), authoritarian constitutions, national police, registration of all citizens, meaningless elections, absence of civil and political rights, many secret police and intelligence groups, extremes of torture and thought reform for dissidents, close neighborhood surveillance by police and resident families

4. *Metaphysical ideology of national essence:* Prewar and postwar Japan, North and South Korea, and Taiwan have all had a metaphysical political ideology emphasizing national *difference* and antiliberalism or anti-Westernism. (Korean, Japanese, and Chinese scholars all read and commented upon the same neo-Confucian texts 150 years ago, which is the common point of origin.) Ultimately these doctrines seek an obliteration of liberal politics in favor of an organic conception, or the merger of state and society such that "civil society" barely exists.

a. In *prewar Japan*, this ideology took the form of *kokutai* (*kukch'e* in Korean), an opaque doctrine often translated as "national polity," emphasizing everything that made Japan different from and morally superior to the West. In *postwar Japan*, the most important intellectual theme has been *shutaisei* (*chuch'esông* in Korean), a theme probing what it means to be modern and Japanese at the same time.[61]

b. North Korea's reigning *chuch'e* doctrine includes the same character (*tai*), and although this is usually translated as "self-reliance," it also means everything that makes North Korea different from, and morally superior to, the West.[62]

c. Taiwan has gone forth under Sun Yat Sen's "Three People's Principles," but much more often it uses the "self-strengthening" metaphysic pioneered by Li Hung-chang in the late nineteenth century,[63] which also reproduces the *tai* character in the formulation "Chinese thought for the base [*tai* or *t'i* in Chinese], Western technology for use [*yung*]."

d. In South Korea, Syngman Rhee offered the "One People Principle" in the late 1940s, and Park Chung Hee fostered *chuch'esông* in the 1970s.

5. *Political economy of administrative guidance and neomercantilism:* state-centered direction of economic activity, state-accumulated and provisioned capital, relying in early stages on maximum extraction from peasant economy, state-guided product cycle through stages of industrialization, import substitution followed by exporting followed by secondary and tertiary import substitution and subsequent exporting, "getting prices wrong" as a means of strangling domestic consumption and capturing foreign markets, highly protected domestic market, national or cartelized industries (rails, roads, steel, chemicals, electricity, banks, etc.); no labor unions or corporatized labor

a. Prewar Japan: the original model (1928–1945); postwar Japan: same model modified by Occupation reforms (1945–1947), single-party democratic politics and semisovereign status within U.S. hegemonic regime (1947–1995), also known as the "developmental state"

b. Prewar Korea and Taiwan: objects and subjects of regionwide application of Japanese industrialization model, late 1920–1945, with strong, centralized colonial state apparatuses, *zaibatsu* investment, and limited but consequential involvement of a few big native capitalists (Kim Sŏng-su, Pak Hŭng-sik, Liu Wei-hung); maximum extraction from peasant economy, colonial division of labor meant heavy industry in northern Korea and textiles, light industry and rice/foodstuff exports in southern Korea, with heavy *zaibatsu* involvement; aluminum, cement, and light industry (rice, sugar, and foodstuff exports) in Taiwan, with much *zaibatsu* involvement but more scope for small native business

c. Postwar South Korea: state-centered direction of economic activity, state-accumulated and provisioned capital, maximum extraction from peasant economy until 1970s; state-guided product cycle through stages of industrialization, ISI followed by ELI followed by secondary and tertiary ISI followed by exporting, "getting prices wrong" as a means of strangling domestic consumption and capturing foreign markets, highly protected domestic market, national or cartelized industries (rails, roads, steel, chemicals, electricity, banks, etc.); no labor unions or corporatized labor

d. Postwar North Korea: state-centered direction of economic activity modified by Stalinist and Korean self-reliance doctrines; state-accumulated and provisioned capital; maximum extraction from peasant economy until 1970s; state-planned product cycle through stages of industrialization, nearly exclusive ISI, nearly closed domestic market (exceptions being Soviet and Chinese machinery and technology, oil, and coking coal), national industries with no private ownership after 1950; state-controlled labor unions

e. Postwar Taiwan: state-centered direction of economic activity modified by KMT "bureaucratic capitalism"; state-accumulated and provisioned capital but much less than in Korea, with significant overseas Chinese investment; maximum extraction from peasant economy until 1970s; state-guided product cycle through stages of industrialization, ISI followed by ELI followed by secondary and tertiary ISI, followed by exporting; "getting prices wrong" as a means of strangling domestic consumption and capturing foreign markets, less protected domestic market, national industries (rails, roads, steel, chemicals, electricity, banks, etc.) and a few big cartels, but larger scope for light industry and small firms; no labor unions or corporatized labor

6. Involvement in closely linked *regional* political economy: this was true a fortiori of Japan's regional empire in the 1930s and 1940s, but was reimposed in modified form after American-sponsored changes beginning in 1947 (George Kennan's reverse course and Dean Acheson's "great crescent," with a decade-long delay caused by Kim Il Sung's attempt to break this developing system in 1950). Japanese economic influence had been reintroduced in South Korea and Taiwan by the mid-1960s, and is being reintroduced in North Korea and Manchuria in the 1990s.

There is more to be said about the northeast Asian BAIR model, but this sketch may serve to whet the appetite of the reader for my forthcoming work.[64] What is missing from this abstract sketch, of course, is the collective force of peoples, which we will examine in the next chapter.

CONCLUSION: STAATSWISSENSCHAFTEN, OR
STATE SCIENCE OF LATE INDUSTRIALIZATION

Our discussion thus far, whether we know it or not, has indulged in a kind of science unknown in America, what nineteenth-century Germans called *Staatswissenschaften*, or state science (as distinct from, say, social science). When Hirobumi Itō came back from Germany and quipped, "I understand the secret of the state, now I can die a happy man,"[65] it was first of all because he had met Lorenz von Stein, author of the classic text *Der Begriff der Gesellschaft und die soziale Geschichte der Französischen Revolution bis zum Jahre 1830*. As Immanuel Wallerstein argues, von Stein understood "society" to be a concept of Staatswissenschaft because it has meaning primarily "in the antimony, society/state."[66] For von Stein, society and state were not simply linked inextricably in meaning, but fused in a number of senses; for example, states decide who constitutes the citizenry ("civil society"). More powerfully, if for Hegel the monarch embodied the state and vice versa (a different fusion), the novelty of the French Revolution was that after it, the state embodied the popular will (or should have). The question then becomes, Who embodies (or creates, or knows) the popular will?

Consider how different this is from our social science, where these questions still predominate and where "the state" either is not taken seriously as a category for analysis or is criticized as something wont to be reified, a hypothetical construct in comparison to a society that we presumably know well: made up of individuals, roles, clusters of interest, pressure groups, and the like. But looked at from von Stein's perspective, "society" is also a hypothetical or mere rhetorical construct, endlessly reified and morally valenced as "civil society," "democratic society," "pluralist society," "only found in the West," and so on.

In any case, American rhetoric is not the rhetoric of mid-nineteenth-century Germany or twentieth-century Japan, Korea, or China. The latter were drawn inexorably toward state science, whether of the von Stein or the Leninist or the Park Chung Hee variety. Sooner or later, all the northeast Asian nations fashioned states worthy of the battle of late industrialization, and all of them did so in conditions ranging from the complete absence to the overwhelming presence of hegemonic American ideology (1930s Japan vs. 1960s Japan; North Korea vs. South Korea; post-1949 China vs. post-1949 Taiwan).

This is why I disagree with Theda Skocpol's point that "state building" is the business of revolutionaries after a conjunctural cataclysm.[67] The meaning of state building in northeast Asia's fused states/societies is that recourse to the state comes first, followed by conscious or unconscious attempts to create industry and then and only then "society," that is, the groups requisite for and appropriate to contemporary imaginings of "modernity." The space may have been semiperipheral or, more accurately, in heaven-sent or carved-out breathing spaces of the world (uncolonized northeast Asia ca. 1850–1910; indulgent America's part of northeast Asia ca. 1945–1970; revolutionary-nationalist East Asia ca. 1945–1975). But the time was "late," with imperial and industrial antagonists breathing hotly on the neck. Nothing concentrates the mind better than grand opportunity combined with overwhelming danger.

It is not the case that "in the beginning was the word." In the beginning, as with the human being, was the conception, something residing in a pre-discursive groping for its own name—Itō searching for the answer to the state.[68] In northeast Asia, that name turned out to be state science. American analysts have not seen this because they haven't been looking for it; they have been preoccupied with the creation of a different space, that space between the rational intellect and theology in the first place, and between the citizen and the state later on—what is now apotheosized by Habermas as "public space" and anathematized for all of East Asia as no "civil society." In some ways, East Asia has meant industrialization without Enlightenment, a crude adoption that strikes at the heart of Western civilization. Behold, they took the baby and not the bath water.[69]

A state science of late industrialization, however, is not hegemonic ideology. It cannot take the world as its oyster and reckon for the whole. It takes the world as its octopus and reckons for the parts. To put it another way, northeast Asia beginning with Japan has not exported universals. It has consumed certain select Western universals and disregarded others—the supreme and unforgivable insult. Our universals have been British universals, artifacts of England's preeminence after Waterloo.[70] The mid–nineteenth century saw not merely England as the workshop of the world, but England as the ventriloquist for the world (especially the American world). Germany was the bête noire of this world, shamelessly copying the inventive wizardry of the English and then dumping the shabby results in British markets. The German and Japanese consciousness was the mirrored reflection of hegemonic thought: a replicative consciousness in search of an elusive perfection, through which the particulars could become not hegemonic, not dominant, but merely equal.

The difference between American and East Asian experience, then, is quite breathtaking: here, replication of the British model thus to supersede; there, selective replication of continental experience thus to pass muster. The first, being hegemonic in intent, was holistic; the second, being egalitarian in intent,[71] was particular. Inevitably the latter would fasten upon *technique* stripped away from Weltanschauung and give us *kokutai, chuch'e,* and the insoluble *t'i-yung* problem. If internally the state would create the "modern," autodisciplined subject, externally it would defend the terrain against the hegemonic power, its products and its worldview.

Wallerstein asserts that after World War II *Staatswissenschaften* disappeared as a school of thought in Germany and elsewhere,[72] but that is far from the case. In Japan and South Korea, the United States fashioned liberal constitutions (albeit with the requisite loopholes in the precarious ROK), but Taiwan got martial law, and in all three countries the interwar bureaucrats continued apace as if nothing had happened. In North Korea and Taiwan, the constitutions were Leninist. But the central bureaucrats perdured, and no doubt will perdure.

Still, the central experience of northeast Asia in this century has not been independence wherein reigns autonomy and equality, but enmeshment in another web: the hegemonic web. This web had a spider: first England-America, then America-England, then war and defeat, then unilateral America, then (about 1975 down to the present) trilateral America. Japan, South Korea, and Taiwan industrialized mostly within this web. North Korea and China defined themselves as outside the web, thereby endowing the web with overriding significance—and so they structured their states to resist enmeshment. Japan, South Korea, and Taiwan have thus had states "strong" for the struggle to industrialize, but "weak" from the web of enmeshment: they are semisovereign states. North Korea had a state "strong" for industrialization and "total" for hegemonic resistance. But as the century ends, it, too, is being drawn into the web; and so, finally, is Vietnam. Heir to French exploitation and Ho Chi Minh's revolution, it now wants to discipline itself thus to follow in the wake of the NICs. Better that it had invited the Japanese to colonize it.

4

CIVIL SOCIETY AND DEMOCRACY IN THE

UNITED STATES AND EAST ASIA

Orient and Occident are chalk-lines drawn before us to fool our timidity.—Nietzsche

In this chapter I take up the problematic of civil society and democracy in the United States and in East Asia (but primarily South Korea). In the first section I examine the work of various people who theorize about civil society (including Harvard theorists Robert Putnam and Michael Sandel, and Jürgen Habermas), and the strengths and weaknesses of their work—including the Western bias and essentialism of their accounts. The next section looks at two alternative critiques of civil society: from the Marxist Left, primarily through the work of Marx and Gramsci, and from the Catholic Right, through the work of Alasdaire MacIntyre and Roberto Unger. I then take up the question of Korean democracy: the popular struggles and elite responses that brought about a particular, Schumpeterian form of democratic system in 1993 and a well-known dissident as president in 1998; the continuing crisis of transition from authoritarianism to democracy, unmatched in the world for its depth and audacity; and the remaining agenda of democratization in Korea. The final section addresses the question, What is democracy? in the light of the American and Korean experiences.

CIVIL SOCIETY IN SEARCH OF ITSELF

In the United States in the 1990s, the political spectrum from right to left is suffused with deeply conflicted concerns about American civil society. All commentators point to the same symptoms: the pathologies and dangers of the public space (i.e., cities), high rates of crime amid a more general breakdown of morality, the disintegration of nuclear families, citizen apathy and disinterest in voting, cynicism about the political system, the debasement of public debate (particularly on television, the primary medium for delivering this debate), and the absence of political and national leadership.

According to a Gallup poll published in February 1994, 80 percent of the American people do not believe that government can be trusted to do what is right; 75 percent are dissatisfied with the way the political process works; and about 75 percent believe that government benefits a few big interests rather than the interests of all. In 1992, 1994, and 1996, protest politicians (Ross Perot, Newt Gingrich, Patrick Buchanan) sought to mobilize voters on the basis of these grievances, usually citing the 1950s as a golden age when everything was fine with America (Gingrich recommended the year 1955 as the apogee of the American system).

Simultaneously, contemporary writers of great influence argue that civil society is inherently a Western concept and therefore absent in the remaining communist countries, most in need of creation in postcommunist countries, and mostly absent in East Asia—in authoritarian Singapore, democratic Japan, and the NICs of South Korea and Taiwan. Samuel Huntington of Harvard University made this view notorious in his essay, "The Clash of Civilizations," which sought to fashion a new paradigm for post–cold war global politics. But perhaps Karel van Wolferen's *Enigma of Japanese Power* is the best recent example of the argument that East Asia industrialized without civil society and without an Enlightenment. This book would merit no more than a footnote were it not so influential in American circles: at one point in late 1993, van Wolferen performed the feat of having articles published simultaneously in *New Left Review, Foreign Affairs,* and *The National Interest,* thereby blanketing the spectrum of intellectual opinion from left to right. The editors of the *New York Times* not only have opened their op-ed page to him several times, but have written editorials based on his work, which they think located a "third system" after capitalism and communism, namely, the East Asian system.

For van Wolferen, "the West" connotes a site of "independent, universal truths or immutable religious beliefs, transcending the worldly reality of social dictates and the decrees of power-holders";[1] Japan, however, is a place where people adjust their beliefs to situations in "a political culture that does not recognize the possibility of transcendental truths" (9). As in nineteenth-century accounts of "the Orient," Japan for van Wolferen is an enigma, opaque, led by a mysterious "System," and "single-mindedly pursuing some obscure aim of its own" (9). The System "systematically suppresses individualism" (3), he writes, and the Japanese do not accept Western logic or metaphysics, going all the way back to "the Greeks" (9). The "crucial factor" that proves these generalizations is "the near absence [in Japan] of any idea that there can be truths, rules, principles or morals that always apply, no matter what the circumstances" (9). Koreans might think the same thing of Japan, but van Wolferen does not like any of the East Asian political systems: "The Japanese, Korean and Taiwanese experiences show that a third category of political economy can exist, beside the Western and communist types" (6). These states represent "a largely uncharted economic and social-political category" (8).

In this discourse, which is quite common in the United States, the ills and pathologies of American civil society curiously disappear, to be replaced surreptitiously by an idealized construction drawn from Locke and Tocqueville. Of course, no one can claim that East Asian countries have the social pathology obvious on almost any street in any American city, and recent elections in Taiwan had rates of voter turnout far above those of American elections. But all that is forgotten in the conjuring of a Western civil society where well-informed citizens debate the important questions of politics and the good life without fear or favor, in contrast to the limited democracies, authoritarian systems, and general illiberalism of East Asia, illustrated mundanely in the caning of Michael Fay in Singapore or more tellingly in the continuing crisis of governance in Japan. Now let's look more closely at the debates about civil society in the United States.

Conservatives believe that American problems lie either with government or with the people themselves. Welfare, entitlements, big government, and sixty years of influence by a "liberal elite" are the causes of America's ills. If not that, then the people themselves lack virtue. In the 1980s, conservatives sought the causes of American economic decline in the demise of a work ethic, but amid general economic growth and continuing social pathology in the 1990s, they now find the cause in an absence of civic virtue. The Cato Institute, for example, a libertarian outfit in Washington that is often more thoughtful than most think tanks, advertised its publications in a 1996 brochure entitled *How You Can Help Advance Civil Society.* A bust of Thomas Jefferson adorned the cover.[2] The brochure began this way: "It is the nature of human beings to be free, and increasingly we are coming to realize that freedom from bureaucratic institutions not only is consistent with human nature but is the source of human progress. . . . the old paradigm of structuring societal arrangements through governmental mechanisms is crumbling." This institute described its mission as one of "expanding civil society" through "a Jeffersonian philosophy" that can best be described as "market liberalism": "It combines an appreciation for entrepreneurship, the market process, and lower taxes with strict respect for civil liberties and skepticism about the benefits of both the welfare state and foreign military intervention."

A liberal counterpoint to the Cato libertarians is *Tikkun* magazine's Foundation for Ethics and Meaning, which sponsored a "summit meeting" in Washington in April 1996.[3] This "summit" would help to create "a progressive alternative to address America's economic, spiritual, and ethical crises." Most people, the summit statement argued, "have a strong desire to live in a society that embodies social justice and that encourages connection, mutual recognition, and ethical and ecological sensitivity." *Tikkun's* progressive program is a more general expression of a profound concern for renewing civil society that animates several recent works of scholarship in political theory.

Harvard political scientist Robert Putnam has been lauded across the American political spectrum, from the leftist *Nation* to the conservative *Economist*, for his book *Making Democracy Work*. A study of civil society in general and in the specific confines of Italy, it begins with a discussion of the widespread despair in the United States about public institutions and democratic possibilities, continues with the exemplary civic virtue of northern Italy and the lack of it in southern Italy, and ends on a pessimistic note: "Where norms and networks of civic engagement are lacking, the outlook for collective action appears bleak. The fate of the Mezzogiorno is an object lesson for the Third World today and the former Communist lands of Eurasia tomorrow, moving uncertainly toward self-government."[4] Putnam thinks that Robert Dahl and Seymour Martin Lipset were right in stressing the contribution of modernization to democracy: "Nothing is more obvious even to the casual observer than the fact that effective democracy is closely associated with socioeconomic modernity, both across time and space." He also rehabilitates Almond and Verba's *Civic Culture*, calling it "a modern classic" in the vein of Tocqueville's *Democracy in America*.[5]

Putnam's own theory draws heavily on the Weberian/Parsonian pattern variables that Almond and Verba used thirty years ago, renaming them as "norms of civic engagement," "social structures of cooperation," and the like. Machiavelli thought the character of a citizenry depended on its "civic virtue," and this "republican school," according to Putnam, gives us the best explanation for well-functioning civil societies and democracies. They rest on civic engagement, political equality, the attenuation of individual striving in the interests of community, "solidarity, trust, and tolerance," and a network of civic or secondary associations: indeed, a key indicator of "civic sociability" is the "vibrancy of associational life." Perhaps we can call this the conservative republican position.

The liberal republican position has its most sophisticated recent exposition in a book by Harvard political theorist Michael Sandel. He begins his account with a discussion of two great American worries: "One is the fear that, individually and collectively, we are losing control of the forces that govern our lives. The other is the sense that, from family to neighborhood to nation, the moral fabric of community is unraveling around us."[6] Together, Sandel writes, these concerns "define the anxiety of the age" (3).

Sandel's argument is that the ills of civil society have arisen from a one-sided emphasis on the rights of the individual (i.e., libertarianism) and a corresponding decline in another form of American liberalism, called republicanism (that is, the civic virtue Putnam found in northern Italy, but which Sandel calls communitarianism). The master theorist of the first tendency is John Stuart Mill; that of the second tendency (for Sandel) is the very person the Cato Institute loves: Thomas Jefferson. The key distinction between Sandel and the Cato libertarians is not their worry about American civil society: they both agree that it is badly in need of repair. The distinction is that Sandel does not privilege the market and seeks to retrieve a liberalism from the past that would control the worst effects of market capitalism through communitarian constraints.

This republican vision stresses the harnessing of individual liberty through the mediating effects of citizen activism, self-government, and the "moral bond" of the community. In place of individualism it offers civic virtue; in place of a procedural political regime that guarantees individual rights, it offers a government that would seek the substantive goal of creating virtuous citizens. The republican tradition, Sandel argues, can thus "offer a corrective to our impoverished civic life" (3), or even "repair the civic life on which democracy depends" (7).

Sandel has cogent passages on the ills of the American public sphere. The older American cities are the obvious examples, of course, with the decline of urban public schools and crime in the streets heading a familiar list of other problems. But he notes that the suburbs, where the majority of Americans now live (often to escape the cities), are no longer open and welcoming but gated and closed "secure zones." Private security services that guard suburban housing compounds and shopping malls are so widespread that their members now outnumber public police officers in the United States. Even public playgrounds for children, first developed during the Progressive Era, have given way to suburban "pay-per-use" playgrounds at $4.95 per hour.[7] The suburb may once have been a site of community and civil society, but today it is a site of withdrawn and encapsulated anomie, suspended between cities that parody the presumed "modernity" of urbanism and small towns that still serve as the fount of American mythology about the pastoral virtues and "town-meeting" civic responsibility of times gone by.

The suffocating contemporary sameness of American suburbs, connected by highways lined with fast-food and other national business franchises and carbon-copy shopping malls, loses that very "sense of place" upon which community and citizenship depends. At most times in the day, the residential districts of these suburbs appear to be uninhabited, but in the evening they light up with the glow of television sets visible through living room windows but little evidence of other community activity. The streets are silent, like the streets of most American city centers after work ends. But in the suburbs the streets are safe: "citizens of nowhere have banded together for their common protection," to anticipate a phrase that we will revisit below.

Jürgen Habermas is the world's preeminent theorist of the public sphere (Öffentlichkeit), and in his work the concerns of people like Sandel and Putnam reach their highest, most sophisticated level. Habermas is the opposite of a romantic reactionary or a skeptical postmodernist: his thought is thoroughly shaped by belief in the Enlightenment project, the uses of human reason, the validity and abundant yield of progress, and the (still unrealized) utopian potential of the modern—however much it may be difficult to believe in that potential in today's world. Educated first in an apprenticeship to Adorno and Horkheimer and their Frankfurt School, his life work has combined a deep knowledge of the continental tradition and its heights (especially for him in the work of Kant, Hegel, Marx, Nietzsche, and Weber), with an unusual interest in positivist and systematic Anglo-Saxon social science. From the latter he draws on precisely the Parsonian concern with norms, roles, and systems that influenced Almond, Verba, and Putnam.[8] Unlike Putnam but similar to Sandel, he is deeply critical of unfettered individualism. The "motivating thought" in all his work, he has said, concerns "the reconciliation of a modernity which has fallen apart, the idea that without surrendering the differentiation which modernity has made possible in the cultural, the social and economic spheres, one can find forms of living together in which autonomy and dependency can truly enter into a non-antagonistic relation, that one can walk tall in a collectivity that does not have the dubious quality of backward-looking substantial forms of community."[9]

Such concerns led Habermas quite naturally to the sphere of civil society, or what he calls the public sphere. It is "the definitive institution of democracy," according to an American theorist: "A public sphere is an arena in which individuals participate in discussions about matters of common concern, in an atmosphere free of coercion or dependencies (inequalities). . . . Habermas' institutional concerns center on empowering voice, and on disenabling other means of collective judgement within democratic arenas—coercion, markets, and tradition."[10] The public sphere by no means consists of just the commonly designated sites of political discussion, like parliament or the newspapers; it is a vast (and theoretically universal) communications network that nonetheless bases itself in procedural democracy—especially in guarantees of basic human rights and political freedoms—and in a pluralism of groups. Autonomous public spheres are formed through the self-organization of myriad social groups, entering into a moral and political relationship with each other through communicative networks, yielding an egalitarian, open, and uncoerced debate. All who participate must be equal, each to the other; the sphere must be completely open, with no barriers to entry; the resultant debate is ipso facto both political and *moral*, since Habermas recognizes no separation of fact and value, or politics and morality (at least in the sphere of debate and decision). But it is also a *rational* sphere, where facts and values can be known. As Peter Dews explains, Habermas distinguishes among " 'three domains of reality': outer nature, inner nature, and society, to which correspond the objective, the subjective, and the intersubjective dimensions of rationality."[11]

The "new social groups" to which Habermas draws attention are environmental and alternative political forces such as the Greens in Germany, feminist organizations, multicultural education, and the antinuclear protests of the 1980s. A movement like that of the 1994 Gingrich Congress, however, does not fit the category because it was not counterhegemonic or liberating, but a protest movement of dominant white male professionals. The contemporary influence of Habermasian ideas is perhaps most evident in the self-description of participants in the Internet or World Wide Web, even if Habermas himself may be remote from their concerns; the more important point is that for Habermas, an intersubjective communicative process featuring dialogue, debate, and even conflict is the medium allowing us to know rationally the uses and ends of civil society.

Habermas's ideal-typical public sphere thus has much in common with the economists' marketplace, where all enter equally to truck and barter according to self-interest and supply and demand, free of coercion or regulation. His insistence on the pathologies of violence in politics, however, is most reminiscent of the Quaker pacifist tradition in America, where all problems must—by definition—be debated and talked through, no matter how long it takes, until that point where consensus is achieved. As Stephen K. White describes it, "Habermas announced that a rational basis for collective life would be achieved only when social relations were organized 'according to the principle that the validity of every norm of political consequence be made dependent on a consensus arrived at in communication free from domination.'"[12] Any intervention by violence, or by the organs of power, thus short-circuits the deliberative process necessary to a democratic public sphere.

CRITIQUE

The key similarity of the libertarians, *Tikkun*, Harvard theorists Putnam and Sandel, and the Habermasians is their disregard of radical, alternative constructions of civil society. From Raymond Williams we can learn that Sandel's reconstruction of republicanism is essentially an anachronistic discourse on the country and the city. The flip side of Jefferson's rural community was disdain for newly risen industrial cities, a resistance to the simultaneous newly structured order and unruly chaos that any number of other critics declaimed in the early industrial era as they witnessed "a social dissolution in the very process of aggregation."[13] The recourse to ideas of civil society born of a bygone agrarian order ignores not only the impossibility of recreating such ideas in our time, but the inequalities of that order when it existed: the isolation and frequent ignorance of the farms and villages; the slaves held by Jeffersonian Virginians; the oppressions of women, itinerant laborers, and the heterodox of all types; and the huge class of victims claimed by Westward expansion. The pastoral ideal, as Williams says, is authentic and moving precisely to the degree of its unreality.[14]

Cato libertarians and Sandel can unite in privileging Jefferson because the political economy of the late eighteenth and early nineteenth century enabled Jefferson to have his cake and eat it too, that is, to be both individualistic and libertarian in regard to the (mostly nonexistent) central government, and to be communitarian through the lateral expansion to the Western frontier of replicative small towns and farming communities based on individual private property and government by "town meeting," yielding freedom and independence vis-à-vis superordinate power and the civic virtues of self-government (so long as the cavalry was not too far away).[15] In short, Sandel's vision is a sophisticated species of atavism. He offers not a single practical policy suggestion as to how republicanism can be reconstituted in 1990s America.

Sandel's anachronism is matched in Putnam's neo-Tocquevillean account of civil society and democracy. However much Italians in certain wealthy regions (harboring cities like Venice and Florence that are showered every year with billions of tourist dollars) may be joiners and civic doers, Tocqueville's account of the 1840s American propensity to join voluntary associations and participate in politics has little relevance to "downsized" suburban couples working two or more jobs to make ends meet, collapsing exhausted into their chairs to let television entertain them before trying to get enough sleep to start the long work day again.

The most disturbing aspect of this recent literature, at least to me, is the cavalier identification of civil society and communitarian democracy with the West: these originated in Western Europe, then migrated to North America and the British Commonwealth and hardly anywhere else. Non-Western societies are simply not suitable settings for civil society and republican democracy, Putnam suggests. *The Civic Culture* reported these Western conceits straightforwardly in 1963, a time of higher American self-confidence and less self-awareness; it was only in the United States and England that the authors found "a pattern of political attitudes and an underlying set of social attitudes that is supportive of a stable democratic process." In the other nations they studied (West Germany, Italy, and Mexico), "these patterns are less evident."[16]

Habermas, a person who certainly ought to know better, also privileges the West as the site of the origin of his "public sphere" and its contemporary problematic, as well as its ultimate redemption. He concluded one of his books on "modernity" with this statement: "Who else but Europe could draw from its own traditions the insight, the energy, the courage of vision—everything that would be necessary to strip from the . . . premises of a blind compulsion to system maintenance and system expansion their power to shape our mentality."[17] This is by no means an unusual emphasis for Habermas, even if it is unusually blunt. His whole work is imbued with "the claim that the modern West—for all its problems—best embodies" the values of rationality and democracy,[18] with a now-evident, now-hidden discourse about modern German history (which I think pushes him toward the privileging of norms of political interaction that are evident in postwar West Germany, but nowhere else in German history—and for that reason may be temporary or precarious in their staying power) and an apparent utter lack of concern for the non-Western experience, except as a species of occasional counterhegemonic practice in the "Third World." Thus he shares the same prejudices of his cherished predecessor, Max Weber (Habermas is most of all a Weberian), but not Weber's passionate and intelligent comparativist project—and in a time when Weber would certainly recognize his own provincialism, were he still talking about "only in the West . . ." But perhaps we better sample the original Weber, what he said then, since we don't know what he would say now: "Only the occident knows the state in the modern sense, with a professional administration, specialized officialdom, and law based on the concept of citizenship. . . . Only the occident knows rational law. . . . Furthermore, only the occident possesses science. . . . Finally, western civilization is further distinguished from every other by the presence of men with a rational ethic for the conduct of life."[19]

Habermas is much more aware than Sandel and Putnam of critical alternatives to his work, however, which is not to say the critiques make a big impact on him. Nancy Love is right to point out that the public sphere of Habermas's construction "asks us to be Gods," to enter the public space free of property, inequality, recourse to force or even to anger; thus is constructed an arena of "ideal speech," recognizing "no sides": no classes, genders, or races to be transcended.[20] In that respect, Habermas's public sphere is no different than the ideality of liberalism. Still, that is an easy criticism, and Habermas is right that in public debate, we do not want the shadow of our class, race, or gender to overwhelm the message we wish to impart. Nor is Habermas's Western essentialism something that distinguishes him from any number of Western theorists. We should try harder to develop an effective critique of Habermas in his own terms.

We have been examining an Anglo-Saxon discourse about civil society, even if the German Habermas agrees with it; now let us examine the continental European discourse of the mid–nineteenth century. If we return to original European debates about state and civil society, in Hegel's work and Marx's critique of it, we see that the first modern representative state also just happens to be found in the hegemonic power of the nineteenth century, England. Its primary industrial rival, Germany, could only produce some unavailing, pale reflection of the liberal state, according to Marx. So, in reality, it produced a strong state that was the flip side of a weak civil society—a "fused state," as we saw earlier. But at the level of theory, Germany could work an elegant and sublime substitution for Anglo-Saxon dominance: namely, Hegel, who towered over any English thinker in his time.

For Hegel, modern society establishes the distinction between public and private, and because individuals are atomized by the market (Marx says of Hegel's theory), the state itself must provide a new form of unity—in Hegel, an abstracted unity that substitutes for a lost organic community. Whereas John Locke presents the state (or "civil government") as the separated "impartial judge" of private conflicts, for Hegel this separation of state and civil society was a contradiction of his deepest understanding of human society.[21] So he hypothesized a state that would restore the lost wholeness for which he yearned, yielding a fusion of what we call state and society.

Hegel seeks to overcome the division between state and civil society also through representative government, whereby delegates are chosen and entrusted to "superintend the state's interests" in civil society. Marx points out that this hardly solves the problem of the state's alienation from civil society: it is the civil service in the form of administration or judiciary or police that in turn represents the state in civil society, and often with force majeure. Hegel thinks he gets around this objection by arguing that the civil servant is not loyal to the monarch but is instead a neutral figure, chosen on the basis of his specialized knowledge; if every citizen has the opportunity to join "the class of civil servants," and there are specified procedures for deciding who joins (civil service examinations), then we need not worry about the arbitrary exercise of state power.[22] Guarantees against arbitrary power are lodged in the official himself, for example, in the civil servant's "dispassionate, upright and polite demeanor." The reader will note that Hegel's reasoning is quite compatible with contemporary doctrine.

Hegel introduces a confusion, however, by saying that not just anybody ought to be a bureaucrat. Where do we find such people? Generally speaking, Hegel says, in the middle class—the "pillar" of the state. Likewise, the bureaucrats are part of the definition of what it means to be middle class. Marx then intrudes Hegel's idea that the state should also develop the middle class, or "grow it," to use a Clintonesque term, if it is weak.[23] And with that, Hegel's argument reveals its circularity and its bourgeois presuppositions; it is a dog biting its own tail: a government of the middle class, by the middle class—and for the middle class?

Marx took Hegel (and not Locke) to be the exemplary theorist of the representative state, and instantly took his measure. However dazzling he was, Hegel merely recapitulated Germany's position vis-à-vis the advanced economies:

> The German *status quo* is the *undisguised consummation of the ancien régime* and the *ancien régime* is the *hidden defect of the modern state.* The struggle against the German political present is the struggle against the past of modern nations. . . . the present German regime . . . [is] an anachronism, a flagrant contradiction of universally accepted axioms. . . .
>
> In Germany, therefore, we are about to begin at the point where France and England are about to conclude. . . . This is a good example of the *German* form of modern problems, an example of how our history, like some raw recruit, has up to now been restricted to repeating hackneyed routines that belong to the past of other nations.[24]

As for Hegel, he supplied the ideality for which there was no reality:

> We Germans have lived our future history in thought, in *philosophy.* We are the *philosophical* contemporaries of the present without being its *historical* contemporaries. . . . What for advanced nations is a *practical* quarrel with modern political conditions is for Germany, where such conditions do not yet exist, a *critical* quarrel with their reflection in philosophy. (249)

I have purposely left out Marx's most important statement, which has a prescience founded in genius and requires no emphasis: In England and France "it is a question of the solution; here [in Germany] it is only a question of the collision" (248). Why a collision? Because a middle class brought into being in hothouse conditions could never establish its hegemony short of a bloody reckoning with its reactionary enemies, such as the Prussian Junkers, classes forged in the long run of "real" history. Germany thus combined the "civilized defects" of the modern world with the "barbaric defects" of the old regime. How can such a country, in one great leap, overcome "not only its own limitations but those also of the modern nations" (252)?

History's answer was that it could not, and those who enjoy pointing out the progressive teleology in Marx's thought need also reckon with Germany's trajectory (Bismarck to World War I to Weimar to Hitler to catastrophe, and then and only then to liberalism) and the diabolical unfolding of barbarism within "civility," foregrounded by Marx in 1844.

Antonio Gramsci, writing in the twentieth century, extended the conception of civil society by arguing that it was not just the sphere of debate, disputation, and politics (that is, the sphere primarily of the intellectuals), but a vast space existing between the ruling groups who inhabit the state and the normal or commonsensical routines of everyday life in the society. It is in this space that state and society come together, with the outcome indeterminate: it might be an organic unity of one and all, or a sharp cleavage of every man for himself, held together by the forces of order. For civil society to have legitimacy, or even to function at all effectively, the goals of the dominant groups must be translated into the quotidian reality of each person, so that civil and political behavior becomes habitual and no longer a matter of conscious reflection.

Gramsci's well-known definition of hegemony emerged from this logic: That civil society is organic which teaches its master ideas through the metaphors of mother's milk or the air we breathe; it is no longer ideology, but ethos (ether, the air we breathe). Absent such hegemonic mediation, the state must exist over and above civil society as a coercive form of domination. State and civil society, therefore, coexist in a curious zero-sum fashion: the less the civil society functions as it ought to, the more the state must grow in power to remedy this defect. The intellectuals are the primary carriers of a self-conscious civil society and therefore populated the salons of eighteenth-century France as the modern conception of civil society developed. But modern society can only be whole when the intellectuals abandon their protected sphere (resting implicitly on state guarantees of basic freedoms, which often do not exist for other people) and constitute themselves as organic with the people. This is for Gramsci the only acceptable "fused state."[25]

From Marx we have learned that civil society is a construct of the early industrializers, and the abortively fused state the product of late industrialization, a political entity seeking to make up for lost time, to substitute for a lost historical evolution. Gramsci understood this historical substitution of the state for the unevolved civil society, but argued that modern society can become whole only when civil society is no longer the vested interest of the intelligentsia but the common property of all. Clearly, Sandel and Putnam, but most importantly Habermas, have much to learn from this critique on the Left.

A critique of the Anglo-Saxon discourse on civil society from the Right, or the Catholic tradition, can be found in Alasdair MacIntyre's influential book, *After Virtue*, and in Roberto Unger's *Knowledge and Politics*. MacIntyre begins his account with the incapacity of Americans to decide questions of morality in the public sphere. Of moral and political debate there is plenty, but the debates are never resolved: they are interminable, because we have "no rational way of securing moral agreement."[26] The debate over abortion, for example, "the right to life" versus "the right to choose," is but one of many such irresolvable issues. MacIntyre and Unger trace the origin of this problem to Anglo-Saxon positivism and its separation of fact and value, of objective knowledge and normative preference. Where Habermas establishes a distinction between instrumental and intersubjective relations in civil society (usually identified as the technocratic rationality of a bureaucracy in contrast to the I-thou relations of a true political community), MacIntyre says that the separation of fact from value in American civil society leaves us with nothing but instrumental relationships. You have your moral or political preference and I have mine, but in choosing between values, reason is silent. Therefore we must agree to disagree and fashion a procedural politics that is unconcerned with substantive ends. Such a politics will then mediate conflicting moral/political positions.

MacIntyre contrasts this procedural regime, which is only concerned with "man as he happens to be," with the Aristotelian notion of "man as he could be if he realized his essential nature": "To say what someone ought to do is at one and the same time to say what course of action will . . . lead toward a man's true end and to say what the law . . . enjoins" (50–51). For MacIntyre, politics is that sphere where human beings realize their true or essential nature. The question must be, What sort of person am I to become? Liberals wish to avoid this question, because reason must be silent before questions of what constitutes the good for human beings; instead, the liberal asks What rules ought we to follow, what procedures will enable us to reach a rough form of justice between conflicting claims of right? But this does not avoid the question of what sort of people we are; every day we answer that question in our practice, through the lives that we lead. Ineluctably, therefore, MacIntyre argues that the presupposition of any civil society must be "the exercise of the virtues and the achievement of the good" (149).

Through this contrast between the liberal and the Aristotelian position, MacIntyre and Unger arrive at a devastating conclusion about the possibilities of civil society in America: We cannot form an intersubjective political community (Habermas's ideal) because not only do we not know what its purpose would be, but we have already agreed not to raise this question. As Unger puts the point, "The political doctrine of liberalism does not acknowledge communal values. To recognize their existence, it would be necessary to begin with a vision of the basic circumstances of social life that took groups rather than individuals as the intelligible and primary units of social life."[27] Or as MacIntyre argues, "a modern liberal political society can appear only as a collection of citizens of nowhere who have banded together for their common protection."[28]

Sandel's communitarian idea is precisely that we should realize ourselves through our political participation, that we attain civic virtue through this practice; he has a liberal vision of how the group or communal life can be or should be, something that transcends individualism. But he cannot tell us why we should do this and has no conception of the end or goal that this community must seek. For MacIntyre, this is a critical liability: "a community which lacks practical agreement on a conception of justice must also lack the necessary basis for political community" (227).

MacIntyre goes on to argue that the civic community is not one defined by a single, reigning conception of virtue: if people sincerely assert their conceptions of the substantive ends of human community in their daily practice, inevitably there will be conflict. Instead of submerging that conflict as an insoluble normative problem, or expecting it somehow to dissolve in the consensus of the ideal public sphere, it is "through conflict and sometimes only through conflict" that we will learn "what our ends and purposes are" (153). But however a community chooses to reach moral or substantive ends, it must do so or risk becoming a mere collection of anomalous individuals: "In any society where government does not express or represent the moral community of the citizens, but is instead a set of institutional arrangements for imposing a bureaucratized unity on a society which lacks genuine moral consensus, the nature of political obligation becomes systematically unclear" (236). From this insight we can understand the increasing tendency of Americans to assume that they have no obligations, from the simplest one of voting to the more important task of shaping a political community that is also a moral bond among people.

From the Catholic Right we have learned that liberalism cannot create the civil society that it privileges as its birthright because of the inherent presuppositions of liberalism itself. MacIntyre and Unger agree with Sandel's argument that civic community must be a value over and above the individual and his or her liberty, but argue that such a community cannot exist without an agreement on its substantive end—which must be to fashion human beings who realize the community's conception of the good. What about Habermas?

It turns out that a person we can call "the early Habermas" had already figured all this out. His 1961 book, *The Structural Transformation of the Public Sphere*, is a tour de force analysis of how the liberal (or bourgeois) public sphere, a limited but vital civil society in the eighteenth century, turned into a bureaucratized, alienated public space still marching under the banner of the French philosophes' ideals of civic virtue.[29] Here we find Habermas saying essentially what Gramsci did, that civil society exists *between* the state and the mass of the people; as it developed in the eighteenth century, it bid fair to be the ideal political space that liberals have always claimed it should be, with the spread of newspapers, journals, salons, and coffeehouses. But by the late nineteenth century, it had become what it is today, a space for competition among plural interests who "negotiate and compromise among themselves and with government officials, while excluding the public from their proceedings."[30] The bourgeois public sphere is thus limited to a particular epoch and is not synonymous with the historical development of civil society itself.

The clarion of the bourgeoisie, the newspaper reporting the latest business information and stock quotes (i.e., *The Wall Street Journal* in our time), was the impetus for an enormous expansion of print media under early capitalism, which later became the carrier of political debate and the creator of political community as a precursor to the arrival of the public sphere.[31] Habermas took from Kant the idea of "publicity" as the bridging principle between politics and morality, something deeply influential to his whole conception and yielding the citizen who can think and judge for himself. Likewise, towns emerged to hold the burgeoning bourgeoisie (now there's a trope), with various markets at the center but with teahouses, coffee shops, and reading and debating parlors growing in the interstices of new cities.

Habermas rather agrees with Marx that Hegel "took the teeth out of the idea of the public sphere in civil society"; Marx's blistering critique "demolished all fictions to which the idea of the public sphere" appealed, a sphere that "contradicted its own principles of universal accessibility" (122–24). Whether it was German "late" development or the arrival of masses of laborers in England's cities, "the bourgeois self-interpretation of the public sphere abandoned the form of a philosophy of history in favor of a common-sense meliorism": "the critique of the idea of the bourgeois public sphere as an ideology was so obviously correct that under the altered social preconditions of 'public opinion' around the middle of the [nineteenth] century, when economic liberalism was just reaching its peak, its social-philosophical representatives were forced almost to deny the principle of the public sphere of civil society even as they celebrated it" (130–31). There is a bourgeois public sphere, in other words, but also a *"plebeian* public sphere" that represents the entrance of the masses onto the political stage—as with Robespierre and his followers.[32] Habermas thought the Chartist movement, when organized labor first burst upon the industrial scene, was the specific cause of this change.

The denial and evasion that followed is best evidenced in John Stuart Mill's reaction to the "pressure of the street" in the form of laborers, women, and (American) blacks pushing for the voting franchise. Mill was by all means in favor "of all movements rebelling against the aristocracy of money, gender and color";[33] they should all have the franchise. But the arrival of this new, flooded public sphere of loud and divided opinion also struck Mill as a new kind of "coercive force" violating the open, nonviolent nature that should characterize the public space, and so he began deploring "the yoke of public opinion" and the compulsion to conformity that the new majority threatened. Or, as Tocqueville put the point (in full if unacknowledged agreement with Mill), "In democracies public opinion is a strange power. . . . It uses no persuasion to forward its beliefs, but by some mighty pressure of the mind of all upon the intelligence of each it imposes its ideas."[34] Now Mill called neither for participation without fear or favor nor for critique of the powers that be by the tribunes of the people, but for tolerance—mostly of the now slim stratum of intellectuals, that is, the elect of the liberal public sphere. Meanwhile, Tocqueville came to understand the genius of the American founding fathers in dividing the political public sphere through checks and balances and the voluntary associations that mediate between leaders and led.

There is a direct line from this surreptitious denial and evasion, this historically shaped yes and no to the massed laborers and the nonelect by Mill and Tocqueville, through Bentley, Dahl, Almond and Verba, and Putnam, down to Huntington's exasperated attack on "the democratic distemper" of the 1970s. Here Sandel's communitarian conundrum is also established, in Mill first saying yes and then no, yielding a procedural politics that gives us "tolerance" but not substance.

Habermas summarizes his account of the decomposition of the liberal public sphere as follows: "Marx shared the perspective of the propertyless and uneducated masses who . . . would employ the platform of the public sphere, institutionalized in the constitutional state, not to destroy it but to make it into what, according to liberal pretense, it had always claimed to be. In reality, however, the occupation of the public sphere by the unpropertied masses led to an interlocking of state and society which removed from the public sphere its former basis without supplying a new one."[35]

Is this a better explanation of the democratic malaise Sandel and Putnam point to, or not? In my view, Habermas delivered in 1961 an unanswerable critique of actually existing liberalism.[36]

DEMOCRACY AND ITS DISCONTENTS IN EAST ASIA AND KOREA

The East Asian state-society configuration that van Wolferen, James Fallows, Chalmers Johnson, and others find so wanting from a modern Western standpoint bears close comparison to a particular Western experience, if not *the* Western experience—namely, continental European development—and therefore is by no means sui generis. As we saw, Marx and Hegel could hardly have been more explicit about Germany's predicament. For Marx, it was that Germany "did not pass through the intermediate stages of political emancipation at the same time as modern nations."[37] For Hegel, the optimist of course, it was the task of the state to overcome Germany's debilities: "It is a prime concern of the state that a middle class should be developed, but this can be done only if the state is an organic unity . . . i.e., it can be done only by giving authority to spheres of particular interests, which are relatively independent, and by appointing an *army of officials* whose personal arbitrariness is broken against such authorized bodies."[38] This is a theory of "late" state formation and of "late" democratization; Marx places the German domestic configuration in the time and space of the world system and declares the task hopeless, whereas Hegel conjures it in the thin air of an ideal type and then foists the problem off on the bureaucrats. What is the problem? To create the middle class that is the presumed basis of democracy.[39]

In German "state science" (*Staatswissenschaften*), the conception of the *fused state* was thus born, as we saw earlier, in the aftermath of the French Revolution as a point of definitional anxiety and political reality. It is then a short step to observe the disorders of that same revolution, to relate them to novel ideas about "popular will," and to conclude, well, who needs that? Of what value is civil society in a race for industrialization? The Germans invented the fused state not to solve the problems of liberty, equality, and fraternity at the dawn of the industrial epoch, but to solve the mid-nineteenth-century problems of the second industrial revolution and, more important, to catch up with England. A fused state is one that both subsumes civil society and tries to build it up—but not if these efforts get in the way of industrialization.

Here, in short, is a political theory of late development that put off to a distant future the magnificent obsession of the Anglo-Saxon early industrializers with questions of popular will, democratic representation, public versus private, and state versus civil society. It is also a theory that explains much about East Asia's democratic trajectory: Japan, a democracy after 1945 but only after the cataclysm of war and occupation; South Korea, a democracy in 1993 but only after the cataclysm of revolution, war, division, and decades of military dictatorship (1961–1987) and sharp political struggle; Taiwan, a democracy in 1996 but only after revolution, war, national division, and forty years of martial law (1947–1987).

To look at it another way, the major power of our time, the United States, was at war in East Asia from 1941 to 1975. In the immediate aftermath of

World War II, it divided Korea, China, and Vietnam, while unilaterally occupying Japan. At bottom, this happened because the United States feared
the anti-imperial, antisystemic, revolutionary nationalists who took power
in North Korea, China, and North Vietnam, and especially their incipient
alliance with the Soviet Union and their addiction to the Soviet model of
industrialization. It fought two of the bloodiest wars in the twentieth century, in Korea (1950–1953) and Vietnam (1961–1975), stalemating with one
enemy and losing to another because of the extraordinary sacrifices of huge
numbers of people, mostly peasants, in Korea, China, and Vietnam.

Through all this, van Wolferen appears to imply, Japan, Korea, and China
also ought to have become liberal, that is, to have developed stable democracies and open civil societies. Viewed from the standpoint of the late 1990s,
one analyst after another now argues that some parts of it did: South Korea
and Taiwan are celebrated as victories for democracy, coming (predictably)
toward the end of a process of "modernization" in which a middle class
emerged triumphant. So do we have the "fused state," or emergent democracy and civil society? The answer is this: We had the fused state in South
Korea and Taiwan, and now we have a limited form of procedural democracy—just like Japan and Germany. But the path to this end was hardly
smooth; instead, it was filled with decades of torment and turmoil—Sturm
und Drang and then, and only then, democracy.

The struggle for Korean civil society and democracy was precisely situated
in MacIntyre's "site of conflict." Democratic struggles began in Korea on the
day that Japan surrendered in August 1945 and have continued down to the
present.[40] The popular forces of the late 1940s wanted both democracy and
social justice, that is, a cleansing revolution that would wipe away the influences of Japanese imperialism. They got a cleansing in North Korea but no
democracy, little if any cleansing in South Korea and little if any democracy,
and after a massively destructive civil war, a thoroughly divided and dis-
jointed nation.

Within the constricted politics of the Rhee regime (1948–1960), where any
sign of a leftist orientation meant a jail term if not death (the inconsequential
progressive Cho Pong-am was executed in 1958, one of the better-known of
many similar examples), a space for the intelligentsia cracked open wide
enough that students, faculty, and intellectuals could be the vanguard for an
overthrow of the First Republic, albeit when Syngman Rhee was on his last
legs and the United States wanted him out. The tepid opposition organized
the Second Republic through a weak cabinet system of government, where
for a year (April 1960–May 1961) civil society on the liberal model mush-
roomed. At this time, South Korea had more college students per capita than
England, more newspaper readers per capita than almost any country in the

world, and a concentration of administrative, commercial, industrial, and educational energies in one great capital city, much like Paris.[41] A very lively salon society animated the capital, publishers brought out thorough rewritings of modern Korean history, and students began to imagine themselves the vanguard of unification with the North.

I lived in Korea in 1967–1968, teaching English as a member of the Peace Corps. The family I lived with, the head of which was a schoolteacher, lacked most of the pathologies that I had come to associate with American family life. The students I taught were models of intelligence and discipline and often studied long into the night. I spent a lot of my time off sitting in the tearooms (*tabang*) that seemed to inhabit every street corner and that were animated by lively political discussions. Everyone in Seoul seemed to know everyone else, and they all had an opinion—often one that excoriated the politicians in power. I was amazed by the depth of interest in political gossip, and everyone seemed to read newspapers obsessively—including those who could not afford them, by way of wall posters in many places in the city. A woman who had taught us Korean in Peace Corps training turned out to be an avid reader of Thomas Hardy novels. Students would stop me on the street to ask me questions like this: "What is the significance of the hose in the basement in Arthur Miller's *Death of a Salesman*?" These same students ran through the streets by the hundreds, protesting some excess by the authorities. Laborers were anything but the docile, poorly paid workforce then being touted in *Fortune* magazine. I slowly came to think that Korean civil society was too vibrant, too raucous for the elites or their American backers to tolerate for very long.

General Park Chung Hee was the Korean agent of the Hegelian conception of the fused state, shutting down civil society with his coup d'etat in 1961 and the three-year emergency junta that followed, and deploying the state as the initiator, guide, and financier of a classic type of "late" industrialization. Strong American pressure from the Kennedy administration forced Park to drop his plans for instant heavy industrialization and to don mufti and run for election (in 1963), yielding "export-led development" and the contentious public sphere that I first encountered in 1967. The Nixon administration enlarged the sphere of Korean autonomy through the Guam doctrine and Nixon's neomercantilist New Economic Policy of August 1971, enabling Park to shut down civil society completely in 1971–1972 with barely a murmur from Washington.[42]

I lived in Seoul in that year, too, and have indelible memories of the extensive and brutal deactivation of politics that ensued from the Garrison Decree of October 1971 to the Yusin system and the martial law of autumn 1972. To make a long and bloody story very short, we can say that Park misjudged the hidden strengths and growing maturity of the public sphere, which was over-developed in relation to the economy but still underdeveloped compared to the ubiquitous agencies of the expanding Yusin state: a vast administrative bureaucracy, huge, distended armed forces, extensive national police, a ubiquitous Central Intelligence Agency with operatives at every conceivable site of potential resistance, and thorough ideological blanketing of every alternative idea in the name of forced-pace industrialization. If you want to experience early 1970s Korea, you can go to China today and see all the same things.

Park's fused state thus set up an unending crisis of civil society that culminated in the disorders of Masan and Pusan in August and September 1979, leading to Park's assassination by his own intelligence chief in October, which led to the "coup-like event" mounted by Chŏn Tu-hwan and No T'ae-u in December 1979 and the denouement at Kwangju in May 1980. The period 1980–1987 will appear in history as a classic Brumairean event,[43] with the luckless "nephew" (Chŏn) acting on behalf of the dispatched "uncle" (Park), using the jail and the knout all the way, but compounding into farce the tragedy of Park Chung Hee (who truly was Korea's industrial sovereign, if not its Napoleon). The real tragedy, of course, had taken place at Kwangju, where an aroused, self-organized, and intersubjective citizenry (i.e., not a bunch of rioters and miscreants) sought desperately to save itself from the new martial law regime that Chŏn had just announced, only to be slaughtered (a minimum of six hundred killed, maximum of two thousand—like Tiananmen in 1989).

Civil society began to waken again with the February 1985 National Assembly elections, and by spring 1987 an aroused, self-organized, and intersubjective citizenry took over the streets of the major cities, with latecoming but substantial middle-class participation, thus forcing Chŏn from office in June. A few months later, the always tepid opposition again split, allowing the emergence of an interim regime under the other, somewhat shrewder "nephew" (No T'ae-u), a regime that first accommodated and then sought to suppress a newly energized civil society now including the liberated and very strong forces of labor (more strikes and labor actions occurred in 1987–1988 than at any other point in Korean history, or most national histories).

In 1990 this regime sought to fashion the Japanese solution to democratic pressures, a Democratic Liberal Party (reversing the characters of Japan's Liberal Democratic Party) that would encompass the moderate opposition in the form of Kim Young Sam and his Pusan-based political machine, bringing them under the tent of the southeastern Taegu-Kyŏngsang elites (or T-K Group) that had dominated the ROK since 1961, thus to form a single-party democracy that would rule for the ages—or at least for the next generation. A host of analysts (not the least being the U.S. Embassy in Seoul) came forward to laud this "pact" between softliners and hardliners among the elite, which seemed to mimic the democratic transitions of the 1980s in Latin America.[44]

This was the Schumpeterian solution to the problems of an enlivened and growing civil society. The Austrian aristocrat Schumpeter never cared much about mass democracy; he was a classic elitist. He valued a democratic system that provided a circulation of elites through periodic elections, enough funds mediated by the banks or the state to keep business growing, enough cash from big business to keep the politicians happy, an occasional circus by the politicians to keep the people entertained, and little more than that. The Liberal Democratic Party followed this model closely in the period 1955–1992, perhaps too closely given its (temporary) loss of power in the summer of 1993; the Democratic Liberal Party was the same (although no one quite imagined that it would provide such a circus!). Soon the DLP was gone, replaced by factions representing the T-K Group and Kim Young Sam's Pusan-based group.

The DLP solution could not last, because unlike Japan's system, it excluded labor (still today no political party has roots in Korea's massive working class, and labor unions were prevented by law from involving themselves in politics until 1998); it failed to reckon with unresolved crises in postwar Korean history (especially Kwangju); and it masked sharp splits within the political elite. Above all, the DLP refused to acknowledge the continuing exclusion of representation for the southwestern Chŏlla people in the politics of Seoul, the continuing repression of anything smacking of a serious Left (through the National Security Law), and the restiveness of the *chaebŏl* (conglomerate) groups under continuing strong state regulation.

In 1995 a series of dramatic events and actions unfolded, with consequences no doubt unforeseen at the time but having the result of an audacious assault on the military dictators who ruled Korea from 1961 onward and their legacies, a reckoning that goes beyond anything in the global transition from authoritarianism that the world has witnessed in the past decade. It goes beyond the Latin American cases, where (often at the urging of American political scientists) the new regimes decided to let bygones be bygones and let the military go back to the barracks. It goes beyond Rumania, where a rough summary justice dispatched dictator Ceausescu but let his system remain. And it goes beyond East Germany, where Honnecker was overthrown and expelled but where West Germany merely absorbed the old East German system, rather than achieving a consensual merger between two rather different civil societies.

Most commentary focused on the actions of President Kim Young Sam in cashiering the generals. His backers argued that he was a sincere reformer all along who now wanted to right the wrongs of modern South Korean history. His detractors claimed that he allowed the prosecution of Chŏn and No on charges of bribery because that would help him overcome the influence of the Taegu-Kyŏngsang group within the ruling party; that he then was forced in November 1995 to allow both of them to be indicted for the December 1979 coup and the suppression of the Kwangju citizenry because the "slush fund" scandal was lapping too close to his own door. More important, in my view, has been the emergence of a new generation of prosecutors, formed by the struggles of civil society as they got educated and came of age, and who now ingeniously use "the rule of law" to go after their dictatorial antagonists.

First, no Liberal Democratic Party solution could work for the reasons given above, and thus we are back to political parties grouped around prominent leaders (namely, the "three Kims," who have dominated Korean politics in the 1990s), based in regional political machines and patron-client ties as always in postwar Korean history. Second, with the continuing exclusion of labor from the governing coalition and the continuing suppression of the nonviolent Left under the National Security Law, the ROK still falls short of either the Japanese or the American model of democracy and civil society. Third, the falling out among the ruling groups and the trials of Chŏn and No, as well as the full glare of publicity on the slush fund scandals, bathing the state and the *chaebŏl* groups in a highly critical light, opened the way to another assertion of civil society and perhaps an authentic democracy that will finally give Korea the noncoercive, intersubjective public sphere it has long deserved, a politics that will go beyond the halting and temporary, jerrybuilt transitions to weak democracy in Latin America, the former Soviet Union and East Europe, and the Philippines.[45] In December 1997, long-time dissident Kim Dae Jung was elected to a five-year term amid a capitalist panic that no one—least of all the cheerleaders for the "Korean miracle"—had predicted. Because he suffered so much in the past from the security organs of the state, one would expect him finally to dismantle them. But he also must revive the Korean economy while accommodating very strong labor unions. How those difficult problems are resolved will determine the future of Korean democracy for a long time to come.

We can conclude this brief consideration of recent Korean history with the observation that the contribution of protest to Korean democracy cannot be overstated; it is a classic case of "the civilizing force of a new vision of society ... created in struggle."[46] A significant student movement emerged in Western Europe and the United States in the mid-1960s and had a heyday of perhaps five years. Korean students were central activists in the politics of liberation in the late 1940s, in the overthrow of the Rhee regime and the politics of the Chang regime in 1960–1961, in the repudiation of Korea-Japan normalization in 1965, and in the resistance to the Park and Chŏn dictatorships in 1971–1988. Particularly in the 1980s, through the mediation of *minjung* ideology and praxis (a kind of liberation theory stimulated by the Latin American example), Korean students, workers, and young people brought into the public space uniquely original and autonomous configurations of political and social protest,[47] ones that threatened many times to overturn the structure of American hegemony and military dictatorship. This was a classic example of Habermas's characterization of student protest in terms of a blurring of lines "between demonstration and civil disobedience, between discussion, festival, and expressive self-presentation."[48] Many students also adopted the Gramscian position, leaving the campuses to merge organically with the working class, often to find themselves jailed and tortured as "disguised workers" and always at the risk of their careers. Even if that part of the Korean public sphere is relatively quiescent now, it made an indelible contribution to Korean democracy in the past two decades.

One other conclusion is irresistible: So much for the Huntington–Lee Kwan Yew–van Wolferen idea that East Asians have a different view of human and civil rights than "we" do, that they prize order and even authoritarian direction, that they industrialized without Enlightenment and civil society, that "Confucianism" makes them this way, and so on and so forth.

What Is Democracy?

This comparative inquiry into American and East Asian democracy has argued that the limited pluralism of American politics is the outcome of an abortive development of civil society under the pressures of the modern project itself over the past two hundred years, and that when it comes to participation without fear or favor in the life of politics, not just the average American but the vaunted student movement of the 1960s cannot hold a candle to those who struggled for democratic rights over the past half century in Korea and many other "developing" countries. But we have not really addressed a question prior to all this: What is democracy?

For Adam Przeworski, democracy exists if another party can win an election.[49] Schumpeter also preferred this form, yielding a circulation of party elites. The premier democratic theorist in the United States, Robert Dahl, would not disagree; although he places more emphasis on political equality as a key prerequisite for democracy than does Schumpeter, their basic schemes of pluralist democracy are quite similar: "the Schumpeter-Dahl axis . . . treats democracy as a mechanism, the essential function of which is to maintain an equilibrium" between "two or more élite groups for the power to govern society."[50] In our terms, this is mere procedural democracy, less interested in developing civic virtue than in restraining civil society. Dahl's account is also marked by the implicit idea that democracy is what you get in the West but not elsewhere for the most part,[51] and it is passively satisfied with the outcomes of procedural justice. Yet Dahl is the main theorist used by the political scientists who have produced most of the "transitions to democracy" literature.

A quite different view is presented by Michio Morishima, who argued recently that postwar Japan is both typically undemocratic in its cleavage between a favored upper stratum and all the rest (like other advanced industrial societies) and more democratic than the Western democracies by virtue of its "bureaucratic democracy," whereby each individual is treated equally and there is little "us versus them" (i.e., little class conflict). The situation of general equality and general education (to a high standard), with smaller maldistribution of wealth as compared particularly to the United States, means that Japan has satisfied a critical demand of Habermas's public sphere: that people enter it equal at the start. Thus the Japan model, Morishima argues, is a challenge both to free market–style development and to Western versions of democracy.[52] South Korea, also, has a more egalitarian distribution of wealth than does the United States, high levels of general education, and, in my view, a much more developed civil society than one finds in Japan. So, once labor and the Left are included in the South Korean system, perhaps it will be more democratic than the American system. But that is still not the democracy we need.

Another unusual perspective is provided in an excellent recent book, *Capitalist Development and Democracy*.[53] The authors begin by agreeing with Seymour Martin Lipset's famous judgment that economic development and pluralist democracy are positively related. But they offer very different explanations for this correlation. The political outcomes of development have to do with four elements, in their view: (1) the pattern of agrarian transition; (2) the empowerment of subordinate classes through industrialization (the middle class, but especially the working class); (3) the type of state structure; and (4) transnational power relations (something all the other accounts of democratization leave out). The authors also have a sense of *timing*, especially the persistence over time in certain "late"-developing countries of particular agrarian social relations, industrialization patterns, roles for the state, and variant positions within the world system. In other words, they have systematized the conception of democracy that Marx was groping toward in his critiques of Hegel.

Capitalist development, according to the authors of this book, is associated with democracy because as a byproduct of growth it transforms class structures, undermining old ones and creating new ones. The new middle classes, however, will fight to the point of their own democratic representation, but not beyond: after that, they will seek to restrict working-class representation (just like Mill and Tocqueville, in other words: a yes, but then again a no). And here we have a nice explanation for the continuing absence of labor representation in South Korea and the fecklessness of the two "labor" parties in Japan, the socialists and the communists. In the United States, the Democratic Party functioned as a business-labor coalition from 1932 through the 1980s, but the "neo-Democrats" now in power in Washington think they must attend to the interests of the middle class, to the detriment of the old Democratic coalition. Perhaps this means that the middle class will also seek to disestablish working-class representation.

As for the international element, Rueschemeyer, Stephens, and Stephens rightly emphasize that geopolitical and other interests of great powers generated direct interventions and support for repressive states. For example, prewar Japan's authoritarianism was in part an outcome of the breakdown of the world economy and outside economic pressure from the United States and England (although neither supported its repressive state). Japan's postwar democracy was "nested" in an American-dominated security regime: American policing of East Asian security left Japan alone to be "developmental," and its status as an "economic animal" deprived of military and political power in the world was a clear and conscious result of American strategy. In the authoritarian regimes that prevailed in South Korea and Taiwan until the end of the 1980s (and almost always supported by U.S. policy), we can also see the completion of a Japan-centered economic and security sphere in northeast Asia. At any rate, perhaps it is only in America that democratic theorists think so little about the external sources of and obstacles to democracy.

C. B. Macpherson's work was imbued with the idea of substantive justice and can therefore serve to unite the critiques by Marx, Gramsci, the young Habermas, MacIntyre, and Unger. For Macpherson, democracy is, first, that system which empowers a conception of men and women as makers, as fully realized human beings. A truly democratic system must encourage the manifold development of human capacities in all people. Second, democracy in the world of inegalitarian distribution we all live in is inseparable from "the cry of the oppressed." Democracy is and must be the means for a redress of human inequality, especially economic inequality. Without these two things, political equality is mostly meaningless.[54]

The East Asia of the late 1990s is far more democratic than it was before. But the best example of such a politics—Japan—cannot be our model of democracy. The same is true of the new democratic systems in Taiwan, South Korea, and the Philippines. But then the American polyarchy cannot be the model to which democrats aspire, either. What is civil society? What is democracy? It has to be more than this, more than the Japan of the Liberal Democratic Party, Korea of the Democratic Liberal Party, or the American system. It is Macpherson's admonition to bring full human development to the many, not just to the few.

5

There is a real crisis brewing in a place the cameras don't go. [It is] the single most dangerous problem, the impending nuclearization of North Korea. . . . None will sleep well with nukes in the hands of the most belligerent and paranoid regime on earth. The North Korean bomb would be controlled by either Kim Il Sung, the old and dying Great Leader, or his son and successor, Dear Leader Kim Jong Il . . . unpredictable, possibly psychotic, [he] would be the closest thing to Dr. Strangelove the nuclear age has seen.[1]

One of the world's most menacing powers [is now] bereft of its cold-war allies and on the defensive about a nuclear-weapons project that ranks among the biggest threats in Asia. . . . "North Korea could explode or implode," said General Robert Riscassi, the commander of the 40,000 U.S. troops who remain here. As the Stalinist Government of Kim Il Sung is driven into a corner, its economy shrinking and its people running short of food, General Riscassi contends, "it is a debatable matter" whether the country will change peacefully or lash out as it once did before. . . . One senior Bush Administration official said last week that North Korea already had enough plutonium to build a crude nuclear weapon . . . this has helped fuel . . . fear that the country that has bombed airliners and tried to kill the South Korean cabinet would make one last lunge for survival.[2]

These two extracts from the two newspapers that come closest to being America's papers of record are typical of the American commentary on North Korea in the early 1990s. A desperate rogue regime run by a paranoid dictator now threatening the world with nuclear attack: these were the tropes, and they appeared time and again in 1991–1994, until North Korea once more sank into the oblivion of media inattention. It is by definition impossible to predict the behavior of a crazy person, and indeed American officials constantly harped on P'yŏngyang's unpredictability. I want to argue, to the contrary, that North Korean behavior was quite predictable, and that an irresponsible and spineless American media, often (but by no means always) egged on by government officials, obscured the real nature of the U.S.-Korean conflict. The media had the wrong tropes in the wrong place at the wrong time; the absurd result was that often one had to read North Korea's tightly controlled press to figure out what was going on between Washington and P'yŏngyang. Because of this severe and often state-induced media bias, it was exceedingly difficult to figure out the real stakes in this conflict.

Two logics clashed in this crisis: the first, a rationality of historically informed, trial-and-error, theory-and-practice *learned* behavior growing out of the Korean civil conflict going back to 1945, yielding intransigent bargaining strategies and extreme conceptions of national sovereignty; and the second, an instrumental reason of superordinate power surveilling and seeking to control the recalcitrant, the heterodox, the enemy, without any felt necessity to know that enemy, thus yielding daily violations of national sovereignty. North Korea's stake in this confrontation, its position, was to use its nuclear program to fashion a new relationship with the United States; its hole card was the possibility that it might already possess one or two atomic bombs. In pursuing a shrewd diplomacy of survival, P'yŏngyang used bluff, sham, and brinkmanship to get what it wanted. The American goal was to stabilize an unruly post–cold war world, one that had already produced a major war in the Gulf. Given an American public that often seemed to think the world's problems were over with the end of the cold war and the collapse of the Soviet Union, successive American administrations constantly exaggerated threats to gain public support in policing intractable nations. The 1990s dealt North Korean leaders a very bad hand, but they played it with surprising skill; the 1990s dealt the United States the best hand imaginable, and it very nearly plunged into another major war, three years after the Gulf war ended.

This experience, I would argue, meets the social science test of certain propositions yielding falsifiable hypotheses that, when tested empirically, prove to be reliable and valid. Both the American and the North Korean logics were clear by 1991 if not earlier, providing testable propositions about the nuclear crisis that ensued for the next three years. The propositions are as follows:

1. The DPRK lives a civil war history and acts according to civil war logic.

    a. The United States denies this history and has dealt with P'yŏngyang as a generic Soviet proxy or rogue enemy.

    b. This yields an advantage to the DPRK, and the disadvantage of inattention and inapplicable logic to the United States.

2. The DPRK has been under American nuclear threat since 1950 and sought to use the nonproliferation regime to escape this threat after bipolarity collapsed.

a. The way to do that was to trade its nuclear program for a new relationship with the United States.

b. Most American analysts assumed the DPRK only wanted to develop nuclear weapons; most ignored the history of American nuclear blackmail.

3. The United States wanted to surveil and discipline the DPRK, using the International Atomic Energy Agency (IAEA) to fill out its surveillance regime.

a. The DPRK responded with a shell game that, over time, allowed its own logic to gain a hearing.

b. United States surveillance overreached itself by making the IAEA an adjunct of American intelligence.

4. The DPRK's self-reliant energy regime required domestic nuclear energy to compete with South Korea and Japan; the United States knew this but chose to ignore it until 1994, in the interest of maintaining the Nuclear Non-Proliferation Treaty (NPT) regime and teaching rogue nations a lesson.

5. Hardliners in both countries drove the crisis to the brink of war in May–June 1994, whereupon the United States relearned the Korean civil war logic and settled for a diplomatic solution.

Realpolitik conceptions of power, interest, and rationality are of little help in figuring out how a country of 22 million people spending about $4 billion per year on defense stood up to and stalemated the single superpower of our time, with 260 million people and spending $260 billion on defense. Therefore, it is predictable that realists have not praised the October 1994 Framework Agreement between the United States and the DPRK and have been waiting for (and predicting) it to fail ever since. As of this writing, however, North Korea is in full compliance with the terms of the agreement, notwithstanding various speed bumps and nettlesome problems that have made implementation difficult. Likewise, a "rational choice" logic on the part of those who privilege game theory, prisoner's dilemmas, and the like was never able to explain P'yŏngyang's behavior (some did try), because this was an abstract rationality devoid of context.

Max Weber taught that the conception of modern legal-rational authority really connotes a *belief* in that rationality. My belief is in a comprehensive rationality that comes with long immersion in a subject, such that the brain and the viscera connect, one shouts Eureka!, and thereby creates a problem-solving logic. We find the same epistemology in Clausewitz, as we saw above. For him, war is a fully political human activity in which a rational intelligence marries the means of warfare to the ends of policy. How this is done involves logic, strategy, and cunning, but also an intuitive knowledge of the battlefield and the totality, the "organic whole," of war and politics that can only come to one fully experienced in both. I want to explore the "organic whole" of the U.S.-North Korean crisis in five parts.

MAD DOGS AND AMERICANS: WAR IS A STERN TEACHER

At a critical point in March 1994 when the United States thought its diplomatic effort vis-à-vis North Korea was collapsing, *New York Times* reporter David Sanger began an article this way: "Say this about North Korea's leaders: They may be Stalinist fanatics, they may be terrorists, they may be building nuclear bombs, but they are not without subtlety. They have mastered the art of dangling Washington on a string." He went on to refer to North Korea as "a country with a mad-dog reputation."[3] Left unexplained was how mad dogs could simultaneously be subtle puppeteers. At a minimum, however, the mad dog had a memory of war, a presumably "forgotten" war; meanwhile, most Americans did not.

A first principle for understanding contemporary Korea is to know that a devastating civil war occurred there in the recent past, and that the war never ended: the warring sides agreed only to stop firing at each other—an armistice. Moreover, the conclusion of the hot phase of that war in 1953 left a split verdict in America. How could the United States get stalemated by fourth-rate North Korea and third-rate China? Why was there "a substitute for victory"? For Clausewitz, as we saw earlier, war "is an act of violence intended to compel our opponent to fulfill our will"—which leads logically to the idea that "complete victory" is the goal of war and to the idea that "moderation in war is an absurdity."[4] This is the passage people cite most often from *On War*, and it yields the logic that the powerful discharge all their power in war. Thus pundits like Harry Summers sprinkle their texts with quotations from Master Clausewitz and argue that the United States failed in Korea and Vietnam because of politically imposed limits on the use of its power.[5]

Summers, like so many others, misreads *On War*. For Clausewitz, as we have seen, the politics of war do *not* dictate the use of every means at one's disposal or the absolute obliteration of the enemy; like everything else about war, the conclusion of the victory is inevitably political. War exists to compel the surrender of the enemy, but surrender is a politically governed activity. The Korean War ended in a stalemate, with the restoration of the status quo ante, because American leaders could not pay the political price that victory would have required (e.g., taking the war to Chinese territory).

If the end of the Korean War is misunderstood in the United States, its origins and its nature likewise are misconstrued. With handfuls of Soviet and Chinese documents spilling out in the 1990s, many analysts are once again sure that Stalin and Kim Il Sung "started" the Korean War in June 1950 (i.e., the original Truman administration position) and that it therefore constituted international aggression. But the civil conflict originated in the division of Korea just as World War II ended, proceeding from sharp political conflict in 1945 to peasant rebellion in 1946–1947 to guerrilla war in 1948 and border wars in 1949, and finally to general war in June 1950. The memorable line from Thucydides' *Peloponnesian War*—"war is a stern teacher"—was prompted by the civil war in Corcyra, as we saw above. The full passage is almost a mnemonic for "Korea": "So revolutions broke out in city after city. . . . What used to be described as a thoughtless act of aggression was now regarded as the courage one would expect to find in a party member; to think of the future and wait was merely another way of saying one was a coward; any idea of moderation was just an attempt to disguise one's unmanly character; ability to understand a question from all sides meant that one was totally unfitted for action. Fanatical enthusiasm was the mark of a real man, and to plot against an enemy behind his back was perfectly legitimate self-defense. Anyone who held violent opinions could always be trusted, and anyone who objected to them became a suspect."[6]

This is a classic statement on civil war. It fits the American Civil War, by far the most devastating of all American wars (to Americans), but one that happened long enough ago that most Americans have no idea what it means to have warfare sweeping back and forth across the national territory.[7] This extended passage fits the Korean civil war with no necessity to dot "i's" or cross "t's"; it explains the continuing blight on the Korean mind drawn by that war, just like a doctor drawing blood: to understand the Korean War "from all sides" is still to go to jail in either North or South. But whatever else one may say about the North Koreans, they were sternly taught by this war.

The logic of this history means that the North Koreans understand how the Korean War began and ended, but Americans do not. The incessant intensity of the confrontation along the Korean demilitarized zone is something the P'yŏngyang leadership deals with every day, as against the handful of witting Americans who know this quotidian conflict from the other side and the mass of Americans always surprised to learn that forty thousand American troops are still in Korea. P'yŏngyang's media drum war stories into the brain so frequently that one might think the Korean War just ended; meanwhile, that same war, never understood at the time and forgotten quickly after its conclusion, yields an American tabula rasa.[8]

It was therefore a simple matter to superimpose onto North Korea all the media tropes by which Americans were led to understand the 1990–1991

Gulf war. North Korea was not our daily enemy of forty years' standing, but a new "renegade state." This transference began in the immediate aftermath of the four-day ground war that defeated Iraq: Leslie Gelb editorialized in the *New York Times* that North Korea was "the next renegade state," a country "run by a vicious dictator" with SCUD missiles, "a million men under arms," and likely to possess nuclear weapons "in a few years." Another Iraq, in short.[9] I was amazed by Gelb's editorial and the mimetic commentary that followed on its heels for three years; it made me understand that my professional knowledge was akin to paleontology or some other arcane and remote discipline, and that the Korean War existed in the American mind under "ancient history"—if not "never happened."

This ahistoricity went hand in hand with assertions that would fail a freshman logic class. North Korea was the greatest security threat in the world, according to the leaders of our foreign policy, and simultaneously on the verge of collapse. How could it be ten feet tall and about to devour the South, with a basket-case economy? A huge military threat and a demolished economy, all led by a nut case? On ABC's *Nightline,* correspondent Chris Bury described Kim Jong Il as "a 51-year-old son about whom little is known other than his fondness for fast cars and state terrorism." As for the country he runs, "North Korea may be growing desperate. Its economy is in shambles. . . . Yet North Korea maintains a huge army, more than a million soldiers on a permanent war footing, nearly 70 percent of them within 60 miles of Seoul."[10]

Chris Bury, like all other mainstream reporters, did not say how many South Korean soldiers are between Seoul and the DMZ, and thus sixty miles from P'yŏngyang: roughly 540,000, or 90 percent.[11] Of course he did not say, because he would not know, that threats of a northern invasion began in March 1946 and have never ceased since.[12] Take this quotation: "There's signs of a big buildup. . . . The [North Koreans] could be in Seoul in four hours if they threw in everything they have." James Wade got this from an American engineer working for the U.S. Army—in 1960.[13] South Korean security services and their American allies are the creators of this one-sided picture; they have succeeded for decades in getting Americans to stare blankly at one side of the Korean civil conflict, like a pigeon with nystagmus such that its head turns only toward the left.

Examining the history of the Korean conflict and the perpetual special pleadings of the two sides—flashing some light into the shadows they hope no one will notice—takes time. Far easier, then, to take the word of an American official. On the same *Nightline* segment, Richard Solomon, Nixon-Bush China expert, said this: "Not a bad way to look at it is to think of the Waco, Texas crisis, when you have a small ideological, highly armed and isolated community."[14] Mad dog Kim Il Sung becomes David Koresh in this rendering, and it is perfectly believable; if you are dealing with insanity, as I said at the beginning, anything is possible. North Korea is an American tabula rasa, and anything written upon it has currency—so long as the words are negative. North Korea ended up thrice-cursed, a Rorschach inkblot eliciting anticommunist, Orientalist, and rogue-state imagery. But then, that was its original image, both in American strategy (Truman called his 1950 intervention a "police action" to catch North Korean criminals) and in Hollywood (in films like *The Manchurian Candidate*).

There is a virtually endless supply of similar quotations from the American media in 1991–1999, so let me stop here and merely argue that history makes a difference, and that only a historically informed analysis can make sense of the relationship between North Korea and the United States. Not just any history, however, but an appreciation of the actual conflict in Korea since 1945, examined dispassionately, as if the two sides were blue and green rather than red and white.

American Nuclear Threats

Part of the problem in resolving the nuclear crisis was (1) the American desire to get P'yŏngyang to commit to the inspection regime of the NPT, administered by the IAEA in Vienna, and (2) P'yŏngyang's desire to get out from under a nuclear threat that had been palpable since the 1950s and that gave it rights of self-defense under the NPT.[15] If we assume that P'yŏngyang's real goal was to build weapons, it had solid justifications for going nuclear; after all, it could argue that it was merely engaged in deterrence, that is, the classic argument that once both sides have nuclear weapons, the resulting standoff negates the possibility of use, and that a DPRK weapon returns the peninsula to the status quo ante 1991, before the USSR collapsed. Moreover, the DPRK was the target of periodic nuclear threats and extended nuclear deterrence from the United States for decades, yet until now has possessed no such weapons itself. To my knowledge, no mainstream reporter in the United States examined this history during the crisis with North Korea.[16] But P'yŏngyang would truly be crazy not to take this history with total seriousness.

After the Korean War ended, the United States introduced nuclear weapons into South Korea in spite of the 1953 armistice agreement that prohibited the introduction of qualitatively new weaponry. How did this come about? The United States took this drastic step primarily to stabilize the volatile civil war. In 1953, Syngman Rhee had opposed any armistice settlement, refused to sign the agreement when it was made, and frequently threatened to reopen the war. In November 1953, Vice President Nixon visited Korea "and sought to extract written assurances from President Rhee 'that he is not going to start the war up again on the gamble that he can get us involved in his effort to unite Korea by force.' "[17] He got no such written assurance, but in the absence of it, the American commander was directed, in a highly secret "annex" circulated only to a few American leaders, to secure "prompt warning of any decision by Rhee to order an attack" and to prevent its issuance or receipt by ROK Army field commanders.

In spite of being hamstrung in this way, Rhee well knew that there were Americans who supported his provocative behavior, critically placed people who advocated the use of nuclear weapons should the war be reignited and the act clearly laid at the communist door. Among them was the chairman of the Joint Chiefs of Staff, Admiral Radford, who at a conference between the State and Defense Departments in September 1956, had "bluntly stated the military intention to introduce atomic warheads into Korea." On 14 January 1957 the NSC Planning Board, at the instruction of President Eisenhower, "prepared an evaluation of four alternative military programs for Korea." A key question was "the kinds of nuclear-capable weapons to be introduced, and the question of storage of nuclear warheads in Korea." In the ensuing six months of discussions, Secretary of State John Foster Dulles agreed with the JCS that such weapons should be sent to Korea. There were two problems, however: the Armistice agreement and Syngman Rhee. A subparagraph in the agreement (section 13d) restricted both sides from introducing new types of weapons into the Korean theater. Radford wanted unilaterally to suspend 13d, since in his view it could not be "interpreted" to allow nuclear weapons. Dulles, ever the legalist, conditioned his support of the JCS proposal on the provision of "publishable evidence confirming Communist violations of the armistice sufficient to justify such action to our Allies and before the UN." The problem was that the "publishable evidence" was not satisfactory, because the communist side had not seriously violated section 13d. It had introduced new jet aircraft, but so had the United States, and neither case was considered a radical upgrading of capabilities. Nuclear weapons were quite a different matter. This point bothered the British, but the United States went ahead in spite of their worries and in June 1957 relieved itself of its 13d obligations.

There remained the problem of Syngman Rhee. Unverified intelligence reports in February 1955 "spoke of meetings in which Rhee told Korean military and civilian leaders to prepare for military actions against north Korea." In October came reports that he had ordered plans for the retaking of Kaesŏng and the Ongjin Peninsula, firmly in North Korean territory since the armistice, and in 1956 came more alarms and diversions. Meanwhile, no doubt unbeknownst to Rhee, the Eisenhower administration in August 1957 had approved NSC 5702/2, a major revision of Korea policy that approved the stationing of nuclear weapons in Korea and, in what one official called "a small change," allowed for the possibility of "U.S. support for a unilateral ROK military initiative in response to a mass uprising, Hungarian style, in north Korea."[18] This is an amazing mouthful, suggesting that in a political crisis in North Korea, the United States might support a South Korean invasion. This may have been a response to rumors around that time that a North Korean general had tried to defect across the DMZ with his whole division in tow, or it may merely have been a harbinger of the thinking that subsequently led to the Bay of Pigs fiasco in Cuba (a small provocation might touch off a general uprising against communism). It was, however, exactly what Rhee and his allies were looking for; who knows if they got wind of it, but John Foster Dulles certainly did.

Dulles was the man, it will be remembered, who famously eyeballed Kim Il Sung across the thirty-eighth parallel a week before the war started. He appears to have spent the rest of his life with unsettling whispers from that sudden Sunday, as if Banquo's ghost were shaking his gory locks. At an NSC meeting in 1954, he worried that the North might start the war up again—and in a rather creative fashion: "[Dulles] thought it quite possible that the Communists would launch their attack by infiltrating ROK units and staging an attack on the Communist lines in order to make it appear as though hostilities had been started on ROK initiative."[18] At several other high-level meetings, Dulles worried aloud that the United States would not know how a new war might start in Korea, and that Rhee might well start it. At the 168th meeting of the NSC in October 1953, Dulles had warned that "all our efforts" must be to forestall a resumption of war by Rhee; in 1957, at the 332nd meeting, he still worried that Rhee might "start a war"; two weeks later, "If war were to start in Korea . . . it was going to be very hard indeed to determine which side had begun the war."[19]

It is in this specific context that Dulles lent his agreement to the JCS desire to place nuclear weapons in Korea. Pursuing the civil war deterrent that Secretary of State Dean Acheson had applied to Korea before the war, he wanted to restrain both sides.[20] Hotheads like Rhee and Kim Il Sung would think twice before starting a war that would rain nuclear destruction on the peninsula. But Dulles's nukes would be kept under exclusive American control and would be used only in the event of a massive and uncontainable North Korean invasion.

In January 1958, the United States positioned 280mm nuclear cannons and Honest John nuclear-tipped missiles in South Korea; a year later, the Air Force "permanently stationed a squadron of nuclear-tipped Matador cruise missiles in Korea." With a range of eleven hundred kilometers, the Matadors were aimed at China and the USSR as well as North Korea.[21] By the mid-1960s, Korean defense strategy was pinned on routine plans to use nuclear weapons very early in any new war. As a 1967 Pentagon war game script put it: "The twelve ROKA and two U.S. divisions in South Korea had . . . keyed their defense plans almost entirely to the early use of nuclear weapons."[22] In January 1968, the North Koreans seized the U.S. spy ship *Pueblo*, capturing the crew and keeping it in prison for eleven months: "the initial reaction of American decision-makers was to drop a nuclear weapon on P'yŏngyang. . . . the fact that all the U.S. F-4 fighter planes held on constant alert on Korean airfields were loaded only with nuclear weapons did not help the leaders to think clearly."[23]

U.S. atomic demolition mines (ADM) were defensive weapons designed to be used in South Korea "to contaminate an advance area and to stop an armored attack," as one ADM engineer put it. ADMs weighed only sixty pounds and yet had a twenty-kiloton explosive force; "you could get two weeks worth of contamination out of it so that an area was impassable."[24] The ADMs were moved around in Jeeps and placed by special teams who carried them in backpacks; meanwhile, U.S. helicopters routinely flew nuclear weapons near the DMZ. That one of them might stray across the DMZ during a training exercise (as a small reconnaissance helicopter did in December 1994) and give P'yŏngyang an atomic bomb was a constant possibility. Meanwhile, forward deployment of nuclear weapons bred a mentality of "use 'em or lose 'em"; even a small North Korean attack might be cause enough to use them, lest they fall into enemy hands.[25]

These weapons also deterred both South Korea and Japan from going nuclear. In 1975 Richard "Dixie" Walker, later the American ambassador to Korea during the Chun Doo Hwan regime, wrote this: "The presence of American conventional and even tactical nuclear forces in Korea helps to confirm strategic guarantees for Tokyo and to discourage any Japanese thoughts about a French solution: a force de frappe of their own. This is a fact well understood by leaders of many political persuasions in Tokyo and also appreciated in Peking."[26] In other words, Korean lives were hostage to an American policy of dual containment: containing the communist enemy and constraining the Tokyo/Seoul ally.

The commander most enamored of nuclear weapons for both defensive and offensive use was General Richard Stilwell, who originated the "Team Spirit" war games that began in the late 1970s and continued into the 1990s. Team Spirit exercises were the largest in the world, often including two hundred thousand troops, of which about seventy thousand were Americans—those already in Korea, and others flown in for the games. In Stilwell's strategy, the games were "a dry run for a retaliatory attack on the north and a precursor of the AirLand Battle doctrine" of the 1980s, emphasizing offensive strikes behind enemy lines.[27]

A famous August 1976 incident illustrated the extraordinary "tripwire" nature of the DMZ confrontation, where a new war could occur on almost any day. Some American and Korean soldiers had entered a forbidden zone of the DMZ near P'anmunjŏm to "trim a poplar tree" that the United States said was obstructing its vision northward. (The poplar stood alone by itself; anyone who has been to P'anmunjŏm knows that the surroundings are largely denuded of trees, since the area took such a pounding in the war.) A North Korean team confronted the trimming team, and in the fight that ensued a North Korean grabbed an axe from one of the Americans and killed two American soldiers with it. This was an unfortunate incident but a completely predictable one given the ratcheted-up tension of this insanely militarized demilitarized zone.

General Stilwell put U.S.-ROK forces on high alert (for the first time since 1953) during this confrontation and festooned the Korean theater with American force: an aircraft carrier task force arrived in Korean waters and a phalanx of nuclear-capable B-52s lifted off from Guam and flew up the peninsula toward the DMZ, "veering off at the last moment"—or as one analyst put it, "we scared the living shit out of them." According to another analyst, Stilwell asked permission from the Pentagon (and received it) to delegate to his subordinates the authority to initiate artillery and rocket fire, should they lose communications with him and be unable to consult, yielding the possibility that tactical nuclear weapons might be used without central command and control. Now a joint U.S.-ROK task force entered the Joint Security Area, with seven helicopter gunships escorting another twenty helicopters carrying a full rifle company protecting them. They proceeded finally to chop down the offending limbs on the poplar tree. Meanwhile, another Washington informant, whom I cannot name, told me that it was actually Stilwell who exercised "restraint" in this episode; he was fearful that back in Washington, Henry Kissinger might want to start a war to further lame-duck Gerald Ford's chances in the upcoming elections.

In 1991 I heard a high-level, retired official and former commander of U.S. forces in Korea give an off-the-record presentation of U.S. strategy as it had developed by the 1980s:

1. The United States planned to use tactical nuclear weapons in the very early stages of a new Korean conflict, at "H + 1," or within one hour of the outbreak of war, if large masses of North Korean troops were attacking south of the DMZ. This he contrasted with the established strategy in Europe, which was to delay an invasion with conventional weapons and

then use nuclear weapons only if necessary to stop the assault. The logic was that we dare not use nuclear weapons in Europe except in the greatest extremity because the other side has them, but we could use them in Korea because it doesn't. South Korean commanders, he said, had gotten used to the idea that the United States would use nuclear weapons at an early point in a war with North Korea.

2. The "AirLand Battle" strategy developed in the mid-1970s called for early, quick, deep strikes into enemy territory, again with the likely use of nuclear weapons, especially against hardened underground facilities (of which there are many in North Korea). In other words, the strategy itself implies "rollback" rather than simple containment of a North Korean invasion.

3. Neutron bombs—so-called enhanced-radiation weapons—might well be used if North Korean forces occupied Seoul, thus to kill the enemy but save the buildings. (The neutron bomb was invented by Samuel Cohen, who first conceived of such a bomb while watching the battle to retake Seoul in 1951; in early 1980s news accounts, he spoke of its possible deployment to Korea.)[28]

4. North Korean forces both expanded and redeployed in the late 1970s as a response to the "AirLand Battle" doctrine. The redeployment led to the stationing of nearly 80 percent of their ground forces near the DMZ. American and South Korean sources routinely cite this expansion and redeployment as evidence of North Korean aggressive intent, as we have seen; in fact, it was done so that as many soldiers as possible could get into the South (regardless of how a war started), to mingle with ROK Army forces and civilians before nuclear weapons would be used, thus making their use less likely.[29]

This harrowing scenario became standard operating procedure in the 1980s, the kind written into military field manuals and the annual Team Spirit military exercises.[30] It implied an initial containment of a North Korean attack, followed by thrusts into the North, ultimately to seize and hold P'yŏngyang and topple the regime. (In December 1993, the *New York Times* detailed such plans in a front-page article, erroneously stating that they had just been developed.) Such war games were also conducted in Korea because in the early 1980s, NATO governments and strong peace movements would not allow similar exercises in Europe.

The Gulf war, however (according to the former commander in Korea), caused a reevaluation of the role of nuclear weapons. Given "smart" bombs that reliably reach their targets, such high-yield conventional weapons are more useful than the messy and uncontrollable effects of using nuclear warheads. The Army, he said, wanted out of battlefield nuclear weapons as soon as possible. Thus American policy reached a point where its own interests dictated withdrawal of obsolescent nuclear weapons from Korea in the fall of 1991. (The weapons removed included forty 203mm and thirty 155mm nuclear artillery shells, plus large numbers of ADMs. Official spokesmen were ambiguous, however, about some sixty nuclear gravity bombs for F-4 and F-16 bombers, reported in 1985 to be stored at an American air base at Kunsan.)[31]

From the Korean War onward, North Korea responded to this nuclear blackmail by building enormous facilities underground or in mountain redoubts, from troop and matériel depots to munitions factories, even to subterranean warplane hangars. American control of the air in that war illustrated a deterrence principle supposedly developed only with the advent of "smart" weapons, namely, that "what can be seen is already lost."[32] The North Koreans have long known this principle and have acted upon it. In the mid-1970s, P'yŏngyang faced more threats as the Park Chung Hee government sought to develop nuclear capabilities; Park ceased the activity only under enormous American pressure, while retaining formidable potentialities. The ROK went ahead with its clandestine program to develop "indigenous ability to build ballistic missiles" capable of carrying nuclear warheads. South Korea also garnered a reputation as a "renegade" arms supplier of pariah countries like South Africa, and Iran and Iraq during their war.[33] Much of this reads as if it were written about North Korea, not South Korea, and puts P'yŏngyang's activity into perspective; much of it was responsive to U.S. pressure and ROK initiatives. In any case, if we understand North Korea as Team Green rather than Team Red, its behavior has been consistent with the logic of the nuclear confrontation in Korea since 1958.

North Korea's Energy Regime

Yŏngbyŏn is a relatively well-known Korean town about thirty-five miles north of P'yŏngyang. Its secluded geographic position led to its fortification at least by the early fifteenth century; later on it became a scenic spot and pleasure resort for the aristocracy. It was a silk-producing town in the old days; the North Koreans built a large synthetic textile (mainly rayon) industry there, accounting for over 50 percent of production in the region—and leading some American intelligence observers to think that alleged nuclear reprocessing facilities observed by satellites might just be textile mills. Here is the way a German geographer described it in 1942: "Out of the way of the modern traffic routes the county seat of Yŏngbyŏn is concealed high above the meandering valley of the Kuryong River in a tremendous, well-preserved old Korean fortress sprawling out across the surrounding . . . dome-shaped granite mountains."[34]

By now, any viewer of American television news will have seen a stock film clip of the Yŏngbyŏn nuclear facility, but never have they been told the meaning of the ubiquitous slogan affixed to the roof: *Charyŏk kaengsaeng.* This is a Maoist term meaning self-reliance (literally, regeneration through one's own efforts). Here was the North Korean justification for Yŏngbyŏn from the beginning: to substitute nuclear power in an energy regime dependent on domestic coal and hydroelectricity and imported petroleum. In other words, P'yŏngyang sought to do what Japan and South Korea have been doing for decades. The difference was that since the big powers refused to ship them any potentially processable nuclear fuel, they built a reactor that would utilize North Korea's substantial deposits of uranium. The problem was that such reactors produce plutonium from uranium, which, with a bit of refining, can become the high-grade fuel for nuclear weapons.

In the 1990s North Korea's per capita use of energy has still been close to South Korea's, and for decades was much higher. Given that so much South Korean energy use goes to private automobiles and home consumption, the per capita energy use for industry and the military is much higher in the North. In an interview in 1978, Kim Il Sung told a delegation of the Japan Socialist Party that in the late 1960s some Korean scientists wanted to start up a petrochemical industry for refining petroleum (probably because Park Chung Hee had similar plans). However, Kim said, "our country does not produce oil," and the United States influenced the world oil regime; ergo, "we are not yet in a position to depend on imports. . . . [To do so] means allowing a stranglehold on our jugular."[35]

Both Seoul and Washington agree that P'yŏngyang is only 10 percent dependent on imported petroleum for its energy use, a major achievement by any comparison. In 1992–1993, the North Korean energy profile looked like this (in units of 10^{15} joules): 226 for petroleum, 1,047 for coal, 176 for hydroelectric, and 38 for "other," yielding a total energy usage of 1,486 10^{15} joules. All petroleum was imported; 75.4 joules of coal was also imported (out of 1,047 total usage); that is, coking coal used in steel mills, coming almost exclusively from China now that the USSR is gone. These data do not count fuel wood, which is also in heavy use, and minor exports to China of hydroelectricity from the huge dams along the Yalu River.[36] This energy regime has been in crisis in the 1990s because of the demise of the USSR and the collapse of trade partners in East Europe, leading to escalating costs for imported oil.[37] All the more reason to go nuclear at home. To figure out this crisis, in short, you need to know P'yŏngyang's energy regime. But you also have to know how to build an atomic bomb.

The DPRK obtained a small nuclear reactor for research purposes of perhaps four megawatts capacity from the USSR in 1962, which was placed under IAEA safeguards in 1977. It then built a thirty-megawatt facility; construction probably began around 1979, and it went into operation in 1987 at Yŏngbyŏn. North Korea has lots of uranium-238, the radioactive element found in nature that has 92 protons and 146 neutrons. This atomic structure is intrinsically unstable; when bombarded with a neutron, the uranium atom will split, giving off two neutrons. Each of these can split an additional uranium atom, and thus a chain reaction is born—or was born in a crude graphite pile under Alonzo Stagg Stadium at the University of Chicago in 1942. North Korea uses a magnox-type reactor which is an improvement on Enrico Fermi's pile, but not by much; natural uranium is made into pellets and stuffed into hollow metal rods of a magnesium oxide alloy called magnox; these tubes are placed in a welded steel vessel, with a graphite pile or core inside, cooled by CO^2 gas. The chain reaction in the tubes generates heat, which is used to generate electricity and move turbines. As this heat is produced, so is plutonium: U-238 absorbs slow neutrons to become U-239, which then decays into fissile plutonium-239. All natural uranium reactors produce plutonium. When the process is finished, hot fuel rods are withdrawn and put in a cooling pond; they are then immersed in nitric acid, which separates the plutonium from the uranium. A Nagasaki-type bomb can be made from as little as five kilograms of such plutonium,[38] but it must first be reprocessed into weapons-grade fuel.

North Korea's reactor is very much like the British model "Calder Hall" of the 1950s, which produced England's first atomic arsenal and which the Soviets and then the North Koreans copied. The Calder Hall generated electricity as a byproduct of plutonium production; generally rated at 50MWe in its second-generation "Chapelcross" type, the size of the core was fourteen meters wide and eight meters high. Inside was a stack of six fuel elements, consisting of massive solid rods of uranium metal. Each fuel element had about 1,691 fuel channels for a total of 10,146 fuel elements (or rods). The magnox alloy is 0.8 percent aluminum, .002–.005 beryllium, .008 cadmium, and .006 iron; when each ton of magnox fuel is irradiated for 1,000 megawatt days, it contains 998 kilograms of unconverted uranium and 0.8 kilogram of plutonium, that is, about one-sixth of the fuel necessary for one atomic bomb. Because the fuel was used for making weapons instead of electricity, the British irradiated and removed the whole core about twice a year; when the fuel is used for generating electricity, the rods are removed only every few years.[39] Although the North Korean version is similar to the Calder Hall, the Yŏngbyŏn reactor was clearly adapted to capture heat for making steam and generating electricity: the fuel load has been removed only twice, in 1989 and

1994; if P'yŏngyang had wanted a usable nuclear arsenal, it would have removed the fuel much more often than this.

Yŏngbyŏn, in short, began in pursuit of energy self-reliance and ended as a bargaining chip to trade for a new relationship with the United States. No one paid much attention to it for several years, including an IAEA that P'yŏngyang asked to come have a look—only to be told that North Korea had missed that year's deadline and would have to reapply for IAEA inspections. Subsequently, in 1989 American spy satellites monitored a 75- to 100-day shutdown of the reactor, while fuel rods were withdrawn and new fuel was added. The satellites also picked up apparent evidence of another reactor under construction, of 50- to 200-megawatt capacity, which some thought would come onstream in the early 1990s; government experts also claimed to have spied a building nearby that looked like a reprocessing facility (but that others thought might be a textile mill).[40] But nothing much happened until the end of the Gulf war enabled prominent American officials to bathe North Korea in a new and threatening light.

"A MILL TO GRIND ROGUES HONEST": THE AMERICAN SURVEILLANCE REGIME

> The Organization is based on the principle of the sovereign equality of all its Members. (United Nations Charter, Article 2.1)[41]

Our understanding of international politics at the end of the twentieth century remains deeply imbued with definitions of power inherited from the sixteenth and seventeenth centuries, namely, that to achieve social peace among highly imperfect human beings, we need a state with an authoritative monopoly on coercion; that societies having such states and collected within (recognized) boundaries merit the name nation-state; that such nation-states (when properly recognized) have something called sovereignty; that no sovereignty exists above that of the nation-state (save what it may willingly delegate to an international body); and finally, that the output of sovereign nation-states is called power. Power itself must also be "recognized," however, for it to have much meaning: "big" powers are the ones that count in international politics. The power of Chad may be relevant for Chadians and the rebels against that state, but it doesn't count for much else in the rest of the world. Still, Chad is a recognized "sovereign state" and that is no small thing; amid the contemporary chaos of micronationalisms, this is what hundreds of peoples in the world want right now: recognition as "sovereign." Sovereignty, once the weapon of the strong, in the last century became a weapon of the weak, a way for small or vulnerable peoples to claim independence and autonomy, that is, self-determination.

It was the British who did the most to propel this doctrine around the world, confounding and undermining their imperial practice with an abstract, idealist theory that transferred ideas about the free market to international politics: if every entrepreneur ought to be the equal of any other entering the marketplace, so every nation was equal and sovereign before the bar of international law. Or as Karl Polanyi put it, "in the liberal theory, Great Britain was merely another atom in the universe . . . and ranked precisely on the same footing as Denmark and Guatemala."[42]

Jeremy Bentham was a great exemplar of British liberalism and was the author of the modern era's definition of "the Good": the greatest good for the greatest number, an idea that propelled the extension of democratic rights and equality and caught the aspirations of masses of people to rise into the middle class, just as it inspired ridicule from England's rivals.[43] But Bentham was also a social engineer; indeed, it was to this that he gave over "his boundless imaginative faculties": decennial population censuses, "frigidariums" for fruits and vegetables, poorhouses converted to armaments manufacture, convict-run textile factories, "Chrestomathic Day Schools" for the upper middle class, contraceptives to keep the poor rate down, and so on.[44]

As Nietzsche noted, there was always "a touch of Tartuffe" about Bentham's idea of "the happiness of the greatest number."[45] Far more representative of the modern positivist project were new power grids and techniques of surveillance and control by which the rational, "modern" individual, understanding himself as the only important subject, held sway over the object: the irrational, the premodern, the colonized, the feminine, the heterodox. Heterodox human objects got defined, constituted, and controlled by "rational" human subjects, their interaction being purely instrumental rather than interactive and intersubjective. The Panopticon was the logical outcome of Bentham's brand of rationality. It combined the genius of a tinkerer with the moral disposition of Aunt Mathilda: techniques of "inspectability" such that the top knows what the bottom is doing at all times.[46] Here Bentham defined not just the modern "Good," but new conceptions of modern power.

Once called a "mill to grind rogues honest, and idle men industrious,"[47] the Panopticon is in fact a prison in which the individual cells surround a watchtower pierced by circular holes that emit light and thereby silhouette every single inmate for the guard in the center. The guard, however, cannot be seen by the inmates, creating "an effect of constant, omniscient surveillance," and thus the prisoners police themselves.[48] Bentham's ingenious device became a metaphor for Michel Foucault, whose lasting contribution was to redefine power for our (modern or postmodern) time by looking not at its central fount (e.g., sovereign state power) but at its distant sources, in the rivulets and eddies where power affects daily life—"those points where it becomes capillary."[49] Foucault's empirical inquiries took him to mental hospitals, church parishes, prisons, and classrooms, with the goal of understanding power at what we might call its point of production. Such power becomes manifest through "the production of effective instruments for the formation and accumulation of knowledge—methods of observation, techniques of registration, procedures for investigation and research, apparatuses of control" (102). Ultimately, you find power exercising itself even through the individual gesture or word, without the body necessarily knowing it.

Our understandings of power are deeply conditioned by where we expect to find it: looking for it at the central source, such as the king, the parliament, or the state, discloses it. This is "sovereign" power, from which most of our theories of sovereignty germinate—and a conception to which P'yŏngyang clings with a passion. But who is the sovereign who takes my video picture in the supermarket line? Who uses my social security number to get a record of my expenditures? Who manipulates the videocameras at the shopping mall or the parking garage? Why does the National Security Agency fear the Internet and wish to put a special chip in every American computer to monitor communications? This omnipresent power is exercised through continuous surveillance; it is indescribable in the traditional language of sovereignty or legal right or in the daily American discourse of freedom and individualism. Instead it is a new kind of power founded and developed with modern society itself and advanced with every novel technology, for which we have little theory and often little awareness. Yet it is a power that ultimately deals in discipline and coercion, just as does any courtroom—and often more effectively, as Bentham knew.[50]

In the 1990s, the United States has been the avatar of the worldwide extension of democracy and the market (i.e., liberalism) and for national self-determination. President Clinton's Wilsonian calls for self-determination of small nations appealed to the many new nations demanding recognition in the post–cold war period. It is almost sacrilege to say that there is anything more to American policy than that: liberalism and self-determination. But the United States has also become the world's singular policeman, seeking to contain and rein in unruly forces on both sides of the old bipolar divide; it has routinely violated other nations' sovereignty in so doing. Our liberalism continues the Benthamite tradition, in other words, but given the potency of contemporary technologies, it does so with a vengeance.

The Gulf war of 1990–1991 was mediated and fought through nosecone cameras, laser-guided weapons, SLAM Walleyes, infrared beams, terrain-mapping cruise missiles, AWACS surveillance aircraft, high-resolution spy satellites, Patriot antimissile missiles, and a Telestrator to explain it all on TV, thus appearing to realize "ubiquitous orbital vision of enemy territory."[51]

The range of vision (or what I call Pentavision)[52] extended to the home front, where Pentagon briefers, compliant journalists, and advanced television technology brought into the living room the Gulf war as a kind of Pentagon hit series. The advance of American technology allowed people to sit home and watch missiles homing onto their Baghdad targets, relayed via nosecone cameras that had the good taste to cease transmitting just as they obliterated their quarry, thus vetting a cool, bloodless war through a cool medium and into the living room. Here was "a kind of video press release," said a pioneer of the use of images to manipulate public opinion:[53] a bomb that was simultaneously warfare, image, news, spectacle, and advertisement for the Pentagon.

The success of George Bush's "television war" in the Gulf propelled utilitarian logic to a new conclusion: a war to end all (post–cold war) wars inaugurates a "new world order" in which the whole Third World must behave and police itself or suffer the consequences from an omniscient, omnipresent, technologically omnipotent America. In the 1990s, the United States replaced the Soviet bloc with new Third World enemies called renegade or rogue states, redeployed the immense intelligence apparatus for surveilling the Soviet bloc against these states, and utilized new technologies to keep rogue states weak. The Pentagon and the intelligence agencies gained from that a continuing (or marginally decreasing) hold on the national budget (worth $28 to $30 billion for the intelligence "black budget," about $260 billion all told in 1998). This prepared a future in which the assumptions of positivism, the technology of smart weapons, and the unseeing but conforming eye of television combine to make a new form of war, simultaneously surveilling the home front and an unruly world.

The cunning of history, however, had provided fewer and fewer enemies to watch in the 1990s. As General Colin Powell put it, "I'm running out of demons. I'm running out of villains. I'm down to Castro and Kim Il Sung."[54] In this sense, therefore, the Yŏngbyŏn facility fueled much more than whatever P'yŏngyang used it for; it fueled the defense budget and the intelligence agencies for several more years in a post–cold war situation where hugely expensive facilities for surveilling the now nonexistent Soviet bloc might otherwise seem obsolescent.[55]

Nayan Chanda has long been one of the best reporters in Asia, writing for the *Far Eastern Economic Review*. In 1993 he prepared a major study of the nuclear crisis, which, for the first time in my reading, dwelled on the IAEA's use of American intelligence imaging to surveil North Korea. On 22 February 1993, the IAEA unveiled for its board at their Vienna home office "a series of amazingly detailed photographs taken by U.S. spy satellites in 1989," which showed North Koreans "working to hook up their plutonium reprocessing plant with a huge waste storage tank."[56] Spy satellite photos from 1992, also displayed at the time, showed that "the entire area around the building had been filled with tonnes of earth gently sloping from the tank and had been landscaped with trees, a parking lot and a road. These extraordinary photographs suddenly threw a flood of light on the mystery of the missing nuclear waste" (23). The waste tanks were said to be eight meters underground, with a concrete slab on top and a building erected aboveground on the slab. Chanda's article contained an artist's rendering of this site in 1989 and how it was subsequently camouflaged.

As we have seen, the used fuel rods from a Calder Hall–style reactor are washed in nitric acid solutions to extract plutonium, and the resultant hot chemical waste is stored in stainless steel tanks. Access to such tanks would enable specialists to determine how much plutonium was extracted in 1989. Chanda wrote that the IAEA had been told that the "time signature" on the plutonium and waste samples that the North Koreans provided did not match: "The isotopic content of reprocessed plutonium and its residue in the waste changes at a fixed rate. This allows scientists to determine the exact time when plutonium was processed." Who told them? This determination also came from U.S. intelligence, not the IAEA.[57] Chanda then drew the IAEA's conclusion: "the North Koreans had obviously processed more plutonium than they had admitted."

The IAEA estimated that North Korea had reprocessed plutonium four times since 1989 (according to Chanda). Meanwhile, the CIA said that the North pulled out 10 to 16 kilograms in one hundred days in 1989, or 22 to 35 pounds; North Korea admitted to experimenting with reprocessing small amounts of plutonium from damaged fuel rods in 1990, telling the IAEA that it only separated 3.5 pounds (98 grams) of plutonium.[58] When the IAEA wanted a better sense of how much plutonium the Koreans had reprocessed in these episodes, "the CIA then came up with the suggestion that the IAEA examine the waste sites"; this is why "the CIA supplied the IAEA with satellite photographs."[59] Chanda's *Far Eastern Economic Review* article quoted Hans Blix (director of the IAEA) saying he didn't worry about North Korean charges that he had compromised the IAEA's impartiality by using American intelligence information: "Satellite imagery today belongs to the realm of conventional sources of information. I don't see any reason why anyone should object to that."

What Blix did not say is that the resources of the U.S. National Reconnaissance Office (NRO—even the name was classified until recently) are vastly superior to private-eye satellite imagery. In a 1994 letter from one of Japan's most experienced nuclear proliferation experts, addressed to a friend of mine who showed it to me on a not-for-attribution basis, we read this: "There is a whole issue of the most delicate [nature: the] international problem of sharing of intelligence across national borders." Delicate in any context, such intelligence sharing was incendiary in the Korean context.

North Korea has been the object of a kind of international proctology since before the Korean War, when surveillance by airplanes began. Every day a variety of satellites surveil its territory, using equipment so sophisticated that it allegedly can record conversations in autos speeding through P'yŏng-yang; even the old U-2 spy plane retains a function in the Korean theater. P'yŏngyang complains mightily whenever it tracks a U-2 or other spy plane above or near its territory—which is about once a day, judging from P'yŏng-yang's Central News Agency reports. Bereft of technologies to control its own air space (and "space" space), over the decades North Korea built underground facilities and engaged in elaborate shell games to confound the eyes intruding from above. For example, much of the reevaluation of DPRK armed strength in 1978–1979 that derailed Jimmy Carter's troop withdrawal strategy was based on reinterpreting reconnaissance photos: tanks and other weapons originally thought to be wooden mockups were redefined as the real thing. "I have always suspected that the facts were doctored" by the Defense Intelligence Agency and others, Carter later told a reporter, "but it was beyond the capability even of a president to prove this."[60]

So, what do we make of this regime unveiling a waste site in 1989 and then camouflaging it by 1992? Do they go about their business unaware of this round-the-clock surveillance? Of course, it meant that they wanted the NRO to witness these events; it wanted to show its ace in the hole, and then put it back in the deck.[61]

FROM NEAR WAR TO RELAXATION: THE CRISIS UNFOLDS

The most dangerous crisis between Washington and P'yŏngyang since the Korean War came in early 1993 and lasted for eighteen months. It began for the American press on 12 March 1993 when North Korea announced that it would withdraw from the NPT. Once again, Leslie Gelb (by then head of the Council of Foreign Relations) held forth, arguing that North Korea's nuclear activity will bring on "the next crisis," where another "bad guy" like Saddam may soon test the mettle of "the sane nation[s]."[62] For Congressman John Murtha (D-Pa.), chairman of the House Appropriations Subcommittee on Defense, North Korea had become "America's greatest security threat"; if it did not let its nuclear facilities be inspected, he said in March, the United States ought to knock them out with "smart weapons."[63] By this time it was routine for influential American analysts to argue that Kim Il Sung was evil or insane or both, that his regime ought to be overthrown, and that if necessary his nuclear facilities should be taken out by force.[64]

For North Korea, however, the crisis began on 26 January 1993, when newly inaugurated President Clinton announced that he would go ahead with Team Spirit war games, which George Bush had suspended a year earlier and then revived for 1993. In late February, General Lee Butler, head of the new U.S. Strategic Command, announced that the Pentagon was retargeting strategic nuclear weapons (i.e., hydrogen bombs) meant for the old USSR on North Korea (among other places). At the same time, new CIA chief James Woolsey testified that North Korea was "our most grave current concern."[65] By mid-March 1993, tens of thousands of American soldiers were carrying out war games in Korea again, and in came the B1-B bomber, B-52s from Guam, several naval vessels carrying cruise missiles, and the like; whereupon the North dropped another hole card on the table, announcing that it was pulling out of the NPT.

It is a basic principle of the nonproliferation regime that countries without nuclear weapons must not be threatened by those that possess them,[66] and since the demise of the USSR, American war games in Korea aimed only at the North. By threatening to leave the NPT, the DPRK played a strong card; implicitly it raised the specter of other near–nuclear powers doing the same, when the current NPT was due for a global renegotiation in April 1995 and major countries like Japan and India were unhappy about it. Yet if North Korea merely wanted nuclear weapons, it would have stayed outside the NPT regime in the first place. Once Team Spirit was over, however, the North agreed to high-level talks with the United States and subsequently (on 11 June 1993) suspended its withdrawal from the NPT—putting that joker back in the deck. That Team Spirit and other U.S. nuclear threats were what motivated the North could not be clearer from reading the North Korean press, which warned against resuming the games since the November 1992 American elections. Yet amid the usual frothy bombast against American imperialism, all during this period P'yŏngyang continued to call for good relations with the United States.

The other issue that energized P'yŏngyang in early 1993 was the IAEA's demand to carry out "special inspections" of undeclared sites in North Korea, including the one that the IAEA said was a nuclear waste dump. The IAEA had never before demanded such an inspection for any other country, but it was under international pressure for not ferreting out several sites in Iraq, discovered after Baghdad was defeated. The North resisted these inspections on two grounds: first, that the IAEA utilized American intelligence to ferret out new sites to visit, and that since the United States was a belligerent in Korea this violated the mandate of the IAEA; second, that the IAEA had passed the results of its inspections to the United States, and should the DPRK allow this to continue, the United States would eventually want to open up all DPRK military facilities to the IAEA.[67] (That is precisely what some high-level American officials advocated; reporters paraphrased un-named officials traveling to Korea with George Bush in January 1992 to the effect that they would require "a mandate to roam North Korea's heavily guarded military sites at will" before they could be sure of DPRK capabilities.[68] Some Defense Department officials wanted to use the special inspections brouhaha as a springboard for finding ways to eliminate the DPRK's "entire nuclear program."[69]

The United States became obsessed with getting the DPRK to comply with the IAEA, and the DPRK voiced its perennial fear that the United States simply wants to obliterate its existence as a state. So, here was the intricately raveled knot of the disagreement in 1993–1994, with the IAEA demanding inspection of an alleged waste site and the North Koreans claiming that the waste site was a military installation and therefore off limits, while lambasting the IAEA for following the desiderata of the DPRK's sworn enemy, the United States, and for not demanding equal time to see what the United States might be doing at its many installations in South Korea. And as if someone had been trying to force-feed North Korean paranoia and tell them to summon even more of the blank recalcitrance for which they are justly famous, the *New York Times* featured an essay by a well-placed expert who referred darkly to "faddish and misguided notions" in Washington's new strategic war plans—such as "forming a nuclear expeditionary force aimed at China and the third world."[70] Little wonder that the DPRK worked assiduously on its medium-range (six hundred miles) missile, the Nodong 1, launching it well into the Japan Sea during a test in June 1993, banging the target precisely at a distance of three hundred miles—and making no bones about its purpose this time.[71] (The Nodong 1 is a SCUD missile with additional engines wrapped around its waist, giving it medium-range thrust; foreign experts were not sure whether the precise targeting of the missile was an accident or an indication of the North's technological prowess.)

When President Clinton took office in 1993, his administration was stuck with Bush's decision to renew Team Spirit, and immediately faced a crisis over P'yŏngyang's threat to withdraw from the NPT—one that Clinton paid little attention to, however, because he had campaigned on the slogan "It's the economy, stupid!" and did not want a foreign policy crisis to interrupt his domestic agenda. The North Koreans brought themselves insistently to Washington's attention, however, and after some months passed, the Clinton administration took the road of negotiation (in spite of much provocation to do otherwise) and accomplished several things no previous administration had ever done. Clinton opened direct, high-level talks with North Korea not just on nuclear weapons, but also on a wide range of policy issues; the administration also proffered a number of potential concessions to the

North, including an end to Team Spirit, a pledge that it would not use force against North Korea, and an upgrading of diplomatic relations (including the opening of liaison offices in both capitals). And, of course, the administration mobilized various governments and the United Nations to warn North Korea of the dangers to the world as a whole should it withdraw from the NPT, while offering to help North Korea with less threatening kinds of nuclear power generation. For once, in other words, the United States used deft diplomacy to defuse a Korean crisis, instead of sending a hailstorm of B-52s, F-4 Phantoms, aircraft carriers, and troop alerts to face down Kim Il Sung, as all previous presidents had done. The Clinton administration deserves much credit for this sober and artful effort.

But this was not a one-way street of American concessions to P'yŏngyang, as often reported. In recent years, North Korea has also made many concessions, diplomatic and otherwise, that have not gone unremarked in our press—they just never seem to influence opinion. North Korea agreed to join the United Nations in 1991, in spite of extant resolutions branding it the aggressor in 1950. It allowed the IAEA to conduct seven regular inspections of its nuclear facilities, a fact many American newspapers ignored, but also one that would have been unthinkable for P'yŏngyang during the heyday of the cold war. It passed several unprecedented joint-venture laws and tax-and-profit regulations, and has a number of ongoing projects with foreign firms, including many from South Korea. (In 1998 South Korean newspapers were filled with reports of business interest in the North, but relations between Seoul and P'yŏngyang were still sufficiently distant that much potential business activity between the two Koreas is still blocked.) P'yŏngyang has also conducted normalization talks with Japan for several years. Above all, it consistently called for better relations with the United States throughout the nuclear crisis and welcomed a wide range of Americans to visit.[72]

Agreement wasn't easy, and much mutual misunderstanding delayed a settlement. The North Koreans had forty years of experience at P'anmunjŏm with brinkmanship negotiations, but the American diplomatic team had to relearn some hard lessons. Clinton's chief negotiator, Robert Gallucci, first met DPRK Vice Foreign Minister Kang Sŏk-ju on 2 June 1993: "Gallucci didn't like the North Koreans and they knew it. When he talked to them, the body language was amazing. Then Kang would look at him like a Cheshire Cat about to claw you in the face, and we'd say 'Oh no, here it comes.' He'd light a cigarette, turn to his interpreter and say, 'What the hell kind of noise is this guy telling you?' Then our interpreter would say, 'Mr. Kang is puzzled by your remarks.' "[73]

Despite what one participant called marathon haggling sessions, the route to an agreement began in June–July 1993, when the North Korean side proposed that their entire graphite reactor nuclear program be replaced by American-supplied light-water reactors (LWRS), which are much less prone to weapons proliferation but which would also require that P'yŏngyang become dependent on external supplies of fuel (mainly enriched uranium).[74] (North Korea had often stated that it was forced to go with graphite reactors and its own uranium because no one would help it with nuclear energy.) P'yŏngyang instantly toned down its anti-American rhetoric, even as the anniversary of the beginning of the Korean War passed. Nothing came of the North Korean LWR proposal in the summer of 1993, however.

The two delegations met again in November 1993, and on 11 November North Korea offered a "package deal" to resolve the confrontation. It demanded an American statement assuring against the threat and use of force against the DPRK, but also included a plan for the general improvement of relations between the United States and North Korea, suspension of Team Spirit, IAEA continuity-of-safeguards inspections (but no more than that), a termination of antagonism and especially American nuclear threats against the DPRK, and a fundamental resolution of the nuclear problem through the provision of LWRS. The DPRK declared its intention to renounce its entire graphite system in return. Other sources say the still unpublished November initiative went even farther, toward a general resolution of all the difficulties remaining between P'yŏngyang and Washington. Selig Harrison, who was the private analyst most aware of the significance of the 11 November proposal, listed ten items in the package deal, including liaison offices, a new peace treaty to replace the armistice, mutual force reductions, removal of trade restrictions and Trading with the Enemy Act items, a consortium to provide the LWRS, American support for Japanese and South Korean aid and investment in the DPRK, the admission of North Korea to Asian Pacific Economic Cooperation (APEC) combined with American encouragement of private-sector investment, and an American willingness to discuss ground force withdrawals from South Korea (timed to North Korean redeployments away from the DMZ).[75]

This was a diplomatic watershed in the history of U.S.-North Korean relations, but it was all mostly secret.[76] South Korea got wind of it, of course, and President Kim Young Sam went ballistic in a meeting with Clinton, fearing that somehow P'yŏngyang might damage Seoul's relations with the United States, or even isolate it.[77] Meanwhile, P'yŏngyang publicly played the game it plays best: saber rattling. At the end of November 1993, P'yŏngyang said, "When we declared our decision to withdraw from the NPT, we had taken into account all possible consequences, and we are fully prepared to safeguard the sovereignty of the country even if the worst such as 'sanctions' or war is imposed on us."[78] In a key statement on 1 February 1994, the Foreign

Ministry in P'yŏngyang stated, "The United States has created a momentous crisis that is likely to develop into catastrophe, at this crucial juncture when prospects are in sight for saving the DPRK-USA talks from the current deadlock and striking a package solution to the nuclear issue."[79] P'yŏngyang blamed the IAEA and "hardline" forces in the United States for creating the obstacles in the path to agreement (e.g., the Pentagon's decision to deploy Patriot missiles in South Korea), rather than Clinton and his advisors. With the United States pushing its allies and DPRK ally China toward supporting UN sanctions, P'yŏngyang played its ultimate trump card: it announced that sanctions would be taken as "an act of war."

The Pentagon had war-gamed a new Korean War many times over the years, but in late 1993, *Newsweek* leaked one outcome that showed the North Koreans winning. Every outcome showed a death toll of at least fifty thousand Americans and hundreds of thousands to millions of Koreans.[80] The North's Nodong-1 missile raised the specter of Japan's being drawn into a new war.

The two sides continued high-level talks trying to get a diplomatic settlement. By mid-1994 there was still no agreement, however, so P'yŏngyang forced Clinton's hand by shutting down its reactor (in May) for the first time since 1989, withdrawing some eight thousand fuel rods and placing them in cooling ponds. This dangerous ploy called Washington's bluff and left administration officials with no apparent room for maneuver.[81] Predictably, this act also occasioned another irresponsible media blitz about a new Korean War. In this case, however, unbeknownst to the media, the alarms were warranted: the United States and North Korea came much closer to war at this time than most people realize. On NBC's *Meet the Press* on 3 April 1994, Defense Secretary Perry said, "we do not want war and will not provoke a war over this or any other issue in Korea," but if U.S. sanctions "provoke the North Koreans into unleashing a war . . . that is a risk that we're taking."[82] By mid-June, the Clinton administration "had devised a plan laying out the first steps the U.S. should take to prepare for war," which included the addition of ten thousand American troops in Korea, dispatching Apache attack helicopters, and moving in more Bradley Fighting Vehicles.[83] Furthermore, "To make sure Clinton understood both the human and the monetary costs of a war, the Joint Chiefs had summoned all the regional commanders and four star generals in the service to Washington in late May [1994] to discuss Korea and brief the President. . . . According to General Luck's estimates, as many as 80,000 to 100,000 American soldiers would die in a new Korean war, and Korean troop casualties could reach the hundreds of thousands. Moreover, if the North struck Seoul as expected, [Thomas] Flanagan notes, 'the number of civilian casualties would be staggering.' The cost of such a war, Luck predicted, could top $1 trillion, far higher than the almost $60 billion spent on Desert Storm, a sum largely borne by U.S. allies."[84]

One way of describing what happened in May and June 1994 is that Clinton and his advisors looked down the barrel of the other side's guns and blinked. Another way is to say that P'yŏngyang did the same thing. It did not want war, either. But it did want to rub American noses in the realities of the Korean conflict so that the United States would pay attention and settle the crisis through diplomacy (i.e., diplomacy in the sense that both sides gave up something, not that one side imposes its will on the other). Former President Jimmy Carter had been invited to visit P'yŏngyang some years before. Alarmed by what he had learned about the depth of the crisis from briefings by Clinton administration officials, he decided to fly off to P'yŏngyang in mid-June 1994 and meet with Kim Il Sung (the first such meeting between Kim and a current or former U.S. president). By a sleight of hand that depended on Cable News Network's simultaneous transmission (direct TV mediation that short-circuited the ongoing diplomacy), Carter broke the logjam. During discussions with Kim Il Sung on a yacht in the Taedong River, he suggested that P'yŏngyang freeze its Yŏngbyŏn facility in return for LWRs and a new relationship with the United States, gaining Kim Il Sung's apparent assent with the TV cameras there to record it. President Clinton appeared in the White House press room soon thereafter and declared that if P'yŏngyang were to freeze its program (i.e., leave the fuel rods in the cooling ponds and halt ongoing construction on new facilities), high-level talks would resume—which they did on 8 July in Geneva. This critical breakthrough made possible the accord that was consummated in October 1994.

The October Framework Agreement promised P'yŏngyang that in return for freezing its graphite reactors and returning to full inspections under the NPT, a consortium of nations (the United States, Japan, South Korea, and others) would supply LWRs to help solve the North's energy problems; the consortium also agreed to supply long-term loans and credits to enable P'yŏngyang to purchase the new reactors, valued at about $4 billion. In the meantime, the United States would supply heating oil to tide over the DPRK's energy problems and would begin a step-by-step upgrading of diplomatic relations. In early 1995, the North balked at accepting South Korean LWRs because of fear of dependency on the South, but high-level negotiations in May solved that problem, essentially by relabeling the reactors. As of this writing, the Framework Agreement is still working, although there are no official liaison offices as yet. The Framework Agreement is predicated on mutual mistrust, and therefore both sides must verify compliance at each step toward completion of the agreement, which will not come until the early part of the next century, since constructing the reactors and bringing them online will take years. By that time, if all goes well, the United States and the DPRK should finally have established full diplomatic relations and the North's nuclear energy program should be in full compliance with the nonproliferation regime. Before the reactor construction is completed, the North Koreans will finally have to open the famous "waste site" to IAEA inspection, and that will show us whether they ever reprocessed enough plutonium for an atomic bomb.

CONCLUSION

Here, in brief, are the principles I derive from this complicated episode. First, those who live a particular history know it in their bones, both because they have to and because of the venerable argument that there is no theory without practice. Thereby the logic of the weak can trump the logic of the powerful, which must be abstract by virtue of the number of abstractions it has to deal with. Robert Manning, a State Department official in the Bush and Clinton administrations, remarked that "the North Koreans had a very weak hand, and they played it brilliantly."[85] But then they had done so in the fall of 1950 as well, when their country was occupied and they got Chinese troops to bail their chestnuts out of a very hot fire. This is the story of the Vietnam War, too. I do not think, however, that it is a story Americans have yet learned, or want to learn.

A second point is that knowing the "rogue" enemy seems difficult but is not so hard because its mind is concentrated by the power asymmetries. Third, historically informed analysis beats abstract "rational-choice" logic and the inveterate presentism of media analysis, but becoming "historically informed" is not easy. Fourth, knowing American foreign policy and the policy process seems easy, but it is extraordinarily difficult because of any number of false or misleading presuppositions placed before the analyst, especially by the American media. Last, in the absence of archival documents (i.e., to understand foreign policy crises in the present), multiple readings of the rogue and the American press constitute a useful empirical method, but only through an optic schooled in principles 1 through 4.

Now that the nuclear crisis seems to have been resolved, North Korea (and Korea in general) has receded to the margins of American media attention, which now reports only when the International Monetary Fund bails out Seoul or psychotic playboy Kim Jong Il inherits another title from his deceased nut case/father. I have no idea what the average American thinks about a media that railed on for years about North Korea's evil intentions only to have been proved completely wrong in its estimates, thence to sink into silence. But I do know that through this drumbeat of media disinformation, a few people who have long studied our problems with North Korea were proved right in arguing that P'yŏngyang was sincere in its desire to give up its nuclear program in return for better relations with the United States. They include Anthony Namkung of the Rockefeller Foundation, Dae-sook Suh of the University of Hawaii, Steven Linton of Columbia University, and the author of this book—but above all, Selig Harrison of the Carnegie Endowment, who was by far the most important private citizen involved in bringing Washington and P'yŏngyang together.[86]

The point of this exercise is not to say that North Korea "won" this recent political and diplomatic struggle, or that P'yŏngyang has a better media policy: quite to the contrary, its policy for half a century has been to pile lie upon lie, exaggeration upon exaggeration, even when it would be more convenient and helpful to its cause to tell the truth. But that is what we have learned to expect from communist regimes. The DPRK is not a nice place, but it is an understandable place, an anticolonial and anti-imperial state growing out of a half century of Japanese imperialism and another half century of continuous confrontation with a hegemonic United States and a more powerful South Korea, with all the predictable deformations (garrison state, total politics, utter recalcitrance to the outsider) and with extreme attention to infringements of its rights as a nation. What is the explanation for a lemminglike, mimetic, and ultimately ignorant media in a raucous democracy like the United States, in spite of their (regrettably post facto) protests about how the Pentagon herded the media like cattle during the Gulf war?

These conclusions deal only with the nuclear crisis as a kind of test case of post–cold war conflict management. The deeper meaning of the North Korean case is the extension of post–Gulf war surveillance techniques to a small, independent Third World state threatening only to do to others what has been done to it for decades, namely, to obtain nuclear weapons and use them to influence political outcomes. Looming behind North Korea is another potential "renegade state," the People's Republic of China, which the United States also surveils continuously and which it would like to involve in nonproliferation and missile-control regimes in spite of China's being a "great power" as conventionally defined. Such surveillance violates not only China's conception of sovereignty, but the traditional conception as well—founded on equality, mutual noninterference in internal affairs, and expectations of reciprocity. After all, the rational and perfectly justifiable response to such American pressures would be North Korean and Chinese demands to inspect American nuclear facilities (to "roam [American] heavily guarded military sites at will"), to monitor the dealings of American firms with countries like Iraq, Iran, and Israel, and to make certain the United States does not permit (or turn a blind eye toward) the export of materials that might be used to build weapons of mass destruction—such as the various American exports that helped build up Saddam Hussein in the 1980s.

Another question: Do we respect those who watch us twenty-four hours a day, or vow to get even with them when we finally escape their prying eye? Is this new pattern of high-tech frontier violation a source of strength or an admission of weakness? Are you powerful when you practice the equivalent of international proctology, or does it mean you cannot elicit compliance any other way? Does it serve the interests of international legality for a single superpower to use "rogue" methods to go after those it unilaterally designates as "rogue states"?

I don't have good answers to these questions, but the simplest answer is probably the one that worked all during the cold war, namely, that when we raise the stakes of the game to a new level, the other side will find a way to do so as well. Surveillance will prompt countersurveillance; violation of sovereignty in one place will lead to violation in another; rogue methods will yield rogue outcomes. Hanging in the balance will be an indispensable conception for the peace of the world, namely, Article 2.1 of the UN Charter, "the principle of the sovereign equality of all its members." Two scholars interpreted the meaning of that phrase in an era much more idealistic than ours, but what they said bears repeating today: "States are sovereign, and for that reason they have an equal capacity for rights as members of the international community. Every state, irrespective of origin, size or form of government, has an equal right to order its own internal affairs and in general to direct its policy within the limits of international law."[87]

6

THE WORLD SHAKES CHINA

> One might trace the history of the *limits*, of those obscure actions, necessarily forgotten as soon as they are performed, whereby a civilization casts aside something it regards as alien. Throughout its history, this moat which it digs around itself, this no man's land by which it preserves its isolation, is just as characteristic as its positive values.—Michel Foucault

In a recent Italian film, *Il Postino*, the Chilean poet Pablo Neruda teaches an uneducated mailman first the word and then the art of *metaforé*. The mailman is a quick study, and soon asks Neruda this intriguing question: "Is the world perhaps a metaphor for something else?" Neruda pauses and then says that he will have to think about this question. But he never gives the postman his answer.

China has not been a nation for Americans, but a metaphor. To say "China" is instantly to call up a string of metaphors giving us the history of Sino-American relations and fifty years of "China watching" by our politicians, pundits, and academics: unchanging China, cyclical China, the inscrutable Forbidden City, boxes within boxes, sick man of Asia, the good earth, agrarian reformers, China shakes the world, who lost China, containment or liberation, brainwashing, the Sino-Soviet monolith, Quemoy and Matsu, the East is Red, containment without isolation, Ping-Pong diplomacy, the week that changed the world, whither China-after-Mao, the Gang of Four, the four modernizations, the China card, silkworm missiles, MFN, Tiananmen, butchers of Beijing, whither China-after-Deng, China shakes the world (again),[1] cycles of rise and decline (again),[2] unchanging China (yet again).[3] Beyond all that, our pundits and experts remain captured by a master metaphor of China's unfathomable-in-a-lifetime vastness,[4] its long history, its huge population, and (therefore) its overriding importance to the world we live in.

The accompaniment to this operatic "China" din is a cacophony of expert opinion offering "scenarios" for where China is going and what we must (by all means) do about it. Pick up almost any journal or magazine of expert opinion and you will read that China is disintegrating, or that it is united and stable; that Sino-American relations are frayed to the breaking point, or that they are just over yet another nettlesome hump; that fearsome China must be "contained," or that outward-opening China must be "engaged"; that its military is growing ominously, or that it is underfunded and fitted out with obsolescent weaponry; that all Chinese now revile Mao, or that periodic "Mao crazes" agitate even the jaded teenagers in Shanghai; that its commerce is drastically overheated and facing crisis, or that it is now or will soon become the world's third largest economy; that China may attack Taiwan, or that Taiwan may soon be China's biggest foreign investor; that China may take over the Spratly Islands, or that it will not because it cannot; that China will subjugate Hong Kong now that it is no longer a British colony, or that Hong Kong has been colonizing China for years; that a budding civil society was crushed at Tiananmen followed by a retreat to a 1990s version of medieval feudalism, or that the protesters themselves did not know what they were doing or wanted; finally that post-Deng China will dissolve into chaos because Tiananmen made the political system's beastliness "hideously apparent," or that the new leadership will pluralize China's politics.[5] Atavistic China seems to be lying in wait for the next trough in history's recurring cycle . . . or not.

Contrast all this with George F. Kennan, who, around the time that Mao mounted the Gate of Heavenly Peace (i.e., Tiananmen) to found the People's Republic, remarked "China doesn't matter very much. It's not very important. It's never going to be powerful."[6] China had no integrated industrial base, which Kennan thought basic to any serious capacity for warfare, merely an industrial fringe stitched along its coasts by the imperial powers; thus China ought not be included in his containment strategy. Japan did have such a base and was therefore the key to postwar American policy in East Asia. Or take Deng Xiaoping, who in the 1980s steered a pragmatic middle course through the fractious and dangerous yin and yang of high Chinese politics by reforming in even-numbered years and conserving in odd-numbered years.[7] It's as good a formula as any. Such clear-eyed thinking, informed by a shrewd *realpolitik*, is a better place to start than with the chorus of alarms and diversions surrounding the China issue. If we can think realistically about where China has been, maybe we can make better judgments about where it is going.

WHERE HAS CHINA BEEN? CASTLE AND MOAT

Michel Foucault's metaphor gives us culture as a feudal castle, protected by a moat of ingrained practices, habitual choices, and conscious or unconscious rejections, through which the heterodox and the alien are kept at bay or subdued. It might be a restatement of the reigning metaphor for Chinese civilization: dignified, aloof, self-contained, content with itself, always ready to reject the barbarian—or if it must succumb temporarily, to dissolve the foreigner in the absorbent sea of Chinese custom and practice. For centuries, this fate awaited the Mongol, the Manchu, and according to many accounts, the Westerner.

The Chinese "castle," however, was a large empire encompassing the known universe, and its "moat" delimited civilization itself. Two hundred years ago, East Asia had two dynasties and two kings, the dynasties apparently destined to rule forever, the kings to be venerated forever for their long and peaceful reigns. Korea's Chosŏn Dynasty, founded in 1392, was led by King Yongjo from 1725 all the way to that pregnant historical year, 1776. Korea was China's most important tributary state, and for most of the century it paid obeisance to the Qianlong Emperor, who ruled from 1736 to 1796. In 1793 King George III (who reigned for fifty-nine years) sent a mission to the Chinese court, asking for the opening of trade relations. The Qianlong Emperor replied, "Swaying the four seas, I have but one goal, which is to establish perfect governance; strange jewels and precious objects do not interest me. . . . the virtue and prestige of the celestial dynasty have spread far and wide, the kings of the myriad nations come by land and sea with all sorts of precious things. Consequently there is nothing we lack." King George, in other words, should take his cues from King Yongjo and get in line with the tribute appropriate for a God-king ruling from the center of civilization. The "Middle Kingdom" *was* the right metaphor—then.

Modern history began for China when the British banged on the door and when, in C. P. Fitzgerald's perfect metaphor, "to the amazement of all, within and without, the great structure . . . suddenly collapsed, leaving the surprised Europeans still holding the door handle."[8] A great structure that could sway the entirety of China was not put together again until a century and a half of debilitation, rebellion, central collapse, and disintegration had transpired, followed by false starts, blind alleys, civil and international wars, and an immense social revolution. When Mao announced atop Tiananmen in 1949 that "China has stood up," he stirred the hearts of Chinese everywhere, for at least China was again unitary, the humiliation had stopped, and the foreigner had been expelled. For fifty years, all Chinese elites, whether Confucianist, nationalist, or communist, had united on the principle of "self-strengthening," taking the famous *ti-yong* formula of Chinese experience and philosophy as the "base," Western learning and technique "for use." What then, after national consolidation?

Following immediately upon the heels of the communist victory came the conflict in Korea, a war of extraordinary destructiveness for Koreans and great peril for China. The war remained limited to the Korean peninsula (although just barely), and in its aftermath China enjoyed high prestige among newly independent or still colonized peoples, at a time when the anticolonial movement was at its height. Lost for a generation because of that war, however, was any chance of Chinese and American reconciliation. The United States now firmly backed Mao's blood enemy, Chiang Kai-shek, and had effectively separated Taiwan from the mainland. This hot war, combined with intensity of the cold war in the 1950s and an American economic blockade, left China with no choice but to embrace the Soviet bloc.

Harry Truman's secretary of state, Dean Acheson, was the architect of a different policy, one that the Korean War put off sufficiently long so that Richard Nixon, Acheson's antagonist in the 1950s, could fulfill it only in the 1970s. That policy was to recognize Communist China as a means of bringing it into the world economy and making it dependent on the West. Acheson, like George Kennan, thought that Moscow could not really do much to rehabilitate and industrialize China; sooner or later it would have to turn to the West for help. An Anglophile and an internationalist, Acheson wanted to work with Britain to keep China open, with the hope that this would split Beijing and Moscow and ultimately scatter China's insurgent impulses in the solvent of free trade. The way to do that was to try to stay on the good side of Chinese anti-imperial nationalism and hope to enmesh China in the world economy.

The Achilles' heel of Acheson's policy was Taiwan. Like his president, Acheson vastly disliked Chiang Kai-shek's regime, which had fled to Taiwan in 1949; neither held out hope that Chiang could do better at containing communism on Taiwan than he had on the mainland. At the same time, Acheson did not want the communists to occupy the island and thus be able to surveil large swatches of the Pacific as Japan had done in World War II. He wanted to contain the island but not the regime, and so he engaged in a long pattern of duplicity in 1949 and 1950. Pretending publicly to a policy of "letting the dust settle" in the Chinese civil war, he told his aides privately that "we must carefully conceal our wish to separate the island from mainland control."[9] The Korean War enabled Truman to accomplish that goal, interposing the Seventh Fleet between Taiwan and the mainland. The two remain divided today.

THREE STRATEGIES

This early 1950s history shaped China's development strategy profoundly. In essence, three broad conceptions of political economy, each with a foreign policy corollary, have animated post-1949 China.[10] All have had the goal on which all Chinese nationalists could agree: to foster China's wealth and power. All have had the stunning and unnerving aspect of thorough change abruptly initiated from the top, first by Mao and then by Deng. And all have sought to contend with the same problem the Qianlong Emperor faced: a vibrant world economy led first by England and then by America.

Through much of this period, revolutionary China acted much like old China: it pulled up the ramparts and closed itself off against the Western challenge, only to fall behind. It adopted the modern world's only significant alternative to industrial capitalism, namely communism, and imagined that it leapt ahead of the decadent West, only to fall behind. It closed itself off in the 1960s to both the Soviets and the West in the name of "self-reliance," and again fell behind. The only untried strategy was to join up with the West, as Japan had done after 1868, whereupon it would fall in well behind Japan, a former tributary.

In the 1980s, Chinese intellectuals were able for the first time in decades to travel to the West and to appreciate the wealth, power, and civic order of societies long caricatured by regime scribes as capitalist nightmares; meanwhile, the very leaders who had penned the caricatures were now looking to the West for a way out of China's developmental impasse. Thus, even the one remaining achievement of the Chinese revolution, the reestablishment of national dignity and pride, seemed a mere illusion. "No foreigner can understand the depth of our pain," a respected intellectual told a visiting American.[11]

In these encounters, spanning two centuries, we can appreciate the alpha and the omega of China's relationship to the modern world. Standing at the center of the only world it knew, supremely confident of the inherent superiority of its own civilization, China has still not overcome the humiliation of encountering a West that prevailed against all Chinese stratagems.

The first phase in the 1950s was orthodox Stalinist industrial policy, something perhaps inevitable but deeply reinforced by mutual hostility and American blockade: extensive, heavy industrial development, taking steel as "the key link," with the foreign policy corollary that China "leaned to one side" in the bipolar conflict. Mao emphasized China's relative backwardness and its "late" industrialization in world time; buoyed by China's strong growth in the mid-1950s, he launched the Great Leap Forward to catch up with England in fifteen years. Instead, he caught up with a profound economic crisis, compounded by the deaths through famine of millions of peasants. The foreign policy corollary of the 1950s program also collapsed, as the Sino-Soviet split deepened and China found itself under threat by both Washington and Moscow. But as a book that circulated widely in China (*Looking at China with a Third Eye*) pointed out, Mao's agrarian policies and institutions also worked to root China's vast peasantry to the soil for thirty years (all the while thinking that they were making revolution), rather than have them flood into the cities as they do in most Third World countries (and as they do in China today).

No statement better captures the reasoning behind China's next dramatic departure than Mao's remark in 1961 on Premier Nikita Khrushchev's doctrine of peaceful coexistence and competition with Washington and with capitalism: "This is changing two de facto world markets into two economic systems inside a unified world market." That is, China's lean-to-one-side policy was predicated on withdrawing from the capitalist market system and building an alternative socialist system, itself in conflict with and seeking to replace the other; Soviet revisionism was responsible for giving up this struggle. What little was left of Stalin's alternative system, moreover, was corrupt, fostered intrabloc dependency, and had lost its original raison d'être; finally, of course, a unified world market, led by the United States, remained as strong as ever. If these four points were valid, China could either go it alone through a self-reliant strategy or join the world market on the best terms China could get. Generally speaking, China chose the first course in the mid- and late 1960s and the second course from the late 1970s down to the present. Both choices assumed a single world economy, but the first spelled withdrawal and the second implied enmeshment.

The self-reliant strategy of the 1960s was preeminently and uniquely a Maoist political economy, drawing on mass mobilization and moral or ideological incentives, with "class struggle" as the key link. Its domestic expression was the Cultural Revolution, and its foreign policy corollary was solidarity with the Third World. Class struggle turned out to mean intense political infighting at the top, however, and growing chaos, violence, and alienation everywhere else. A certain nadir was reached in 1971 when "Mao's chosen successor," Lin Biao, sought to flee to Russia in a plane after a failed coup attempt, only to be shot down. After that, few Chinese could believe anything the central regime said, and the dictatorial elite did not know what it was doing.

In that same year, Nixon and Kissinger opened relations with China, seeking to reinforce Sino-Soviet differences, thus to contain communism by communism. It was a grand diplomatic success, and soon Sino-American relations warmed almost to the point of strategic alliance. In December 1975, Deng Xiaoping welcomed Gerald and Betty Ford to a sumptuous dinner in the Great Hall of the People. With *maotai* glasses held high, they heard Deng offer this toast to the presidential party:

There is great disorder under heaven and the situation is excellent. . . .
The factors for war and revolution are increasing. Countries want inde-

pendence, nations want liberation, and people want revolution. . . . The wind in the belltower heralds a storm in the mountains.[12]

But Deng might really have wanted to say this:

There is great disorder under heaven and the situation is terrible. The factors for war are decreasing and those for revolution nonexistent. Countries want interdependence, nations want wealth, and people hate revolution. The wind in the belltower heralds a catastrophe in China.

THE MAN WHO LOVED CROISSANTS

Within ten months of President Ford's visit, Mao would die and his mandate would end, punctuated by China's most destructive earthquake in this century. Slowly, gradually, all the metaphors with which we had come to understand the Chinese revolution reversed: Mao was not the titan who brought revolution, national unity, and egalitarian prosperity to "the sick man of Asia," but a murderous despot to be ranked with Hitler and Stalin—except that he liked to molest little girls. China's intellectuals were not the effete scholar-officials who had delivered their nation to nineteenth-century imperialism, let alone the "stinking ninth category" abused by Mao's wife, Jiang Qing, but the new hope for an incipient civil society, the green shoots emerging after a revolutionary nightmare. Deng was not a "capitalist-roader" renegade who said it didn't matter if a cat was yellow or black as long as it caught the rat, but a bridge-playing, soccer-loving family man who had developed a taste for croissants when he lived for five years in France as a youth (Ho Chi Minh showed him where to find the best ones).[13] *Time* magazine's "Man of the Year" twice (in 1978 and 1985), Deng was the folksy reformer and would-be democrat who in 1979 toured a Houston rodeo waving a ten-gallon hat. His economic reforms, helped along by a supportive United States, had finally opened the path to the wealth and power all of China's reformers had long sought. Then came the massacre of young people at Tiananmen on 4 June 1989, and all the metaphors reversed again.

After the watershed deaths of Mao and Chou in 1976, the first response of the post-Mao leadership to China's continuing economic backwardness was an axiomatic and predictable one: to turn back to the allegedly halcyon days of the mid-1950s, when the Soviet model, high growth rates, and general political stability held sway. China's predicament, of course, could not be overcome by a return to Stalinist panaceas and massive "leaps forward." Furthermore, Chairman Hua Kuo-feng's "two whatevers" ideology (that the people should always defend whatever instructions Mao had issued and whatever policies he had promoted) alienated a population now inured to believing that whatever Mao said was probably wrong and that only a schizophrenic could follow his zigzag policy pronouncements. A major shift away from Maoism and the command political economy thus began at the end of 1978.

The Third Plenum of the Eleventh Central Committee in December 1978 was the birthday of this extraordinary turnabout, signaling a definitive end to Mao's political economy, but modestly termed a program of readjustment and reorientation. No change has been deeper, or more systematically sustained, than China's reform strategy since 1978. With the exception of Tiananmen (which had little effect on the economy), it would be hard to cite a single lurch or tortuous passage since then that is comparable to the pre-1978 period; instead, there has been a comparatively steady tendency, almost a textbook example, of how to introduce a developing country into the world economy. Hu Yaobang, general secretary of the Communist Party in the 1980s, later stated that the Third Plenum was a turning point in CCP history comparable only to the changes in 1927 and 1936. In February 1980, high-ranking critics of the new reforms were removed and Cultural Revolution pariah Liu Shaoqi was rehabilitated; later in the year, Hua Guofeng was officially demoted to a respectable obscurity, Zhao Ziyang became premier, and the celebrated trials of the Gang of Four began. A new political leadership, led by Deng Xiaoping, had established firm control of the Chinese state.

Always thorough when embarking on major new programs, the Chinese leadership made the requisite revisions in basic theory and assumptions. In place of the Maoist emphasis on class struggle and the relations of production, Deng Xiaoping pushed the "theory of productive forces" and the epistemological doctrine of "seeking truth from facts." The motive force in history was not class conflict, it turned out, but an all-round development of human and material forces of production. Deng deemed science and technology to be politically neutral, thus contradicting Jiang Qing, who had declared that a socialist train running late was better than a capitalist train on time. China's economists began studying Keynes and Friedman, but preferred the former since he blessed a central role for the state in the economy. More subtly, the determinist "productive forces" theory nudged communist China toward learning from capitalist Japan, which had always emphasized the acquisition of advanced technologies in its march to economic prowess.

In 1981, Zhao Ziyang said, "We must abandon once and for all the idea of self-sufficiency. . . . all ideas and actions based on keeping our door closed to the outside world and sticking to conventions are wrong." He continued: "Greater exports are the key. . . . we should boldly enter the world market." Zhao cited China's vast labor pool as its key advantage in world markets, and was not above waving the fabled China market in the face of Western businessmen: "Farsighted personages . . . abroad understand the enormous potentialities of the China market." (Indeed. A Monsanto representative once exclaimed, "Just one aspirin tablet a day to each of those guys—that's a lot of aspirin!") By that time, China had joined the IMF and the World Bank and had most-favored-nation status with the European Community. The broader logic, of course, was that there was but one world, not three as Mao had said: the world of global capitalism, Acheson's world.

At crucial junctures, Deng Xiaoping personally blessed the reform process—if only in even-numbered years. In 1978 came the campaign to emancipate the mind; in 1984, Deng proudly toured China's "Special Economic Zones" (described elsewhere as "golden triangles" of development to accompany the "golden necklace" of fifteen cities centered on Tianjin, the industrial city near Beijing). These were, in his words, windows "to technology, management, knowledge, and foreign strategies. . . . the special zones will become the foundation for opening up to the outside world." He also blessed a slogan he had observed on his visit: "Time is money." In 1986, he averred that "to get rich is no sin." He codified these vast changes, including the designation of fourteen "open cities" along China's coast, in the Seventh Five-Year Plan (1986–1990).

Deng's even-year zigs had their odd-year zags: in 1979, the crackdown on Democracy Wall; in 1981, the campaign against "bourgeois liberalism"; and in 1983, that against "spiritual pollution." In 1987, he again "conserved" by getting Premier Zhao to redefine China's current "stage" of history as "socialism with Chinese characteristics" for the next one hundred years (another Keynesian idea—in the long run we'll all be dead, so no one will be around to see if Deng is wrong). In 1992, he said that experience had proved "the correctness of the line" adopted in December 1978, and then unintentionally mocked the stereotype of changeless China: "Changelessness is what is needed. We should not make people think that [these] policies are going to be changed." In 1994, Deng uncharacteristically allowed a bit of conservatism in an even year: Jiang Zemin now spoke of "the three stabilities," namely, that rice and other staples, basic services, and major producer goods would remain under state control for a long time, thus to keep inflation and people's livelihoods under control. In 1995, Jiang launched a huge campaign against rampant corruption; about forty-eight thousand people, including several high officials, had been punished by the end of the year.

Slowly the staggering nature of China's "reform" became apparent. Agriculture was virtually privatized in a massive decollectivization, prices were decontrolled, the currency fluctuated against the dollar, central planning moved in the direction of Keynesian macroeconomic regulation, and the massive state sector began to cut free of the government's subsidies and umbilical cord. It would take an unreconstructed determinist to have predicted, however, that the same treaty ports that fueled China's economy in the imperial era would now be touted as models to emulate. Yet in April 1981, the State Council called on everyone to "learn from Shanghai, the coastal provinces, and the advanced"—not the Shanghai that was a radical bastion in the Cultural Revolution, but the Shanghai that provides about 15 percent of China's exports and 70 percent of its textile and light-industrial exports (bicycles, clothes, sewing machines). Soon high communist leaders were referring to "China's gold coast," while hardliners drew the analogy of the old treaty ports and foreign concessions. Today China's treaty-port region is becoming another country, a rapidly growing, vast market that both fuels and benefits from the export program.

Those experts who project Chinese disintegration have no trouble locating several "Chinas" already: the inland provinces where the peasant majority lives, with a per capita GNP of around $300; coastal provinces with perhaps twice as much wealth per capita; and selected enterprise zones and big cities (especially Shanghai and Canton), where huge fortunes are being made and where average wealth is at least 50 percent higher than in the nonurban coastal provinces. But that is a limited perspective: What about still other Chinas? The proximity of Taiwan, Hong Kong, and overseas Chinese in Southeast Asia, all now making enormous investments in China, suggests that ever-increasing involvement with the several countries of "greater China" is a far more likely outcome than domestic disintegration. Counting Taiwan, Hong Kong, Singapore, and the Southeast Asian Chinese diaspora (particularly active in Malaysia and Indonesia), a Chinese population of nearly fifty million deploys a per capita GNP averaging about $15,000; here is the advance guard for the ongoing transformation of the livelihoods of perhaps five hundred million Chinese in the coastal provinces. This is why Hong Kong will remain as a capitalist entrepôt, the centerpiece of the productive sphere of Chinese capitalism. It will continue to be a nodal point where the world economy continues to shake China.

Many China watchers seem to think that something is amiss because so much of the "exporting" from the new zones has been to China's interior, yet this merely recapitulates within China the triangular nature of China's trade in the world economy: generally speaking, it buys from the core and sells in the periphery, and inner China is still very much peripheral in the world system. In 1985 the World Bank found that the industrial market economies took 32 percent of China's manufactured exports, the developing economies 63 percent; its imports were overwhelmingly from the former.[14] This trend has only deepened since then. Furthermore, a potentially huge domestic market gives China a great advantage over other newly industrializing countries, who run into trouble when protectionism limits their access to the American or Japanese market because of low purchasing power at home. The five hundred million people of the coastal zones alone represent ten times as many potential consumers as South Korea, twenty-five times as many as Taiwan.

The debacle at Tiananmen in 1989 predictably energized many aging Stalinists and Maoists, now termed "conservatives" in the literature. They counterattacked with the battle cry of communist orthodoxy, claiming that Tiananmen proved that the noxious, polluting influences of capitalism could not be blocked while importing Western technologies and ideas "for use." Four months later, Jiang Zemin, Party secretary (and now Deng's successor), said this about Tiananmen: "Hostile forces at home and abroad created this turmoil to overthrow the leadership of the Party, subvert the socialist system, and turn China into a bourgeois republic and into an appendage of big Western capitalist powers once again. The victory and nature of this struggle represent an acute opposition between the Four Cardinal Principles and bourgeois liberalization, and it is a political struggle bearing on the life and death of our party, state, and nation. It is also a serious class struggle."

The "four upholds," as these principles were known, constituted "the foundation of the nation," Jiang said, "whereas reform and opening to the outside world are means of strengthening the nation." It was a restatement of the century-old *ti-yong* formula of Chinese experience and philosophy as the "base," Western learning and technique "for use"—except that the "four upholds" seemed to have been fabricated by a madman from one of Lu Xun's short stories: as China deepened its export-led developmental program, bringing bankers and businessmen running from all corners of the globe, it was also to uphold "Marxism–Leninism–Mao Zedong thought, socialism, the dictatorship of the proletariat, and the supremacy of Party leadership." All this connoted, said Deng in 1992, a "social market economy." The four principles were appropriate for a communist country like North Korea, which remained closed (and constantly harped on similar themes), but merely became the butt of after-dinner jokes in 1990s China, when they were not occasions for despair about the utter absence of a moral center, made worse by the regime's harping on maintaining a "socialist spiritual civilization." The one constant "moral center" since 1949 is China's zealous and absolute concept of national sovereignty, about which it has been a good deal more sensitive than the Western powers who introduced the idea to China in the first place. But then, it is the only principle China has left.

WHERE IS CHINA GOING?

Prognostication about China is no easy task, as shown by the well nigh infinite collection of bad predictions that Americans of every political persuasion have made over the years. Whether it was the Right arguing for inflicting Chiang Kai-shek against the mainland when he had just contrived to lose a nation there, or the Left claiming that Mao had invented a new form of democracy—or simply Richard Nixon saying all things about China, from "unleash Chiang" to "the week that changed the world"—the record is abysmal. Usually the cause is bad thinking or the projection of hopes and fears onto a Rorschach inkblot called "China," with both tendencies compounded by shock at China's latest plunge into the trough of its presumably inescapable history.

Almost all thinking about China today, whether by trained expert or grazing pundit, remains colored by the events of June 1989. In a game that might be called What's My Atavism? after the old TV program *What's My Line?*, we have heard everything from Henry Kissinger lamenting the 1989 events "with the pain of a spectator watching the disintegration of a family to whom one has a special attachment," to China expert W. J. F. Jenner's judgment that "the experience of medieval Europe" should be our guide to "Chinese futures." Observers simply could not fathom that croissant-lover Deng, the man in the ten-gallon hat, knew how to play hardball.

In 1994 the "butcher of Beijing" took his last even-year stroll through one of his "open cities," the marvelous Sino-European treaty port of Qingdao. Here is what Deng said then: "The policy of taking economic construction as the key link must never be changed; the reform and open-door policy must never be altered. The party's basic line must not be shaken for 100 years. . . . We must properly draw the lesson from the former Soviet Union. . . . the Chinese Communist Party's status as the ruling party must never be challenged. China cannot adopt a multi-party system."[15]

There you have it: economic perestroika and glasnost, but no political counterparts of either. Our newest capitalist "miracle" just happens to be run by communists. Deng's persistent hypothesis was that if China's living standards keep rising, his party can rule forever. He is probably wrong about his party, but right about the equation between prosperity and political legitimacy. Since 1978 the economy has grown at the average rate of 9 percent, quadrupling China's GNP. If the growth is stunning, his vision makes him no visionary; Deng was really nothing more than the Park Chung Hee of China.

I do not make this comparison lightly.[16] Anyone who knows South Korea's history from 1965 to the present should know that all manner of political disorder can proceed without disrupting economic growth or dislodging the ruling groups. Park declared martial law and promulgated a frankly authoritarian constitution in 1972, bivouacked his army on the campuses, ran thousands of dissidents off to jail or the torture chamber or merely to military boot camp, and meanwhile pushed a radical, state-dominant heavy-industry strategy against all the best advice of our economists. Always his theory was that economic growth would buy political legitimacy. His own security chief blew Park's brains out in 1979; his protégé Chun Doo Hwan took over the security agencies and then (probably) provoked an uprising in the southwestern city of Kwangju in May 1980 that can be compared in precise detail to what happened in June 1989 in Beijing, complete with regular military units exterminating students (the Kwangju death toll was, if anything, higher). Seven years later, Chun was overthrown in massive street protests by students, workers, and ordinary middle-class citizens. Meanwhile, through the entire period, Korea's growth rates were usually the highest in the world, and Park sits atop Korean public opinion polls as the most respected former president. Taiwan was always Korea's rival in growth rates; its economic transformation went on under a full martial law regime enforced from 1947 to 1987.

China is quite frankly pursuing the latest version of the theory of the developmental state, a theory our economists cannot understand but that makes sense to Asians as diverse as former Japanese Prime Minister Kishi Nobosuke, Chiang Kai-shek, Park Chung Hee, Lee Kwan Yew, and Deng Xiaoping. The *Economist* notes that consumption patterns in China today mimic those of Taiwan around 1970, and Chinese analysts point to Harvard political scientist Samuel Huntington's theory that political instability can be expected as per capita GNP moves from $300 to $4,000—but it will end after that, and therefore so will Communist Party rule (or so they hope).[17] Korea and Taiwan both had a huge state economic sector that owned the banks and most large industries, courtesy of a half century of Japanese colonialism; the state sector produced 57 percent of Taiwan's industrial production in 1952, 40 percent in 1964, and 15 percent in 1975. Rapid growth rates in Taiwan and Korea occurred in spite of this state sector, with private firms often expanding by nearly 20 percent per year. Now when we examine China in the 1990s, we find a state sector that is a drag on the economy (but a huge employer of its people), retarding a private-sector growth rate of as much as 20 percent, but also slowly giving way: the state sector is expected to be 30 percent of industrial production by the year 2000, and 18 percent or less by 2010.

The current leadership's model of preference is Singapore, not Korea or Taiwan, and indeed, several newly emerging cities (designed to absorb huge rivers of peasants leaving the villages), such as Zhangjiagang near Shanghai, are laid out on the fastidious and totally managed Singapore pattern, in search of "a China that doesn't smell." (Jiang Zemin once asked how a China that put satellites into space could not make a public bathroom that didn't stink.) When we move from the half-country of South Korea to the island of

Taiwan to the city-state of Singapore, we see that China is not another "Asian tiger" but a ten-thousand-pound elephant proposing to clean up its act while squatting in the middle of the world economy. I can't imagine what that will ultimately mean, but perhaps our economists can explain how 1.2 billion people pursuing their "comparative advantage" will avoid trampling on all the rest of us. (Shades of "China shakes the world." Could Beijing's goal be to break capitalism by capitalism?)

At any rate, this is the unarguable and inevitable direction of contemporary China. Beijing's vintage "conservative," central planner Chen Yun, is about as smart as our economists: he illustrated his worldview by likening state planning to a cage and the market to a bird flying around inside it; rarely has an analogy so confirmed an utter misunderstanding of the world market's inexorable logic, which is "to batter down all Chinese Walls" (in Marx's 1848 metaphor). In this sense, the Colonel Sanders dummy standing in front of the Kentucky Fried Chicken outlet at Tiananmen Square knows more than all the leaders who have stood atop the Gate of Heavenly Peace, scratching around for another way to wall in their people.

This Chinese elephant will not be a liberal. When television's window opened on the terrible events of Tiananmen, experts and pundits called Deng a "hardliner," a "conservative," a "reactionary," and a "fascist," while the deposed premier Zhao Ziyang became a "softliner," a "moderate," and a "liberal." This same Zhao Ziyang personally sponsored the 1980s campaign for "the new authoritarianism," as did economic reformer Zhu Rongji, the person who was incessantly fingered as a "moderate" successor to Deng (and who became prime minister in 1998). This campaign also took Korea and Taiwan as a model, arguing that both examples showed how an echelon of technocrats under strong state guidance could transform a backward economy through financial subsidies, cheap state credits, and successive multi-year economic plans. As Zhao put it, "the major point of the theory is that the modernization of backward countries inevitably passes through a phase . . . centered on strong, authoritarian leaders who serve as the motivating force for change." Deng was typically shrewder, telling Zhao that the theory wasn't bad, but the name wouldn't make for good politics.

China today uses the full panoply of authoritarian measures that Park pioneered in the early 1970s to keep people's noses to the economic grindstone and out of politics: ubiquitous surveillance by enormous security agencies, prompt deployment of riot police, expulsions from elite universities, blacklists of forbidden books, absence of habeus corpus, and the torture of recalcitrant dissidents. China's "socialism with Chinese characteristics" mimics Park's "Korean-style democracy"; dissidents and foreign critics are labeled "anti-China," just as any critic of Park was called "anti-Korean."

Meanwhile, under Deng's 863 Plan, put into effect in 1986, China's technocrats (who constitute around 25 percent of new Party members since 1980) figure out how to move into the high-technology industries of semiconductors, genetic engineering, and materials science.

Today Americans lament the millions of peasants flooding into China's cities, cluttering the train stations and sleeping on the streets (Beijing has had a "floating population" as high as three million); public manners have degenerated into shoving old ladies and breaking queue lines for buses and taxis; vast clouds of black pollutants spew from overcrowded buses chugging down the streets; a spirit of pettiness and moneygrubbing seems to affect everybody. Recently China was judged by businesspeople to be second only to Nigeria as the most corrupt major economy in the world. The only refuge is down the back alleys, where the worst thing one might encounter is an open sewer or an old man brushing his teeth. This is Beijing today. These are also my indelible memories of Seoul when I first lived there in 1967. In brief, to figure out where China will be in the next couple of decades, look at where Korea and Taiwan have been since about 1970.

CHINA AND THE TIGERS

These days no country suffers the slings and arrows of human rights activists more than China, but from Beijing's point of view all the criticism is the sheerest hypocrisy. Where were the activists when Korean troops ravaged Kwangju, only to find General Chun's reward to be a quick state visit to Washington? Beijing argues that the British never allowed anything resembling democracy in their Hong Kong colony until it looked like it might go back to China (true), and that Taiwan only rescinded the "Period of Mobilization for the Suppression of Communist Rebellion" in 1991, four years after it ended Taiwan's forty-year martial law regime (also true). But that was then and this is now. The developmental states of East Asia have moved toward direct elections and basic political freedoms, even if their preferred model is Japan's long-term system of single-party democracy. Therefore China can look forward to a never-ending conflict between advocates of human rights and democracy on the one hand and economic growth on the other, as long as it fails to decompress its political system.

More significant for China's future, however, will be the strong economic undertow that Taiwan and Hong Kong will exercise on China's open cities and "golden necklace" for many years to come. China's export zones were not placed by accident: Zhuhai is opposite Macao, Shenzhen is across from Hong Kong, and Shantou and Xiamen face the Taiwan Straits. They are export entrepôts and pivots for China's involvement in the world economy (China's exports rose an astonishing 62 percent in the first quarter of 1995, with fully 40 percent of the value coming from Guangdong Province, opposite Hong Kong), but much less cloistered and controllable than the old *cohongs* of Canton that succeeded the Qianlong Emperor's rejection of King George, set up to carry on a modest trade while keeping out Western contaminants.

The top two foreign investors in China before 1997 were Hong Kong and Taiwan, followed by the United States, with Hong Kong (and Macao) accounting for 63 percent of all foreign investment by the end of 1994; Taiwan's investment in China totaled $4 billion in the same year. Will this strong counterinfluence provoke China forcibly to shut down Hong Kong's politics or to use force against Taiwan? Will Hong Kong's posthaste democracy begin to colonize China's near reaches, as its economy has done? Will China continue to fire its Dongfeng (East Wind) medium-range missiles across the bow of General MacArthur's "unsinkable aircraft carrier" (as it did in March 1996), or will it deepen the $20 billion worth of trade it now does with Taiwan, a trade heavily in China's favor? (China's trade with Taiwan rose by more than 500 percent from 1990 to 1994, with the mainland getting 15 percent of Taiwan's exports but Taiwan getting only 2 percent of the mainland's exports.) The growing exchange across the Taiwan Straits is the dominant tendency, reinforced by the surprising strength of a party favoring reunification with the mainland in Taiwan's recent elections. This burgeoning exchange has already reduced Taiwan's "three no's" policy (no contact, no negotiation, no compromise) to merely the last: no compromise. But that is a big no.

Roosevelt and Churchill decided to give Taiwan back to Chiang Kai-shek at the Cairo Conference in 1943, more to punish Japan than to reward China. Until recently, as we have seen, Japan did much better than the nationalists at winning the hearts and minds of the natives. But a deal is a deal, and the Cairo deal was deeply reinforced by the decisions of two presidents, Nixon in 1972 and Carter in 1978, to trade away the island for a new relationship with China. China is completely within its international rights when it says, as it often does, that any sovereign state "is entitled to use any means it deems necessary, including military ones, to uphold its sovereignty and territorial integrity." This is a sacred principle to China, precisely because it has so few left. Thus China clings to the formula that in the final instance it is willing to use force if the people of Taiwan declare their independence.

Deng Xiaoping's foreign policy echoed the pragmatism of his reform program, however, just as China's foreign policy under Mao was always cautious and calculating (as Allen S. Whiting has shown), despite its loud bluster. Deng's "one China, two systems" formula was meant to imply long-term autonomy for Taiwan. In 1984 he stated that China needs peace for the next two decades to develop itself, and proceeded to slash spending for the People's Liberation Army. The share of the state budget going for defense was halved from 1977 to 1986, dropping to 9.3 percent; it rose by an average of about 12 percent from that point to the present, with the figures skewed by early-1990s spending increases to placate and assure the loyalty of the military and to assuage the military's shock at the effectiveness of American weaponry in the Gulf war. Deng made sure to control the military with his own confidants: nineteen full generals were promoted in 1994, but the key appointees were Deng loyalists rather than career soldiers. Much of China's recent saber rattling over Taiwan and the Spratlys is by military figures hoping for more funds or by civilians hoping to placate the military with tough rhetoric.

Today the People's Liberation Army spends little more than South Korea and Taiwan combined on defense and imports only a quarter of the weaponry that they do ($1.5 billion for China in 1988–1992, compared to $5.8 billion for South Korea and Taiwan). It mostly has Soviet equipment like that the United States devastated in the Gulf war and lacks the amphibious and air cover capability to take over Taiwan.[18] But even if Beijing should attempt to invade Taiwan, the United States is in no position once again to intervene in the Chinese civil war, nor should it. Taiwan has been given the wherewithal to defend itself; to fight for democracy in Taiwan when we turned a blind eye to its absence for four decades would be absurd. To do so because Senator Jesse Helms says we should would be equally absurd, since one never knows if his hostility to China is based on Beijing's politics or the effects of Chinese exports on North Carolina's textile industry. The better wisdom is C. P. Fitzgerald's: "There is no real possibility of dividing China peacefully into two or more states. The attempt, repeated throughout history in times of confusion, has always led to war."[19]

Still, the question of democracy will bedevil China's growing economic relationship with Taiwan as long as it bedevils China itself. The real question in the final reunification of China rests in the foundation of Taiwan's return. It is inconceivable that the Taiwanese majority, finally able to disabuse itself of the mainlanders who imposed their rule at the point of a gun in the late 1940s, would succumb to the straitjacket of Beijing's authoritarian politics in the 1990s. Therefore, a reunification without bloodshed will be possible only when some successor to Deng's handpicked leadership (Jiang Zemin and Li Peng in particular) decompresses Chinese politics.

CONCLUSION: IS CHINA A METAPHOR FOR SOMETHING ELSE?

Charles Krauthammer argued in an essay in *Time* magazine that "we must contain China." China, led by a "ruthless dictatorship," seeks "relentlessly to expand its reach" and must be stopped. Moreover, "containment of such a

bully must begin early in its career," that is, now. Other prominent observers, such as Karen Elliott House writing in *The Wall Street Journal*
in 1995, have argued that the United States and China "are on a collision
course." Whereas other East Asian countries "have pursued the U.S. model of
economic and political development" and value the U.S. presence in the
region, China's political economy is deeply insecure, she thinks, and thus it
"pursues a foreign policy that is part petulance and part paranoia." Various
"realists" have also been quick to argue that China's growing capabilities
will soon yield an assertive China intent on dominating East and Southeast
Asia, or even the world; powerful China will want its place in the sun.

The burden of this chapter is that China is different: its history has been
singular, confining its expansion to its near reaches and constraining its
choice of means. When China used force after 1949, it did so within its
historic region, and more than once it did so judiciously and effectively.
Chinese leaders may still proclaim the inherent superiority of their culture,
but that heritage also teaches them the ultimate weakness of a power that
only expresses itself militarily. Nor can military force solve China's deepest
problem, which is the continuing predominance of the West. The answer to
that challenge is civilizational, not military.

Going directly against George Kennan's conviction about China's relatively modest weight in global politics, the United States fought two Asian
wars with the goal of containing the Chinese revolution. Rough peasant
armies, Chinese and North Korean, fought our troops to a standstill in Korea;
another tough peasant army, led by the man who showed Deng Xiaoping
where to find the best croissants in Paris, defeated us outright. Both wars left
about 110,000 Americans dead for our efforts, and now we are advised to try
once again, with a China now armed with nuclear-tipped ICBMs that can
reach the American heartland. From 1990 to 1994 the Pentagon thought
many times about fighting North Korea again, as we saw, egged on constantly by the very hard line taken by Charles Krauthammer, Karen Elliot
House, and many other commentators. Instead, for the first time the Clinton
administration engaged North Korea diplomatically, and the policy worked
successfully against nearly all the advice of our experts and pundits.

Americans cannot recognize a victory when they see one. In two decades of
peace since 1975, Vietnam has become the country we always wanted it to
be: pro-American, opening to the world market, a buyer of American goods.
China has moved in the same direction, to a depth inconceivable in 1975, and
even moat-builder North Korea now wants entry to the only game in town.
They all just happen still to be led by communists. Having said that, not a
single East Asian country pursues "the U.S. model." As the IMF told us in
1997 (but only in 1997), they follow Japan, which has truly proven to be a

disease of the heart (and communism a mere disease of the skin, sure to disappear if we allow it to do so). Imagine what it must have been like for Chinese and Koreans to watch the empire that ravaged their nations and their souls get rich after World War II, while they fought bloody wars and agrarian misery beyond American comprehension.

Kennan was right, however: Japan is the active factor in East Asia. It is still today the sole comprehensively industrialized Asian nation operating at a technologically advanced level, and thus the only real rival to the Western powers. We have been busily if surreptitiously containing Japan since 1945, and if anything this has deepened in the 1990s, when the Pentagon's main object of containment, the USSR, disappeared. How do we now propose also to contain China—which wants to contain Japan? A rough balance of power now obtains in East Asia and will for many years, with Japanese economic might offset by China's nuclear arsenal and huge conventional armies in both Koreas, China, Taiwan, and Vietnam, not to mention the industrial growth that has built power throughout the region. Why not let well enough alone?

We cannot, because China is a metaphor for something else: for an enormously expensive Pentagon that has lost its bearings; for neoconservatives who no longer have a Left worthy of serious attack; for American idealists in search of themselves, in a country that also has lost its moral center; for an American polity that imagines itself coterminous with mankind and therefore cannot understand true difference.[20] China has had many vices, true, but one virtuous difference through history has been its benign neglect of its neighbors. As a civilization widely perceived to have given much more than it took away—especially in contrast to Japan—China assumed that a great civilization leads by example (Kennan has often said the same), that all who wish to come to the Middle Kingdom may do so, and that all the rest can stay put: George III of England, for example. This generality excludes China's subordination of Tibet since 1949, of course, but it helps to explain the long-term orientation toward the Middle Kingdom of several tributary states.

For a great scholar, C. P. Fitzgerald, the first pillar of Chinese civilization was the empire, long the combined Greece and Rome of East Asia. Settled agriculture was the second pillar, Pearl Buck's "good earth," placing an implicit limit on the reach of the empire. The third was Confucian orthodoxy. The peasant cultivated the soil and the scholar-official the classics, thus to satisfy the body and soul of all under heaven and maintain the moat of self-sufficiency. No emperor could have his mandate without the support of both classes.

Whatever else one says about him, Mao matched the old emperors on all fronts: he unified a China expanded to its historical full breadth with the conquest of Tibet and the intervention in Korea; he deployed a communist orthodoxy that was increasingly Chinese, and thus very quickly at odds with Moscow's orthodoxy; he had a policy for the peasantry, and he vastly expanded the reach of the officials (if not the scholars); above all, he built the necessary moat that enabled China to remain isolated for another generation.

Thus it is not a matter of small concern that China today has neither empire nor orthodoxy, earns the contempt of the scholars, and projects for its vast peasantry a daily disappearance of both the soil and the ancient livelihood that it sustained. Orville Schell lamented that "there is almost nothing that is fixed or certain" in today's China.[21] Imagine how the Chinese must feel about that. At the end of this century, the ancient pillars crumble and only the expediency of "getting rich" remains. Still, China does have the officials, long accustomed to the delivery of goods and services whether under Confucianism or communism. The central state is now transforming itself along the lines of Japan's model; it will try to ride the capitalist tiger in the interest of a China that is both rich and powerful. Like its near neighbors, it will reach unforeseen limits placed on it by the world economy, and will have to join rather than dominate the hierarchy of advanced industrial states. Then we will see if China has established, in two hundred years, a principle allowing it to be modern and Chinese at the same time.

China's contemporary leaders desperately want a moat, any moat, to establish distance between China and the world economy, but to have one they must have a principle of Chinese difference to enforce, and there is none at hand. Predictably, China fragments into imperialists who want to use China's military power to forge a new suzerainty, intellectuals who want their internal island of freedom, party bureaucrats who harp about "bourgeois liberalism," reactionaries nostalgic for peasant China, and officials who want to repress heterodoxy in the name of a lost orthodoxy. None of these programs can win, but they can cause endless trouble. Yet if the economy continues to grow in the context of greater China, they will be merely troublesome; none will shake the world. The domestic race will go to the bureaucrats and the corporate leaders, who will complete the circle of capitalism with an East Asian difference. The world will then have shaken China.

China is a country whose central leaders have swayed it this way and that for two centuries in search of a principle for involvement with the modern West. Today China still has no principle for interacting with that world while retaining its dignity; but maybe one day it will find that balance as it finally becomes the nation it has wanted to be through two centuries of humiliation. Certainly no foreigner can suggest what that principle might be; rather, the route to understanding China is through self-knowledge. A wise policy begins with China's long-term humiliation at the hands of the

West, and therefore Western humility: we have shaken China enough as it is; we should do what little we can to encourage a less dominant central government, the rule of law, and basic political rights for China's citizens—without illusions that we will make much of a difference. The main theme in our relations with China should be a long period of economism that allows both peoples to discover a new relationship. Do we want a China shooting missiles across Taiwan's bow, or a China that polishes its application to the World Trade Organization with trade concessions to the United States? This is not a hard choice, and illustrates how far China has come in two decades. It will all probably end merely with China captured by the gravity of the world market. But it might end with both peoples rediscovering the core of their own, different, civilizations. Then "China" will finally become, for Americans, simply China. And perhaps China will have finally shaken the world.

7

BOUNDARY DISPLACEMENT: THE STATE, THE FOUNDATIONS, AND INTERNATIONAL AND AREA STUDIES DURING AND AFTER THE COLD WAR

It is a curious fact of academic history that the first great center of area studies . . . [was] in the Office of Strategic Services. . . . It is still true today, and I hope it always will be, that there is a high measure of inter-penetration between universities with area programs and the information-gathering agencies of the government.—McGeorge Bundy, 1964

The late Mr. Bundy would know what he was talking about. At a time when he was dean of Arts and Sciences at Harvard, making life difficult for young scholars with political backgrounds that he or the FBI found suspect, he was also working closely with various Central Intelligence Agency projects.[1] The declassification of American archival materials on the service to the state provided by many prominent academics during the cold war has barely be-gun, but there is enough to suggest that Bundy was not the exception, but rather the rule—a rule particularly evident at the most prestigious American universities. It is now fair to say, based on the declassified evidence, that the American state and especially the intelligence elements in it shaped the entire field of postwar area studies, with the clearest and most direct impact on those regions of the world where communism was strongest: Russia, central and eastern Europe, and of course East Asia. A surge of opposition to the Indochina War in the 1960s directed some light into this academic-intelligence nexus, but by no means enough to disrupt the ongoing dailiness of its exchanges. But the collapse of Western communism and the end of the cold war have set major changes in motion, ones that have threatened exist-ing area programs and that have called into question the connection between the state's need for information and academe's capacity and willingness to provide it. If we are not in a new era, we are in a time when the consumers of area-studies knowledge are fewer, the provisioners of its ongoing funding are stingy, and scholars with competing paradigms of analysis claim pride of place.

In this chapter I examine the displacement and reordering of the boundaries of scholarly inquiry in the postwar period in two phases: the first, determining burst of academic work on East Asia and communism more generally that began during World War II but vastly expanded in the early years of the Soviet-American confrontation, which is the necessary prelude to understanding the second phase, namely, the contemporary revaluation of American studies of the rest of the world occasioned by the watershed changes since 1989. If space permitted I would also examine the interim period, the war of movement on the campuses that began around 1965 and continues today between hegemonic and counterhegemonic forces; here I simply want to acknowledge its existence and its role in making tenuous any claim that the intelligence-university nexus is determining of the work that scholars do (depending on the university or the field, academics who work with the intelligence arms of the state may feel beleaguered or even marginalized over the past thirty years).[2] I would still argue that the ultimate force shaping scholarly studies of what used to be called "the non-Western world" is economic and political power; this power is concentrated in the central state, but the most interesting effects of such power are often the least observed. They reside in those local points or "ultimate destinations" where power "becomes capillary" (in Foucault's words), such as universities and academic departments and the organizations that mediate between academe and the foundations—for example, the Social Science Research Council (SSRC). A Foucauldian understanding of power also helps us understand that conscious agency is not always, or even usually, the point in these relationships; people do things without being told, and often without knowing the influences on their behavior. In observing power "going capillary" in newly rearranged rivulets, we can discern both the origin of the "area" boundaries that expanded and contracted academic knowledge, the disordering occasioned by watershed changes in power politics and the world economy, and in the 1990s, emergent new relationships between power and knowledge.

Although the first phase (the 1940s) has been much studied, it is still rare to find an acknowledgment of the often astonishing levels of collaboration among the universities, the foundations, and the intelligence arms of the American state that accompanied that phase.[3] As the second phase unfolds intermittently before our eyes (and with only partial information, much as in the late 1940s), it is remarkable how central the intelligence function has been to it. Because I offer an assessment of such relationships, among others, let me say that in this chapter I do not assume a moral position, nor do I wish to indict individual academics or take to task the foundations or the SSRC, nor am I involved in "conspiracy theory." In earlier public presentations of versions of this chapter,[4] such comments have predictably come up: I must be trying to single out and blame scholars who worked at some point in their careers for the government, and in so doing I must be asserting an evil conspiracy. Rather, what I wish to do is evaluate contemporary boundary displacements in the unblinkered light of what we now know about the early years of area and international studies.

Perhaps I should also make clear my position on academics in government service. In an earlier draft of this chapter, I stated that working for the government against Hitler was different from doing the same thing during the cold war; the difference, it seems to me, is that between a crisis that drew nearly every American to the effort against the Nazis and Japan in conditions of total war to Washington and overseas posts distinct from campus positions, and the very different requirements placed on scholars and universities in peacetime to uphold their independence and academic freedom and to make full disclosure of possible biases deriving from clandestine sponsorship and privileged access to research funds.[5] To join, say, an Office of Strategic Services (oss) inhabited by Paul Baran, Cora DuBois, John King Fairbank, Hajo Halborn, Charles Kindleberger, Wassily Leontif, Herbert Marcuse, Barrington Moore Jr., Franz Neumann, and Paul Sweezy[6] was almost to be asked to join the best faculty the United States could assemble, thus to defeat Hitler. (The luminous names do not provide their own justification for such service, of course; historian Charles Beard set a different sort of example, by resigning from Columbia University in protest of Woodrow Wilson's drafting of college students in World War I, and then interrogating Franklin Roosevelt's pro-war policies in publications written both before and after World War II.)

One commentator argued that by saying such things I had given up a principled position of academic independence: Working for the state is always wrong. I disagree; to offer one's expertise to the Research and Analysis (R&A) branch of the oss does not compromise academic integrity, in my view, if we stipulate that (1) the war is one of total mobilization against an enemy clearly determined to take away all our freedoms, including academic ones; (2) one takes a leave of absence from the classroom to serve this war effort, establishing a clear difference between the two domains of the state and the university; and (3) classified work does not continue after reentry to the university. These same principles, of course, argue for a complete separation of the intelligence and the academic functions in ordinary times. Nothing should be more sacred to faculty offered tenure-to-the-grave security and full legal protection for their viewpoints, however heretical, than honesty and full disclosure before their colleagues and students—something unavailable to those who sign agreements never to speak or write about what they do for intelligence agencies.[7] But then, what are "ordinary times"? Would the cold war struggle against the Soviet Union qualify? The oss "faculty" in R&A appear to have split over that question; Herbert Marcuse and Paul Sweezy were not, to say the least, enlisted in that cause. If we nonetheless stipulate that the cold war fit the first criterion above, doing intelligence work during the four decades of the cold war's life clearly did not meet the second and third criteria. Instead, such activities compromised academic freedom.

These prefatory points are necessary because it was the OSS director, William "Wild Bill" Donovan, who in 1941 enunciated the rationale for employing the nation's expertise "to collect and analyze all information and data which may bear upon national security." Present at this creation were representatives of the SSRC and the American Council of Learned Societies (ACLS) who helped Donovan come up with "a slate of [academic] advisors" for the OSS.[8] Donovan's relationship to left-leaning academics was similar to General Leslie Groves's collaboration with Robert Oppenheimer on the Manhattan Project (i.e., they had nothing in common), but it yielded a political spectrum in OSS from an anticommunist like Philip Mosely to the Marxist founders of *Monthly Review*, Baran and Sweezy. The R&A branch was widely thought to be the most successful program in the OSS. It thus presented a model for postwar collaboration between intelligence and academe and influenced the division of the Central Intelligence Agency into separate research and operations branches. In many ways, it also helped to create the basic division between the academic disciplines and something else, a catchment area for interdisciplinary work that soon came to be called "area studies."[9]

For a generation after World War II, the bipolar conflict between Moscow and Washington and the hegemonic position of the United States in the world economy drew academic boundaries that had the virtue of clarity: "area studies" and its sibling, "international studies," had clear reference to places or to issues and processes that became important to study, backed by enormous public and private resources. The places were usually countries, but not just any countries: Japan got favored placement as a success story of development; China got obsessive attention as a pathological example of abortive development. The key processes were things like modernization, or what for many years was called "political development" toward the explicit or implicit goal of liberal democracy.

East Asian studies is what I know best, and it will be my main focus. The Association for Asian Studies (AAS) was the first "area" organization in the United States, founded in 1943 as the Far Eastern Association and reorganized as the AAS in 1956. Before 1945 there had been little attention to and not much funding for such things; but now the idea was to bring contemporary social science theory to bear on the non-Western world, rather than continue to pursue the classic themes of Oriental studies, often examined through philology.[10] Political scientists were often the carrier of the new "theory" (modernization), and they would begin talking to Orientalists. In return for their sufferance, the Orientalists would get vastly enhanced academic resources (positions, libraries, language studies)—and soon, a certain degree of separation, as the social scientists inhabited institutes of East Asian studies and the Orientalists occupied departments of East Asian languages and cultures. This implicit Faustian bargain sealed the postwar academic deal—and meant that the Orientalists didn't necessarily have to talk to the social scientists after all. If they often looked upon the latter as unlettered barbarians, the social scientists looked upon the Orientalists as spelunkers in the cave of exotic information, chipping away at the wall of ore until a vein could be tapped and brought to the surface, to be shaped into useful knowledge by the carriers of theory.

So, which "areas" did we study, and how did we do it? Countries inside the American hegemonic system, such as Japan, and those outside it, such as China, were clearly placed as friend or enemy, ally or adversary. But national boundaries were not sufficient to the task. A part of Korea and a part of Vietnam had one epistemology, and the other parts a totally different one. In both direct and indirect ways, the American government and the major foundations forged these boundaries by directing scholarly attention to distinct places and distinct ways of understanding them: in academe, communist studies for North Korea, North Vietnam, and China; modernization studies for Japan and the other halves of Korea and Vietnam; on the National Security Council, one expert to cover China and North Korea, and a different one for Japan and South Korea. To be in "Korean studies" or "Chinese studies" was daily to experience the tensions that afflicted Korea and China during the long period of the cold war. Over the decades of the cold war this revaluation by power gave us two tropes, yielding an entire inventory of East and Southeast Asia. The first trope was "Red China," yielding a red blotch on the map that spilled over to the northern part of the DMZ in Korea; the second was "Pacific Rim," a trope bequeathed by the Nixonian transition in response to defeat in Vietnam (opening relations with China, etc.). Each trope valued and revalued East and Southeast Asia, as Westerners (mostly Americans) recognized and defined it, in ways that highlighted some parts and excluded (or occluded) others. This change happened in the 1970s, and most of the area scholars came trundling along in its wake.

When East Asia was "painted Red," it held an apparent outward-moving dynamic whose core was "Peiping." Four hundred million Chinese armed with nuclear weapons, in Dean Rusk's 1960s scenario, threatened nations along China's rim with oblivion: South Korea, South Vietnam, Taiwan, Indonesia, Thailand, and the big enchilada, Japan. "Pacific Rim" was the post-1975 artistry, an era of forward movement and backward occlusion, as Americans sought to "put Vietnam behind us." The new trope looked forward; suddenly the rim became the locus of a new dynamism, bringing pressure on the mainland of Asia. Organized into the new inventory were "miracle" economies in Japan, South Korea, Taiwan, Hong Kong, Malaysia, and Singapore, with honorable mention for Thailand, the Philippines, Indonesia, and post-Mao (but pre-Tiananmen) China—signified by "Beizhing" (which is the Ted Koppel–approved way to pronounce Beijing). But "Pacific Rim" also heralded a forgetting, a hoped for amnesia in which the decades-long but ultimately failed American effort to obliterate the Vietnam revolution would enter the realm of Korea, "the forgotten war." The many working-class and antisystemic movements of the East Asian region in the past decades remained poxes, irrationalities that illustrate immature "political development" in the Rim. The constant element was that Rimspeak, like modernization theory, continued to look with curiosity if not disdain on anyone who did not privilege the market. And the centerpiece in the region was still Japan, a newly risen sun among advanced industrial countries—indeed, "number one" in Ezra Vogel's perfectly timed book published in 1979.[11] From the 1950s through the late 1980s it was almost heretical to utter a critical word about postwar Japan, or to point out that in the midst of the Korean "miracle" Park Chung Hee and Chun Doo Hwan were beating the brains out of thousands of workers and students, bivouacking their troops on elite university campuses, and jailing and torturing professors.

When the cold war ended and Western communism collapsed in 1989–1991, a third revaluation unfolded. One set of rationales for studying "areas" (or areas in particular kinds of ways, namely communist studies) collapsed, while another—"development," whether economic or political—deepened. In effect, the previous boundaries disappeared as the framework of inquiry distended to approximate the reach of the world market; the dawning "world without borders" collapsed area studies into international studies. Even "Pacific Rim" gave way to a new globalism, as Japan's economic bubble burst and the United States emerged finally as the mature hegemonic power of the century. It turned out that we were now living in a world economy, something that radicals had written about for decades but that now materialized as the essential domain of American activity and academic endeavor.

The state and the foundations were the quickest to sense this displacement and to redirect practical and scholarly efforts. The Clinton administration moved toward a major emphasis on foreign economic policy, spinning off one alphabet-soup organization after another (Nafta, APEC, etc.). Lacking a clear enemy and worried about their budgets, forces within the national security state sought to reposition China as another Soviet Union requiring "containment." But they were vastly weaker than the enormous weight of the multinational business forces wanting to "engage Beizhing." The foundations moved to attenuate their support for area studies, emphasizing instead interregional themes (such as "development and democracy"). The SSRC and the ACLS, long the national nexus for raising and administering funds for area studies, found their very existence threatened and began a major restructuring for the first time in more than thirty years. The source of power had shifted in the 1990s, from the state's concern with the maintenance of cold war boundary security to transnational corporations that, as the organized expression of the market, saw no geographic limit on their interests. Sponsors' expectations of area experts likewise changed quickly; a Kremlinological opinion about "China after Deng" was less interesting than informed judgments on "China's economic reforms: whither the old state sector?" and the like. The entire field of communist studies found itself alone with the intelligence agencies and the Pentagon, searching for a function after the object of their desire had rolled itself back to nothing. A government publication that had exemplified the age now exemplified the transition: changing *Problems of Communism* to *Problems of Post-Communism* delimited and even announced a certain post–cold war marginality.

As postwar history unfolded, in other words, scholars caught up in one historical system and one discourse that defined discipline, department, area, and subject suddenly found themselves in another emerging field of inquiry, well in advance of imagining or discovering the subject themselves. To put a subtle relationship all too crudely, power and money had found their subject first, and shaped fields of inquiry accordingly. But I have given you my conclusions without the evidence. I will now revisit in more detail the origins of area and international studies in the early cold war period, examine how both changed with the end of the cold war, and suggest how we might rethink boundaries (of area and discipline) and reengage our minds with the task of understanding the world outside American boundaries.

Area and International Studies in the Early Cold War

> The channel is more important than that a lot of water should be running through it.—McGeorge Bundy

After World War II ended, the new area programs and associations (such as the AAS) instantly confronted the existing boundaries of the social science and humanities disciplines; this often made for interesting intellectual confrontation as well. William Nelson Fenton was present at the creation of area studies, and in 1947 he wrote that area programs "faced fierce resistance from the 'imperialism of departments' since they challenged the fragmentation of the human sciences by disciplinary departments, each endowed with a particular methodology and a specific intellectual subject matter."[12] The anthropologist Cora DuBois thought that the OSS's collaborative work during the war was the prelude to a new era of reformist thinking on an interdisciplinary basis: "The walls separating the social sciences are crumbling with increasing rapidity. . . . People are beginning to think, as well as feel, about the kind of world in which they wish to live."[13] Area studies, much maligned as the precinct of atheoretical navel-gazing and Orientalia, was beginning to challenge the parochialism of the disciplines in the name of interdisciplinary work or even unified knowledge.

Still, these were not the power lines that counted. The state was less interested in the feudal domains of academe than in filling the vacuum of knowledge about a vast hegemonic and counterhegemonic global space, and it was the capillary lines of state power that shaped area programs. This was effected in the first instance by the relocation of the OSS's Soviet division to Columbia University as the basis for its Russian Institute, which opened in September 1946, and in the second instance by a Carnegie Corporation grant of $740,000 to Harvard to establish its own Russian Research Center in 1947.[14] Soon the Ford Foundation put in much more money, a total of $270 million to thirty-four universities for area and language studies from 1953 to 1966.[15]

This munificent funding created important area programs throughout the country and provided numerous fellowships that allowed scholars to spend years in the field acquiring difficult languages and other forms of area knowledge. McGeorge Bundy, however, was much closer to the truth in linking the underpinnings of area studies to the intelligence agencies: the OSS, and subsequently the CIA. William Donovan may have directed the wartime OSS and then returned to Wall Street, but he was also in many ways the founder of the CIA.[16] In his papers, combed through by the CIA and then deposited at the Army War College, there is a brief account of the original development of "foreign area studies," in which Donovan, George F. Kennan, and John Paton Davies played the major roles. Davies had a plan to transform area studies and bring enormous amounts of government and foundation funding into American universities through what was originally to be an Institute of Slavic Studies but that subsequently became a model for the organization of studies of the communist world and threatened Third World areas.

Donovan, who was then with the Wall Street firm Donovan, Leisure, was at the center of this effort, working with Davies in 1948 and helping him get foundation funding. The organizers specified that the government was not to be involved publicly in developing area studies, thus to allay suspicions that such programs were little more than "an intelligence agency." Their work should be "impartial and objective," clear of conflicts of interest, and so on. (Indeed, the files on this project are full of concern with academic independence and proper procedure.) However, in a letter to Donovan, Clinton Barnard of the Rockefeller Foundation—which with the Carnegie Corporation funded this effort at the beginning—wrote, "the most compelling aspect of this proposal is the intelligence function which the Institute could perform for government."[17]

Sigmund Diamond greatly expanded our understanding of the establishment of area studies centers during the early years of the cold war in his book, *Compromised Campus*. Diamond paid particular attention to the Russian Research Center at Harvard, which, following Columbia's Russian Institute and Davies's Slavic studies institute, became a model for other area programs on Eastern Europe and China. It was also a model of cooperation with the CIA and the FBI. Although Diamond's government documents on Harvard in this period have been greatly expurgated—and Harvard's own papers remain closed to scholars under a fifty-year rule—he was able to document that the Harvard Russian Research Center was based on the wartime OSS model (like Columbia's); that the Center was deeply involved with the CIA, the FBI, and other intelligence and military agencies; that several foundations (Carnegie, Rockefeller, Ford) worked with the state and the Center to fund projects and, in some cases, to launder CIA funding; that the same scholars who undertook this activity often were subjects of FBI investigations themselves; that some of these scholars, in turn, were responsible for denouncing other scholars to the FBI; and, finally, that these academics were major figures in the postwar development of Russian area studies in the nation as a whole.[18] By 1949 Harvard and the Center had established a mutually satisfactory relationship with the local FBI office; indeed, results of the Russian Research Center's work were "made available to the Bureau officially through contact with President James B. Conant of Harvard University, who has on occasion indicated his respect for the Bureau's work and his understanding for its many and varied interests in connection with internal security matters." At roughly the same time, Conant also negotiated basic arrangements between Harvard and the CIA.[19]

I frequently chide myself for running afoul of what I might call the fallacy of insufficient cynicism. I had not, for example, imagined that J. Edgar Hoover enjoyed being wined and dined by major figures in organized crime, or that the Mafia had blackmailed him (either because of his closet homosexuality or his gambling debts) into refusing for years to investigate organized crime, even into denying that there was such a thing.[20] Nor had I imagined the lengths to which the FBI would go to investigate even the most trifling aspects of life in academe in the early cold war period. It is only a bit of an exaggeration to say that those scholars studying potential enemy countries either consulted with the government or risked being investigated by the FBI; working for the CIA thus legitimized academics and fended off J. Edgar Hoover (something particularly important for the many scholars born in foreign countries and the many one-time communist émigrés now engaged in anticommunist research).[21]

Diamond's papers contain large files of FOIA material on FBI investigations of academics in the early 1950s throughout the country. Although most of the files are still thoroughly blacked out by "declassification" censors (in truth, there has been hardly any declassification on this issue), there is enough to indicate that any hearsay, any wild charge, any left-of-center organization joined, any name entered on a petition for whatever cause unacceptable to the FBI (e.g., peace or racial integration), any subscription to a magazine the FBI didn't like (e.g., *The Nation* or *The New Republic*) was enough to get an entry in the file. The FBI routinely checked the credit records of academics, tailed them, monitored their lectures, questioned their colleagues and students, and sought out reliable campus informants (William F. Buckley Jr. distinguished himself at Yale by becoming an important source for the FBI, as did Henry Kissinger to a lesser degree at Harvard).[22]

One FBI memorandum on Harvard goes on for forty-two pages with a detailed account of its courses on the USSR, complete with syllabi, teachers, and the content of the courses.[23] Another has extensive reports on lectures at Harvard sponsored by the John Reed Club (which future Japan scholar Robert Bellah chaired and whose membership included future China scholars Albert Feuerwerker and Franz Schurmann).[24] Academics working on East Asia, of course, were particularly vulnerable to FBI harassment; those working on the USSR were as well, but for reasons deeply involved with the history of those fields (e.g., the USSR never inspired much sympathy among academics in the postwar period, but China, pre- and post-1949, did), more Asianists seemed to have come to the FBI's attention. The Korean War, for example, had an immediate impact on Harvard's policies toward the John Reed Club. Two months after the war began, Harvard banned the club from using Harvard facilities unless it went through a lot of formalistic procedures (membership lists, sources of funds, etc.) not required of other groups. In the same period Harvard security people blocked China hand Israel Epstein from speaking at a club gathering. An FBI informant in the Reed Club reported that the war in Korea was the cause of this new policy and that some club members did not want to register with Harvard for fear that their names would be turned over to the government.[25]

If Harvard's Russian Research Center were the only place where such intelligence ties and government interference went on, it could be dismissed as an aberration. Unfortunately, it was a central model for area programs around the country, as was the one at Columbia University (to which OSS R&A transferred its Soviet division, as we have seen). Philip Mosely ran Columbia's Russian Institute for many years; an R&A branch veteran, he was one of the most important figures in Russian studies and American foreign policy in the 1950s. In addition to directing Columbia's Center, he was head of the Council on Foreign Relations from 1952 to 1956, a member of various boards and committees at the Ford Foundation, and a prominent leader of the American Political Science Association. His papers raise the same question Sigmund Diamond did in his book: Why did so many of the major figures in academe and the foundations, and particularly the leaders of area centers, have CIA ties and background?

Although Mosely's papers contain little formerly classified material, they document his nearly constant involvement with secret government agencies from the late 1940s through his retirement from Columbia in the early 1970s.[26] The sketchy and incomplete nature of his papers makes it impossible to know exactly what he did for the CIA and other agencies, or whether he had such clearances at all times. But his continuing relationship with intelligence groupings is clear. One example is his communication with W. W. Rostow in 1952 about which portions of Rostow's "classified project" on the "dynamics of Soviet society" should be released for publication, a project for which Mosely was an advisor.[27] Another is Frederick Barghoorn's letter to Mosely in the same year, asking for Mosely's help in getting government work for the summer: "In addition to some sort of official interview project or intelligence operation, it has occurred to me that perhaps I might obtain some connection with the State Department's educational exchange project."[28] In 1955 John T. Whitman of the CIA wrote to Mosely, asking that Mosely schedule recruitment interviews for him with students at Columbia's Russian Institute, "as you so kindly did for Messrs. Bloom, Bradley and Ferguson last year." Mosely was happy to oblige.[29] Mosely was also an active partisan in the politics of the McCarthy era. He testified before the Subversive Activities Control Board in 1953, for example, that an unnamed "respondent's" views and policies "do not deviate from those of the Soviet Union." This testimony was part of the Justice Department's attempt to get the CPUSA to register under the McCarran Act, whereupon its members could be jailed.[30] The McCarthy era, of course, produced the most widespread wave of political repression in American history, according to Ellen Schrecker, a wave that was especially effective in eliminating dissent over America's role in the world.[31]

Mosely was a central figure at the Ford Foundation throughout the formative years of American area studies centers, which Ford supported to the tune of $270 million. On 5 May 1953 Ford's Board on Overseas Training and Research approved an agenda for implementing a program of "Coordinated Country Studies." Shortly thereafter, Paul Langer wrote to Mosely, stating that the first item in regard to implementation would be consultation with CIA Director Allen Dulles. After suggesting that a person high in the Foundation should consult with Dulles, the other items to be discussed were listed as follows:

(b) In what terms are the projects to be presented to the CIA?

(c) To what extent will the Foundation assume responsibility toward the government in regard to the political reliability of the team members?

(d) Should mention be made of the names of persons tentatively selected?

(e) Should the directors of the proposed study projects be informed of the fact that the CIA has been notified?[32]

Another memorandum from the Ford Foundation concerning "implementation of the proposed country studies" said in the second paragraph that "Carl Spaeth [of Ford] offered to call Allen Dulles to explain in general terms the nature of the proposed studies," to be followed up by a more detailed presentation of the projects in a meeting between Cleon Swayze, also of Ford, and Allen Dulles. (Here, however, the purpose of these contacts with the CIA was said to be "merely to keep interested government agencies informed.")[33]

Other memoranda in Mosely's files show that plans for these country studies spawned some of the most important works later published in the field of comparative politics; for example, Langer recommended Lucian Pye for work on guerrillas in Malaya, and suggested "a broadly conceived" study of Burmese government and politics (which Pye also did somewhat later, although he was not recommended for it in this memorandum). Langer also wanted a study of Turkey as "a special case in the Near East" of "smooth development toward democracy" and immunity "to the appeals of communism." Among other scholars, he thought Dankwart Rustow would be good for the task; Rustow, together with Robert Ward, later published a central work on how Japan and Turkey modernized successfully.[34] (There is no evidence in these memoranda that Pye or Rustow knew that they were under consideration for such tasks.)

Later in 1953 the Ford Foundation sponsored a Conference on Soviet and Slavic Area Studies to discuss a program of fellowships in that field. Major academic figures in Soviet studies such as Mosely, Merle Fainsod, Cyril Black, and Frederick Barghoorn attended; also attending was China specialist

George Taylor. Government figures present included George Kennan, Paul Nitze, Allen Dulles, and several CIA officials. Pendleton Herring of the SSRC also attended.[35] Among other things, the conferees fretted about "loyalty" checks on fellowship grantees and therefore suggested denying fellowships to "partisans of special Soviet movements and recognized supporters of political parties inimical to the best interests of the United States." Although this stricture was directed primarily at the CPUSA, the language was broad enough to include, say, supporters of Henry Wallace's Progressive Party. The Carnegie Corporation also applied such concerns to a variety of liberal academics.[36]

One apparent result of this program was a CIA-sponsored study entitled "Moslems of the Soviet Central Asia" done by Richard Pipes, a well-known Harvard historian of Russia who eventually became responsible for Soviet affairs on Ronald Reagan's first and most ideologically committed National Security Council.[37] Langer, Mosely, and others also sought in 1953 and 1954 to develop Chinese studies along the lines of their previous work in Russian studies.[38] The Ford Foundation's decision in the late 1950s to pump at least $30 million into the field of China studies (to resuscitate it after the McCarthyite onslaught, but also to create new China watchers) drew on the same rationale as the Russian programs examined above: "The investment strategy was based on the model designed just after World War II by cooperation on the part of the Carnegie Corporation of New York and the Rockefeller Foundation in supporting Soviet studies, initially and principally through grants to Columbia and Harvard Universities."[39]

That Mosely provided a working linkage among Ford, the CIA, and the ACLS/SSRC well into the 1960s is suggested by Abbot Smith's 1961 letter to him, referring to lists of possible new CIA area studies consultants whom he wished to clear with Mosely, William Langer, and Joseph Strayer. (Smith was described as the director of the CIA's "consultants' group.")[40] In Mosely's response, he recommends among other people China scholar John M. Lindbeck of Columbia, A. Doak Barnett (China watcher then with the Ford Foundation but soon to join the Columbia faculty), and Lucian Pye of MIT ("my first choice").[41] In 1962 Mosely told James E. King of the Institute for Defense Analyses (IDA, an academic arm of government security agencies), who had proposed a three-year program of some sort to Ford, that "of the major foundations, only Ford has shown a willingness to mingle its money with government money, and even it is rather reluctant to do so"; Mosely counseled King that "the question of 'end-use,' i.e., whether classified or publishable, is important to the foundation."[42] Other evidence suggests that Columbia professors such as Mosely and Zbigniew Brzezinski worked closely with the IDA, both in supporting students completing dissertations such as former

CIA employee Donald Zagoria, and in bringing IDA people into Brzezinski's Research Institute on Communist Affairs.[43]

This incomplete but important evidence from the Mosely papers suggests that the Ford Foundation, in close consultation with the CIA, helped to shape postwar area studies and important collaborative research in modernization studies and comparative politics that were later mediated through well-known Ford-funded SSRC projects (ones that were required reading when I was a graduate student in the late 1960s.)[44] According to Christopher Simpson's study of declassified materials, however, this interweaving of foundations, universities, and state agencies (mainly the intelligence and military agencies) extended to the social sciences as a whole: "For years, government money ... not always publicly acknowledged as such—made up more than 75 percent of the annual budgets of institutions such as Paul Lazarsfeld's Bureau of Applied Social Research at Columbia University, Hadley Cantril's Institute for International Social Programs at Princeton, Ithiel deSola Poole's CENIS program at MIT, and others." Official sources in 1952 reported that "fully 96 percent of all reported [government] funding for social sciences at that time was drawn from the U.S. military."[45] My own work in postwar American archives over the past two decades has taught me how many books central to the political science profession in the 1950s and 1960s emerged first as internal, classified government studies.

ALLEN AND TAYLOR AT WASHINGTON

The University of Washington in Seattle has one of the oldest area studies centers, with parts of it established well before World War II. But the cold war transformed it as well, beginning with a case that made headlines all over the country. In January 1949 the Board of Regents of the University of Washington fired three tenured professors for their political views: two because they initially denied and then later admitted membership in the Communist Party, and one—Ralph Grundlach, a national figure in the discipline of psychology—who was not a Party member but a radical who was uncooperative with University and state legislature inquiries. Ellen Schrecker wrote that this decision "had nationwide repercussions," not only as the first important academic freedom case in the cold war period, but one that also established a model for purges at many universities thereafter. President Raymond B. Allen was the prime mover behind this influential case; Schrecker takes particular note of how careful Allen was to assure that proper academic procedure be followed in all political cases.[46]

There is no suggestion in Schrecker's definitive account, however, or in the more detailed study of this case by Jane Sanders,[47] that as the case unfolded Allen had extensive contact with J. Edgar Hoover and his close aides in the FBI, or that he was advised by William Donovan on the crucial matter of how to construct a model argument against these professors, an argument that would make it possible to fire them but still be consistent with contemporary doctrines of academic freedom, and one that would stand up in a court of law.[48] By far the most disturbing aspects of this case, therefore, begin at the top: not in what this president did in the early cold war period to protect academic freedom and threatened faculty or to arouse the suspicions of the FBI, but in what he did to facilitate such suspicions and deliver up such faculty.

I came across Donovan's role in shaping Allen's argument in the former's papers,[49] but the FBI's involvement was much greater. For unknown reasons, the FBI file on the University of Washington (UW), is relatively unexpurgated.[50] This relationship apparently began with President Allen's request to meet with Hoover or a top assistant in May 1948 to express his concern that the so-called Canwell Committee (Washington State's early and vicious version of the House Un-American Activities Committee) was not abiding by agreements he had made with it.[51] Allen had instructed UW faculty to assist in Canwell's investigation and to speak with Everett Pomeroy, one of Canwell's chief investigators (whom Allen wrongly believed to be a former FBI agent). In return, Allen said, Canwell had agreed to turn over the names of faculty to be hauled before his committee so that the UW could carry out its own internal investigation first (thus to avoid public embarrassment).

Allen was also interested in an arrangement that he thought obtained at UCLA, whereby an on-campus FBI representative "cooperates with university officials"; he wished to have a similar arrangement at UW, so that he could get current FBI information on UW faculty and check the names of potential new faculty with the FBI. Hoover scrawled on this document, "make sure this isn't being done" at UCLA, apparently a comment for the file since the FBI proceeded to set up for Allen what can only be called the arrangement Allen asked for—the one he persistently thought existed at UCLA in spite of FBI denials, and in any case one that provided him the information he wanted on UW faculty. By November 1948 an FBI agent was seeing Allen weekly, and Allen in return was giving him privileged information on what the relevant faculty committee and the Board of Regents were likely to do about politically suspect professors. Allen even provided to the FBI the entire transcript of the University's internal proceedings, including privileged testimony assumed to be strictly confidential.[52]

In a case of particular interest to the Korean field at UW (an area it has specialized in since 1945), Allen told the FBI that "although Harold Sunoo appeared to be an innocent dupe of the Party, he [Allen] was not entirely satisfied with the information available with respect to Sunoo" and asked for more from the FBI.[53] Sunoo taught at the University in the early cold war period and subsequently was forced to resign. Many years later, he told me that he thought George Taylor, for decades the director of the Russian and Far Eastern Center at the University, had turned him in to the FBI as a security risk because of his membership in a small faculty group critical of the Syngman Rhee regime.

I later verified that information independently with another Korean employed by UW at the same time, who participated in the same group and who said that Taylor's denunciation of him to the FBI was responsible for getting him fired (from a department having to do with the arts and thus utterly unrelated to any possible security problem). For nearly two decades thereafter he was unable to obtain a passport. Worse happened to other Koreans who ran afoul of the FBI in other states: according to Sunoo and other Korean Americans from that era with whom I have spoken, some Koreans who were active politically in the United States were deported to South Korea, where they were subsequently executed. (FBI files on these cases were still closed when I sought access to them several years ago.)

Declassified documents demonstrate that George Taylor did indeed collaborate with the FBI. An example is a conference he helped to organize in 1955 (the same year that, in a celebrated case, UW cancelled a speaking invitation to Robert Oppenheimer[54]). At first the conference was to be titled "World Communism and American Policy." Taylor invited a local FBI agent to attend, assuring the agent that "there would be no improper interference from the presence of the agent," and offering to synopsize the conference for the FBI. Subsequently, the name of the conference was changed to "American Policy and Soviet Imperialism," with the public invited to attend and with verbiage such as this in conference fliers:

DO YOU KNOW that over half your income taxes are due to the aggressive nature of Communist imperialism?

DO YOU KNOW what Lenin and Stalin intended regarding world domination? . . .

DO YOU KNOW the kinds of private American Cold War operations and what they are doing?[55]

One only begins to understand the early cold war period by learning that Taylor and his colleague Karl Wittfogel were also attacked as left-wingers or communist sympathizers by right-wing groups who noted Wittfogel's past communist affiliations and Taylor's presence alongside China hand John Service in the Office of War Information and Taylor's membership in the Institute for Pacific Relations. President Allen chose to stand by them, however, and shortly Allen accepted the directorship of the Psychological Strategy Board, a CIA position Taylor had turned down in 1950.[56] (Once again, one senses that in this period you either consulted with the CIA or got investigated by the FBI.) Meanwhile, Taylor and Wittfogel offered hostile testimony against Owen Lattimore in the McCarran inquisition.

Nikolai Poppe also taught for decades at UW and also testified against Lattimore. Originally a specialist on Mongolia, he defected from the USSR to the Nazis on the first day they arrived in his town in 1942 and "actively collaborated" with the quisling government in the Karachai minority region in the Caucasus—the first acts of which consisted of expropriating Jewish property, followed by a general roundup of Jews for gassing. He later worked at the Nazis' notorious Wannsee Institute in Berlin, which involved itself primarily in identifying ethnic peoples of the USSR and Eastern Europe. He was picked up after the war first by British intelligence and then by American intelligence as part of "Operation Bloodstone" to make use of Nazis who might aid the United States in the developing cold war struggle.

Poppe was brought to the United States in 1949 as part of the same areas studies institute program presided over by John Davies and George Kennan, described above. Placed first in Harvard's Russian Research Center (where sociologist Talcott Parsons had been his big backer), he soon went to UW. There, George Taylor introduced him to Benjamin Mandel, chief investigator for the House Un-American Activities Committee and then for the subsequent McCarran inquisition of the China field; Mandel at the time was preparing a perjury indictment against Lattimore. None of this came out at the time of Poppe's testimony against Lattimore, and Lattimore's role in blocking an American visa for Poppe until 1949 (on the grounds that he had been a Nazi ss officer) also remained unknown.[57]

INTERNATIONAL STUDIES DURING THE COLD WAR

International studies has been a more muddled field than area studies, although for many, the two labels are synonymous.[58] One can count on most members of area programs to have competence on those areas, but international studies is such a grab bag that almost any subject or discipline that crosses international boundaries can qualify for inclusion. The annual meetings of the International Studies Association have an extraordinary range of panels, with political scientists predominating but with a profusion of disciplines and subfields typically represented on the program. It is anything and everything, perhaps with a bias toward international relations and policy-relevant research. International studies is an umbrella under which just about everything gathers, from fine work and fine scholars to hack work and charlatans.

Among the earliest and the most important of international studies centers was MIT's Center for International Studies, or CENIS; it was a model for many subsequent international studies centers, and it was a model of CIA involvement; in CENIS's early years in the 1950s, the CIA underwrote this Center almost as a subsidiary enterprise. CENIS grew out of "Project Troy," begun by the State Department in 1950 "to explore international information and communication patterns." It later broadened its agenda to "social science inquiry on international affairs,"[59] but narrowed its sponsorship mostly to the CIA. This is evident in the transcript of a visiting committee meeting at MIT in May 1959, attended by MIT faculty W. W. Rostow, Ithiel deSola Poole, Max Millikan, and James Killian (president of MIT for several years); the visitors included Robert Lovett, McGeorge Bundy, and several unidentified participants.[60] One assumes there must be many similar CENIS transcripts; in any case, this one (from which are drawn the quotations through the end of this section) offers a vintage example of CIA-university collaboration and the problems such affiliations raised.

Queried as to whether the Center served just the CIA or a larger group of government departments, Millikan remarked that over the five years of the Center's relationship with the CIA, "there has been some continuing ambiguity as to whether we were creatures of CIA or whether CIA was acting as an administrative office for other agencies." He also admitted that the Center had "taken on projects under pressure" to have work done that the CIA wanted done (these were among "the least successful projects" from MIT's standpoint, he thought). At one point in the transcript, Millikan also says that "[Allen] Dulles allowed us to hire three senior people," suggesting that the CIA director had a hand in CENIS's hiring policies. The Center provided an important go-between or holding area for the CIA, since "top notch social scientists" and "area experts" had no patience for extended periods of residence at CIA headquarters: "A center like ours provides a way of getting men in academic work to give them [sic] a close relationship with concrete problems faced by people in government."

This transcript predictably shows that the two big objects of such work were the Soviet Union and China, with various researchers associated with the Center doing internal, classified reports that subsequently became published books, for example Rostow's *Dynamics of Soviet Society*. The primary impetus for this, of course, was the professional desire to "get a book out of it." But Millikan also noted another motivation: "In an academic institution it is corrosive to have people who are supposed to be pursuing knowledge and teaching people under limitations as to whom they can talk to and what they can talk about." One way to remedy that problem was to take on no project "whose material we can't produce in some unclassified results." McGeorge

Bundy, however, thought that the value of classified work was not in its "magnitude" or in the number of books produced, but in the connection itself: "The channel is more important than that a lot of water should be running through it."

Lovett acknowledged that there could be "very damaging publicity" if it were known that the CIA was funding and using CENIS, since the CIA provided "a good whipping board"; he thought they could set up a "fire wall" by making the NSC "our controlling agent with CIA the administrative agent." Killian responded, "I have a strange animal instinct that this is a good time to get ourselves tidied up. We shouldn't take the risk on this." Another participant named McCormack said he had always thought "that others would front [for] the CIA"; a participant named Jackson said that the NSC could be "a wonderful cover." In the midst of this discussion (which recalls Hollywood versions of Mafia palaver), card-carrying "Wise Man" Robert Lovett provided the bottom line: "If this thing can be solved you will find it easier to get more money from the foundations."

Area and International Studies after the Cold War

Perhaps there is enough detail above to convince independent observers that several major American centers of area and international studies research came precisely from the state-intelligence-foundation nexus that critics said they did in the late 1960s—always to a hailstorm of denial then, always to a farrago of "Why does this surprise you?" today. CIA-connected faculty were so influential that they made critics who stood for academic principle look like wild-eyed radicals in the 1960s; today, critics merely appear to be naifs who didn't know what was going on.[61]

If we now fast-forward to the 1990s, we find that the first proponents of the state's need for area training and expertise (thus to meet the challenges of the post–cold war era, etc.) decided to put the intelligence function front and center, with a requirement that recipients of government fellowships consult with the national security agencies of the same government as a quid pro quo for their funding. I refer, of course, to the National Security Education Act (NSEA, also known as the Boren Bill, after former Senator David Boren). Several area associations went on record in opposition to this program, and it nearly fell beneath Newt Gingrich's budget-cutting axe in 1995.

In a useful summary of the issues that scholars raised about the NSEA,[62] the administrator in charge of the program in 1992, Martin Hurwitz (whose background is in the Defense Intelligence Agency, an outfit that makes the CIA look liberal and enlightened by contrast) suggested that everyone should be open about the intelligence aspects of the program; even though "the buffer approach is 'traditional clandestine tradecraft,' " Hurwitz thought that "aboveboard is the way to go" for the NSEA in the 1990s.

The NSEA was something less than "aboveboard," however, since its public board was supplemented by a "shadow board"; some also complained that "aboveboard" was not quite descriptive of the Defense Intelligence College that was to house the NSEA. People worried about such affiliations therefore hoped to find a non-Pentagon house and call this new office, with a certain ineffable predictability, The David L. Boren Center for International Studies (with no substantive changes otherwise). On 14 February 1992, three area associations (not including the AAS) wrote to Senator Boren, expressing worries about "even indirect links to U.S. national security agencies." Each of those three organizations had extant resolutions on their books urging members not to participate in defense-related research programs.

The secretary-treasurer of the AAS, L. A. Peter Gosling, introduced the issue to the membership as follows: "The goal of our continued discussions about and with the NSEA [he refers to discussions with Martin Hurwitz] has been to make it as useful and acceptable to the scholarly community *as possible*, which in turn involves insulating it *as much as possible* from the Department of Defense where it is funded and located" (emphasis added).[63] Gosling went on to fret that "there are *no* [sic] other sources now, nor in the immediate future" for funding international or area studies, and that although the NSEA only supplemented Title VI funding, "there are those who fear that the traditional Defense Department/intelligence community whose support has so often saved Title VI funding from extinction may [now] be less motivated to do so." Gosling thought the program would benefit Asian studies at both the undergraduate and graduate levels and noted that all Asian languages were included in the NSEA's list of priority languages (and isn't that wonderful, etc.). Even though the NSEA Board "sets the priorities for the program," this could be mitigated, Gosling thought, by "the use of re-grant organizations" in administering parts of the program, such as the Fulbright program; through such modalities the program might escape from Defense Department control. Gosling closed his statement by saying that the AAS has "made clear the desirability of distancing this program from Department of Defense design and control."

At least three major area associations (for the Middle East, Latin America, and Africa) refused participation in this program, as we have seen. Anne Betteridge, an officer of the Middle East Studies Association, had argued that "academic representatives do not wish to obscure the source of funding, but do wish to assure the integrity of academic processes."[64] Others commented that some academics worry that students in the program "may appear to be spies-in-training," and that the program would compromise field research in many countries around the world.

A fair reading of these statements, it seems to me, suggests that Betteridge and the area associations from Latin America, Africa, and the Middle East raised important objections to the NSEA, whereas the secretary-treasurer of the AAS seemed concerned primarily with (1) getting the money, (2) showing AAS members how important the NSEA would be for Asian studies, and (3) evincing no concern whatever for the "traditional clandestine tradecraft" that makes "re-granting agencies" mere window dressing—perhaps because of a different "tradition" in Asian studies: that of intelligence agency support for Title VI funding, a tradition that I, for one, had never heard of before Gosling brought it to my attention.

Important changes have also come to SSRC and the ACLS in the 1990s. These organizations have been the national, joint administrative nexus of American academic research since the 1930s. The SSRC has not been a center of social science research as most social scientists would define it (the Survey Research Center at Michigan, for example, would come much closer), but a point at which the existing disciplines find a meeting ground with area studies. (I have walked on that ground many times myself, as a member of various SSRC committees and working groups over the years.) As such, of course, it is a more important organization than any of the area associations. Therefore we can hearken to how the SSRC vice president, Stanley J. Heginbotham, appraised the NSEA.

First, he welcomed it by saying that "new forms of federal support for higher education" have been "extremely difficult to mobilize" in the recent period of spending cuts, budget deficits, and the like.[65] Senator Boren, he explained, wanted the NSEA to facilitate area studies education at the graduate and undergraduate levels and had hoped the program would be part of an independent governmental foundation. However, the Office of Management and Budget blocked this, and instead ruled that for defense funds to be disbursed for the NSEA under the 1992 Intelligence Authorization Act, it would have to be located in the Department of Defense. Heginbotham added in a footnote that Boren decided further to strengthen "the credibility of the program in academic circles" by putting the administration of the program under the Defense Intelligence College; "few observers were reassured by this provision," Heginbotham wrote, but the Defense Intelligence College retained what he called a "nominal" role in the program.

Heginbotham expressed particular concern about "merit review" provisions in the NSEA: "The academic and scholarly communities need firm assurance that selection processes will be free from political or bureaucratic interference beyond assuring compliance with terms of reference. . . . It would not *seem* acceptable, for example, to have candidates screened on the basis of their political views . . . [or] their ability to obtain security clearances" (emphasis added). Heginbotham went on to recommend that grants to individuals be made by "independent panels of scholars," and that the academics on the "oversight board" be selected by a means "transparently independent" of the state agencies making up the same board. But "most worrisome," Heginbotham wrote, were the service requirements of the NSEA. He described the postgrant requirements for individuals as follows: "Finally, the legislation includes important but ambiguous 'service' requirements for individuals who receive funds. . . . Undergraduates receiving scholarships covering periods in excess of one year, as well as all individuals receiving graduate training awards, are required either to serve in the field of education or in government service for a period between one and three times the length of the award. The legislation also prohibits any department, agency, or entity of the U.S. government that engages in intelligence activities from using any recipient of funds from the program to undertake any activity on its behalf while the individual is being supported by the program." Heginbotham suggested that the postgrant term be limited to a year, and limited not just to positions in "government and education," but enabling any employment that used the training to benefit the nation's international needs.[66]

Heginbotham's analysis is similar to Gosling's in three respects, but superior in others. First, the analysis and recommendations are almost entirely procedural; neither Heginbotham nor Gosling defends international and area studies as important apart from what the state (let alone the "intelligence community") may want. Both also leave the impression that any funds of such size are ipso facto worth having, regardless of provenance, assuming that the procedures can be "as good as possible" in Heginbotham's words. And of course, the guarantees that Heginbotham asks for have not only been routinely bypassed by the state and area studies academics that we examined above (and used as a cover), but even powerful senators complain that the very "oversight" committees responsible for monitoring the CIA have been ignored and subverted—especially in the most recent period. (I refer mainly to the revelations of the "Iran-Contra" scandal and the murders of Americans by CIA-associated militarists in Central America.)

The SSRC's Heginbotham, however, seems both more responsible and more concerned than the AAS's Gosling about "re-granting agencies" being little more than laundries for DOD funding; his calls for merit review, academic independence, recognition of the difference between scholarship and government "service," and so on would seem to be basic principles for any kind of fundraising, and were the ones I observed in action on several SSRC committees. Heginbotham should be praised for enunciating them again— even if few seem to be listening, as sources in South Korea, Taiwan, and Japan have become major funders of Asian studies in this country, usually without proper peer and merit review.[67] Subsequently, the SSRC decided to have nothing to do with the NSEA, a welcome if belated decision.

The *Bulletin of Concerned Asian Scholars* (*BCAS*) provided periodic coverage of the NSEA, whereas (so far as I can tell) the other alternative journal in the field—*positions: east asia cultural critique*—has been silent. Mark Selden argued correctly that the NSEA "poses anew the issue of scholarship and power that lay behind the origin" of the Committee of Concerned Asian Scholars and its *Bulletin,* and noted that unlike earlier such activities, this one "saw no reason to conceal the military and intelligence priorities and powers shaping the field."[68] The *BCAS* drew particular attention to Article 3 of the "purposes" section of the NSEA, calling for it "to produce an increased pool of applicants for work in the departments and agencies of the U.S. Government with national security responsibilities." The *BCAS* also noted the similarity between the issues posed by the NSEA and those that the Columbia chapter of CCAS took up in regard to the contemporary China committee of the SSRC in a controversial set of articles in 1971.

As a graduate student, I participated in preparing that report, the main author of which was Moss Roberts of New York University. We were interested in Ford Foundation funding of the China field, the SSRC's Joint Committee on Contemporary China (JCCC), and an organization formed in the State Department in 1964 to coordinate government and private area studies research, called the Foreign Areas Research Coordinating Group, or FAR. From our inquiry it appeared that FAR played a role in shaping the field of contemporary Chinese studies, in line with the state's needs and with Ford Foundation funding.[69] It did this by suggesting appropriate research and dissertation subjects, in hopes that, together with Ford funding, the expertise of the government's China-watching apparatus would be enhanced (with obvious benefits also to China watchers in academe).

We were able to establish that FAR had grown out of the Army's concern for the "coordination of behavioral and social science" in and out of government, which had long been sponsored by the Special Operations Research Office of Johns Hopkins University. FAR had been in contact with the JCCC, which had been one of many beneficiaries of the Ford Foundation's decision to reconstitute the China field. Our report also drew attention to the first chair of the JCCC, George Taylor of the University of Washington, who, we argued, was a partisan in the McCarthy-McCarran inquisition that had nearly destroyed the China field, and therefore a strange choice to preside over a committee hoping to heal wounds and reconstitute the field. We questioned as well why non-China scholars like Philip Mosely were included on the first JCCC.[70]

The report brought a vituperative response from John Fairbank of Harvard which evokes in me today the same emotions it did in 1971: it is a political attack, designed to ward off such inquiries rather than to provide a sincere and honest response to the many questions of fact that we raised. He began by saying that our report "raises an issue of conspiracy rather than an issue of values," and ended by accusing us of offering "striking parallels to the Mc-Carran Committee 'investigation'"; that is, we were left-McCarthyites. In between, precious few of our questions were answered.[71] Ultimately a precise specification of the relationship and responsiveness of FAR and the JCCC to government or intelligence agendas could not be judged in the absence of access to classified materials. But the issues are strikingly similar to those raised by the NSEA today.

In November 1994 the cunning of history gave us the "Gingrich Revolution" and a chainsaw approach to cutting budgets; thus the NSEA appeared to get what it deserved, namely, a quick burial. No doubt Newt thought the NSEA was just another boondoggle for academia (and maybe he was right). At first, Congress cut all its funds, but then restored some of them—or so it seems, since NSEA scholarships were again available to students in early 1996. Still, the NSEA is limping along into the post-Gingrich era.

If government funding for area studies seems to be drying up, so is that from the foundations. One result is the contemporary restructuring of the SSRC. For forty years SSRC and ACLS committees have been defined mostly by area: the Joint Committee on China, or Latin America, or Western Europe; there were eleven such committees as of early 1996. That is all changing now, under a major restructuring plan.[72] The SSRC has justified this effort by reference to the global changes and challenges of the post–cold war era, the "boundary displacements" that I began this chapter with. These include a desire (1) to move away from fixed regional identities (i.e., the area committees), given that globalization has made the "'areas' more porous, less bounded, less fixed" than previously thought;[73] (2) to utilize area expertise to understand pressing issues in the world that transcend particular countries, which is the real promise of area studies in the post-1989 era; (3) to re-introduce area knowledge to social science disciplines that seem increasingly to believe that they can get along without it (an implicit reference to the rational-choice paradigm and to "formal theory" in economics, sociology, and political science); (4) to integrate the United States into "area studies" by recognizing it as an "area" that needs to be studied comparatively; and (5) to collapse the SSRC and ACLS projects themselves, given the increasing cross-fertilization between the social sciences and the humanities. (I do not know if the restructuring will actually yield just one organization, but refer only to the justifications I have seen for the new plans).

Major funding organizations like the Mellon Foundation and the Ford Foundation have recently made clear their declining support for area studies and their desire to have cross-regional scholarship. In that subtly coercive context, item 1 in this plan becomes obligatory (some say that the SSRC has been teetering on the edge of bankruptcy for several years). Item 2 is no different from the original justification for area studies. Items 3 and 4 are laudable, however, for anyone conversant with the daily life of the social sciences in American universities in the 1980s and 1990s.

Rational-choice theory is the academic analogue of the "free-market" principles that Margaret Thatcher and Ronald Reagan represented in the 1980s and that are now offered to the "world without boundaries" as the only possible paradigm of economic development. Like the putative free market, rational choice collapses the diversity of the human experience into one category, the self-interested individualist prototype that has animated and totalized the economics profession in America. As this paradigm now proposes to colonize political science and sociology, it has no use for (and indeed views with deep hostility) anyone who happens to know something about a "foreign area" or, for that matter, the United States. They are all threats to the university of this model, which can explain everything from how Japanese Diet members control the Ministry of Finance to why Indian widows throw themselves onto funeral pyres—with every explanation contingent on the listener knowing little or nothing about the subject itself. So-called formal theory takes this paradigm one step further: "soft" rational choice seeks to verify the claims of its model empirically, through the collection and testing of data, the estimation of regression coefficients, and the like; "formal theory" is a simpler matter of the researcher staring at the game-theoretic mathematical formulas that appear on the computer screen, thus to determine how the real world works. If the theory does not explain political, social, or economic phenomena, it is the real world's fault.

The rise of these two paradigms of social science inquiry have put at risk the subfields of economic history, historical sociology, and comparative politics, and the entire area studies project. Why do you need to know Japanese or anything about Japan's history and culture, if the methods of rational choice will explain why Japanese politicians and bureaucrats do the things they do?[74] If some recalcitrant research problems nonetheless still require access to Chinese or Swahili, why not get what you need from a graduate student fluent in those languages rather than an academic expert on China or Africa? The "soft" rational-choice practitioner may in fact have language and area training, or if not, will still find value in the work of area specialists; once again, they are the spelunkers who descend into the mysterious cave to mine a lode of "facts," which the practitioner will then interpret from a superior theoretical vantage point. The formal theorist, however, has no use for either of them.

This is hardly an idle matter of one paradigm contesting another in the groves of academe. Rational-choice people are determined to have the social sciences their way, to dominate them and exclude those who disagree. This is evident in Harvard political scientist Robert Bates's injunction to the profession concerning which young scholars should get tenure. Political science departments ought to "re-think their approach to evaluating junior personnel," he writes: "Unless fortunate enough to be a native speaker of a foreign language or to possess an unusually strong mathematical background, most junior faculty will not be able to consolidate both area and analytical skills prior to facing the tenure hurdle, much less to produce research demonstrating a confident command of both. In making promotion decisions, therefore, rather than focusing purely on product, attention will have to be placed on investment."[75]

Rational-choice proponents have no idea what "area specialists" actually do, but ritually caricature and cubbyhole their scholarship anyway. A scholar like Barrington Moore is certainly an expert on an "area"—originally, Russia. He is also a theorist of the first order. But his best-known work, *Social Origins of Dictatorship and Democracy*, is a classic of the comparative method precisely because of his deft mix of abstract theory and thoroughly known and thought-through history. Scholars who work on Japan, India, China, France, the United States, and England—his six "case studies"—have all had to come to grips with his analysis for the past three decades, whether they agree with it or not. But above all, it is the modern experience of Germany that breathes through this work, and yet there is no German chapter. There need not be, since Moore's analysis of lord and peasant in the modern world is also a social science meditation on how the greatest catastrophe of modern times could possibly have occurred. Rational choice has never produced, and will never produce, a book that holds a candle to Moore's *Social Origins*. Yet Barrington Moore came out of the same oss–Ford Foundation–"area studies" nexus that I discussed earlier. If it is a choice between the slim pickings of contemporary rational choice and the oss-spawned likes of Moore, Cora DuBois, John Fairbank, Franz Neumann, and yes, Phillip Mosely, I say gimme the oss old boys' network any day of the week.

Item 4 in the ssrc's new program proposes to turn the United States into an "area," and were it ever to succeed, it would also transform the disciplines. Research on the United States is indeed an "area study" just as any other; but then it's our country and has all manner of idiosyncrasy and detail that the nonexpert or foreigner could never possibly understand. And following on that insight, you arrive at the dominance of Americanists in almost any history, political science, or sociology department. That they might be as blithely ignorant of how the world beyond American borders influences the things they study as any South Asian area specialist makes no dent in their departmental power. Much more important, the ancient injunction to "know thyself" and the doctrine that there is no "thing in itself" make comparative study obligatory. So, to have a "Joint Committee on the United States" under the ssrc/acls rubric would be a big step forward.

Kenneth Prewitt, president of the ssrc until 1998, wrote that for all the aforesaid reasons, and no doubt others that I am not aware of, the ssrc/acls has come to believe "that a number of discrete and separated 'area committees,' each focused on a single world region, is not the optimum structure for providing new insights and theories suitable for a world in which the geographic units of analysis are neither static nor straightforward."[76] Instead of eleven committees, the new plan apparently proposes three, under the following general rubrics: area studies and regional analysis; area studies and comparative analysis; area studies and global analysis. There may also be a fourth committee designed to support and replenish the existing scholarly infrastructure in the United States and to develop similar structures in various other parts of the world. Nonetheless, Prewitt still envisions an important function for area specialists: "If scholarship is not rooted in place-specific histories and cultures, it will miss, widely, the nuances that allow us to make sense of such phenomena as international labor flows, conflicting perspectives on human rights, [etc.]."

As this restructuring project got off the ground (before Prewitt became president in 1996), the ssrc's Heginbotham sought to justify it by reference to the unfortunate cold war shaping of area studies in the early postwar period, and the need for "rethinking international scholarship" now that the cold war is over.[77] This odd return of repressed knowledge stimulated a sharp response: several scholars associated with Soviet and Slavic studies weighed in to deny that political pressures deriving from the cold war agenda of U.S. foreign policy had much effect on their field, which often produced scholarship "strikingly independent of assumptions driving U.S. political preferences." Various area institutes may have been formed "partially in response to the cold war," but nonetheless were able to conduct scholarship "without compromising their academic integrity." The authors also argued that the new ssrc framework "will tear international scholarship from the rich, textured empirical base that has been assiduously developed through decades of research, moving it instead to a nebulous 'global' framework for research."[78]

This is a nice statement of the likely outcome of the current ssrc/acls restructuring, but, as we have seen, Heginbotham is clearly right about the state's role in shaping the study of "foreign areas." Honest and independent scholarship was possible in the early area institutes, but the academic integrity of the institutes themselves was compromised by a secret and extensive network of ties to the cia and the fbi. It is a bit much, of course, for the ssrc to acknowledge this only now by way of justifying its new course, when it spent all too much time in the 1960s and 1970s denying that the state had any influence on its research programs.[79] More important, however, is the contemporary denial of the same thing, and here the SSRC's critics had a point.

If the current American administration has one "doctrine," it is a Clinton doctrine of promoting American-based global corporations and American exports through the most activist foreign economic policy of any president in history. Clinton's achievements in this respect—Nafta, APEC, the new World Trade Organization and many other organizations, and the routine, daily use of the state apparatus to further the export goals of U.S. multinationals—are all justified by buzzwords that crop up in the new SSRC plans: a world without borders, increasing globalization, the wonders of the Internet and the World Wide Web, the growth of multiculturalism, the resulting intensification of subnational loyalties and identities, and so on. Furthermore, the SSRC drafts of its restructuring plan make clear the concern not just for scholarship, but for policy relevance and encouraging better capacities for "managing" the new global issues of the 1990s—a clear rationale for scholarship and "area expertise" to be at the service of national security bureaucrats.

I am by no means a purist on these matters, and see nothing particularly wrong with scholars offering their views on policy questions, so long as the practice is not openly or subtly coerced by funding agencies and does not require security clearances (as the NSEA clearly does). The post-1960s SSRC, in my limited experience, has managed the nexus where state power and scholarship meet about as well as could be expected, assuming that there is some necessity to do it in the first place if the organization hopes to be funded as a national organizer of social science research. Many SSRC research projects and even a couple of its joint committees (notably, the Latin American group) have had clear counterhegemonic agendas and produced scholarship of enormous relevance to political struggles around the world.[80]

The SSRC/ACLS area committees have also been fertile ground for interdisciplinary scholarship; for decades, they offered a rare venue where one could see what a historian thought of the work of an economist, or what a literary critic thought of behavioralist sociology. Meanwhile, my own experience in the university has led me to understand that an "area specialist" is as unwanted in the totalized world of Friedmanite economics as a zek from the Gulag would be at a meeting of Stalin and his secret police chief, Beria. To the extent that the more diverse discipline of political science has produced any lasting knowledge about the world beyond our shores, it has almost always been done through the contributions of area specialists to the subfields of comparative politics and international relations.[81]

In 1994 Northwestern University won a grant from the Mellon Foundation to run two year-long interdisciplinary seminars in the hopes that they would bridge the areas and the disciplines. I participated in writing that grant proposal and directed the first seminar in 1995–1996, on "The Cultural Construction of Human Rights and Democracy." The results of this effort are not completely in yet, but it seems to me that this funding succeeded in providing a useful and important forum for interdisciplinary work, getting people to talk to each other across areas and disciplines, and I hope that the book growing out of it will be valuable.[82] To the extent that the Mellon Foundation views such seminars as an addition to the funding of existing area programs, the seminars are wonderful. To the extent that they represent a redirection of funding away from area studies, the seminars are no substitute for the training of people who know the languages and civilizations of particular places. You win with people, as football coach Woody Hayes used to say, and had there not been people already steeped in the regions we studied, inventing them would have been impossible—or at least forbiddingly expensive when compared to the level of funding provided by Mellon.

In one of the ssrc restructuring plans, there is this sentence: "There is no making sense of the world by those ignorant of local context-specific issues; and there is no making sense of the world by those indifferent to cross-regional and global forces." I think this is true, even if I would phrase the point differently. Although "area programs" trained many scholars and made possible a rare interdisciplinary intellectual program, the sad fact is that most area specialists were not interested in it. There is no reason, of course, why a person working on Chinese oracle bones should have anything in common with an expert on the Chinese Communist politburo; their common habitus in a Chinese studies program was the result of a historical compromise between the universities and the state in the early cold war period. In return for not complaining about the predominance of Kremlinologists or communist politics specialists, the oracle bone or Sanskrit or Hinduism specialist got a tenured sinecure and (usually) a handful of students in his or her classes. The state, the foundations, and the universities supported scholars who spent their entire lives translating the classics of one culture or another into English, often with next to no interaction with their colleagues. Many were precisely as monkish and unyielding to the intellectual life outside their narrow discipline as a micro-economist. I have never thought it too much to ask that a person like this find something to teach that would attract enough students into the classroom to pay the bills, but it happens all the time, and now the area studies programs are paying the price; often representing enormous sunk costs, the faculty and the sinecures are very expensive now and unlikely to be sustained at anything like current levels in the future. If we end up having no Sanskrit, no Urdu, no oracle bones, and no Han Dynasty history, it will not just owe to the ignorance of the foundations, the government, and the university administrators, but will also reflect the past privilege of the hidebound, narrow scribblers themselves.

Perhaps the most disappointing aspect of the new SSRC/ACLS restructuring and the apparent new direction of the major foundations is the absence of any reference to the basic motivation for so many of the new tendencies in the 1990s world that they hope to adapt themselves to, namely, the global corporation.[83] This is the motive force and modal organization for "globalization" and the technologies that speed it. Bill Gates's Microsoft is as dominant in this new sphere as John D. Rockefeller's Standard Oil was a century ago; and no doubt our grandchildren will vote for various governors and senators, if not presidents, named Gates—and the ones who become academics will go to the "Gates Foundation" for their research grants. Another symbolic American corporation, Coca-Cola, has become the first U.S. multinational to place overall corporate management in the hands of its world office rather than its historic national center in Atlanta. In that sense, SSRC is merely following Coca-Cola's lead by making the United States of America just another subsidiary, just another "area committee." All the globally competitive American corporations are all-out for multiculturalism, multiethnic staffs, a world without borders, and the latest high technology, no matter what its impact on human beings, something evident in their media advertising. "Oil for the Lamps of China" may have been Standard Oil's slogan for selling kerosene worldwide, but now Michael Jordan as the high-flying, globe-trotting logo for Nike might as well be the logo for America, Inc. (Jordan and his Chicago Bulls are particularly popular in "Communist China"—just as they are in my household.)

This is not a matter of the SSRC raising a challenge to the global corporation, which is hardly to be expected, but it is a matter of not abandoning hard-won scholarly knowledge and resources that we already have—and here I am not speaking simply of the existing area programs. Because of the ferment of the 1960s, social science scholarship of the 1970s met a high standard of quality and relevance. In political science, sociology, and even to some extent economics, political economy became a rubric under which scholars produced a large body of work on the multinational corporation, the global monetary system, the world pool of labor, peripheral dependency, and American hegemony itself. A high point of this effort was Immanuel Wallerstein's multivolume *Modern World-System*, but there were many others.

I would say that one of the shocks of my adult life was to see the alacrity with which many social scientists abandoned this political economy program, especially since the abandonment seemed roughly coterminous with the arrival of the Reagan and Thatcher administrations. Often the very social scientists who produced serious scholarship in political economy in the

1970s became the leaders of a march into the abstractions of rational choice and formal theory in the 1980s. One of the SSRC committees that sought to sustain this 1970s agenda was the States and Social Structures Committee (my bias: I was a member); it was summarily eliminated by a new SSRC president in 1991. Be that as it may, there remains a fine body of work in American political economy that could be the basis for a revival of scholarship on the global corporation and the political economy of the world that it creates before our eyes.

CONCLUSION

What is to be done? Immanuel Wallerstein recently offered some useful, modest suggestions, which I fully support: Encourage interdisciplinary work by requiring faculty to reside in two departments; bring faculty together for a year's work around broad themes; reexamine the epistemological underpinnings of the social sciences in the light of the eclipse of the Newtonian paradigm in the hard sciences; and reinvent a university structure still strongly shaped by the conditions of the eighteenth and nineteenth centuries.[84] I have some additional modest suggestions, in the interest of continuing discussion and debate:

1. Abolish the social sciences and group them under one heading: political economy (if economics will not go along, connect it to the business school).
2. Regroup area studies programs around a heterodox collection of themes that allow us all to stand "off center"[85] from our native home and the (foreign?) object of our scholarly desires.
3. Raise funds for academic work on the basis of the corporate identity of the university as that place where, for once, adults do not have to sell their souls to earn their bread, but can learn, write, produce knowledge, and teach the young as their essential contribution to the larger society.
4. Abolish the CIA, and get the intelligence and military agencies out of free academic inquiry.

Several commentators on earlier versions of this chapter thought I was being much too hard on the social sciences. Actually, I was being satirical; I don't expect anyone to follow my injunctions. Of course there is much scholarship of lasting value in the social sciences, and the subfields of historical sociology, comparative politics, and economic history are eminently worth preserving, from my point of view. But economic history has been abolished from most economics departments, and the formalist hounds are hot on the heels of the other two subfields. The point I stress is not my likes and dislikes, though, but rather that the historically limited and contingent theory of the rational, interest-maximizing individual is colonizing all the social sciences—and in so doing, abolishing them as creators of worthwhile knowledge, whether we like that outcome or not.

As we began this chapter with McGeorge Bundy, it is best to close it with one of the few scholars to speak out against the FBI purge in the early postwar period—and for his efforts, to suffer his due measure of obsessive FBI attention: historian Bernard A. DeVoto. In 1949 he wrote words as appropriate to that era as to the NSEA and the "globalized" world of today:

> The colleges . . . have got to say: on this campus all books, all expression, all inquiry, all opinions are free. They have got to maintain that position against the government and everyone else. If they don't, they will presently have left nothing that is worth having.[86]

8

EAST ASIA AND THE UNITED STATES:

DOUBLE VISION AND HEGEMONIC EMERGENCE

In the first chapter, I argued that Japan nested through almost all of the twentieth century in an international structure that offered first England and then the United States a diffuse, outer-limit leverage over its behavior. An American nest has also sheltered South Korea and Taiwan since 1945. In this concluding chapter, I suggest that this structure will last at least into the first couple of decades of the twenty-first century.

Hegemony is the name of the American game, but hegemony is a complex human practice and therefore cannot be defined precisely.[1] Our world has a hierarchical structure where those on top get the most of what there is to get, but the hierarchy is by no means one of domination, subordination, direct dependence, closed opportunity for others, or a matter of winning all the time. (Obviously Japan was "winning" in trade for many years, but it was never, and is not, hegemonic.) One of the hardest things in understanding hegemony is to distinguish it from crude Hobbesian notions of power and to mark the critical turning point at which winning actually changes to losing. The "policy" of the hegemon often consists of establishing outer limits on the behavior of those within the hegemonic realm; the outer limits must be wide enough to allow talent to rise or the system will not last (it will polarize and explode), and it must be strong enough to prevent orientation away from the realm. But we can hardly call this humdrum day-to-day "policy," since the last structural change in the system of U.S.–northeast Asian relations came with the Allied victory in World War II and its consequences in the period 1945–1950, and this structure still defines the situation today.

Hegemonic power is ultimately conditioned by technological and industrial power, which helps us understand its beginnings; that advantage is locked in by military power, which helps us understand the long middle years of a hegemonic cycle; and the requirements of military supremacy and a (probable) later tendency toward financial speculation and resultant capitalist torpor helps us grasp its decline.[2] But just as no episode of industrialization has been identical to a previous one (as Alexander Gerschenkron endeavored to teach us), so no two hegemonies are exactly alike: what happened to England may or may not help us to understand America's hegemonic cycle. Daniel Moynihan once said that we don't know how we achieve consensus but we certainly know when it is gone; similarly, there is no magic path to hegemony but we do know when it is gone. Indeed, we can date it precisely in our time: the baton was definitively passed from London to Washington when Dean Acheson got a message from the British Embassy in February 1947 saying that England could no longer defend Greece and Turkey, and he then walked off to a club for lunch, remarking to a friend that there were only two powers now (the United States and the USSR). If in the 1990s Japan's prime minister was bailing out Mexico or South Korea or choosing the new head of the World Bank or threatening Iraq with punitive sanctions, we would know that American hegemony had ended. Of course it hasn't: Japan is still a piker in the system of states and a cipher in the global regime of popular culture (which does so much to propel American influence around the world).

The strong system and the ideal hegemony, as Gramsci and any aristocrat worth his salt understood, is that realm in which people do the right thing out of habit, that is, by inhaling ethos, exhaling social action, and thinking that their action is voluntary and comes from within. The weak hegemony wields the knout and opens the jails and the gallows, a signal that power is unsure and defensive. (This is in fact no hegemony at all; imperative domination or subordination would be a better name.) Hegemony is signaled when people do what you want them to do, without having to be told or, better yet, asked. Japan, South Korea, and Taiwan have done what the United States wanted them to do for most of the postwar period: China moved dramatically away from its prior course and toward an American-shaped path since 1978, and the preeminent industrial power in northeast Asia, Japan, has followed either the Anglo-American core or the European continental alternative (e.g., the German model) in most of its industrial development since 1868.

Realms of autonomy open up within this international system, particularly for alternative organizational forms of capitalist profit making, just as bouts of inattention and fits of apparent or real decline affect the hegemonic power. As the American capacity unilaterally to manage the global system declined in the 1970s, a clear realm of enhanced autonomy did open for Japan, and instantly a new duality afflicted the U.S.-Japan relationship: Japan should do well, yes . . . but not so well that it hurt American interests. This is not, of course, a duality that the United States can dominate or control, since people are people, their comparative advantages come and go, and things change; it merely tells us that the U.S.-Japan relationship entered a new and less predictable phase. American thinking about Japan remains firmly within that duality today, a "double vision" symbolized by the inability of elites and pundits to do more than oscillate between lauding free trade and criticizing protectionism, between admiration for Japan's success and alarm at its new prowess.[3] Intellectually this takes the form of putative watershed divisions between Japanese and American capitalism. As there is much discussion lately about the ostensibly great or even "civilizational" divide between American and East Asian capitalism (state vs. market, Lockean liberalism vs. Confucian authoritarianism, individualism vs. the group life, etc.), here again I want to continue my discussion of the mainstream or "liberal" view of Japan.

The liberal view is not one held by an American known as a "liberal," such as Senator Ted Kennedy (although he may hold it). By liberal I mean the worldview of Anglo-Saxon positivism (Mill, Bentham, and all that), the idea that politics ought to be vote-driven, and the assumption that economic activity is or ought to be market-driven. We saw earlier that the liberal view in political economy has many American adherents. For the system of states, however, the liberal view is exemplified by Robert Scalapino, whose large oeuvre on the U.S.-Japan relationship operates on a discursive plane far removed from the fundamentals of this relationship. Speaking usually in the passive tense, a tense where the "agent" gets to act without regard to the "principal" and vice versa, Scalapino finds things happening over time in this relationship that may occasion a smile here and a frown there—here a shimmer and there a sunspot—but from 1945 to the present the U.S.-Japan relationship mostly yields a twinkle in his eye.

In a locus classicus for this liberal optic circa 1977, Scalapino finds a Japan firmly committed to internationalism and to the internationalist ideology of those years, called trilateralism.[4] If some analysts fret about a return to "xenophobia and exclusiveness," he wrote, and others about a declension to "continental involvement" (connoted in 1977 as "Pan-Asianism"; 399), any Japanese venture in such directions would be "hopelessly unrealistic" (407).

Every once in a while, Scalapino delivers himself of a value judgment, however, for example, in the second sentence of this same essay: "In the early nineteenth century, the Japanese islands were in a remote, nearly inaccessible part of the world, totally removed from a larger economic or political context" (391).

It is my belief that the Japanese islands were located then exactly where they are now, but that is not the Eurocentric picture—and thus Perry's black steamships can "discover" Japan in 1853, etcetera. Scalapino's essays rarely tell the reader why things happen in this relationship; they just happen, with no particular origin and no particular structure. This all-seeing liberal eye floats above the realities of postwar U.S.-Japan relations on a discursive plane that reflects only what it wishes the reader to see (with some subjects placed front and center and others in the shade). I do not mean to single out Scalapino; his essays on this theme are representative of (and often better than) a vast policy-related literature that could reverse all the valences of approval/ disapproval the minute Washington or Tokyo acted to change the fundamentals hammered out after World War II. Perhaps the best proof of this point is that no Japanese, no matter how pro-American or committed to internationalism, can write with the same blithe disregard for origin and structure.

Thus in the same 1977 volume we find mainstream political scientist Seisaburo Sato saying that nineteenth-century Japan was indeed remote—to the Western powers—and therefore too remote and too unpromising "to subjugate effectively" (Perry may have "discovered" Japan, but all he wanted was coaling stations).[5] This idea, of course, is part of the world-system dictum that the imperial powers winked at Japan enough to energize its reformers, but the imperial glare was not strong or sustained enough to incorporate Japan, and therefore Japan got the precious systemic "breathing space" that E. H. Norman was the first to highlight, and that distinguishes Japan from China and Korea in the modern period.[6]

From Sato we learn also of a regime of technology and resources, in which for most of the twentieth century Japan has been dependent on advanced Western technology, for all of the postwar period has depended on the United States for its defense and its military technology, and for all of this century has depended on crucial imported raw materials, especially oil. And here we get a punchline: according to Sato, it was oil that made the difference in Japan's singularly autonomous foreign policy decision, namely, the "move south" in July 1941 that culminated in Pearl Harbor. In 1977 Sato thought that Japan remained a fundamentally weak country among the hallowed circle of advanced industrial states, and could not *but* cooperate in any regime the other powers developed, whether trilateralism, Nafta-APEC, the newly formed World Trade Organization, or something else. Scalapino's docile and compliant Japanese foreign policy becomes Sato's "irresponsible immobilism"—"ad hoc, reacting, and equivocating."[7] (It is well to remind the 1990s reader who watched Japan's catatonia at the time of the Gulf war or Prime Minister Hosokawa's hand-wringing or Prime Minister Hata's empty rhetoric about Japan becoming a "normal power" or Prime Minister Murayama's "socialist" recapitulation of all three, that Sato wrote these lines more than two decades ago.)

Sato also had a mathematically precise conception of Japan's place in the twentieth-century hierarchy of states: number eight after it defeated Russia in 1905, number three under the Washington system of the 1920s, and number two (maybe) in 1977. Furthermore, he wrote, Japan almost always sought an alliance with a stronger industrial country: England from 1902 to 1923, the American-defined Washington System from 1922 to 1931, Germany from 1940 to 1945, and the United States throughout the postwar period (379). We have seen these same emphases in the work of Akira Iriye.

Earlier in this book, I argued that if we excavate "Japan as number two" in the international realm, where states are arrayed in a hierarchy of power, sometimes known as the balance of power, and states are both autonomous and penetrated (their state structures being the outcome of both domestic and international forces), we get the structure of a world system in which Japan has played an important but always secondary part. Let us revisit the archaeological timelines of Japan in the twentieth-century system:

A. 1900–1922: Japan in British-American hegemony

B. 1922–1941: Japan in American-British hegemony

C. 1941–1945: Japan as regional hegemon in East Asia

D. 1945–1970: Japan in American hegemony

E. 1970–1990s: Japan in American-European hegemony

There are always problems with a division of human history by years and decades; I am just as capable as the reader in pointing out inconsistencies or errant facts in this one (and there are many in the decade of the 1930s). Like any other division into decades, this one is driven by a conception more than by daily empirical fact. For my purposes here, the schema has the virtue of highlighting the long-running trilateral partnerships that Japan joined (like it or not), which corresponded to the rising and declining phases of transitional hegemonies (1902–1947 for England, 1970–20?? for the United States).

The American trajectory is instructive for grasping the historical system known as hegemony and the turning point in the early 1920s that Iriye connoted as "the Washington system." By 1900 if not earlier the United States was the dominant industrial power in the world. It is only in 1941, however, that we can see a conscious American drive to hegemony under Roosevelt, and only in 1947 did the United States finally replace England as the hegemonic power (with no terrible result for England, just an American-cushioned decline to the point where now the only English comparative advantage appears to be the editorships of American intellectual magazines).

As I have argued elsewhere,[8] the dynamic mechanism that moves within the hegemonic nesting both temporally and geographically is the product cycle, a constant motion of industrial and technological innovation and decline: American rolling stock in Manchuria in the 1910s, American technology in Japanese mines in the 1920s, American-blueprinted refineries in Wŏnsan, Korea, in the 1930s, American steel and electronic technology in Japan in the 1950s, Japanese light electronic technology in Korea in the 1960s, Japanese steel technology in P'ohang, South Korea, in the 1970s, Japanese technology solicited by North Korea to renovate old American mines in the 1980s, Japanese technology in Manchuria in the 1990s. Because Japan has been the core of this regional product- and technology-proliferation system, some analysts such as Kaname Akamatsu came to see it as the lead goose in a flying formation of nearby geese. It was a truth, but only a partial truth. It is true only if one's optic misses the real lead goose or the ceiling above which the regional formation does not fly. And here, of course, we can see why the "flying geese" formation much talked about in the early 1990s was not the Greater East Asia Co-Prosperity Sphere revisited, and will not be until the world (and not just Korea or Taiwan or Thailand) sources its technology from a hegemonic Japan.

In 1941 the lead goose invoked the outer limits of its hegemonic power by embargoing oil to Japan, which came as a tremendous psychological shock and made its leaders assume that the only alternative was war. Yet even in the midst of that terrible war, the leaders of Japan's "New Order" complained that Anglo-American ideas "cling to us like fleas," and there never was substance to either the philosophy or the reality of the "Co-Prosperity Sphere."[9] You had to go all the way to Burma to find an Asian people that bought Japan's wartime ideology (perhaps it looked good only at a great distance from Japan's risen sun). As H. D. Harootunian has pointed out, Imperial Japan's ideologues failed miserably at a subjective or *shutaisei* (*chuch'esŏng* in South Korean, *juche* in North Korean) program for being both Asian and modern at the same time.[10]

THE GREAT CRESCENT AND THE KENNAN RESTORATION

The definition of Japan's place in the postwar world occurred in the period 1947–1950 and still governs the situation today. It was in that period that the tectonic plates of the international structure found their resting place after the earthquake of World War II. Dean Acheson, George Kennan, and John Foster Dulles—to take three of the most important American planners— wished to situate Japan structurally in a global system shaped by the United States, so that Japan would do what it should without having to be told—by remote control, as it were. In so doing they placed distinct outer limits on Japan's behavior, and these limits persist today.[11]

Japan was demilitarized and democratized during the early Occupation years, if with less thoroughness than the proponents of the policy had hoped for. It is thus proper to view the years 1945–1947 as an exception to the general thrust of American policy toward Japan in the postwar period, a policy elaborated during the war years by Japanophiles in the State Department who looked forward to reforms that would quickly restore Japan's position in the world economy and that would not penalize Japan's industrial leaders for their support of the war. Indeed, these plans got going within six months of Pearl Harbor, illustrating the point that 1941 was a brief, temporary hiatus in the general pattern of hegemony in East Asia.[12] It is also important to remember, however, that the twin goals of democratization and demilitarization were not antithetical to the subsequent strategy,[13] but in fact represent the extraordinary reach of American hegemony in the late 1940s: restructuring both the world system and the internal political economies of major industrial competitors Japan and Germany (something that England tried but failed to do in regard to Germany after World War I).

The United States was the one great power with the central economic, financial, and technical force to restore the health of the world economy. Although hegemony usually connotes "relative dominance" within the group of core states, as we have seen, by 1947 it was apparent that the United States would have to exercise unilateral dominance for some time, given the gross asymmetry between the robust American industrial system, then producing half of all the world's output, and the poverty of nearly all the others. It was this critical problem of industrial revival, spanning Western Europe and Japan, that detonated basic shifts in 1947; the so-called reverse course in Japan was thus an outcome of global policy—as William Borden has aptly demonstrated. The new goal was the reconstitution and flourishing of the German and Japanese industrial economies, but in ways that would not threaten hegemonic interests.[14] But the revival of Axis industry also spelled out a new regional policy.

Soviet-American conflict in central Europe had erected barriers to almost any exchange, a great divide known to Americans as the Iron Curtain. This sliced up marketing and exchange patterns that had underpinned important regional economies. The bulwarks dropped across the central front in Europe, and the developing cold war in Asia cut off the Western European and Japanese economies from peripheral and semiperipheral sources of food, raw materials, and labor: in Eastern Europe, grain from Poland and Hungary, meat and potatoes from Poland, oil and coal from Rumania and Silesia; in East Asia, rice and minerals from Korea, sugar from Taiwan, coking coal and soybeans from Manchuria, tungsten from South China. With the European recovery so sluggish, Japan still dormant, and communist parties threatening in Italy and France, China and Korea, this structural problem was newly perceived and demanded action in 1947. The East Asian expression of this policy had an elegant metaphor.

The foundation of "containment" in East Asia was a world economy logic, captured by Dean Acheson's notion of a "great crescent" stretching from Japan through Southeast Asia and around India, ultimately to the oil fields of the Persian Gulf.[15] Although containment was thought to be preeminently a security strategy against communist expansion, in East Asia it mingled power and plenty inextricably. To complement and to achieve their security goals, American planners envisioned a regional economy driven by revived Japanese industry, with assured continental access to markets and raw materials for its exports. This would kill several birds with one stone: it would link together nations threatened by socialist state-controlled economies (containment), make Japan self-supporting (not incontinent), weave sinews of economic interdependence with Japan and the United States (plenty), and help draw down the European colonies by getting a Japanese and an American foot in the door of the pound and franc blocs in Asia (power and plenty).

The archaeology of Acheson's great crescent thus uncovers a world-system conception of multiple, overlapping tripartite hierarchies: the United States was the dominant core economy in the world; Japan and Germany would underpin regional core systems and help reintegrate peripheral areas as exclusively held empires disintegrated. The "high-tech" industries of the 1940s, represented in world-competitive American firms like Westinghouse, General Electric, IBM, General Motors, Ford, Lockheed, and the multinational oil firms, had nothing to fear from Japan and Germany as long as both countries were kept on political, technological, defense, and resource dependencies. As the Rooseveltian design of enmeshing the Soviet Union in the world economy failed, Acheson and others devised a second-best strategy of regional concentrations of strength within the noncommunist "grand area" to forestall the greater catastrophe of further expansion by exclusively held, independent, state-controlled socialist economies. (Of course, they were also dead set against a less formidable type of political economy, the nationalist autarkies of the 1930s.)

After the victory of the Chinese revolution, the search for Japan's hinterland came to mean mostly Southeast Asia, but in 1947–1948 Korea, Manchuria, and north China were all targets of potential reintegration with Japan. In a stunning intervention at the beginning of the famous "fifteen weeks" that inaugurated the Truman Doctrine and the Marshall Plan, Secretary of State George Marshall himself scribbled a note to Acheson that said, "Please have plan drafted of policy to organize a definite government of So. Korea and connect up its economy with that of Japan," a pearl that cannot be brought to the surface and examined without demolishing much of the diplomatic history on Korea in this period.[16] It captures pithily and with foresight the future direction of U.S. policy toward Korea from 1947 to the normalization with Japan in 1965.

The irony, of course, is that Japan never really developed markets or intimate core-periphery linkages in East and Southeast Asia until the 1960s. It was the Korean War and its manifold procurements, not the "great crescent," that pushed Japan forward along its march toward world-beating industrial prowess (indeed, Chalmers Johnson has called the Korean procurements "Japan's Marshall Plan"). A war that killed three million Koreans was described by Prime Minister Yoshida as "a gift of the Gods,"[17] giving the critical boost to Japan's economy; the Tokyo stock market fluctuated for three years according to "peace scares" in Korea. Yet the logic of an Asian hinterland persisted through the Korean War; it is remarkable to see how vexed the Eisenhower administration still was with "the restoration of Japan's lost colonial empire."[18] Ultimately this logic explains the deep reinvolvement of Japanese economic influence in Korea and Taiwan from the 1960s onward, as we will see.

In short, Japan in the postwar period has been a workshop of the world economy. Japan's sun was to rise high but not too high; high enough to cause trade problems for the allies in declining industries (textiles, light electronics, automobiles, steel), but not so high as to threaten leading-edge industries, let alone confer comprehensive industrial advantage. The logic for such a policy was hammered out in 1947, coterminous with the emergence of the cold war, and it deepened as Japan benefited from America's wars to lock in an Asian hinterland for Japan and the "free world" in Korea and Vietnam. For the next quarter century, Japan was a dutiful American partner, and America was tickled pink at Japan's economic success; American planners may have fretted about Japanese, Korean, and Taiwanese import substitution and the strong roles for the state in their economies, but the United States supported and indulged these same northeast Asian allies with massive and unprecedented transfers of technology and capital.[19]

Historians such as John Gaddis have spoken of a "long peace" in the postwar era, but they neglect the security underpinnings of that peace in a system of *dual containment:* containment of the communist enemy and of the capitalist ally. Here was what I have called "the Kennan Restoration." George Kennan played the key role in conceiving the logic of this security structure, first in papers done in 1947, and then in long negotiations with MacArthur in Tokyo in 1948. The real reason for the long peace between the superpowers was that the Soviet Union shared hidden American security goals to a much greater degree than is generally recognized. Stalin's doctrine, which became the life-long doctrine of Foreign Minister Andrei Gromyko, was to contain not just the United States, but also any hint of revanche in Germany and Japan. While the United States laid siege against the Soviet bloc, Moscow laid siege against West Germany (360,000 Soviet Army troops in East Germany) and against Japan (10,000 soldiers on windswept Iturup Island, plus large deployments in the Kamchatka Peninsula region).

Thus when the United States found itself in the best of all possible worlds in the 1990s, having won the cold war but still retaining significant leverage vis-à-vis Germany and Japan, it was not by accident, because the cold war consisted of two systems: the containment project, providing security against both the enemy and the ally, and the hegemonic project, providing for American leverage over the necessary resources of our industrial rivals. Both the hegemonic project and the allied-containment system survive—even flourish—today.

The postwar settlement is also the reason why northeast Asia, when compared to Europe, has so few multilateral institutions and mechanisms today, with even fewer through most of the postwar period. There was and is no NATO and no OSCE; the OECD (Organization for Economic Cooperation and Development) was remote, and the United Nations was an American operation in East Asia. This outcome was the result of a unilateral American military occupation of defeated Japan in 1945, followed within five years by a general division of the region corresponding to the bipolar structures of the cold war. General Douglas MacArthur issued General Order Number One on 15 August 1945, excluding allied powers from the occupation of Japan, dividing Korea at the thirty-eighth parallel and Vietnam at the sixteenth parallel, and seeking to unify China under Chiang Kai-shek's rule by requiring Japanese soldiers to surrender to Nationalist forces. The only part of that East Asian military division that did not hold was China, and as the communists cleared the mainland in 1948–1949 a new division took place, that between Taiwan and the mainland. MacArthur ruled Japan as a benevolent emperor, while policing the fault lines of great power conflict in Korea and China.

The Korean War erupted in June 1950, resulting in a vastly deepened division of northeast Asia. A heavily fortified demilitarized zone replaced the thirty-eighth parallel in Korea and remains to this day as a museum of the defunct global cold war; the two Koreas remade themselves as garrison states, with very high ratios of military-to-civilian population. For a generation China was excluded from the postwar global system by blockade and war threats. Japan also remilitarized, if modestly, as a result of the Korean War. Above all, the Korean War left an archipelago of American military installations throughout the noncommunist part of the region, bases like those in South Korea and Okinawa that hold one hundred thousand troops, and which are rarely discussed in the literature. Yet they are the coercive structure that locked in the American position in northeast Asia, offering a diffuse leverage over allies that I once likened to "a light hold on the Japanese jugular."

The long-term result of this American unilateralism may be summarized as follows: The capitalist countries of the region tended to communicate with each other *through the United States*, a vertical regime solidified by bilateral defense treaties (with Japan, South Korea, Taiwan, and the Philippines) and conducted by a State Department that towered over the foreign ministries of these four countries. All became semisovereign states, deeply penetrated by American military structures (operational control of the South Korean armed forces, Seventh Fleet patrolling of the Taiwan Strait, defense dependencies for all four countries, military bases on their territory) and incapable of independent foreign policy or defense initiatives. All were in a sense contemporary "hermit kingdoms" vis-à-vis each other, if not in relation to the United States.

The capitalist countries "communicated" with the communist countries primarily through the American military, symbolized by the military talks at P'anmunjŏm, minicrises like Quemoy and Matsu in the Taiwan Straits, the developing war in Vietnam, periodic fracases with North Korea (the seizure of the *Pueblo* in 1968, the downing of an EC-121 plane in 1969, the "tree-cutting incident" in 1976), and all-round containment of the (relatively weak) Soviet position in northeast Asia. There were minor demarches through the military curtain beginning in the mid-1950s, for example, low levels of trade between Japan and China or Japan and North Korea. But the dominant tendency until the 1970s was a unilateral American regime heavily biased toward military forms of communication and correspondingly biased against the multilateral mechanisms that emerged in Europe.

There was no NATO. There was a SEATO, but it never amounted to much, never spawned a "NEATO," and died after two decades. There was a rump Marshall Plan (the ECA, or Economic Cooperation Administration, which aided South Korea and Taiwan from 1947 onward). Like the Marshall Plan itself, it was superseded by the revival of the advanced industrial economies, in this case the only one in the region, Japan. Still, until the mid-1960s the political economy of the region was primarily bilateral with the United States, with the smaller countries sustained by American bulk aid grants (five-sixths of ROK imports in the late 1950s, for example).

JAPAN IN NORTHEAST ASIA, 1960S–1990S

The decade of the 1960s was a watershed in beginning the transformation back to "normality" of the northeast Asian system. Thenceforth and down to the present, economic exchange would be the driving force restitching ties among the nations of the region. The Kennedy administration was pivotal in this regard, inaugurating many policies directed toward drawing down the

multifurcated military structures and bringing into play new economic relationships. In some ways, this was a fulfillment of Acheson's "great crescent"
conception linking Tokyo, "island Asia," and the Middle East, which was
temporarily demolished by the North Korean invasion in 1950; in other
ways, it anticipated changes later implemented by the Nixon administration, especially the Nixon Doctrine and the opening to China. It was also in
the Kennedy period that for the first time American leaders began criticizing
Japan for its "free ride" in security affairs.[20] (It is daunting to realize that this
rhetoric is now about to enter its fourth decade, with Japan still recalci-
trantly limiting defense spending to about 1 percent of its GNP, and with
American politicians still carping about it.)

The leitmotif of Kennedy's strategy, one scripted by national security advisor W. W. Rostow, was to bring Japan's economic influence back into the
East Asian region. This resulted in the normalization of Japan-ROK relations
in 1965 (under enormous American pressure), and both Taiwan and South
Korea began industrializing under the banner of export-led development,
typically using obsolescent Japanese light-industrial technology.[21] Now the
International Monetary Fund and the World Bank became involved in a kind
of transnational planning that was particularly evident in the case of South
Korea's second five-year plan in the mid-1960s, its recovery from the export-
led doldrums in the mid-1980s, and the IMF bailout in 1997–1998. Nixon
opened relations with China in 1971, initially to draw down American involvement in the Vietnam War and to contain communism by communism,
but after the normalization of relations and the epochal reforms instituted by
Deng Xiaoping (both policies were decided in December 1978), the economic
character of China's interaction with East Asia and the world economy became dominant. Once again, in came the World Bank and the IMF, this time
to help reform a communist economy. The 1990s have seen the further inclusion of Vietnam and an attenuation of North Korea's economic isolation
through joint ventures and limited foreign investment. Since the mid-1960s,
in short, economic forces drove past or ran roughshod over the previously
impervious security barriers hardened by the Korean War. Japan has been the
major regional leader in providing that economic force, but it is still not close
to being the regional political or military hegemon. Indeed, the American
cold war military structure still holds down regional security, even as the
cold war's abrupt end fades into history.

The temporary result of the 1985 Plaza Accord (which greatly boosted the
yen's value) was a vastly enhanced Japanese position in Southeast Asia (in
1989 Japanese firms on average opened one new factory for every working
day in Thailand). All this seemed to suggest that if any tightly linked interdependence emerged it would be Japan-led, predictably raising again the specter

of the Greater East Asian Co-Prosperity Sphere.[22] This was merely another round in the typically overblown and alarmist reactions that have greeted every Japanese emergence in the Western mind; in fact, Japanese investment maintains a global rather than purely regional direction, and when Thailand and Indonesia faced collapse in 1997–1998, it was the United States and U.S.-led organizations like the IMF that bailed them out.

Even today, when compared to the European Community, northeast Asia lacks intense horizontal contact and continues to do without the expected multilateral institutions. The APEC council made a big splash at the Vancouver summit in November 1993 and its members account for 35 percent of world trade, but it remains a merely consultative grouping, a weak assemblage of eighteen countries that do not interact with each other well or often. (Malaysia's preferred option of an exclusive regional economic grouping generated a lot of heat and attention, but it is much less advanced compared to APEC; by 1999 it was going nowhere, while attracting the occasional attention of Japanese nationalists.) There is no equivalent to Nafta, but if a "Neafta" comes into being, it will most likely be an enlargement of Nafta to include selected northeast Asian or Pacific Rim economies. Thus it is right to conclude that the Asian "web of interdependence" is weak; "Asia appears strikingly under-institutionalized," without the "rich 'alphabet soup' of international agencies."[23]

Today the main organization linking the northeast region together is still the private business firm, and it is business firms that drive the dynamics of the region (e.g., in 1994 a huge coalition of American firms ended the Clinton policy of linking most-favored-nation status for China to its domestic human rights situation; in 1997–1998, large American banks rode herd on the rescheduling of debt throughout the region). There is nothing like the European Customs Union or the European Parliament or the Organization on Security and Cooperation in Europe (OSCE), although there was some activity toward creating an OSCE-like forum in the mid-1990s. Some observers also thought they saw a coalescence of the small states of ASEAN against Chinese military expansion, in the form of ARF, the Asian Regional Federation. But ARF is still not barking.[24]

Travel is no longer restricted for businesspeople traversing the East Asian region, but it is for ordinary citizens who may wish to go from Taiwan to China, or South Korea to China, let alone South Korea to North Korea and vice versa. External observers might think that China, Korea, and Japan are linked by a common written language in Chinese idiographs, but in fact the common language of the region is English. China uses simplified characters, whereas Taiwan does not; South Korea seeks to eliminate characters from its written language altogether, and North Korea did so in 1948. Meanwhile,

Japanese and Chinese are as different grammatically as two languages can be (by comparison, French, Italian, and Spanish seem like dialects of English). Even the presumed common cultural background in Confucianism does not create cultural ties between, say, Korea and Japan or Japan and China; the lingering animosities of colonialism and war, combined with the dominance of American mass culture, tend to override this traditional heritage and to make of northeast Asian popular culture a hodgepodge of national constructions united only by American-style pop songs and videos.[25]

Throughout the postwar period, as new work by Richard Samuels and others illustrates, the technological regime was one of the few places that Japan could seek autonomy, given that autonomy in the system of states was off-limits, thereby precluding to this resource-bereft island nation autonomy in regard to resources (and I don't even want to start with discursive autonomy,[26] which Japan has never achieved in the modern era). Japan therefore launched itself along the path of least resistance, assiduously acquiring and husbanding technology from the 1950s down to the present—with results even today that I view as decidedly mixed (Japan number one here, number two there, number three in the next place). Of course, this was only the path of least resistance relative to the others; the United States kept its best technologies from Japanese hands, just as Japan has long tried to keep its Asian neighbors on technological dependencies, and just as South Korea now tries to work North Korea into technological dependency via the light-water reactor controversy of 1994–1995 and other such means.

Although I do not have the space to prove my case here, I do not think Japan in the late 1990s is irreversibly or even significantly ahead of the United States in any important technology. Jean-Claude Derian saw this coming in 1990, a time when the Clyde Prestowitzes of the world were railing on about Japan's being ahead in every important technology and about to become the hegemonic power of the globe, if it wasn't already.[27] Derian expressed concern about America's technological lead in several areas, including semiconducters, supercomputers, gigaflop processors, high-definition television, and the airbus. Yet the Japanese lead in these areas has been overcome by now or no longer matters. In spite of these perceived problems, Derian was generally optimistic that the United States would retain or regain the global technological lead because of critical Japanese weaknesses in what he calls the "sheltered culture" of technology. He was right.

In the late 1980s, globe-straddling giant IBM seemed deeply threatened by Japan's NEC,[28] only to get savaged at home by small, entrepreneurial companies that put personal computers in everyone's office and home and supercomputers on the desktop in the 1990s. Boeing remains preeminent in global aircraft and has back orders well past the year 2000, in spite of much 1980s punditry about its inevitable decline. American computers are now faster,[29] American chips such as Intel's Pentium are better than the Japanese versions, and in software (which is after all the brains of a computer), the United States has a gigantic lead and a flagship monopoly every bit as good as Standard Oil or U.S. Steel in 1900—namely, Microsoft. Even American automobiles—even 1980s weak sibling Chrysler—are back.

Japan, Inc. has a weak scientific tradition, as Derian shows, with few Nobel prize-winners and significantly lower absolute levels of R & D expenditure when compared to the United States. It is in the "exposed" technological culture that Japan has done well, where the key is technical acquisition and product innovation rather than discovery of new technologies.[30] Furthermore, Derian argues, the United States held two trump cards that Japan did not. The first was its prowess in both the sheltered and the exposed cultures, a result in part of enormous American military-related spending. The second was its hegemonic birthright: the privileged position of the dollar as "the cornerstone of the world monetary system" (175). By allowing the dollar to decline, according to Derian, the United States rebuilt its exports and since 1985 has "forced the rest of the world . . . to share the cost of reestablishing the U.S. balance of trade" (267). Though many economists would quibble with Derian, he is right to point out that no other nation has seen prices of some of its exports decline by 50 percent in two years in its competitors' markets. Of course, his argument looked even better in 1995, as the dollar plunged to new postwar lows against the yen while central bankers filed their fingernails, or in 1998, when Clinton administration officials urged Japan to open more of its market and goose consumer spending. Even when the yen was at 80 to the dollar in 1995, yen-denominated world trade was a mere 9 percent of world foreign exchange, compared to 55 percent for the presumably mega-weak dollar;[31] by 1998 the dollar had waxed to the equivalent of 130 yen.

Above all, apart from the regional momentum of economic development, it is still the United States that drives the countries of the region together (or helps to keep them apart, as with North and South Korea). The APEC summit held in Vancouver in November 1993 reflected another lurch by Washington toward a "fundamental shift" in U.S. foreign policy from the Atlantic to the Pacific (the first try since MacArthur's era was during the Reagan administration in the mid-1980s), but the dominant tendency is more a diminution of Atlanticism than a real shift toward the Pacific. In March 1994, U.S. Treasury Department officials exuberantly compared the significance of the contemporary growth spurts in East and Southeast Asia to "the Industrial Revolution and the Renaissance," a rhetorical flourish showing that a little history is a bad thing. (The article admitted that "the finance ministers of these economies have never met all together in one room."[32]) In the same vein, the only tangible result of the November 1993 APEC meetings was that East Asian heads of state met with an American president in one room for the first time. This merely underlines the point that multilateral relations, even today, are still at an incipient stage in northeast Asia.

TWENTY-FIRST-CENTURY NORTHEAST ASIA:
"THE LINCHPIN THAT HOLDS JAPAN IN PLACE"

Simply because American hegemony has defined the region since 1945 does not mean it will continue to do so indefinitely. Indeed, many analysts see an impending shift in the balance of power in East Asia, which almost all of them lament—because they are Americans. The other side of this discourse is an ineffable triumphalism affecting almost everyone in 1990s America, beginning with superficial judgments about how the cold war was won, why the USSR collapsed, and what it all means for an American liberalism now said to be the solution to everyone's problems. (In a sense, the American gaze has temporarily lost its bifocal quality; the all-seeing liberal eye cannot find significant "difference" and therefore neither can the Pentagon, yielding marginally lower defense spending.) The American Century, thought to be waning in the 1980s, is once again at high noon. In many ways, the cold war ended in East Asia a generation ago (except for Korea), and tendencies already well under way in recent decades have merely deepened in the 1990s. But that does not stop American analysts—most of them from the *realpolitik* school—from smugness with regard to northeast Asia, either.

We can see it in Richard Betts's condescending statement, "So should we want China to get rich or not?", or his frank recommendation that Americans should continue being "voluntary Hessians" for Japan for "as long as possible," since the only alternative is for Tokyo to "start spending blood as well as its treasure to support international order," and when that time comes "it will justifiably become interested in much more control over that order." It is a lot better, in other words, if Americans police the world and let Japan remain, in Betts's words, "a uni-dimensional superpower"; otherwise, he says, mixing metaphors, "a truncated End of History in East Asia could be destabilizing rather than pacifying." Stability is equated with a revived American hegemony. Meanwhile the United States should continue enmeshing Japan in mechanisms of "neoliberal institutionalism."[33] The pièce de résistance, though, is Betts's assertion that "a China, Japan, or Russia that grows strong enough to overturn a regional balance of power would necessarily also be a global power that would reestablish bipolarity on the highest level" (74). In other words, no matter which of them came to commensurable power with the United States, that country would be our enemy.

Aaron Friedberg has also argued that the United States must remain the key player in East Asia; in spite of the end of the Soviet threat, it must keep its troops deployed in East Asia, because "American power is the linchpin that holds Japan in place."[34] Samuel Huntington characteristically outdid everyone else in claiming that continued American hegemony is not merely in the American interest, but also the world's: "No other country can make comparable contributions to international order and stability." Japan, however, is not to be trusted because it unremittingly pursues "economic warfare" against the rest of the world, and is, in his view, already dangerously close to hegemonic predominance.[35]

Yet Huntington's argument is yesterday's porridge. If in the recent past most American foreign policy analysts focused on Japan as the rising power—even on "the coming war with Japan"[36]—many now think China is more threatening. Here is Betts again: "The state most likely over time to disturb equilibrium in the region—and the world—is China." Betts seems to think that if current projections hold up, China will not only soon be rich, but will be "the clear hegemonic power in the region."[37] Pentagon planners, ever in search of enemies now that the USSR has disappeared, went so far as to suggest that American war plans be rewritten to target China and other Third World "renegade states."[38] A national public opinion survey conducted in late 1994 disclosed that while the American public still worried mightily about Japanese economic competition, only 21 percent of foreign policy elites thought likewise; many more elites worry about China's rise to global power.[39]

Once again, however, Japanese political scientists find it impossible to agree with the American realists. Takashi Inoguchi, like Sato and Iriye a well-known moderate, somehow found a way to voice what Betts and Huntington would prefer that we forget in the U.S.-Japan relationship. Inoguchi suggested, for example, that American hegemony will give way to a cooperative "bigemony" with Japan long before it devolves into serious conflict,[40] which would be the predictable result of declining hegemony, just as for decades England reached out to the United States for a partnership, thus to restrain the rising power. In the post–cold war era, Inoguchi found the United States seeking to use its security position to prolong its hegemony and to push for its own trade philosophy in northeast Asia.[41] In 1998 that was an understatement, as American officials sought to use the Asian crisis to rewrite the rules of economic exchange throughout the region. Inoguchi and other Japanese and Korean political scientists also have a far more benign view of China's contemporary emergence as a regional power; from the regional perspective, it is not such a terrible thing if Chinese military power balances Japanese economic power, since it is a guarantee that what happened in the 1930s will not happen again.

I have a different view from that represented by the assembled "realists" who have told us how much we will miss the bipolar stability and "long peace" of the cold war, some of whom are cited above. Elsewhere I have argued that if we go "back to basics," we can sketch a world system that for the first time since 1917 is structured as follows:[42]

—It is fully capitalist, there no longer being an effective socialist challenge or an alternative socialist common market.
—It has six advanced capitalist economies (the United States, Japan, Germany, England, France, and Italy) that are reasonably prosperous and cooperative, and that have no compelling revanchist grievances (unlike Germany at the end of World War I).[43]
—The main threat to the system, the cold war, is over, ending the system of bipolarity and carrying the potential for a truly plural world politics.
—A divided Europe and a divided Germany, both outcomes of the 1945 settlement and representing the greatest threat to peace throughout the cold war, are now reunited (or reuniting).
—The system has a United Nations that is fully inclusive and supported by the United States and Russia, and that in August 1990 successfully implemented a collective security response to Iraq's aggression and has followed that up with less effective but no less collective responses in Somalia and Bosnia and in regard to the problem of North Korean nuclear facilities.
—The Third World is fully decolonized, a process also set in motion by the end of World War I and greatly hastened by World War II, and has widely if not completely realized the principle of self-determination.

If we now look at the domestic scene, inside the nations that make up the world system, we find this:

—All the advanced industrial states are democracies, unlike the traditional autocracies in pre–World War I Western Europe, the post–World War I autocracies in Eastern Europe, or the dictatorships of the 1930s.
—Conflicts between capital and labor are by and large accommodated within established systems and mechanisms for negotiation and accommodation, especially when contrasted to pre–World War II class struggles.
—Ideological cleavages and swings are narrow compared to the pre–World War II situation, caught between a Left that cannot but accommodate to capital and a Right that cannot but accommodate to social welfare entitlements.
—In all the advanced industrial countries (if more so in Western Europe), various well-organized people's movements condition and constrain state power.[44]
—The ongoing technological revolution in communications has made each domestic economy acutely aware of its interdependence with other econo-

mies, symbolized by the twenty-four-hour stock market and the ubiquitous trope, "globalization."

Seven decades ago, after the terrible bloodletting of "the war to end all wars," Woodrow Wilson and V. I. Lenin offered competing models for a new world system, which nonetheless had much in common: both held to an internationalist vision, to opposition to Old World imperialism, and to self-determination for colonial peoples. Today Bill Clinton, Tony Blair, Gerhard Schröder, Japan's prime minister, and even Boris Yeltsin do not compete so much as unite on principles of internationalism, collective security, open systems, and a world under law—the latter being the personification of the unfulfilled vision of Wilsonian idealism.

Like the long peace of the nineteenth century, today we also find several great powers of roughly equivalent weight, with a stronger interest in creating wealth than in accumulating power. It is remarkable that in 1996, Britain, France, and Italy were all economies of about the same size, hovering around $1.1 trillion in purchasing-power-equivalent GDP; allegedly, gargantuan Germany was at $1.45 trillion.[45] Over time, Germany may come to dominate its historic terrain in Eastern Europe, but it will have many competitors: American, British, French, and Italian investors, not to mention Japanese and South Korean. In other words, it is unlikely that one nation will have its way in Europe, given that the other industrial economies, whether alone or in concert, are also formidable.

The domestic social configuration in the advanced industrial countries is also vastly different from what it was in the prewar period. The very idiosyncrasies through which the 1930s "withdrawals" from the world system were defined and that detonated fascist and communist revolutions in several explosive domestic configurations[46] no longer exist. The idiosyncrasies derived from different social formations in the various countries; if Japan and Western Europe's ultimate trajectory was liberal, that was not clear until 1945.[47] Until that time, liberal progressivism had to contend with romantic reaction on the Right and social revolution on the Left, both of them anti-market; out of this collision came Nazi Germany and militarist Japan. World War II finished off this conjuncture, however, leaving universal bourgeois democracy in Western Europe. Liberal hegemony had been realized, and the revolutionary prospect slowly faded away. I cite this analysis also to suggest why the "discourse of eternal mistrust" is likely to fade in regard to Japan and Germany: they had their democratic revolutions, even if it took World War II to produce them.

Realists, as we have just seen, have been quick to argue that "West-West" conflicts would quickly replace the East-West conflict,[48] and many others worry that Germany and Japan have not fully learned the lessons of their defeat in World War II,[49] or that intercapitalist rivalry will only be deepened by the end of the cold war, or that a "reemergent threat" (signified by the Pentagon as REGINT) will take over Russia. As of 1999, however, we cannot say that West-West conflict has deepened since 1989; rather, it has lessened. Germany and Japan have given little evidence that their postwar democratic revolutions are in jeopardy; the neo-Right in Germany is more worrisome than anything that has happened in Japan, however, where the cold war structure of conservative political rule collapsed in 1993, thus deepening Japan's democratic commitments and even bringing the eternally oppositional socialists to power (whereupon they jettisoned their socialism, which makes my point about a Left that cannot but accommodate).

In short, a "realistic" comparison of our 1990s world with that of the past seven decades illustrates why cooperation among the advanced capitalist countries is predictable, at least for the near term of the next decade or two. Changes in the structure of the world system since 1989–1991 have produced a world that corresponds to the one liberals always wanted to see, going back to Woodrow Wilson; therefore, global capitalism has as strong or stronger a "peace interest" today as it did in the nineteenth century, and the two combined make possible something that looks like a liberal world order—not vice versa.[50]

Realists also argued in the early 1990s that the world economy would separate into three great regional blocs.[51] But much of this commentary dissipated when Japan's bubble economy burst and Europe's vaunted "1992" turned out merely to be 1992; the European Community was never likely to be a regional economy to put the rest of the world in the shade anyway, and thus stir regional counteraction elsewhere. Furthermore, this community will be no larger (and probably smaller) than the combined markets of North America and the middle and laboring classes of Latin America, or the Pacific community embracing northeast Asia, capitalist-connected regions of China, the ASEAN countries, and Australia.[52] Movement toward enhanced integration has continued in Europe, of course, especially with the dawning age of the euro currency. But there is nothing to suggest that the European Community will cut itself off from non-European markets. All three great markets are and will be interdependent with each other, with everyone wanting access to each other's markets.

This is the essence of my argument about West-West cooperation in the post–cold war era. All we have so far in the way of evidence, of course, is the history of the years since the "revolutions of '89," but that history bears out the virtue of my position and that of Peter Katzenstein and other scholars who peer inside the "black box" of the nation—which hardly can be said for the predictions of the hard-nosed realists.

In this book, I have argued that Japan and its neighbors in northeast Asia (mainly Korea and Taiwan) have nested for most of this century in a Western hegemonic regime and are nowhere near the self-definition and comprehensive autonomy that local nationalists have long sought. How long this regime will last is not "anybody's guess," but will depend on when the United States truly enters its period of hegemonic decline and when, accordingly, Japan escapes from the postwar settlement. Both are, in other words, questions for the next century.

In the early and mid-1990s, East Asia appeared to see itself differently, as finally emerging from the American nest. In Japan, South Korea, and China, it was not hard to find a mirror image of American triumphalism, with many commentators dismissing the United States as yesterday's problem: a declining power, a decrepit economy, a mass culture that cannot compare to the heritage of East Asian civilization. China in particular chose to confront the United States on several issues in the mid-1990s, beginning with the glimmering possibility that Taiwan might once again gain substantial American and international recognition. The current Chinese regime, however, is every bit as ham-handed, brittle, and badly led an authoritarian system as that of Park Chung Hee in the 1970s; mistaking a newfound economic strength for real influence, it overplays its hand at almost every opportunity. The overwhelming influence on China is not its current political regime or its 1990s growth spurt, but the dramatic undertow and gravity of a world capitalist system finally getting its way in this vast and legendary market. Japan is far closer to hegemonic transition than is China and for many years to come will remain the most important factor in East Asia.

Still, though Japan crested to the top of the regime of technology for a period of years, it fell back and today appears as weak in relation to the United States as it was in 1975. If the archipelago of U.S. military bases in northeast Asia appears in the 1990s to have the classic attribute of the Schumpeterian definition of imperialism as an atavism, that is an illusion caused by our former fixation with containing communism. The Pentagon and its bases may indeed by Schumpeter's perpetual-motion machine, but they do have a function and it is not new: containing Japan, South Korea, and China.

American liberals may see sunspots when they gaze upon Japan, but imagine how the Japanese must feel, after a century of modernity and a very long but perpetually secondary role as an American partner. The United States is the only hegemonic power also to have been a continental economy, and it only fully completed its national market with the industrialization of the

Western states in World War II. From that standpoint, 1941 may indeed have been the beginning of the American Century (as Henry Luce had it), and American industry may still be driving Americans "from the rising to the setting sun," in John Fiske's words.[53] The sun that sets in the Seattle of Microsoft and Boeing rises in Japan's east, and a restless America is still there on the horizon, just as it was in 1853.

Notes

Introduction

1   Friedrich Nietzsche, *The Birth of Tragedy*, trans. Walter Kaufmann (New York: Vintage Books, 1967), 67.

2   James Fallows, *Looking at the Sun: The Rise of the New East Asian Economic and Political System* (New York: Pantheon, 1994), 179. On the book jacket is this blurb from John Judis of *The New Republic:* "As Tocqueville did for the French, James Fallows now does for Americans—explaining the validity of a new world to the old."

3   E. H. Norman, *Origins of the Modern Japanese State*, ed. John W. Dower (New York: Pantheon Books, 1975), 451.

4   Karl Marx, "Bastiat and Carey," in *The Grundrisse, Foundations of the Critique of Political Economy*, trans. Martin Nicolaus (New York: Vintage Books, 1973), 885–86.

5   Samuel Huntington, *The Clash of Civilizations and the Remaking of World Order* (New York: Simon & Schuster, 1996).

6   Friedrich Nietzsche, *The Genealogy of Morals*, trans. Walter Kaufmann (New York: Viking, 1969), 119.

7   Masao Miyoshi, *Off Center: Power and Culture Relations between Japan and the United States* (Cambridge: Harvard University Press, 1991); Roland Barthes, *The Empire of Signs*, trans. Richard Howard (New York: Noonday Press, 1983).

8   Barthes, *Empire of Signs*, 48.

9   Benedict Anderson, *Imagined Communities* (New York: Verso, 1991), 16.

10   See Bruce Cumings, "Chinatown: Foreign Policy and Elite Realignment," in *The Hidden Election*, ed. Thomas Ferguson and Joel Rogers (New York: Pantheon Books, 1981), 196–231.

11   I used the term "hegemonic discourse" in a lecture to a large group of Midwestern college professors from different disciplines in January 1998. When I was done, the first questioner asked why I used "conspiracy theory" in my work. I responded that I didn't. Whereupon the professor said, "But you said 'hegemonic discourse.'" This is by no means the only sign that the educators still need education.

12   Louis Hartz, *The Liberal Tradition in America: An Interpretation of American Political Thought since the Revolution* (New York: Harcourt, Brace, 1955).

13   *Novus ordo seclorum* is on the American national seal and the dollar bill, although in the latter case it resides under a cyclops eye hovering above a pyramid, a Masonic or

Illuminati symbol that has drawn the blank stares of American conspiracy theorists from the origin of the nation right down to the local-yokel "militias" that came to the media's attention in the aftermath of the 1995 bombing of the federal building in Oklahoma City.

14 Clemenceau once remarked that "America is the only nation in history which miraculously has gone directly from barbarism to degeneration without the usual interval of civilization."

15 Mike Davis, *City of Quartz: Excavating the Future in Los Angeles* (New York: Vintage Books, 1992).

16 Warren Susman, "The Smoking Room School of History," in Paul Buhle, ed., *History and the New Left: Madison, Wisconsin, 1950–1970* (Temple University Press, 1990), 44.

17 Marx, "Bastiat and Carey," 885.

18 Fredric Jameson, *Postmodernism, or, The Cultural Logic of Late Capitalism* (Durham: Duke University Press, 1991), xix.

1 ARCHAEOLOGY, DESCENT, EMERGENCE

1 Walter Benjamin, "Theses on the Philosophy of History," in *Illuminations*, ed. Hannah Arendt (New York: Schocken Books, 1969), 257–58.

2 Max Horkheimer and Theodor W. Adorno, *Dialectic of Enlightenment*, trans. John Cumming (New York: Continuum, 1990).

3 Immanuel Wallerstein, *Historical Capitalism* (London: Verso, 1983), 98.

4 Christopher Lasch, *The True and Only Heaven: Progress and Its Critics* (New York: W. W. Norton, 1991), 13.

5 Davis, *City of Quartz*, 12.

6 Alasdair MacIntyre, *After Virtue* (South Bend, Ind.: University of Notre Dame Press, 1981), 38.

7 Wallerstein, *Historical Capitalism*, 80–82.

8 Immanuel Wallerstein, *The Modern World-System*, Vol. 3: *The Second Era of Great Expansion of the Capitalist World-Economy, 1730–1840s* (New York: Academic Press, 1989).

9 MacIntyre has effectively done the latter, both in *After Virtue* (which is in many ways a polemic against the modern project via a polemic against Nietzsche, whom MacIntyre rightly takes to be the great interlocutor of the modern—see especially the chapter "Nietzsche or Aristotle?") and *Three Rival Versions of Moral Enquiry: Encyclopaedia, Genealogy, and Tradition* (South Bend, Ind.: University of Notre Dame Press, 1990). The three "versions" are euphemisms for empiricism, Nietzsche and his follower Foucault, and "Thomism" or Catholic thought.

10 This is a central point in the opening argument of MacIntyre's *After Virtue:* "What we possess . . . are the fragments of a conceptual scheme, parts which now lack those contexts from which their significance derived" (1–2).

11 I follow Gary Gutting's discussion in his *Michel Foucault's Archaeology of Scientific Reason* (New York: Cambridge University Press, 1989), 270–72. As he puts it, "The simultaneous application of archaeology to discursive practices . . . and to nondiscursive practices . . . enables Foucault to establish an essential symbiotic relation between knowledge and power" (271).

12 Edward Greer, *Big Steel: Black Politics and Corporate Power in Gary, Indiana* (New York: Monthly Review Press, 1979), 78–82.

13 Douglas MacArthur Archives, Record Group 6, box 78, Allied Translater and Interpreter Service, Issue no. 23, 15 February 1951, quoting original Korean and Russian documents captured in Wŏnsan.

14 These would be the William Randolph Hearsts, the Mills/Reid family of New York (Ogden Mills was Hoover's treasury secretary), the Fassett family of New York Republican fame, and the Adolph Coors family of Denver. See Bruce Cumings, *Origins of the Korean War* (Princeton, N.J.: Princeton University Press, 1990), 2:chap. 5. North Korea requested Japanese technological help for reopening Ŭnsan in April 1987, according to Economist Intelligence Unit, *Country Report: China, North Korea*, no. 2 (1987): 46.

15 Foster Bain, "Problems Fundamental to Mining Enterprises in the Far East," *Mining and Metallurgical Society of America*, 14, no. 1 (January 1921): 1–34. Also Boris P. Torgasheff, *The Mineral Industry of the Far East* (Shanghai: Chali Co., 1930), 131.

16 Carter Eckert, *Offspring of Empire* (Seattle: University of Washington Press, 1991).

17 See Robert S. Schwantes, "America and Japan," in *American–East Asian Relations: A Survey*, ed. Ernest May and James Thomson (Cambridge, Mass.: Harvard University Press, 1972), 112–16. General Electric, of course, provided everything from electric machinery to equipment to manufacture the lightbulbs; Kirin was based on the Spring Valley Brewery set up in Yokohama about 1872 by William Copeland. Marx thought Henry Carey was the only original American economist (see his essay "Bastiat and Carey," in *The Grundrisse* [New York: Vintage Books, 1973], 887); actually, Carey was a protectionist who learned much from Friedrich List, whose theories were also favored at the time in Japan.

18 Information from Angus Hamilton, *Korea* (New York: Charles Scribner's Sons, 1904).

19 Stuart Hall, "The Hinterland of Science: Ideology and the 'Sociology of Knowledge,'" in *On Ideology*, ed. Stuart Hall (Birmingham, England: University of Birmingham, 1978), 29–30. I am indebted to H. D. Harootunian for this reference.

20 See Alasdaire MacIntyre's commentary on Foucault's *L'Archeologie du Savoir* in *Three Rival Versions of Moral Enquiry*, 52; also Gutting, *Foucault's Archaeology*, who notes that *L'Archeologie du Savoir* provided "no serious discussion of the nature of the nondiscursive factors and of the influence they exert"; "there is no elucidation of the fundamental nature and ultimate significance of the link between the discursive and the nondiscursive" (259). There is also the "prediscursive," but I leave the difference between that and the nondiscursive to the Foucault specialists. Somehow, powerful forces in the nondiscursive or prediscursive shape discourse, and that is what I am interested in.

21 Of course, the modernization literature created by the Japanophiles of the 1950s and 1960s (Robert Ward, James Morley) dismissed the 1930s and 1940s as aberrational to the long march of Japanese progress, privileging instead the halcyon years of Meiji and "Taisho democracy." I argue a different point, that Japan in the 1930s and 1940s was aberrational in its relation to British-American hegemony; I would argue for continuity in Japanese imperialism from 1895 to 1945—as would any of Japan's neighbors.

22 For the postwar period see also Bruce Cumings, "Japan in the Postwar World System," in *Postwar Japan as History*, ed. Andrew Gordon (Berkeley and Los Angeles: University of California Press, 1992), 34–63.

23 Thomas Carlyle, quoted in Daniel T. Rodgers, *The Work Ethic in Industrial America, 1850–1920* (Chicago: University of Chicago Press, 1978), 230.

24 J. P. Morgan, quoted in Rodgers, *Work Ethic*, xiv.

25 Article from the *Edinburgh Review*, quoted in Jean-Pierre Lehmann, *The Image of*

Japan: From Feudal Isolation to World Power, 1850–1905 (London: George Allen & Unwin, 1978), 46.

26 Mathew Perry, *Narrative of the Expedition*, quoted in Peter Booth Wiley, *Yankees in the Land of the Gods: Commodore Perry and the Opening of Japan* (New York: Viking, 1990), 164.

27 Some British socialists, writing in 1897, quoted in Lehmann, *Image of Japan*, 120.

28 A missionary's observation (ca. 1900), quoted in ibid., 132.

29 Phillip Lyttleton Gell, quoted in Colin Holmes and A. H. Iron, "Bushido and the Samurai: Images in British Public Opinion, 1894–1914," *Modern Asian Studies* 14, no. 2 (1980): 304–29.

30 See Oliver Lodge, quoted in ibid., 321. Lodge was a Fabian.

31 Sidney and Beatrice Webb, quoted in J. M. Winter, "The Webbs and the Non-White World: A Case of Socialist Racialism," *Journal of Contemporary History* 9, no. 1 (January 1974): 181–92.

32 A British businessman, speaking in 1936, quoted in Isohi Asahi, *The Economic Strength of Japan* (Tokyo: Hokuseido Press, 1939), 207–209.

33 *Gazetta del Populo* (Turin), quoted in *Time*, 22 December 1941.

34 Ruth Benedict, *The Chrysanthemum and the Sword: Patterns of Japanese Culture* (Boston: Houghton Mifflin, 1946), 2.

35 General Douglas MacArthur, speech given in Seattle, Washington, 1951, quoted in Michael W. Miles, *The Odyssey of the American Right* (New York: Oxford University Press, 1980), 170.

36 Ezra F. Vogel, *Japan as Number One: Lessons for America* (Cambridge, Mass.: Harvard University Press, 1979), vii.

37 Ibid., viii.

38 Ezra Vogel, "Transcript of Seminar on U.S.–Japan Relations" (Harvard University, 1982).

39 Samuel Huntington, "Transcript of Seminar on U.S.–Japan Relations" (Harvard University, 1982).

40 Karel van Wolferen, *The Enigma of Japanese Power* (New York: Alfred A. Knopf, 1989), 9.

41 Ibid., 23.

42 Jude Wanniskie, "Some Lines on the Rest of the Millennium," *New York Times*, 24 December 1989.

43 Okita Saburo, quoted in Wiley, *Yankees*, 483. Okita is a former Japanese minister of foreign affairs.

44 Andrew J. Dougherty, "Japan 2000" (Rochester Institute of Technology, 1991, photocopy), 151. This is a summary of a 1990 project funded by the Central Intelligence Agency.

45 Quoted in J. M. Winter, "The Webbs and the Non-White World: A Case of Socialist Racialism," *Journal of Contemporary History*, 9, no. 1 (January 1974): 181–92.

46 Ishihara Shintaro, *The Japan That Can Say No* (New York: Simon & Schuster, 1991).

47 Hannah Arendt, paraphrasing Benjamin, in "Introduction," in Benjamin, *Illuminations*, p. 38.

48 Ibid.

49 Walter Benjamin, *Schriften* I, in ibid., 571.

50 Friedrich Nietzsche, *On the Genealogy of Morals*, ed. and trans. Walter Kaufmann (New York: Vintage Books, 1969), 77–78.

51 Michel Foucault, "Nietzsche, Genealogy, History," in *Language, Counter-Memory, Practice*, trans. Donald F. Bouchard and Sherry Simon (Ithaca, N.Y.: Cornell University Press, 1977), 139–64.

52 "The true picture of the past flits by," Benjamin wrote: "The past can be seized only as an image which flashes up at the instant when it can be recognized and is never seen again. . . . To articulate the past historically does not mean to recognize it 'the way it really was' (Ranke). It means to seize hold of a memory as it flashes up at a moment of danger" ("Theses," 255). See also Hayden White's critique of Rankean history in *Tropics of Discourse: Essays in Cultural Criticism* (Baltimore: Johns Hopkins University Press, 1978), 51–53.

53 MacIntyre, *Three Rival Versions*, 35. See also my discussion of Dean Acheson's "apprehension of imponderables" in *Origins of the Korean War*, 2:chap. 13.

54 Good examples may be found on the cover of *Fortune*, "The Big Split" (6 May 1991), and in George Friedman and Meredith Lebard, *The Coming War with Japan* (New York: St. Martin's Press, 1991).

55 Marx, "Bastiat and Carey," 887.

56 By 1894, American kerosene exports to Japan had reached 887,000 barrels of 42 gallons each. Standard entered the production field in Japan with its International Oil Company. See Harold F. Williamson and Arnold R. Daum, *The American Petroleum Industry, 1859–1899: The Age of Illumination* (Evanston, Ill.: Northwestern University Press, 1959), 675; see also *Sōritsu shichijū-shūnen kinen Nihon sekiyu shi* [Seventieth anniversary history of Japanese petroleum] (Tokyo, Nihon Sekiyu K. K., 1958).

57 James B. Duke formed British-American Tobacco in 1902, in league with a chief rival, the British Imperial Tobacco Company; Duke held two-thirds of the stock. By 1915, British-American Tobacco had almost $17 million in investments in China and was one of its two largest employers (Michael H. Hunt, *The Making of a Special Relationship: The United States and China to 1914* [New York: Columbia University Press, 1983], 282–83).

58 William Wray, "Japan's Big-Three Service Enterprises in China, 1896–1936," in *The Japanese Informal Empire in China, 1895–1937*, ed. Peter Duus, Ramon H. Myers, and Mark Peattie (Princeton, N.J.: Princeton University Press, 1989), 35, 57–59; see also Ramon H. Myers, "Japanese Imperialism in Manchuria: The South Manchurian Railway Company, 1906–1933," in ibid., 105–107.

59 Kiyoshi Kojima, *Japan and a New World Economic Order* (Boulder, Colo.: Westview Press, 1977), 14–15, 120–21; see also Hugh Patrick and Henry Rosovsky, eds., *Asia's New Giant: How the Japanese Economy Works* (Washington, D.C.: The Brookings Institution, 1976), 8–9.

60 Lehmann, *Image of Japan*, 128.

61 Ibid., 178.

62 Holmes and Ion, "Bushido and the Samurai," 320; also Winter, "The Webbs," 181–92.

63 Sidney and Beatrice Webb, quoted in Winter, "The Webbs," 188.

64 Holmes and Ion, "Bushido and the Samurai," 314, 328.

65 Ernest Edwin Williams, *Made in Germany* (London: William Heinemann, 1896), 8–9, 162–63.

66 See John W. Dower's introductory essay in *Origins of the Modern Japanese State: Selected Writings of E. H. Norman*, ed. John W. Dower (New York: Pantheon, 1975), 3–102.

67 Henry Stimson, *The Far Eastern Crisis* (New York: Council on Foreign Relations, 1936), 8–9, passim.

68 Guenther Stein, *Made in Japan* (London: Methuen & Co. Ltd., 1935), 188, 191, 205.

69 Asahi Shimbun, *Present-Day Nippon* (Tokyo: n.p., 1936), 23.

70 Ibid., 119. When I presented an earlier version of this paper in Paris, two French eco-

nomic historians exclaimed that I was wrong, that this could not be the case: Japan had
made no automobiles until the 1950s. The 1935 Datsun was important because it came
off an assembly line, but was by no means the first Japanese automobile: Isuzu and other
Japanese firms made autos in the teens of this century.

71 Jesse F. Steiner, *Behind the Japanese Mask* (New York: Macmillan, 1943). The com-
    manding interpretation of this dark period in U.S.-Japan relations is John W. Dower, *War
    Without Mercy: Race and Power in the Pacific War* (New York: Pantheon Books, 1986).

72 Terence K. Hopkins and Immanuel Wallerstein, "Patterns of Development of the Mod-
    ern World-System," *Review* 1, no. 2 (fall 1977): 120–21, 130–31.

73 For more elaboration see Bruce Cumings, "The Origins and Development of the North-
    east Asian Political Economy," *International Organization* (winter 1984): 1–40. Theo-
    retically this means that "the continued further mechanization of productive processes
    is linked to the continual redefinition of 'core'-type productive activities and the con-
    tinual relocation of core, semiperipheral, and peripheral zones" (Hopkins and Waller-
    stein, "Patterns of Development," 126).

74 Wallerstein, *Historical Capitalism*, 56–59.

75 Especially in Akira Iriye, *Across the Pacific: An Inner History of American–East Asian
    Relations* (New York: Harcourt, Brace, and World, 1967), his most brilliant and original
    book; but see also *Pacific Estrangement: Japanese and American Expansion, 1897–
    1911* (Cambridge, Mass.: Harvard University Press, 1972), *After Imperialism* (Cam-
    bridge, Mass.: Harvard University Press, 1965), and the deeply revisionist *Power and
    Culture: The Japanese-American War, 1941–45* (Cambridge, Mass.: Harvard University
    Press, 1981). All these books operate on the terrain of intercultural imagery and conflict.

76 Iriye, *Pacific Estrangement*, viii, 18–19, 26–27, 35–36. In fact, the United States was for
    the Japanese both "a model and an object of their expansion." Iriye has a remarkably
    benign view of both American and Japanese expansion, terming the former "peaceful"
    and "liberal" because it sought only commercial advantage—that is, what we call hege-
    mony (see 12–13, 36).

77 Iriye, *Power and Culture*, 1–2. From the Meiji Restoration to 1941, he writes, Japan
    wanted to integrate itself with the regime of the great powers, which he connotes as a
    policy of "international cooperation" or "interdependence."

78 Ibid., 3–4, 15, 20, 25–27. Iriye dates Japanese plans for an exclusive northeast Asian
    regional hegemony from 1936, but according to him it still did not have a blueprint in
    1939 and was dependent on the core powers in the system until the middle of 1941.

79 Ishii Kanji and Sekiguchi Hisashi, eds., *Sekai shijō to bakamatsu kaikō* [The world
    market and Japan's opening in the Bakamatsu period] (Tokyo: Tokyo Daigaku Shup-
    pankai, 1982); for an older Marxist interpretation, see Ishii Takashi, *Meiji ishin no
    kokusaiteki kankyō* [*The International Environment of the Meiji Restoration*] (Tokyo:
    Yoshikawa Kōbunkan, 1957). The latter views the famous American diplomat Town-
    send Harris as a representative of American commercial capital, which wanted Japan as
    a base for trading vessels in the Pacific; the British, however, wanted Japan as a market
    for British products, and because they were the dominant capitalist power, they even-
    tually got what they wanted in a revision of customs rates that gave England control of
    Japan as a market (371–72). See also Wiley, *Yankees in the Land of the Gods*, 482–500.

80 The standard work is Ian Nish, *The Anglo-Japanese Alliance: The Diplomacy of Two
    Island Empires, 1894–1907* (London: Athlone Press, 1966), and his second volume,
    Alliance in Decline: A Study in Anglo-Japanese Relations, 1908–1923 (London: Ath-
    lone Press, 1972).

81 Yasuoka Akio, "The Opening of Japan to the End of the Russo-Japanese War," in *Japan and the World, 1853–1952*, ed. Sadao Asada (New York: Columbia University Press, 1989), 94.

82 William Appleman Williams, *The Tragedy of American Diplomacy*, 2d ed. (New York: Delta Books, 1972).

83 Hunt, *Special Relationship*, 279.

84 Iriye, *Pacific Estrangement*, 47–48. Yale professor Trumbull Ladd, for example, sanctified Japan's reforming (if colonial) role in his *In Korea with Marquis Ito* (New Haven, Conn.: Yale University Press, 1908); the dominant diplomatic historian of the period, Tyler Dennett, and the well-known publicist George Kennan did the same.

85 Hunt, *Special Relationship*, 151–52, 198, 206–207, 209–10.

86 Charles E. Neu, "1906–1913," in *American–East Asian Relations: A Survey*, ed. Ernest R. May and James C. Thomson Jr. (Cambridge, Mass.: Harvard University Press, 1972), 155–72.

87 Hunt, *Special Relationship*, 211–14.

88 Neu, "1906–1913." The best study of the naval rivalry is William R. Braisted, *The United States Navy in the Pacific, 1909–1922* (Austin: University of Texas Press, 1971).

89 See Harry N. Schreiber, "World War I as Entrepreneurial Opportunity: Willard Straight and the American International Corporation," *Political Science Quarterly*, 84 (September 1969), 486–511; more generally, see Carl P. Parrini, *Heir to Empire: The United States Economic Diplomacy, 1916–1923* (Pittsburgh: University of Pittsburgh Press, 1969).

90 Williams, *Tragedy*, 78–84.

91 Iriye, *After Imperialism*, 10–22.

92 Hosoya Chihiro and Saitō Makoto, eds., *Washington taisei to Nichi-Bei kankei* [The Washington System and Japanese-American relations] (Tokyo: Tokyo Daigaku Shuppankai, 1978), introductory essay by Hosoya.

93 Chalmers Johnson, *MITI and the Japanese Miracle* (Berkeley: University of California Press, 1982); William Miles Fletcher III, *The Japanese Business Community and National Trade Policy, 1920–1942* (Chapel Hill: University of North Carolina Press, 1989).

94 Gō Seinosuke, formerly head of the huge Oji Paper Co. and director of the Tokyo Stock Exchange for twelve years, drafted a report in 1929 recommending, among other things, "a new national committee . . . to rationalize industrial production in order to 'aid industrial development' "; Gō endorsed the principle of export planning—selecting products that might sell well abroad and fostering their growth. The plan led to the Export Compensation Act of May 1930 and other measures to aid export industries; the plan was to increase export to Central America, Africa, the Balkans, "central Asia Minor," and the USSR, and it later expanded to include "the whole world except for Europe, the U.S., India, and the Dutch East Indies" (Fletcher, *Japanese Business Community*, 59, 61–62).

95 Fletcher, *Japanese Business Community*, 28.

96 Ibid., 2, 98–99.

97 Iriye, *Power and Culture*, 15.

98 A. M. Rosenthal, "MacArthur Was Right," *New York Times*, 19 October 1990.

99 Iriye, *Power and Culture*, 15, 25–27, 65, 81, 83, 97, 148–49.

100 I have written about this in my *Origins of the Korean War*, vol. 2, and in "Japan in the Postwar World System."

101 Horkheimer and Adorno, *Dialectic of Enlightenment*, 92.

1   Some scholars think that the Koreans, who gaze upon Japan from the West, were the ones who christened it Ilbon, that is, Nippon. See Bruce Cumings, *Korea's Place in the Sun: A Modern History* (New York: W. W. Norton, 1997), 38.

2   The theme of American exceptionalism is one of the oldest in American history. For recent discussions see Ian Tyrrel, "American Exceptionalism in an Age of International History," *American Historical Review* 96, no. 4 (October 1991): 1031–55; and Michael McGerr, "The Price of the 'New Transnational History,'" ibid., 1056–67.

3   Godfrey Hodgson, *America in Our Time* (New York: Random House, 1976), 113–14, 116–17.

4   Thucydides, *History of the Peloponnesian War*, trans. Rex Warner (New York: Penguin Books, 1954), 242–43.

5   Although this tradition is well-known in the West, the Eastern tradition is less so. For an excellent compendium of classical East Asian thought on warfare, its ends, and its means see Ralph D. Sawyer, trans., *The Seven Military Classics of Ancient China* (Boulder, Colo.: Westview Press, 1993), esp. 115–20.

6   Anatol Rapaport, "Editor's Introduction," in *On War*, by Carl von Clausewitz (New York: Penguin Books, 1968), 21. Rapaport's essay is quite brilliant and timely, even if written thirty years ago.

7   Carl von Clausewitz, *On War* (New York: Penguin Books, 1968), 101–102.

8   Rapaport, "Editor's Introduction," 14.

9   See Clausewitz, *On War*, 199–200, 366–67, and esp. 404–407.

10   Ibid., 108.

11   Swedberg, *Schumpeter*, 156–58.

12   See Quincy Wright, *A Study of War* (Chicago: University of Chicago Press, 1964).

13   Bernard Brodie, *War and Politics* (New York: Macmillan, 1973), 1–28.

14   Rapaport, "Editor's Introduction," 29; emphasis in original.

15   See Karl Polanyi, *The Great Transformation: The Political and Economic Origins of Our Time* (New York: Beacon, 1944), chap. 1; see also Charles Kindleberger, *The World in Depression, 1929–1939* (New York: Free Press, 1973).

16   Polanyi, *Great Transformation*, 27, 266–67.

17   For an extended argument on Japan as a "late" industrial and imperial power see Bruce Cumings, *Origins of the Korean War: Liberation and the Emergence of Separate Regimes, 1945–1947* (Princeton, N.J.: Princeton University Press, 1981), chap. 1.

18   Dower, *Origins*, 118, 144. Seisaburo Sato makes essentially the same point when he says that nineteenth-century Japan was too remote and too unpromising for the Western powers "to subjugate effectively." See Seisaburo Sato, "The Foundations of Modern Japanese Foreign Policy," in *The Foreign Policy of Modern Japan*, ed. Robert Scalapino (Berkeley and Los Angeles: University of California Press, 1977).

19   See Lloyd Gardner, *Economic Aspects of New Deal Diplomacy* (Madison: University of Wisconsin Press, 1964), 85–86.

20   Gareth Stedman Jones, "The History of U.S. Imperialism," in *Ideology in Social Science*, ed. Robin Blackburn (London: NLB, 1972), 216–17.

21   Richard Drinnon, *Facing West: The Metaphysics of Indian-Hating and Empire-Building* (New York: New American Library, 1980), xiii–xiv.

22   Quoted in ibid., 278.

23   Walter LaFeber, *The New Empire: An Interpretation of American Expansion, 1865–1898* (Ithaca, N.Y.: Cornell University Press, 1967), 69–71.

24 Clausewitz, *On War*, 101.

25 Michael Walzer, *Just and Unjust Wars: A Moral Argument with Historical Illustrations* (New York: Basic Books, 1977), 110. On the influence of Walzer's analysis in the United States see Jean Bethke Elshtain, ed., *Just War Theory* (Oxford: Basil Blackwell, 1992).

26 Walzer, *Just and Unjust Wars*, 58–63.

27 Ibid., 117–22; for my critique see Cumings, *Origins*, 2:chap. 22.

28 See Studs Terkel, *The Good War: An Oral History of World War II* (New York: Pantheon, 1984).

29 Nietzsche, *Genealogy of Morals*, 57–58.

30 Friedrich Nietzsche, *Beyond Good and Evil*, trans. Walter Kauffman (New York: Vintage Books, 1966), 80.

31 When new victims were needed, Unit 731 personnel called local police offices and said, "Send us a communist." See *New York Times*, 4 April 1995.

32 For an argument relating this vast, usually forced mobilization to the origins of the Korean national division and the subsequent civil war see Cumings, *Origins*, 1:chap. 2.

33 John Dower, "The Bombed: Hiroshimas and Nagasakis in Japanese Memory," *Diplomatic History* 19, no. 2 (spring 1995): 275; Richard H. Minear, "Atomic Holocaust, Nazi Holocaust," ibid., 347–66.

34 See Gordon Prange, *At Dawn We Slept: The Untold Story of Pearl Harbor* (New York: Penguin Books, 1981), 539.

35 Clausewitz, *On War*, 258–62.

36 Ibid., 397–98. He goes on, "Let us suppose a small State which is involved in a contest with a very superior power, and foresees that with each year its position will become worse: should it not, if War is inevitable, make use of the time when its situation is furthest from the worst? Then it must attack, not because the attack *in itself* ensures any advantages . . . but because this State is under the necessity of . . . bringing the matter completely to an issue before the worst time arrives" (398). This might be a primer for Admiral Yamamoto's Pearl Harbor strategy as outlined by Prange (*At Dawn We Slept*, 917, 98–106).

37 Clausewitz, *On War*, 258.

38 Seisaburo Sato, "The Foundations of Modern Japanese Foreign Policy," in Robert Scalapino, ed., *The Foreign Policy of Modern Japan* (Berkeley: University of California Press, 1977), 381; Ienaga Saburo, *The Pacific War* (New York: Pantheon Books, 1978), 132–33; Akira Iriye, *Power and Culture: The Japanese-American War, 1941–1945* (Cambridge: Harvard University Press, 1981), 31.

39 Jonathan Marshall, *To Have and Have Not: Southeast Asian Raw Materials and the Origins of the Pacific War* (Berkeley and Los Angeles: University of California Press, 1995).

40 See Cumings, *Origins*, 2:chap. 13.

41 Clausewitz, *On War*, 114–15, 128–29; U.S. State Department, Office of Chinese Affairs, box 15, "Two Talks with Mr. Chou En-lai," no date but probably late 1949, attached to document no. 350.1001.

42 Charles Beard, *President Roosevelt and the Coming of the War, 1941: A Study in Appearances and Realities* (New Haven, Conn.: Yale University Press, 1948), 244–45. See also Richard N. Current, "How Stimson Meant to 'Maneuver' the Japanese," *Mississippi Valley Historical Review* 40, no. 1 (1953): 67–74.

McGeorge Bundy, a collaborator with and sometime ventriloquist for Henry Stimson and a man responsible for using specious "incidents" to escalate the Vietnam War, made a remarkable slip in an article written on the fiftieth anniversary of Pearl Harbor: "We can say for Hiroshima that it put an end to the necessary war for which Pearl Harbor was the necessary ignition" (*Newsweek*, 16 December 1991). That is, the U.S.-Japan war was a necessary war; it was not made necessary by Pearl Harbor alone.

43 Friedrich Nietzsche, *Ecce Homo*, trans. Walter Kaufmann (New York: Vintage Books, 1969), 232.

44 Jean Bethke Elshtain, "Reflections on War and Political Discourse," in *Just War Theory*, ed. Jean Bethke Elshtain (Oxford: Basil Blackwell, 1992), 275–77.

45 Hannah Arendt, *The Human Condition* (Chicago: University of Chicago Press, 1958), 238–42, quoted in Elshtain, *Just War Theory*, 332 n.

46 Or, as Admiral Yamamoto Isoroku put it, "It is the custom of *bushido* to select an equal or stronger opponent" (quoted in Prange, *At Dawn We Slept*, 344).

47 Walzer, *Just and Unjust Wars*, 21.

48 Oppenheimer told Stimson in May 1945 that an atomic explosion "would be equivalent to about 2,000 to 20,000 tons of TNT." Barton Bernstein, "Understanding the Atomic Bomb," *Diplomatic History* 19, no. 2 (spring 1995): 234 n. The higher estimate proved accurate.

49 Journalist Kato Masuo, quoted in Michael Sherry, *The Rise of American Air Power: The Creation of Armageddon* (New York: Yale University Press, 1987), 276.

50 Tokyo police cameraman Ishikawa Koyo, quoted in Thomas Havens, *Valley of Darkness: The Japanese People and World War Two* (New York: University Press of America, 1986), which in turn is cited in Mark Selden's excellent essay, "The 'Good War' and the Logic of Exterminism" (forthcoming). I am indebted to Professor Selden for allowing me to cite this essay.

51 Sherry, *Rise of American Air Power*, 276.

52 Ronald Schaffer, *Wings of Judgment: American Bombing in World War II* (New York: Oxford University Press, 1985), 134.

53 Sherry, *Rise of American Air Power*, 277, 406; Selden, " 'Good War,' " has figures from various sources that range from 87,000 to 97,000 dead and upwards of 125,000 wounded.

54 Curtis E. LeMay with MacKinlay Kantor, *Mission with LeMay: My Story* (Garden City, N.Y.: Doubleday, 1965), 466–67.

55 Robert L. Holmes, *On War and Morality* (Princeton, N.J.: Princeton University Press, 1989), 117–32, 260–94. I am indebted to Michael Loriaux for calling this book to my attention.

56 Rapaport, "Editor's Introduction," 62–63. This is not the only point at which Rapaport adduces a similarity between Nazi and American exterminist doctrine (see 411–12).

57 See, for example, LeMay with Kantor, *Mission with LeMay*, 460–64, where (in 1965) LeMay tells crude jokes about "Japs" and "Chinamen" and writes that "human attrition means nothing to such people." In this passage, LeMay is talking about the Korean War, and no doubt such racist beliefs emboldened him to call for burning North Korea to a crisp as a means of ending the war overnight. Is it possible that even in this dull pit of a mind, a murmur of guilt over his legendary pyromania calls forth the reprehensible rationale So what? They don't care about human life anyway?

58 Committee for the Compilation of Materials on Damage Caused by the Atomic Bombs in Hiroshima and Nagasaki, *Hiroshima and Nagasaki: The Physical, Medical, and Social Effects of the Bombings*, trans. Eisei Ishikawa and David L. Swain (New York: Basic Books, 1981), 21–56.

59 Ibuse Masuji was the first to use the term *black rain* (*kuroi ame*) as a metaphor, in what Dower ("Hiroshimas and Nagasakis," 292) says is "without question the classic Japa-

nese literary reconstruction of the atomic-bomb experience." See Ibuse Masuji, *Black Rain*, trans. John Bester (Tokyo: Kodansha, 1969). There is also a well-known film version that came out in 1988.

60 Hachiya Michihiko, *Hiroshima Diary: The Journal of a Japanese Physician, August 6– September 30, 1945*, trans. Warner Wells (Chapel Hill: University of North Carolina Press, 1955), 14.

61 Committee for the Compilation of Materials on Damage, *Hiroshima and Nagasaki*.

62 Takashi Nagai, *The Bells of Nagasaki*, trans. William Johnston (Tokyo: Kodansha International, 1984), xviii. It is fitting that the first effective writing about Nagasaki after the easing of censorship in 1948 was by Takashi Nagai, a devout Catholic who also happened to be a medical specialist on radiology and who died of radiation poisoning in 1951. See Dower, "Hiroshimas and Nagasakis," 285. See also Takashi Nagai, *We of Nagasaki: The Story of Survivors in an Atomic Wasteland*, trans. Ichiro Shirato and Herbert B. L. Silverman (New York: Duell, Sloan and Pearce, 1951).

63 An early argument along these lines was made by G. E. M. Anscombe in an essay titled "Mr. Truman's Degree," which she wrote in protest of the honorary doctorate Oxford University bestowed on President Truman in 1957. See Thomas Nagle, "War and Massacre," in *War and Moral Responsibility*, ed. Marshall Cohen, Thomas Nagle, and Thomas Scanlon (Princeton, N.J.: Princeton University Press, 1974), 7. The change that occurred during World War II is easily visible in the protests that various governments, and especially the Roosevelt administration, directed at Japanese bombing of Chinese cities and Franco's bombing of Spanish cities (especially Guernica) in 1937–1939, before the global war began. Here is what the U.S. Department of State said about Japanese aerial bombing in 1937: "Any general bombing of an extensive area wherein resides a large population engaged in peaceful pursuits is unwarranted and contrary to principles of law and humanity."

64 The best account of how historians have thought about history (and about their calling) is Peter Novick, *That Noble Dream: The 'Objectivity Question' and the American Historical Profession* (New York: Cambridge University Press, 1988).

65 J. Samuel Walker, "The Decision to Use the Bomb," *Diplomatic History* 19, no. 2 (spring 1995): 321. Walker is the chief historian of the U.S. Nuclear Regulatory Commission.

66 Martin Sherwin, *A World Destroyed: The Atomic Bomb and the Grand Alliance* (New York: Knopf, 1975). For Sherwin's analysis of Nagasaki see 233–34.

67 Hans Bethe (foreword to Sherwin, *World Destroyed*) drew the conclusion that Nagasaki "was . . . unnecessary" (xiv). Other historians agree. For example, Barton Bernstein argues that without the Nagasaki bombing "Japan would have surrendered—very probably on the 10th [of August]" (Bernstein, "Understanding the Atomic Bomb," 255).

68 Herbert Bix, "Japan's Delayed Surrender," *Diplomatic History* 19, no. 2 (spring 1995): 201–203.

69 Ibid., 218 n. See also Bernstein, "Understanding the Atomic Bomb," 247. Bix and Bernstein both frame the issue as a narrow empirical one of how soon Japan would have surrendered if not for the bomb, instead of grasping the moral virtue that would come from restraining the hand of power.

70 Gar Alperovitz, *Atomic Diplomacy: Hiroshima and Potsdam*, rev. ed. (Boulder, Colo.: Pluto Press, 1994); Alperovitz, *The Decision to Use the Atomic Bomb* (New York: Knopf, 1995). The author's views may be sampled in Alperovitz, "Hiroshima: Historians Reassess," *Foreign Policy* 99 (summer 1995): 15–34. This argument has been vigorously contested in the careful archival work of Barton Bernstein. See, for example, Bernstein,

"Understanding the Atomic Bomb." Both Alperovitz and Bernstein have been pejoratively labeled "revisionist."

71 Alperovitz, "Hiroshima: Historians Reassess," 28–29.

72 Sherwin, *World Destroyed,* 67–68, 83–84.

73 David McCullough, *Truman* (New York: Simon & Schuster, 1992), 436–44.

74 See Barton Bernstein, "Misconceived Patriotism," *Bulletin of the Atomic Scientists* 51, no. 3 (May–June 1995): 4.

75 The most egregious example of this is Paul Fussell, *Thank God for the Atom Bomb and Other Essays* (New York: Random House, 1988).

76 A recent example is the front-page article, "Japan Expresses Regret of a Sort for the War," *New York Times,* 7 June 1995.

77 See Saburo Ienaga, "The Glorification of War in Japanese Education," *International Security* 18 (winter 1993–1994): 113–33.

78 Walker, "Decision to Use the Bomb," 322–26.

79 Harry S Truman, letter to Samuel McCrea Cavert, 11 August 1945, quoted in Bernstein, "Understanding the Atomic Bomb," 268.

80 Wallace diary, 10 August 1945, quoted in Bernstein, "Understanding the Atomic Bomb," 257.

81 Robert Lifton, *Death in Life: Survivors of Hiroshima* (Chapel Hill: University of North Carolina Press, 1991), 14. I know of no better statement on the immorality of nuclear war and its inevitable exterminism than the *Pastoral Letter on War and Peace* produced by the American Catholic Bishops in 1983. For an excerpted version see Elshtain, *Just War Theory,* 77–168. Because the nuclear era raises the possibility of annihilating all human life, the bishops wrote, "we read the book of Genesis with a new awareness; the moral issue at stake in nuclear war involves the meaning of sin in its most graphic dimensions. Every sinful act is a confrontation of the creature and the Creator" (107). Richard Minear has written that "the words of the bishops allow us to see Hiroshima in a new light. Hiroshima was *the* first use of atomic weapons in war; that we always knew. But Hiroshima was also *a* first use, on a predominantly civilian target, against an enemy already demonstrably in the throes of defeat: it was 'a deliberate initiation of nuclear warfare'" (Minear, "Atomic Holocaust, Nazi Holocaust," 362).

82 Holmes, *On War and Morality,* 195. Holmes goes on to say that the argument about the intentions of war makers (which is central to Christian just-war doctrine) cannot be carried out consistently (196–97). But that is a different point from mine.

83 Walzer, *Just and Unjust Wars,* 155–56.

84 Ibid., 268.

85 Schumpeter diary, 1945, quoted in Richard Swedberg, *Schumpeter: A Biography* (Princeton, N.J.: Princeton University Press, 1991), 276 n.

86 Bernstein, "Understanding the Atomic Bomb," 236, 261.

87 Acheson Seminars, 14 March 1954, Harry Truman Library, Princeton University.

88 Prange, *At Dawn We Slept,* 6. Nomura was the Japanese ambassador to Washington who handed a message to Cordell Hull on 6 December 1941; Shigemitsu was the Japanese foreign minister who signed the surrender documents aboard the U.S.S. *Missouri* in Tokyo Bay on 2 September 1945. As such, the two men bracket Japan's involvement with the United States in World War II.

89 This phase of the end of the Pacific War is discussed and documented in Cumings, *Origins,* 1:chap. 4.

90 See ibid., 2:chap. 21. For additional information on the nature of the bombs shipped to

Guam and on the relationship of these plans to the relief of General MacArthur see Richard Rhodes, *Dark Sun: The Making of the Hydrogen Bomb* (New York: Simon & Schuster, 1995), 449–52. Rhodes notes that LeMay appointed the Strategic Air Command's deputy commander, Thomas Power, to direct this mission. Power was the very person who had led "the first and most destructive firebombings of Tokyo," a person described in LeMay's biography as "a man so cold, hard and demanding" that several colleagues "described him as sadistic" (LeMay with Kantor, *Mission with LeMay*, 451).

91 Oe Kenzaburo, "Denying History Disables Japan," *New York Times Magazine*, 2 July 1995.

92 Saburo Ienaga, *The Pacific War* (New York: Pantheon Books, 1978). (The Japanese version was first published in 1968.)

93 Ibid.

94 Fredric Jameson, *Sartre: The Origins of a Style* (New York: Columbia University Press, 1984), 13.

95 Kuak Kwi Hoon, "Father and Son Robbed of Body and Soul," in *The Atomic Bomb: Voices from Hiroshima and Nagasaki*, ed. Kyoko Selden and Mark Selden (Armonk, N.Y.: M. E. Sharpe, 1989), 200–204.

96 Akizuki Tatsuichiro, *Nagasaki 1945*, trans. Nagata Keiichi (New York: Quarter Books, 1981), 24–25, 31, 155.

3   COLONIAL FORMATIONS AND DEFORMATIONS

1 See the articles in 1996 and 1997 in *World Development* by Atul Kohli and Stephan Haggard, Steven Moon, and David Kang.

2 See Douglas Mendel, *The Politics of Formosan Nationalism* (Berkeley and Los Angeles: University of California Press, 1970). If one compares Mendel's book to Chong-sik Lee, *Politics of Korean Nationalism* (Berkeley and Los Angeles: University of California Press, 1963), one reaches the conclusion that Formosan nationalism, at least compared to Korean, does not exist.

3 Alexander Woodside, lecture, University of Washington, 1978.

4 See Bruce Cumings, "Webs with No Spiders, Spiders with No Webs: The Genealogy of the Developmental State," in *The Developmental State in Comparative Perspective*, ed. Meredith Woo-Cumings (Ithaca, N.Y.: Cornell University Press, 1999).

5 Ting-Yee Kuo tries to argue that Taiwan was more developed than any Chinese province except Chihli in the 1890s because of Liu Ming-chuan's tenure as governor from 1884 to 1891. See Ting-Yee Kuo in *Taiwan in Modern Times*, ed. Paul K. Sih (New York: St. John's University Press, 1973), 236. Taiwan did get a railway, an arsenal, a coal mine, and some new schools during this period, but only Chinese nationalists (such as Kuo) could argue that this amounted to much, and other sources paint a much more dismal picture of Taiwan in 1895.

6 Angus Hamilton, *Korea* (New York: Charles Scribner's Sons, 1904), 8.

7 Timothy Mitchell, *Colonising Egypt* (Berkeley and Los Angeles: University of California Press, 1991), ix.

8 See, for example, Ngo Vinh Long, *Before the Revolution: The Vietnamese Peasants under the French* (Cambridge, Mass.: MIT Press, 1973); Martin J. Murray, *The Development of Capitalism in Colonial Indochina (1870–1940)* (Berkeley and Los Angeles: University of California Press, 1980); and Nguyen Kac Vien, *Tradition and Revolution in Vietnam*, trans. Jayne Werner (Ithaca, N.Y.: Cornell University Press, 1975).

9 See, above all, Paul Mus, *Viet-Nam: Sociologie d'une guerre* (Paris: Éditions du Seuil, 1952).

10 Eckert, *Offspring of Empire*, 83.

11 Hyman Kublin, "Taiwan's Japanese Interlude, 1895–1945," in *Taiwan in Modern Times*, ed. Paul K. Sih (New York: St. John's University Press, 1973), 35.

12 See Mendel, *Politics of Formosan Nationalism*, 7.

13 See Eckert, *Offspring of Empire*, 44, 82–84.

14 Ibid., 115.

15 Ibid., 128.

16 See Jung-en Woo, *Race to the Swift: The State, Finance, and Industrialization in the Republic of Korea* (New York: Columbia University Press, 1991), 23–30.

17 Ibid., 28.

18 Ibid., 29–30.

19 Ibid., 31, 34–36, 41.

20 Hermann Lautensach, *Korea: A Geography Based on the Author's Travels and Literature*, trans. Katherine Dege and Eckart Dege (Berlin: Springer-Verlag, 1988), 204–207.

21 See Cumings, *Origins*, 1: chaps. 1 and 2.

22 Japanese botanists introduced many flowers, but especially orchids, to Taiwan and Korea; they labored over ingenious new hybrids to be presented to the emperor on his birthday.

23 Gustav Ranis, "Industrial Development," in *Economic Growth and Structural Change in Taiwan: The Postwar Experience of the Republic of China*, ed. Walter Galenson (Ithaca, N.Y.: Cornell University Press, 1979), 222–25.

24 Kublin, "Taiwan's Japanese Interlude," 339. Another source, however, says that most of the bombs fell on Japanese residential neighborhoods, not on industrial plants (Mendel, *Politics of Formosan Nationalism*, 31).

25 Kublin, "Taiwan's Japanese Interlude," 337.

26 Maurice Scott, "Fiscal and Investment Policies," in *Economic Growth and Structural Change in Taiwan: The Postwar Experience of the Republic of China*, ed. Walter Galenson (Ithaca, N.Y.: Cornell University Press, 1979), 313; see also Maurice Scott, "Foreign Trade," in ibid., 345, 349.

27 Mendel, *Politics of Formosan Nationalism*, 66–67.

28 Susan Greenhalgh, "Supranational Processes of Income Distribution," in *Contending Approaches to the Political Economy of Taiwan*, ed. Edwin Winckler and Susan Greenhalgh (Armonk, N.Y.: M. E. Sharpe, 1988), 70–71.

29 Arthur F. Raper, Han-shen Chuan, and Shao-hsing Chen, *Urban and Industrial Taiwan—Crowded and Resourceful* (Taipei: Foreign Operations Administration, Mutual Security Mission to China and National Taiwan University, 1954), 8, 111.

30 Scott, "Fiscal and Investment Policies," 314–15, citing research by Samuel Ho and Lin.

31 Rong-I Wu, *The Strategy of Economic Development: A Case Study of Taiwan* (Louvain: n.p., 1971), 191; see also Erik Lundberg, "Fiscal and Monetary Policies," in *Economic Growth and Structural Change in Taiwan: The Postwar Experience of the Republic of China*, ed. Walter Galenson (Ithaca, N.Y.: Cornell University Press, 1979), 304–305.

32 George W. Barclay, *Colonial Development and Population in Taiwan* (Princeton: Princeton University Press, 1954).

33 Lundberg, "Fiscal and Monetary Policies," 278–79.

34 Ibid., 292–93.

35 Harry A. Franck, *Glimpses of Japan and Formosa* (New York: Century, 1924), 183–84.

36 Kublin, "Taiwan's Japanese Interlude," 336.

37 E. Patricia Tsurumi, "Taiwan under Kodama Gentarō and Gotō Shimpei," *Papers on Japan* (Harvard University, East Asian Research Center, 1967), 4:117–18.

38 Franck, *Glimpses*, 144.

39 Andrew Grajdanzev, *Formosa Today: An Analysis of the Economic Development and Strategic Importance of Japan's Tropical Colony* (New York: Institute of Pacific Relations, 1946).

40 Barclay, *Colonial Development*, 50.

41 Ibid.

42 Ibid., 7.

43 Greenhalgh, "Supranational Processes," 92.

44 From November 1945 to January 1947, commodity prices rose 700 percent for food, 1,400 percent for fuel, and 25,000 percent for fertilizer. Mainlanders wanted bribes for any public service, including passports; a huge black market opened for stolen goods, which included everything from doorknobs to water pipes (Mendel, *Politics of Formosan Nationalism*, 29).

45 Edwin A. Winckler, "Mass Political Incorporation, 1500–2000," in *Contending Approaches to the Political Economy of Taiwan*, ed. Edwin A. Winckler and Susan Greenhalgh (Armonk, N.Y.: M. E. Sharpe, 1988), 61.

46 Thomas Gold, "Colonial Origins of Taiwanese Capitalism," in *Contending Approaches to the Political Economy of Taiwan*, ed. Edwin A. Winckler and Susan Greenhalgh (Armonk, N.Y.: M. E. Sharpe, 1988), 101–18.

47 Murray, *Development of Capitalism*, 35–36, 168–70, 196.

48 Robert Sansom, *The Economics of Insurgency in the Mekong Delta* (Cambridge, Mass.: MIT Press, 1973); see also Cumings, *Origins*, 1:chap. 1.

49 Long, *Before the Revolution*, 73.

50 Murray, *Development of Capitalism*, 75–77, 80–81.

51 Long, *Before the Revolution*, 72–73; Murray, *Development of Capitalism*, 86.

52 Long, *Before the Revolution*, 102, 140.

53 Murray, *Development of Capitalism*, 124–31.

54 John T. McAlister Jr., with Paul Mus, *The Vietnamese and Their Revolution* (New York: Harper & Row, 1970), 7–8; on local elections, see 57–59.

55 Long, *Before the Revolution*, 73.

56 Vietnamese figures in ibid., 74. In 1934, 374,000 Taiwanese children were in elementary school; by 1939, there were more than 557,000 (Grajdanzev, *Economic Development*, 173). About half of all Chinese children were in primary school in the early 1930s and 70 percent by 1940, compared to a maximum of 10 percent of Vietnamese children.

57 Murray, *Development of Capitalism*, 42–43; see also Jeffrey Paige, *Agrarian Revolution* (Berkeley: University of California Press, 1978).

58 Murray, *Development of Capitalism*, 194–95. There were some exceptions: cement, for example, was produced in quantity in Vietnam (235,000 tons in 1937), but that was still only about 40 percent of what Taiwan produced in the same year. The Vietnamese textile industry had about ten thousand workers in 1938, but many of them worked irregularly and in small French and Chinese-owned plants (349–50).

59 Simon Kuznets, "Growth and Structural Shifts," in *Economic Growth and Structural Change in Taiwan: The Postwar Experience of the Republic of China*, ed. Walter Galenson (Ithaca, N.Y.: Cornell University Press, 1979).

60 One of my former students, who later became a dean at one of Seoul's elite universities

during the heyday of student activism, told me he reported weekly to seven different police, intelligence, and government offices.

61 See especially Miyoshi, *Off Center.*

62 These days it is used to explain why Western communism failed and North Korean communism did not. An example is this extract from *Nodong Sinmun* (Worker's Daily), "Ideological Consciousness Is Decisive in Man's Activity," of 1 August 1995 (Korean Central News Agency, P'yŏngyang):

> The Great Leader Kim Jong Il, in his famous work 'Giving Priority to Ideological Work Is Essential for Socialism,' elucidated the idea that ideological consciousness plays a decisive role in human activity. . . . ideological consciousness governs all his activities and serves as the prime mover which propels him to struggle to transform the world. . . .
>
> Parties in some countries which were building socialism in the past clung to economic construction alone. They took the dogmatic approach to preceding [i.e., Marxist-Leninist] theory that man's activity is decided by objective material conditions, and attached decisive significance to the objective material and economic conditions in socialist society. The collapse of socialism in those countries goes to show how important the role of ideology and ideological work are in man's activity.

63 See for example the many uses of "self-strengthening" in Sih, *Taiwan in Modern Times.*

64 Bruce Cumings, *Industrial Behemoth: The Northeast Asian Political Economy in the 20th Century,* long promised to Cornell University Press and sure to be out in the twenty-first century.

65 Itō Hirobumi, quoted in Jon Halliday, *A Political History of Japanese Capitalism* (New York: Pantheon Books, 1975), 37.

66 Von Stein's title is rendered in English as "The History of the Social Movement in France, 1789–1850." Wallerstein aptly points out that the English title omits "the *concept* of society" (Immanuel Wallerstein, *Unthinking Social Science: The Limits of Nineteenth-Century Paradigms* [New York: Blackwell, 1991], 65–67).

67 Theda Skocpol, *States and Social Revolutions: A Comparative Analysis of France, Russia, and China* (New York: Cambridge University Press, 1988). See also Wallerstein, *Unthinking Social Science,* 66.

68 Or, as Schumpeter put it in discussing his notion of "vision," it is a "preanalytic cognitive act that supplies the raw material for analytic effort" (quoted in Swedberg, *Schumpeter,* 181).

69 Schumpeter would have said Bravo! The individual, social, and class conflict of contemporary "civil society," he thought, represented "a profound error": "In the normal group or society, these conflicting elements are integrated with the cooperative elements harmoniously in the framework of a common culture and faith. . . . As soon as the members of any group, a family for example, lose sight of the framework of individual values and beliefs and see among them only conflicts of interest we witness a social disintegration, that is, a pathological phenomenon . . . namely, our society is falling apart" (Schumpeter, "The Future of Private Enterprise," in *The Economics and Sociology of Capitalism,* ed. Richard Swedberg [Princeton: Princeton University Press, 1991], 403).

70 Wallerstein, *Unthinking Social Science,* 191.

71 That is, the point of late industrialization is to achieve equality and thereby protect one's own national space within the world system, not to become hegemonic throughout the globe. Obviously this is a controversial contention, but it seems to me a better

description of Japan and Germany since the 1850s than the typical recourse to their pathological and failed attempts at hegemony in the 1930s and 1940s.

72 Wallerstein, *Unthinking Social Science*, 195.

4 CIVIL SOCIETY AND DEMOCRACY IN THE UNITED STATES AND EAST ASIA

1 van Wolferen, *Enigma of Japanese Power*, 9.

2 Available by writing to Cato Institute, 1000 Massachusetts Avenue NW, Washington, D.C. 20001.

3 See advertisement in the *New York Times*, 22 March 1996.

4 Robert D. Putnam, *Making Democracy Work: Civic Traditions in Modern Italy* (New York: Princeton University Press, 1994), 183. In my reading no reviewer of this book pointed out that many or even most northern Italian cities have had communist mayors in much of the postwar period.

5 Ibid., 11. Putnam disagrees with Almond and Verba, however, on consensus as a prerequisite for stable democracy. A profusion of disparities, cleavages, and fragmentations of various sorts was no bar to "good government" in northern Italy (116–17).

6 Michael J. Sandel, *Democracy's Discontent: America in Search of a Public Philosophy* (Cambridge, Mass.: Harvard University Press, 1996), 3.

7 Ibid., 332. Long ago, William H. Whyte likened suburbs to "a lay version of Army post life," a brilliant observation. See Whyte, *The Organization Man* (New York: Simon and Schuster, 1956), 280.

8 See, for example, Jürgen Habermas, "Toward a Reconstruction of Historical Materialism," in *Communication and the Evolution of Society*, trans. Thomas McCarthy (Boston: Beacon Press, 1984). Habermas is eminently more sophisticated about such matters than Almond and Verba or Putnam, however; for an interesting discussion of Habermas and Parsons, see Anthony Giddens, "Reason without Revolution? Habermas's Theorie des kommunikativen Handelns," in *Habermas and Modernity*, ed. Richard J. Bernstein (Cambridge, Mass.: MIT Press, 1985), 95–121.

9 Quoted in Peter Dews, ed., *Autonomy and Solidarity: Interviews with Jürgen Habermas*, rev. ed. (London: Verso, 1992), 125.

10 Mark E. Warren, "The Self in Discursive Democracy," in *The Cambridge Companion to Habermas*, ed. Stephen K. White (New York: Cambridge University Press, 1995), 171.

11 Peter Dews, *Logics of Disintegration: Post-Structuralist Thought and the Claims of Critical Theory* (London: Verso, 1987), 103.

12 Stephen K. White, "Reason, Modernity and Democracy," in *The Cambridge Companion to Habermas*, ed. Stephen K. White (New York: Cambridge University Press, 1995), 6.

13 Raymond Williams, *The Country and the City* (London: Oxford University Press, 1973), 142–64, 216. It is too bad that Williams is not around to write a needed revision for the 1990s: the country, the city, and the suburb.

14 Ibid., 44.

15 See Sandel's discussion in *Democracy's Discontent*, 137–42.

16 Gabriel Almond and Sidney Verba, *The Civic Culture: Political Attitudes and Democracy in Five Nations* (New York: Little, Brown and Company, 1963), x. *The Civic Culture* makes interesting reading thirty years later. Seeking to quantify the Tocquevillean propensity of Americans to join voluntary associations, the authors found that 57 percent of Americans were joiners, compared to only 44 percent in West Germany. Union

membership was at 14 percent in the American stratified sample of 970 respondents, and 15 percent among 955 West Germans. Today union membership in the United States is still at about 14 percent, whereas 40 percent of German workers are members of unions. No doubt a similar survey today would find that far more Germans are members of voluntary associations than are Americans. If, for Almond and Verba, "weak democracy" is characterized by "the passive citizen, the nonvoter, the poorly informed or apathetic citizen" (338), the United States would certainly qualify in the 1990s, according to Sandel and many others.

17 Jürgen Habermas, *The Philosophical Discourse of Modernity*, trans. Frederick Lawrence (Cambridge, Mass.: MIT Press, 1987), 367.

18 White, "Reason, Modernity and Democracy," 9.

19 Max Weber, *General Economic History*, trans. Frank H. Knight, introduction by Ira J. Cohen (New Brunswick, N.J.: Transaction Books, 1981), 312–14. Weber went on to contrast "the occident" not simply with "the Hindu and the Chinese," as was his wont, but with the three civilizations of East Asia. The "mandarin" was, according to Weber, "a humanistically educated literatus . . . but not in the least trained for administration"; furthermore, in China, the mandarins were merely "a thin stratum of so-called officials," existing above "the unbroken power of the clans and commercial and industrial guilds" (338). In Japan, "the feudal organization" led to a "complete exclusiveness as regards the outer world"; Korea, too, had an "exclusive policy," which was "determined" there on "ritualistic grounds" (344). Of Weber's judgments here on China, Korea, and Japan, it need only be said that he was wrong on all counts. Mandarins were trained, not to mention highly skillful, in administration; Japan was more feudal before the Tokugawa isolation than after; Korea's isolation in the same period was "determined" by a devastating international war in the 1590s, just as was Japan's, with no precedent before that for a "hermit kingdom."

20 Nancy S. Love, "What's Left of Marx," in *The Cambridge Companion to Habermas*, ed. Stephen K. White (New York: Cambridge University Press, 1995), 58–61.

21 Lucio Colletti, introduction to *Karl Marx: Early Writings*, ed. Lucio Colletti, trans. Rodney Livingstone and Gregor Benton (New York: Vintage Books, 1975), 31–32.

22 Karl Marx, *Critique of Hegel's Doctrine of the State*, in *Karl Marx: Early Writings*, ed. Lucio Colletti, trans. Rodney Livingstone and Gregor Benton (New York: Vintage Books, 1975), 111–12.

23 Ibid., 115–16.

24 Karl Marx, *Critique of Hegel's Philosophy of Right*, in *Karl Marx: Early Writings*, ed. Lucio Colletti, trans. Rodney Livingstone and Gregor Benton (New York: Vintage Books, 1975), 247–48.

25 Antonio Gramsci, *The Prison Notebooks* (New York: Columbia University Press, 1992).

26 MacIntyre, *After Virtue*. For analogous points in Unger's work see *Knowledge and Politics* (New York: The Free Press, 1975), 38–49. For Habermas's critique of *After Virtue* (which struck me as quite weak), see Dews, *Autonomy and Solidarity*, 248.

27 Unger, *Knowledge and Politics*, 76.

28 *After Virtue*, 147.

29 Jürgen Habermas, *Strukturwandel der Öffentlichkeit* (Frankfurt: Hermann Luchterhand Verlag, 1961), trans. by Thomas Burger as *The Structural Transformation of the Public Sphere* (Cambridge, Mass.: MIT Press, 1989). This book was published around the same time as Almond and Verba's *Civic Culture* and represents a profound (if implicit) critique of their project. But it was not translated into English until 1989.

30 Thomas McCarthy, introduction to *The Structural Transformation of the Public Sphere* by Jürgen Habermas, trans. Thomas Burger (Cambridge, Mass.: MIT Press, 1989), xii.

31 Habermas, *Structural Transformation*, 20–24.

32 McCarthy, introduction to *Structural Transformation*, xvii–xviii.

33 John Stuart Mill, quoted in Habermas, *Structural Transformation*, 135.

34 Habermas, *Structural Transformation*, 133–36, quoting Tocqueville. And on Mill: he "turned against the idea of a public sphere," advocating instead that political questions be decided not by "an uninformed multitude," but only "by appeal to views, formed after due consideration, of a relatively small number of persons specially educated for this task" (136). The Chartist newspaper was the first one with a mass edition of over fifty thousand copies (168).

35 Ibid., 177.

36 The early Habermas is also brilliant on suburbs (ibid., 157–64), seeing in them a "refeudalization" according to the "technical requirements of traffic flow," and "the shrinking of the private sphere into the inner areas of a conjugal family largely relieved of function and weakened in authority." The resultant "travesty" turned the privacy of the eighteenth-century bourgeois sphere, whose only reference was the public, into a privacy for the sake of refuge from that same sphere (a privacy whose only referent is shelter from the madding crowd), with the raucous new public sphere violating the hallowed family space via a mass media that was part of the sphere of consumption, not the sphere of civility and political debate. Habermas was under the influence of the Frankfurt School at this time, of course, but his conclusion that "the world fashioned by the mass media is a public sphere in appearance only" (170) perfectly anticipates the postmodernist argument that the mass media do not convey reality but only a semblance of reality. It becomes, in his words, "the manipulated public sphere" (217).

37 Marx, *Critique of Hegel's Philosophy of Right*, 252.

38 Hegel, quoted in Marx, *Critique of Hegel's Doctrine of the State*, 116.

39 Scholars as diverse as Zygmunt Bauman and Immanuel Wallerstein have argued that Stalinist states took the German fused-state project to its logical conclusion in their "late-late development," which was to strangle civil society altogether while building the sinews of industry and modern urban society (Immanuel Wallerstein, *After Liberalism* [New York: The New Press, 1995], 220–26). Meanwhile, these Stalinist states created a middle class in spite of themselves, by virtue of bringing forth a new generation of young people in the 1980s—their children.

40 See Cumings, *Korea's Place in the Sun*, chaps. 4, 7.

41 A good source on this period is Gregory Henderson, *Korea: The Politics of the Vortex* (Cambridge, Mass.: Harvard University Press, 1968). One would never understand Seoul at this time by examining aggregate or per capita economic figures, which placed South Korea around $100 per capita GNP. Middle-class families all had maids, and wealthy families employed phalanxes of maids, cooks, drivers, and handymen. Masses of the population were dirt poor, of course, but the society had a material wealth that could not be measured using the empirical methods of developmental economists.

42 The best source on this is Woo, *Race to the Swift*.

43 Karl Marx, *The Eighteenth Brumaire of Louis Bonaparte*, trans. Eden and Cedar Paul (New York: International Publishers, 1966).

44 The key texts in this literature are Guillermo O'Donnell, Phillipe C. Schmitter, and Laurence Whitehead, eds., *Transitions from Authoritarian Rule: Comparative Perspectives* (Washington, D.C.: Johns Hopkins University Press, 1986); *Transitions from Au-*

thoritarian Rule: Latin America (Washington, D.C.: Johns Hopkins University Press, 1986); and *Transitions from Authoritarian Rule: Tentative Conclusions about Uncertain Democracies* (Washington, D.C.: Johns Hopkins University Press, 1986). For my critique, which compared several Latin American cases with South Korea, see Bruce Cumings, "The Abortive Abertura," *New Left Review* (spring 1989).

45 Professor Kim Kwang-woong arrives at a similar conclusion by a different path in his recent paper, "Assessing the Impact of Kim Young Sam's Political Reforms on Korean Democratization," Northwestern University, March 1996. I am indebted to Professor Kim for showing me this paper.

46 Williams, *Country and City*, 231.

47 Simply at the level of political cartoons, the students showed great inventiveness. I remember one mid-1980s mural painted at Yŏnsei University, which showed Chŏn Tu-hwan's bust on Mount Rushmore, Jimmy Carter guarding the mountain with an M-16 automatic rifle, the "three Kims" sitting in an American military Jeep, staring blankly at the scene from a distance, and (the only anomalous part) Ronald Reagan performing oral sex on his wife, Nancy.

48 Habermas, *Autonomy and Solidarity*, 234.

49 See, for example, Adam Przeworski and Fernando Limongi, "Political Regimes and Economic Growth," in *Democracy and Development*, ed. Amiya Bagchi (New York: St. Martin's Press, 1995), 3–24, and Salvador Giner, "Comment" in ibid., 24–27.

50 C. B. Macpherson, *Democratic Theory: Essays in Retrieval* (New York: Oxford University Press, 1973), 78.

51 See Robert Dahl, *Democracy and Its Critics* (New Haven, Conn.: Yale University Press, 1989), 322–23 (on political equality), and 264, where Dahl lists a number of conditions for democracy (or polyarchy, in his terms). The conditions listed barely go beyond the categories elaborated by Almond and Verba in their early 1960s work, *Civic Culture*.

52 Michio Morishima, "Democracy and Economic Growth: The Japanese Experience," in *Democracy and Development*, ed. Amiya Bagchi (New York: St. Martin's Press, 1995), 157–60.

53 Dietrich Rueschemeyer, Evelyne Huber Stephens, and John D. Stephens, *Capitalist Development and Democracy* (Chicago: University of Chicago Press, 1992).

54 Macpherson, *Democratic Theory*, 3–8, 78–90.

5 NUCLEAR IMBALANCE OF TERROR: THE AMERICAN SURVEILLANCE REGIME AND NORTH KOREA'S NUCLEAR PROGRAM

1 Charles Krauthammer, "North Korea: The World's Real Time Bomb," *Washington Post*, 6 November 1993.

2 David E. Sanger, *New York Times*, 16 December 1992.

3 David E. Sanger, "News of the Week in Review," *New York Times*, 20 March 1994.

4 Clausewitz, *On War*, 101–102; Rapaport, "Editor's Introduction," 14.

5 Harry Summers, *On Strategy: A Critical Analysis of the Vietnam War* (Novato, Ca.: Presidio Press, 1982).

6 Thucydides, *Peloponnesian War*, 242–43.

7 In my childhood, I lived for a time with cousins in Memphis, Tennessee, and was shocked by the label "Yankee" that was instantly attached to me at the age of twelve, and the way in which memories of the South's rebellion were kept alive. But such sentiments are mostly gone now.

8 Bruce Cumings, *War and Television: Korea, Vietnam and the Gulf War* (New York: Verso, 1992).

9 Leslie Gelb, "The Next Renegade State," *New York Times*, 10 April 1991; see also Gelb, *New York Times*, 16 April 1991. Gelb appeared to have based his articles on Stanley Spector and Jacqueline Smith, "North Korea: The Next Nuclear Nightmare," *Arms Control Today* (March 1991): 8–13. Gelb's language is very similar to that in the Spector and Smith article without identifying this source.

10 *ABC Nightline*, 16 November 1993, transcript 3257.

11 It is exceedingly rare ever to find a public statement about the distribution of South Korean troops, but in June 1994 *Time* featured a map showing 90 percent of the ROK Army between Seoul and the DMZ.

12 General John R. Hodge, commander of U.S. forces in Korea, first warned of a North Korean attack in March 1946. See Cumings, *Origins*, 1:236.

13 James Wade, *One Man's Korea* (Seoul: Hollym Publishers, 1967), 23.

14 Solomon was the first high official to highlight North Korea as "the number one threat to Asian security," in a speech on 11 October 1990 that got wide media coverage.

15 Or under international law. On 8 July 1996, the International Court of Justice at the Hague stated that the use or threat of nuclear weapons should be outlawed as "the ultimate evil." It could not decide, however, whether the use of nuclear weapons for self-defense was justified: "The Court cannot conclude definitively whether the threat or use of nuclear weapons would be lawful or unlawful in an extreme circumstance of self-defense, in which the very survival of a state would be at stake" (*New York Times*, 9 July 1996). By this standard, North Korea is far more justified in developing nuclear weapons than the United States is in threatening P'yŏngyang with nuclear annihilation.

16 I sought to do so in Bruce Cumings, "Spring Thaw for Korea's Cold War?", *Bulletin of the Atomic Scientists*, 48, no. 3 (April 1992): 14–23, and "It's Time to End the Forty-Year War," *The Nation*, 257, no. 6 (23–30 August 1993): 206–208.

17 Donald Stone Macdonald, *U.S.-Korean Relations from Liberation to Self-Reliance, the Twenty-Year Record: An Interpretive Summary of the Archives of the U.S. Department of State for the Period 1945 to 1965* (Boulder, Colo.: Westview Press, 1992), 18, 200.

18 Dwight Eisenhower Library, Anne Whitman file, NSC, 179th Meeting, box 5, 8 January 1954.

19 Ibid., boxes 4 and 9.

20 See Cumings, *Origins*, 2:chap. 13.

21 Peter Hayes, *Pacific Powderkeg: American Nuclear Dilemmas in Korea* (Lexington, Mass.: Lexington Books, 1991), 35.

22 Ibid.

23 Ibid., 47–48.

24 Quoted in ibid., 49.

25 Hayes, *Pacific Powderkeg*, 50, 58.

26 Quoted in ibid., 59.

27 Hayes, *Pacific Powderkeg*, 60.

28 Samuel Cohen was a childhood friend of Herman Kahn; see Fred Kaplan, *The Wizards of Armageddon* (New York: Simon and Schuster, 1983), 220.

29 Peter Hayes also makes this point in *Pacific Powderkeg*, 148–49.

30 Ibid., 91.

31 Ibid., 94–95. A Kennedy School case study asserted (without offering the evidence) that air-launched nuclear weapons were removed one month after the ground-launched

weapons. See Susan Rosegrant in collaboration with Michael D. Watkins, "Carrots, Sticks, and Question Marks: Negotiating the North Korean Nuclear Crisis" (Cambridge, Mass.: Harvard University, John F. Kennedy School of Government, 1995), 7 n.

32   See President Clinton's former Defense Secretary William Perry quoted to this effect in Paul Virilio, *War and Cinema: The Logistics of Perception*, trans. Patrick Camiller (New York: Verso, 1989), 4.

33   Janne E. Nolan, *Trappings of Power: Ballistic Missiles in the Third World* (Washington, D.C.: The Brookings Institution, 1991), 48–52.

34   Lautensach, *Korea: A Geography*, 258.

35   Report on an interview with Kim Il Sung, 22 December 1978, in *Tokyo Shakaito*, March 1979, 162–68 (U.S. Joint Publications Research Service translation 073363). Don Oberdorfer effectively links North Korea's nuclear program with its historic strategy of self-reliance (especially in energy and the chemical industry) in *The Two Koreas* (New York: Addison-Wesley, 1997), 253–54.

36   Information from Energy Data Associates, cited in Economist Intelligence Unit, *China, North Korea Country Profile 1992–93* (London, 1993).

37   One source estimated that in 1993 China provided 72 percent of North Korean food imports, 75 percent of oil imports, and 88 percent of its coking coal; the North's energy regime required 52 million metric tons of brown coal or anthracite to provide 84 percent of its energy needs at close to full capacity. In 1993 it produced only 29 million tons. North Korea has the capacity to refine 3.5 million metric tons of oil, but only imported 1.5 million tons in 1993. See Ed Paisley, "Prepared for the Worst," *Far Eastern Economic Review* (10 February 1994).

38   This information is culled mostly from Richard Rhodes's two books, *The Making of the Atomic Bomb* (New York: Simon & Schuster, 1986), and *Dark Sun: The Making of the Hydrogen Bomb* (New York: Simon & Schuster, 1995).

39   This information is from Peter Hayes, "Should the United States Supply Light Water Reactors to Pyongyang?" Nautilus Research Center, Carnegie Endowment, 16 November 1993.

40   *New York Times*, 10 November 1991.

41   Leland M. Goodrich and Edvard Hambro, *Charter of the United Nations: Commentary and Documents* (Boston: World Peace Foundation, 1946), 64.

42   Polanyi, *Great Transformation*, 207.

43   Perhaps Nietzsche put "the German view" best: "ultimately [the utilitarians] all want *English* morality to be proved right—because this serves humanity best, or 'the general utility,' or 'the happiness of the greatest number'—no, the happiness of England" (Nietzsche, *Beyond Good and Evil*, 157).

44   Polanyi, *Great Transformation*, 119–21.

45   Friedrich Nietzsche, *The Will to Power*, trans. Walter Kaufmann and R. J. Hollingdale (New York: Vintage, 1968), 267.

46   Polanyi, *Great Transformation*, 140; see also Foucault's discussion in *Discipline and Punish* (London: Verso, 1977), 192–206; also the excellent discussion in Dews, *Logics of Disintegration*, 148–56.

47   Sir L. Stephen, quoted in Polanyi, *Great Transformation*, 121.

48   Dews, *Logics*, 149.

49   Michel Foucault, *Power/Knowledge*, ed. and trans. Colin Gordon (New York: Pantheon Books, 1980), 96.

50   Ibid., 104–106.

51   Virilio, *War and Cinema*, 2.

52 Cumings, *War and Television*.

53 The phrase is David Gergen's, a former Reagan aide known for his deft use of images, who also had the job of sprucing up Bill Clinton's image (quoted in *New York Times*, 6 May 1991).

54 Quoted in *Newsweek*, 22 April 1991.

55 We saw at the beginning of this chapter that General Riscassi, commander of U.S. forces in Korea, warned many times that the DPRK might "explode or implode." This became an all-purpose trope for testimony before Congress when annual appropriations were being considered. Riscassi's replacement, General Gary Luck, told Congress in March 1996 that what concerned him most about a possible DPRK collapse was "whether it will be an implosion or explosion" (*Digital Chosun Ilbo*, 18 March 1996).

56 Nayan Chanda, "Bomb and Bombast," *Far Eastern Economic Review* (10 February 1994): 21–24.

57 One source reported that a senior member of the IAEA had said that the IAEA shipped plutonium samples from North Korea to the United States, "where they were tested for their isotopic content." See Kenneth R. Timmerman, "Going Ballistic," *The New Republic* (24 January 1994): 14. Timmerman called the American tests on the waste samples—which allegedly showed three separate reprocessing runs according to him—"a smoking gun" proving that North Korea was after a bomb. Chanda, *Bomb and Bombast*, says there were four reprocessing runs.

58 *Vantage Point*, 17, no. 1 (Seoul, January 1994): 19.

59 Chanda, "Bomb and Bombast," 24.

60 Quoted in Oberdorfer, *The Two Koreas*, 103.

61 Kent Wiedemann, who was on Clinton's National Security Council as a senior director for Asia, said in 1995, "We finally came to recognize that from the North Korean perspective, it's in their interest to maintain an ambiguity about this whole thing"—that is, the purpose of their Yŏngbyŏn program (quoted in Rosegrant and Watkins, "Carrots, Sticks, and Question Marks," 29). That recognition came about four years late by my reckoning.

62 Leslie Gelb, *New York Times*, Op-Ed page, 21 March 1993.

63 Quoted in *Chicago Tribune*, 18 March 1993.

64 See for example Fred C. Ikle, "Response," *The National Interest*, 34 (winter 1993–1994): 39.

65 Quoted in *New York Times*, 24, 25 February 1993.

66 This was expressed in UN Security Council resolution 255, 7 March 1968. To obtain the requisite votes from nonnuclear states to get the NPT through the UN, the United States, UK, and USSR committed themselves to aid any "victim of an act or an object of a threat of aggression in which nuclear weapons are used" (quoted in Hayes, *Pacific Powderkeg*, 214).

67 Korean Central News Agency, P'yŏngyang, 22 February 1993. In fact, as we have seen, the IAEA had sent its plutonium samples to Washington for examination, since its technology was not good enough to determine how much reprocessing the North might have done. I do not know if P'yŏngyang was aware of this, but in my reading of their press, they never mentioned it.

68 Quoted in *New York Times*, 6 January 1992. Such demands enter the realm of the unnegotiable, of course, since the North Koreans will not allow this, nor would any sovereign state. These officials were also quoted as saying "what we don't know about the North is still terrifying."

69 Rosegrant and Watkins, "Carrots, Sticks, and Question Marks," 13.

70 Bruce D. Blair, "Russia's Doomsday Machine," *New York Times*, 8 October 1993. Blair is a senior fellow at the Brookings Institution. See another article on the front page of the *Times* on 6 December 1993, saying that American officials were retargetting strategic weapons onto "rogue" Third World states, with Russian targets now relegated to "secondary" status.

71 The Korean Central News Agency in September 1993 referred to a "regular missile launching exercise in the DPRK," which Japanese authorities were "making quite a noise about," wishing to add "a 'missile problem' to the 'nuclear problem,'" thus to block normalization of relations. It justified the missile test as a necessary measure of self-defense, given that Japan is dotted with American military bases of all kinds. See Korean Central News Agency, DPRK Foreign Ministry statement issued 24 September 1993. (It is highly unusual for the Korean Central News Agency to report any DPRK military exercise.)

72 For example, at the height of U.S.-DPRK tension, Billy Graham toured North Korea for the first time, preaching before large audiences and meeting Kim Il Sung in a "most memorable" visit (Korean Central News Agency, 1, 2 February 1994).

73 An anonymous American participant in the talks, quoted in Rosegrant and Watkins, "Carrots, Sticks, and Question Marks," 17–18.

74 The best source that I have found on the LWR issue is Peter Hayes, "Should the United States Supply Light Water Reactors to Pyongyang?", Nautilus Research Center, Carnegie Endowment, 16 November 1993. North Korean negotiators raised the issue of LWRS at the second round of high-level talks in June 1993; the United States at this time said North Korea should discuss LWRS with South Korea and Russia (the latter had already agreed to supply four such reactors when the North complied fully with its NPT obligations). LWRS again came up in high-level talks in Geneva in July 1993, when Kang Sŏk-ju offered to give up the Yŏngbyŏn facility in return for U.S. provision of LWRS; on 16 July, the United States agreed that LWRS would be a good idea, but said that LWRS could only work after the NPT safeguards were implemented fully (Rosegrant and Watkins, "Carrots, Sticks, and Question Marks," 20–21).

75 Selig Harrison, "Breaking the Nuclear Impasse: The United States and North Korea," testimony to the Subcommittee on Asian and Pacific Affairs, U.S. House of Representatives, 3 November 1993.

76 There was next to no information about this package deal in the American press in the winter of 1993–1994. The Korean press in both Seoul and P'yŏngyang was more thorough: see the summary in *Vantage Point*, 17, no. 1 (Seoul, January 1994): 16–17; on the DPRK's "package solution," see also the pro-P'yŏngyang *Korean Report*, no. 280 (Tokyo, November 1993), and Korean Central News Agency, reporting a Foreign Ministry statement of 1 February 1994.

77 Rosegrant and Watkins, "Carrots, Sticks, and Question Marks," 25.

78 Press Release, 30 November 1993, DPRK Mission to the UN, New York.

79 Korean Central News Agency, 1 February 1994.

80 Rosegrant and Watkins, "Carrots, Sticks, and Question Marks," 1–2. Apparently, this war game had been crafted in the Pentagon in the fall of 1991 and then shelved (27).

81 Thomas Flanagan, the JCS's representative on Clinton's interagency working group on Korea, believes this act was the key element that got everyone to focus on resolving the nuclear crisis. See ibid., 9.

82 Quoted in *The Chicago Tribune*, 4 April 1994. In a memorandum to the UN dated 10 April 1996, the DPRK stated that "a second Korean War would have broken out

had the United Nations chosen to repeat its past by unilaterally imposing 'sanctions' against the DPRK" (Press Release, 10 April 1996, DPRK Mission to the UN, New York).

83 Rosegrant and Watkins, "Carrots, Sticks, and Question Marks," 2, 33–35.

84 Ibid., 34–35. Although this study discounts Pentagon desires to remove Yŏngbyŏn entirely with a "surgical strike" (15, 32–34), State Department negotiators with North Korea told me they were constantly confronted with Pentagon and CIA officers who would say "Why negotiate with these people? We can handle the Yŏngbyŏn problem overnight." Another informant told me that General Colin Powell played a critical role in pointing out the costs of a new Korean War to Clinton. See also Oberdorfer's harrowing account of how close Washington and P'yŏngyang were to going to war, in *The Two Koreas*, 305–36.

85 Quoted in Rosegrant and Watkins, "Carrots, Sticks, and Question Marks," 11.

86 It was Harrison who first got Kim Il Sung to think about freezing the Yŏngbyŏn facility, during a meeting in P'yŏngyang in May 1994. I remember one appearance by Anthony Namkung on the *McNeil/Lehrer News Hour*, where he said P'yŏngyang would give up its nuclear program for better relations with the United States, and Lawrence Eagleberger of Kissinger Associates responded, "If you believe that, I have a bridge in Brooklyn I'll sell you."

87 Goodrich and Hambro, *Charter of the UN*, 65.

6 THE WORLD SHAKES CHINA

1 Napoleon is alleged to have said that "When China wakes up, it will shake the world." Jack Belden made that the title for his classic account of the Chinese revolution, but two new books on China by our best experts open with Napoleon yet again: Nicholas Kristof and Sheryl WuDunn use this aphorism for their title in *China Wakes: The Struggle for the Soul of a Rising Power* (New York: Times Books, 1994); also Kenneth Lieberthal, *Governing China: From Revolution Through Reform* (New York: W. W. Norton, 1995), xv; see also Harry Harding, *China's Second Revolution: Reform after Mao* (Washington, D.C.: The Brookings Institution, 1987), 239.

2 Harry Harding frames his useful account of Sino-American relations with cyclical metaphors in *A Fragile Relationship: The United States and China since 1972* (Washington, D.C.: The Brookings Institution, 1992), as does Suzanne Ogden in *China's Unresolved Issues: Politics, Development and Culture* (Englewood Cliffs, N.J.: Prentice-Hall, 1995), 6.

3 W. J. F. Jenner, who by his own account once sympathized with the Chinese revolution, argues that Tiananmen proved that China was still captured by its ancient, unchanging and probably irremediable tendency toward tyranny. See *The Tyranny of History: The Roots of China's Crisis* (New York: Penguin Books, 1994), 1–11.

4 Vaclav Smil begins his important study of China's environmental calamities this way: "For knowing China—really knowing this continent-like country of diverse environments, ancient habits, contradictory leanings, and unpredicted challenges—even a lifetime is not enough." One is tempted to say, Well, a lifetime will still have to do. See *China's Environmental Crisis: An Inquiry into the Limits of National Development* (Armonk, N.Y.: M. E. Sharpe, 1993), vii.

5 Nearly all the alarmist images are present in a recent book by one of Hong Kong's foremost China watchers, Willy Wo-Lap Lam, in *China after Deng Xiaoping* (New York: John Wiley & Sons, 1995), 383–430. Medieval feudalism and "hideously apparent" are Jenner's phrases, *Tyranny of History*, 35, 54.

6　Quoted in Cumings, *Origins*, 2:55.

7　Ruan Ming, *Deng Xiaoping: Chronicle of an Empire*, ed. and trans. Nancy Liu, Peter Rand, and Lawrence R. Sullivan (Boulder, Colo.: Westview Press, 1994), 142–50. This is the best single book on Deng Xiaoping.

8　C. P. Fitzgerald, *The Birth of Communist China* (Baltimore: Penguin Books, 1964), 30.

9　Harry Truman Presidential Library, National Security Council file, box 205, NSC 37/5 deliberations, 3 March 1949.

10　For an expanded version of this argument see Bruce Cumings, "The Political Economy of China's Turn Outward," in *China and the World*, 2d ed., ed. Samuel Kim (Boulder, Colo.: Westview Press, 1989), 203–36.

11　Richard Madsen, *China and the American Dream: A Moral Inquiry* (Berkeley: University of California Press, 1995), 185.

12　"Quarterly Review," *The China Quarterly* (spring 1975).

13　According to David S. G. Goodman, *Deng Xiaoping and the Chinese Revolution: A Political Biography* (New York: Routledge, 1994), 25.

14　World Bank, *World Development Report 1987* (New York: Oxford University Press, 1987), 228.

15　Quoted in Lam, *China after Deng*, 386.

16　Nor do Chinese economists who write in China's premier economic journal, *Jingji yanjiu* (Economic studies). For a recently translated sampling of their views on East Asian development in Korea, Taiwan, and elsewhere, see the special issue of *Chinese Economic Studies* (July–August 1994).

17　For Japan, the pioneering work on the developmental state was done by Chalmers Johnson, *MITI and the Japanese Miracle*; for the same in regard to South Korea, see Woo, *Race to the Swift*. For China, see Chen Yizhi, "The Developmental Model for Establishing a 'Hard Government and Soft Economy,'" a 1988 article cited in Ruan Ming, *Deng Xiaoping*, 205. Huntington's theory used different figures; Chen seems to be thinking of the income trajectory and subsequent democratic opening of Taiwan and Korea. Another article from *Jingji yanjiu* in 1992 lauded Keynes for understanding the special role of the state in regulating and controlling the economy.

18　Michael C. Gallagher, "China's Illusory Threat to the South China Sea," *International Security* (summer 1994): 169–93. South Korea and Taiwan spent $29 billion on defense in 1995, compared with China's official figure of about 70.2 billion yuan, or $8.4 billion (U.S. Central Intelligence Agency, *World Factbook* [Washington, D.C.: 1997]. Western estimates put China's real defense spending at somewhere between $25 and $30 billion.

19　Fitzgerald, *Birth of Communist China*, 30.

20　I highly recommend Madsen's *China and the American Dream*, where these themes are explored with great sensitivity.

21　Orville Schell, *The Nation* (17–24 July 1995): 98.

7　BOUNDARY DISPLACEMENT: THE STATE, THE FOUNDATIONS, AND INTERNATIONAL AND AREA STUDIES DURING AND AFTER THE COLD WAR

1　For ample evidence of Bundy's intimidation of young scholars, see Sigmund Diamond, *Compromised Campus: The Collaboration of Universities with the Intelligence Community* (New York: Oxford University Press, 1992), 3–6, and passim; on Bundy's contemporaneous CIA work see Christopher Simpson, *The Science of Coercion: Communications Research and Psychological Warfare, 1945–1960* (New York: Oxford University

Press, 1994). Bundy was particularly involved in the "Soviet Vulnerabilities Project" that W. W. Rostow ran for the CIA, along with Philip Mosely, Adam Ulam, and several other well-known Soviet studies scholars.

2   Robin W. Winks shows how the nexus between area programs and the state broke down in the 1960s as (some) specialists on Southeast Asia condemned the American intervention in Vietnam. On the one hand, he writes, "the dog bit the hand that fed it," leading to a predictable decline in support for area studies programs; on the other, it was not and is not "the function of a university to be supportive" of state policies (Winks, *Cloak and Gown: Scholars in the Secret War, 1939–1961* [New York: William Morrow, 1987], 447–49).

3   Barry Katz has written an informative, well-researched book that nonetheless barely scratches the surface in examining the problems inherent in professors doing intelligence work; furthermore, he ends his story in the late 1940s. See Katz, *Foreign Intelligence: Research and Analysis in the Office of Strategic Services, 1942–1945* (Cambridge, Mass.: Harvard University Press, 1989). Robert B. Hall's seminal study done for the SSRC in 1947 still makes for interesting reading, but Hall, of course, would not have had access to classified intelligence documentation on the government's relationship to area studies (Hall, *Area Studies with Special Reference to Their Application for Research in the Social Sciences* [New York: Social Science Research Council, 1947]).

4   I presented some of the ideas in this chapter at the Association for Asian Studies (AAS) in 1993, on a panel held in honor of the twenty-fifth anniversary of the *Bulletin of Concerned Asian Scholars*. I presented a much-revised version at the 1996 AAS meetings and then published an earlier version of this chapter in a symposium in this same *Bulletin* (29, no. 1 [January–March 1997]: 6–26). Various other people offered comments on my essay in this symposium, comments to which I responded in the subsequent issue (29, no. 2 [April–June 1997]: 56–60). As I said in the latter essay, my work on these matters is in no sense definitive, nor could it be. The subject is not what I am working on, nor is it part of my ongoing research, nor could it be. Why? Because we are nowhere near the truths of our profession and its relation to power, or the evidence that would allow us to assess and debate that relationship. The evidence that I have gathered is incidental to archival research on other subjects; my choice was to leave the information in the files, or find a way to get it out so that it could be discussed in hopes that others will come forward with more information. Moreover, that evidence was just a fragment of what exists in the unmoving bowels of the national security state, especially the Central Intelligence Agency, which still declassifies next to nothing of real importance on the events of the postwar period (e.g., the destabilization of Mossadeq in Iran in 1953, the overthrow of the Arbenz regime in Guatemala the following year, the Bay of Pigs). Thus, it is simply not possible to offer definitive answers to questions about the relationship of area studies to the state in the past half century. Because some foundations (e.g., Ford) and some universities (not Harvard) have opened their archives to varying degrees, it may be possible to look at one or two sides of that triangle. But the most important side would still be missing. For their helpful comments on the different versions of this chapter, I thank Arif Dirlik, Bill and Nancy Doub, Harry Harootunian, Richard Odaka, Moss Roberts, Mark Selden, Chris Simpson, Marilyn Young, Masao Miyoshi, and Stefan Tanaka. Obviously, I am responsible for the views presented herein.

5   My ambivalence, it appears, was shared by Confucius. In the *Analects*, book 18, his judgement is *wu ke, wu buke*, namely "no [absolute] acceptance or rejection" of serving the state. I am indebted to Moss Roberts for bringing this to my attention.

6   Katz, *Foreign Intelligence*, 11, 29, 99, 115.

7 The CIA, for example, enjoins its employees from ever writing about anything to do with their work for the Agency without a prior security vetting, and prosecutes or hounds forever employees who write about their experiences anyway (such as Frank Snepp and Phillip Agee).

8 Katz, *Foreign Intelligence*, 2–5.

9 Ibid., 159–61; see also Winks, *Cloak and Gown*, 60–115.

10 Immanuel Wallerstein, "Open the Social Sciences," *Items*, 50, no. 1 (Social Science Research Council, March 1966): 3.

11 Vogel, *Japan as Number One*.

12 William Nelson Fenton, *Area Studies in American Universities: For the Commission on Implications of Armed Services Educational Programs* (Washington, D.C.: American Council on Education, 1947), paraphrased in Ravi Arvind Palat, "Building Castles on Crumbling Foundations: Excavating the Future of Area Studies in a Post-American World" (University of Hawaii, February 1993). (I am grateful to Dr. Palat for sending me his paper.)

13 Cora DuBois, *Social Forces in Southeast Asia* (Minneapolis: University of Minnesota Press, 1949), 10–11, quoted in Katz, *Foreign Intelligence*, 198.

14 Katz, *Foreign Intelligence*, 160.

15 Ibid.; see also Palat, "Building Castles on Crumbling Foundations"; Richard Lambert et al., *Beyond Growth: The Next Stage in Language and Area Studies* (Washington, D.C.: Association of American Universities, 1984), 8–9.

16 See Betty Abrahamson Dessants, "The Silent Partner: The Academic Community, Intelligence, and the Development of Cold War Ideology, 1944–1946," Organization of American Historians annual meeting, 28–31 March 1996. Katz (*Foreign Intelligence*, 57–60) argues for a break between the antifascist politics of the OSS and the anticommunist politics of the CIA, but a close reading of his text suggests many continuities into the postwar period, in the persons of Alex Inkeles, Philip Mosely, W. W. Rostow, and many others; an alternative reading would be that the antifascists, many of them left-liberals, were either weeded out or fell by the wayside, distressed at the turn taken by American cold war policies after 1947.

17 The letter is dated 28 October 1948. Those who wish to pursue this matter can find additional documentation in the William Donovan Papers, Carlisle Military Institute, box 73a. Others included in this effort were Evron Kirkpatrick, Robert Lovett, and Richard Scammon, among many others. Christopher Simpson terms this same operation "the Eurasian Institute," listing it as a special project of Kennan and Davies, in which Kirkpatrick participated. See Simpson, *Blowback: America's Recruitment of Nazis and Its Effects on the Cold War* (New York: Weidenfeld & Nicolson, 1988), 115 n; Diamond also has useful information on this matter in *Compromised Campus*, 103–105.

18 Diamond, *Compromised Campus*, chaps. 3 and 4. Diamond also has several chapters on Yale. Robin Winks (in *Cloak and Gown*) documented in some detail the extraordinary role that Yale played in providing faculty participants and student recruits for America's clandestine services, a phenomenon with which he is considerably more comfortable than a critic like Diamond. Like other analysts, Winks locates the origin of area studies in wartime intelligence work, especially for the R&A branch of OSS: "It is no exaggeration to say that the rapid growth of area studies programs . . . grew out of the structure of the foreign service, the OSS, and the work of ancillary groups. . . . One finds the alumni of the OSS scattered throughout typical area studies programs" (114–15).

19 Boston FBI to FBI Director, 9 February 1949, quoted in Diamond, *Compromised Campus*, 47; see also 109–10.

20 Anthony Summers, *Official and Confidential: The Secret Life of J. Edgar Hoover* (New York: G. P. Putnam's Sons, 1993). Summers's evidence on Hoover's cross-dressing homosexual encounters is thin and offered mainly to titillate, but his extensive information on Hoover's suborning by organized crime seems undeniable.

21 For example, the Sigmund Diamond Papers (at Columbia University) contain an enormous file on Raymond A. Bauer's inability to get a security clearance to consult with the CIA in 1952–1954 because he had once been an acquaintance of William Remington, whom the FBI thought was a communist (see box 22).

22 Ibid., box 15.

23 Memo from SAC Boston to J. Edgar Hoover, 7 March 1949, ibid., box 13.

24 Boston FBI report of 1 February 1949, ibid.

25 Boston FBI report of 1 November 1950, ibid. Box 14 also has an extensive file on Robert Lee Wolff's security check before he became a consultant to the CIA in 1951.

26 Mosely's files show that he worked with the Operations Research Office of Johns Hopkins on classified projects in 1949; that he had a top secret clearance for CIA work in 1951 and 1954; that in 1957 he had CIA contracts and was a member of the National Defense Executive Reserve assigned to the Central Intelligence Agency Unit, and that he renewed his contracts and status in 1958; that he worked on an unnamed project for the Special Operations Research Office of American University in 1958; that he was cleared for top-secret work by the Institute for Defense Analysis (IDA, a major academic arm of government security agencies) in 1961; and that in the same year he kept Abbot Smith of the CIA informed about his travel to the USSR in connection with ACLS/SSRC work on academic exchanges with that country. See Philip Mosely Papers, University of Illinois, box 13, Operations Research Office to Mosely, 28 February 1949 and 2 November 1949 (the latter memo refers to "the optimum use of the social sciences in operations research"); also "National Defense Executive Reserve, Statement of Understanding," signed by Mosely 19 December 1957 and renewed 26 June 1958 (the latter memo also refers to a "contract" that Mosely has with the CIA, separate from his activities in the Executive Reserve); also Mosely to Abbot Smith, 10 March 1961. (Mosely begins the letter to Smith, "In accordance with the present custom I want to report my forthcoming travel plans.") Smith, an important CIA official and colleague of Ray Cline and William Bundy among others, is not here identified as a CIA man. But he is so in Ludwell Lee Montague, *General Walter Bedell Smith as Director of Central Intelligence* (University Park: Pennsylvania State University Press, 1992), 138–39, where information on Abbot Smith's CIA work can be found. In 1961 Mosely worked with the IDA on a secret project on "Communist China and Nuclear Warfare" (Mosely Papers, S. F. Giffin, Institute for Defense Analysis, to Mosely, 24 November 1961, and Mosely to Giffin, 6 December 1961). See also various memoranda in box 2, including a record of Mosely's security clearances.

27 Mosely Papers, box 4, letter from W. W. Rostow, MIT, to Mosely, 6 October 1952.

28 Ibid., Frederick Barghoorn (Yale University) to Mosely, 17 January 1952.

29 Ibid., Whitman to Mosely, 5 October 1955; Mosely to Whitman, 10 October 1955.

30 Ibid., box 13, Nathan B. Lenvin, U.S. Department of Justice, to Mosely, 20 April 1953.

31 Ellen Schrecker, *The Age of McCarthyism: A Brief History with Documents* (Boston: Bedford Books of St. Martin's, 1994).

32 Mosely Papers, box 18, Langer to Mosely, 11 May 1953.

33 Ibid., Paul F. Langer to Mosely, Carl Spaeth, and Cleon O. Swayze, 17 May 1953.

34 Ibid., "Report Submitted by Paul F. Langer to the Director of Research, Board on Overseas Training and Research, the Ford Foundation," 15 April 1953. The books Pye later authored were *Guerrilla Communism in Malaya* and *The Spirit of Burmese Politics.* One could also include in this group Daniel Lerner's *The Passing of Traditional Society* (New York: The Free Press, 1958), another central text in comparative politics; Lerner had worked with Pye, Ithiel deSola Poole, and other political scientists at MIT's CENIS on projects dealing with communications and society, insights from which were later used in the CIA's Phoenix program in Vietnam. Much of this research was funded under CIA or government contracts for psychological warfare. On this see Christopher Simpson, "U.S. Mass Communication Research and Counterinsurgency after 1945: An Investigation of the Construction of Scientific 'Reality,'" in *Ruthless Criticism: New Perspectives in U.S. Communications History,* ed. William S. Solomon and Robert W. McChesney (Minneapolis: University of Minnesota Press, 1993).

35 The conference was held 9–10 October 1953. See the list of those who attended, Mosely Papers, box 18.

36 Ibid. As Diamond shows, such considerations extended to Carnegie's acknowledged policy of excluding scholars who were "way to the left," which at one point led to worries about Derk Bodde and Arthur Schlesinger Jr. and major fretting about Gunnar Myrdal; however, these cases paled before Carnegie's concerns about the Institute for Pacific Relations and Owen Lattimore (*Compromised Campus,* 299–301).

37 Mosely Papers, box 18, George B. Baldwin to Mosely, 21 December 1954.

38 Ibid., Swayze to Mosely, 21 October 1954; Langer said he was involved in developing Chinese studies in Langer to Mosely, Spaeth, and Swayze, 17 May 1953.

39 Joint Committee on Contemporary China, *Report on the Conference on the Status of Studies of Modern and Contemporary China* (SSRC, New York, March 1968), quoted in Diamond, *Compromised Campus,* 98.

40 Mosely Papers, box 13, Smith to Mosely, 28 February 1961; see also notations on Mosely to Smith, 10 March 1961.

41 Ibid., Mosely to Smith, 16 March 1961.

42 Ibid., Mosely to King, 17 April 1962.

43 Ibid., Mosely to John R. Thomas (of the IDA), 19 July 1963, where Mosely refers to Rand funds going to help Zagoria complete his dissertation and IDA funds that helped support Zagoria for a postdoctoral project; see also Mosely to Brzezinski, 20 August 1963.

44 I refer for example to the Studies in Political Development series, sponsored by the Committee on Comparative Politics of the SSRC, yielding by my count seven books, all published by Princeton University Press in the mid-1960s and all of which became required reading in the political science subfield of comparative politics: Lucian W. Pye, ed., *Communications and Political Development;* Joseph LaPalombara, ed., *Bureaucracy and Political Development;* Robert Ward and Dankwart Rustow, *Political Modernization in Japan and Turkey;* James S. Coleman, ed., *Education and Political Development;* Joseph LaPalombara and Myron Weiner, eds., *Political Parties and Political Development;* Lucian W. Pye and Sidney Verba, eds., *Political Culture and Political Development;* and Leonard Binder, Lucian W. Pye, James S. Coleman, Sidney Verba, Joseph LaPalombara, and Myron Weiner, eds., *Crises and Sequences in Political Development.*

Gabriel Almond and James S. Coleman authored the ur-text in this literature, *The Politics of the Developing Areas* (Princeton, N.J.: Princeton University Press, 1960).

Almond also was an academic participant in intelligence projects at the time. Documents in the Max Millikan Papers at MIT show that Almond was a member of a classified Working Committee on Attitudes toward Unconventional Weapons in 1958–1961, along with Air Force General Curtis LeMay, Harvard academic Thomas Schelling, and MIT's deSola Poole, among others. The committee studied "a variety of types of unconventional weapons, nuclear, biological, and chemical, for use in limited war." The social scientists were expected to find ways of "minimizing" unfortunate reactions by target peoples to the use of such weapons—or as Millikan put it in his letter to Almond inviting him to join the committee, the committee would discuss measures to be taken that "might reduce to tolerable levels the political disadvantages of the use of a variety of such weapons," and how to use weapons of mass destruction and still have "the limitability of limited conflict" (Max Millikan Papers, box 8, Millikan to Almond, 3 November 1958). Millikan's long memorandum of 10 January 1961 to the committee stated clearly that use of such weapons might include crop-destroying agents that would cause general famine; the covert use of this and other unconventional weapons would be accompanied by overt denial that the United States had used them. The key case he mentioned would be use of such weapons against a conventional Chinese attack on a country in Southeast Asia (Millikan Papers, box 8).

45 Simpson, "U.S. Mass Communication Research and Counterinsurgency." Simpson has long lists of social scientists who worked for the OSS and other intelligence agencies during the war; they include Harold Lasswell, Hadley Cantril, Daniel Lerner, Nathan Leites, Heinz Eulau, Elmo Roper, Wilbur Schramm, Clyde Kluckhohn, Edward Shils, Morris Janowitz, and many others. After the war, "a remarkably tight circle of men and women" continued to work for the state, including Lasswell, Lerner, Cantril, Janowitz, Kluckhohn, and Eulau.

46 Ellen Schrecker, *No Ivory Tower: McCarthyism and the Universities* (New York: Oxford University Press, 1986), 97–104, 125.

47 Jane Sanders, *Cold War on the Campus: Academic Freedom at the University of Washington, 1946–64* (Seattle: University of Washington Press, 1979). She has two entries for J. Edgar Hoover and three for the FBI in her index, none related to the 1949 case.

48 Allen's influential argument—"soon [to] be embraced by the academic world"—was, in Schrecker's presentation, "that academics 'have special obligations' that 'involve questions of intellectual honesty and integrity.' Communism, because of its demand for uncritical acceptance of the Party's line, interferes with that quest for truth, 'which is the first obligation and duty of the teacher.' . . . [Thus] Allen concluded that . . . 'by reason of their admitted membership in the Communist Party . . . [the two teachers were] incompetent, intellectually dishonest, and derelict in their duty to teach the truth' " (Schrecker, *No Ivory Tower*, 103).

49 See Donovan's advice to President Allen in Donovan Papers, box 75A, item 889, handwritten notes dated 3 February 1949 (the advice was given earlier than this date). George Taylor also worked with Allen in devising an effective strategy for firing communists and radicals. See Sanders, *Cold War on the Campus*, 79.

50 See Diamond Papers, box 15.

51 Ibid., Lew Nichols to Charles Tolson, 18 May 1948.

52 Ibid.; see also other memos in this file in May 1948, and FBI Seattle to Hoover, 4 November 1948. Allen met with Hoover on 6 May, and made several subsequent visits to the FBI in 1948 and 1949. According to Clyde Tolson's memo to Nichols of 19 May 1948, a Los Angeles FBI agent named Hood had no special relationship with UCLA, but was

"personally friendly with the Dean and just a few days ago the Dean wrote him regarding an individual and wanted certain information." The memo says Hood didn't give him the information. When President Allen later asked the local FBI agent responsible for contacts at UW to furnish information on six professors, however, Tolson told the agent to give it to him (see Tolson to Nichols, 21 June 1948). Allen also asked the FBI for information on Melvin Rader, a stalwart radical whom I remember from when I taught at Washington, and who was never accused of being a CP member—although as FBI information shows, Allen told the FBI he thought Rader was "closely connected with the Communist Party"—while offering no evidence. It later turned out that the Canwell Committee had faked evidence on Rader (Sanders, *Cold War on Campus*, 86).

53 Diamond Papers, box 15, Seattle FBI to Director FBI, 26 January 1949.

54 On that episode, which tarnished UW's reputation among scientists for years thereafter, see Sanders, *Cold War on Campus*, 138–42. Oppenheimer had been invited to lecture at both Washington and the University of Oregon; he arrived in Portland and was told two things: (1) Einstein had died while he was en route; (2) the University of Washington had rescinded its invitation.

55 Diamond Papers, box 15, Seattle FBI to Director FBI, 8 June 1955; Seattle FBI to Director FBI, 24 August 1955. The invited conference guests included representatives from the State Department, the Voice of America, and Radio Free Europe; Alex Inkeles was a featured speaker, as were Taylor and historian Donald Treadgold.

56 Sanders, *Cold War on Campus*, 94. The best study of the Psychological Strategy Board is Gregory Mitrovich, "The Limits of Empire" (New York, 1997). I am grateful to Dr. Mitrovich for letting me read his manuscript, which shows that McGeorge Bundy and Walt Rostow were deeply involved in the CIA's psychological warfare programs, one of which was Radio Free Europe, a covert program in which the Ford and Rockefeller Foundations were also heavily involved (70–71).

57 Simpson, *Blowback*, 118–22; Robert P. Newman, *Owen Lattimore and the 'Loss' of China* (Berkeley: University of California Press, 1992), 363–64. On Taylor's introduction to Mandel, see Diamond, *Compromised Campus*, 308. (Poppe has always denied that he was an SS officer, saying that as a foreigner he could not have joined the SS; he also claimed that his "research" had nothing to do with the "final solution"—which was announced at the Wannsee Institute in January 1942 by SS leader Reinhard Heydrich, with Adolph Eichmann in attendance. See Simpson, *Blowback*, 48 n.)

58 See for example Richard D. Lambert, *Points of Leverage: An Agenda for a National Foundation for International Studies* (New York: Social Science Research Council, 1986).

59 Guide to the Max Franklin Millikan Papers, MIT.

60 This transcript was provided to me by Kai Bird, who got it from David Armstrong, who is writing a dissertation on the Rostow brothers. The first few pages of the original document are missing, so some of the participants are hard to identify; furthermore, their statements were truncated and paraphrased by the transcriber. The meeting was held on 18 May 1959. (All quotations in the text come from this transcript.) Millikan was an assistant director of the CIA in 1951–1952, and director of CENIS from 1952 to 1969, the year in which he died.

61 Professor Diamond begins each of his chapters on Harvard's Russian Research Center with the "official stories" given out to the public about its activities: "we have no classified contracts"; "all our research is generated out of our own scholarly interests"; the various centers and institutes were established by disinterested foundations; and, in

general, all views to the contrary reflect some sort of conspiracy theory (Diamond, *Compromised Campus*, 50–51, 65).

62 The summary is by Anne Betteridge, executive officer of the Middle East Studies Association, and is found in *Asian Studies Newsletter* (June–July 1992): 3–4.

63 Ibid., 4–5; quotations throughout this paragraph are found in ibid.

64 Ibid.

65 Stanley J. Heginbotham, "The National Security Education Program," *SSRC Items*, 46, nos. 2–3 (June–September 1992): 17–23; subsequent quotations from Heginbotham are found in ibid.

66 "Area scholars are extremely sensitive to the damage that can be done to their personal reputations and to their ability to conduct scholarship abroad when they come to be perceived as involved with intelligence or defense agencies of the U.S. government" (ibid., 22).

67 See Amy Rubin, "South Korean Support for U.S. Scholars Raises Fears of Undue Influence," *The Chronicle of Higher Education* (4 October 1996): 10–11.

68 Mark Selden, James K. Boyce, and the *BCAS* Editors, "National Security and the Future of Asian Studies," *Bulletin of Concerned Asian Scholars*, 24, no. 2 (April–June 1992): 84. See also the updated information in *Bulletin of Concerned Asian Scholars*, 24, no. 3 (July–September 1992): 52–53.

69 See the report of our work, a response by John Fairbank, a further response by Moss Roberts, and David Horowitz's essay, "Politics and Knowledge: An Unorthodox History of Modern China Studies," in *Bulletin of Concerned Asian Scholars*, "Special Supplement: Modern China Studies," 3, nos. 3–4 (summer–fall 1971): 91–168.

70 Ibid., 127.

71 Ibid., 105.

72 I saw drafts of the restructuring plan and some of the various Joint Committee responses, all dated in late 1995 and early 1996, but cannot cite the documents under the terms of their provision to me; this is not because of secrecy so much as the provisional and evolving nature of the restructuring itself, as SSRC administrators respond to suggestions and complaints about their new plans. I will also refer to Kenneth Prewitt's "Presidential Items," in the March 1996 issue of the SSRC's newsletter, *Items*, which reflected the essence of the restructuring drafts which I have seen.

73 Prewitt, "Presidential Items," 15.

74 See Chalmers Johnson and E. B. Keehn, "Rational Choice and Area Studies," *The National Interest*, no. 36 (summer 1994): 14–22.

75 Robert Bates, contribution to *PS: Political Science and Politics*, 30, no. 2 (June 1997): 169. This is the newsletter of the American Political Science Association.

76 Prewitt, "Presidential Items," 16.

77 Stanley J. Heginbotham, "Rethinking International Scholarship: The Challenge of Transition from the Cold War Era," *Items* (SSRC, June–September 1994).

78 Robert T. Huber, Blair A. Ruble, and Peter J. Stavrakis, "Post–Cold War 'International' Scholarship: A Brave New World or the Triumph of Form over Sustance?", *Items* (SSRC, March–April 1995).

79 Heginbotham wrote: "Those who shaped the emerging institutions of international scholarship in the early years of the Cold War should have been more attentive to a range of issues involving the autonomy and integrity of scholars and scholarly institutions" ("Rethinking International Scholarship"). The response of Huber, Ruble, and Stavrakis to this truth was to ask Heginbotham to name names: "Which individuals

were inattentive to scholarly autonomy and integrity?" they ask, since such people should have "an opportunity to defend themselves" ("Post–Cold War 'International' Scholarship").

80 One good example is a book that grew out of a conference sponsored by the Latin American committee, David Collier, ed., *The New Authoritarianism in Latin America* (Princeton, N.J.: Princeton University Press, 1979).

81 Heginbotham's critics refer to "the damage done by the exceptionally strong behavioral wave that swept through the social sciences in America thirty years ago," but the damage has been at least as great from the rational-choice wave of the 1980s and 1990s.

82 Bruce Cumings and Meredith Woo-Cumings, eds., *Contending Cultures of Human Rights and Democracy* (forthcoming).

83 Also noteworthy is the similarity between the rhetoric of globalization that Ken Prewitt uses to justify the new SSRC course and that used a decade ago by Richard Lambert in his *Points of Leverage* (for which Prewitt wrote the preface; see for example 1–2, 7, 27–31). "Globalization" may be the new mantra, but maneuvering to find ways to meet the needs of our global corporations is getting old by now.

84 Wallerstein, "Open the Social Sciences," 6–7.

85 Miyoshi, *Off Center.*

86 Quoted in Diamond, *Compromised Campus,* 43.

8 EAST ASIA AND THE UNITED STATES

1 For a recent, closely reasoned account of postwar American hegemony and how it was built, see Robert Latham, *The Liberal Moment* (New York: Columbia University Press, 1997).

2 I acknowledge a debt to Immanuel Wallerstein and Giovanni Arrighi for many publications and discussions, which have shaped my view of hegemony. I say "probable" in the text because it is by no means clear to me that the rampant financial speculation of the 1980s and 1990s can be separated out as an element of hegemonic decline in the midst of a technological revolution worthy of the steam engine, namely, the information revolution, led by the United States and clearly an element of contemporary hegemonic advance.

3 See, for example, Adam Smith's review of two books on the Japanese political economy in *The New York Times Book Review,* 19 March 1995.

4 Robert Scalapino, "Perspectives on Modern Japanese Foreign Policy," in *The Foreign Policy of Modern Japan,* ed. Robert Scalapino (Berkeley: University of California Press, 1977), 400.

5 Sato, "Foundations of Modern Japanese Foreign Policy," 372.

6 Norman, *Origins of the Modern Japanese State,* 118, 144. Now compare Scalapino: Japan's "uniform spread of common culture . . . may even have been the decisive factor that enabled Japan to avoid the kinds of subordination to the West that affected much of Asia" ("Perspectives," 395). For an original and neglected application of world-system theory to Japan and China, see Frances V. Moulder, *Japan, China and the Modern World Economy* (New York: Cambridge University Press, 1977).

7 Sato, "Foundations of Modern Japanese Foreign Policy," 374.

8 For more elaboration see Cumings, "Origins and Development of the Northeast Asian Political Economy."

9   Iriye, *Power and Culture*, 65, 68. Iriye comments on the "orthodoxly Western" nature of Japan's development in northeast Asia after 1941 and finds various Japanese "cultural essence" arguments to be vacuous (95). *Shutaisei* means something like a master principle of putting Japan (or Korea) first in all things, being ever subjective about and absorbed with each nation's putative uniqueness and eternal essence (and so on).

10 H. D. Harootunian, *Overcoming Modernity* (forthcoming).

11 At the time, the leader of the small "Japan Lobby," Harry Kern, said of the U.S.-Japan relationship, " 'remote control' is best" (Harry Kern, "American Policy toward Japan," 1948, a privately circulated paper, in Pratt Papers, box 2). Kern's quotation marks on "remote control" refer to George Sansom's use of the term.

12 Cumings, *Origins*, 1:chap. 3. Iriye has made similar points in *Power and Culture.*

13 The exception is industrial reparations policy, which was a key element in the early development of the cold war in Europe, and which was rejected outright in East Asia by late 1946 because it would benefit Japan's communist or communizing neighbors at the expense of democratizing Japan.

14 See William S. Borden, *The Pacific Alliance: United States Foreign Economic Policy and Japanese Trade Recovery, 1947–1955* (Madison: University of Wisconsin Press, 1984).

15 William Borden and Michael Schaller have done original work on the "great crescent" program (Acheson and the State Department used the term several times in 1949–1950). See Borden, *Pacific Alliance*, and Michael Schaller, *The American Occupation of Japan: The Origins of the Cold War in Asia* (New York: Oxford University Press, 1985). I have set out my ideas here at greater length in *Origins*, 2:chaps. 2 and 5.

16 National Archives, 740.0019 Control (Korea) file, box 3827, Marshall's note to Acheson of 29 January 1947, attached to Vincent to Acheson, 27 January 1947.

17 John W. Dower, *Empire and Aftermath: Yoshida Shigeru and the Japanese Experience, 1878–1954* (Cambridge, Mass.: Council on East Asian Studies, Harvard University, 1979), 316. Japan lost about two million people during the entire Pacific War.

18 At the 139th meeting of the NSC, 8 April 1953, "The President expressed the belief that there was no future for Japan unless access were provided for it to the markets and raw materials of Manchuria and North China." Secretary of the Treasury Humphrey wanted the United States to be "aggressive" in providing Japan and West Germany with a secure position where they could "thrive, and have scope for their virile populations." In some respects, it seemed to him, "we had licked the two wrong nations in the last war." Whereupon, "Mr. Cutler [special assistant to the president] inquired whether the Council wished to go further than this and adopt a policy which would look to the restoration of Japan's lost colonial empire." Ike said no, probably not (Eisenhower Presidential Library, Eisenhower Papers [Whitman file], National Security Council Series, box 4).

19 Woo, *Race to the Swift*, chap. 3.

20 Senator Frank Church's speech of 22 April 1963 was probably the opening curtain in this long-running drama. See Makato Momoi, "Basic Trends in Japanese Security Policies," in *The Foreign Policy of Modern Japan*, ed. Robert Scalapino (Berkeley: University of California Press, 1977), 353.

21 See the analysis of documents from the Kennedy Library in Woo, *Race to the Swift*. A neglected older source on this period is Kim Kwan Bong, *The Korea-Japan Treaty Crisis and the Instability of the Korean Political System* (New York: Praeger, 1968). For Scalapino, Japan's new economic influence in the 1960s also "just happened" to have occurred: "Within less than three decades [after World War II], Japan had reemerged on the

Asian mainland. In Northeast Asia, reemergence took the form of a commanding economic presence in South Korea" (Scalapino, "Perspectives," 397).

22 Lester Thurow, *Head to Head: The Coming Economic Battle among Japan, Europe and America* (New York: Morrow, 1992), 84. This account is quite dated now.

23 Aaron L. Friedberg, "Ripe for Rivalry: Prospects for Peace in a Multipolar Asia," *International Security*, 18, no. 3 (winter 1993–1994): 19–23.

24 See articles in the *New York Times*, 23 May and 24 July 1993. Takashi Inoguchi offers some additional cogent reasons for the lack of regional integration in northeast Asia in "Dialectics of World Order," in *Whose World Order? Uneven Globalization and the End of the Cold War*, ed. George Sorenson and Hans-Henrik Holm (Boulder, Colo.: Westview Press, 1996), 10–12.

25 On this point see the excellent discussion by Masao Miyoshi in *Off Center*.

26 Discursive autonomy is another privilege of hegemony; the hegemonic power always has the right to speak (and in the case of England and the United States, speaks some version of Anglo-Saxon positivism), whereas the right to speak of everyone else in the system ranges from not fully guaranteed to nonexistent. Thus we get Ishihara's 1989 best-seller under the title, *The Japan That Can Say No*, and in 1996, *The China That Can Say No*.

27 Jean-Claude Derian, *America's Struggle for Leadership in Technology*, trans. Severen Schaeffer (Cambridge, Mass.: MIT Press, 1990); Clyde Prestowitz, *Trading Places* (New York: 1989). Prestowitz wrote as if Japan were already hegemonic, and claimed that the United States "had effectively lost its consumer electronics industry by the mid-1970s" and faced a "crisis" in the semiconductor industry in 1985 (92–93).

28 Derian, *America's Struggle*, 285.

29 In September 1996, the United States announced that Scandia Labs was able to build a Janus parallel supercomputer with teraflop (one trillion calculations per second) capability, by far the fastest computer in the world.

30 Derian, *America's Struggle*, 5–6.

31 Figures from David D. Hale, quoted in *Business Week* (10 April 1995): 120.

32 *New York Times*, 19 March 1994; Treasury Secretary Lloyd Bentsen told a California audience, "Asia is a continent that economically could be larger than Europe and the U.S. combined within the next fifty years." Such exaggerations assume that current growth rates can be extrapolated into the future. Similarly, in 1993 the IMF claimed that China's economy was four times larger than usually thought and therefore ranked third in the world; others have suggested that China might be the biggest economy in the world by 2010. Left unexplained is how this will happen while 70 percent of the population remains tied to a peasant agrarian economy, or what industrial or urban jobs will accommodate them if they leave the farms. See Steven Greenhouse, "New Tally of World's Economy Catapults China into Third Place," *New York Times*, 20 May 1993. For similar hyperbole see "When China Wakes," *The Economist*, 28 November 1992.

33 Richard K. Betts, "Wealth, Power and Instability: East Asia and the United States after the Cold War," *International Security*, 18, no. 3 (winter 1993–1994): 55–59.

34 Friedberg, "Ripe for Rivalry," 31–32.

35 Samuel Huntington, "Why International Primacy Matters," *International Security*, 17, no. 4 (spring 1993): 72–73, 82.

36 George Friedman and Meredith LeBard, *The Coming War with Japan* (New York: St. Martin's Press, 1991). For other suggestions that Japan might be replacing the United States as global hegemon, see Ezra Vogel, "Pax Nipponica," *Foreign Affairs*, 64, no. 4

(spring 1986): 752–67; also Ron Morse, "Japan's Drive to Pre-Eminence," *Foreign Policy,* 69 (winter 1987–1988): 3–21.

37 Betts, "Wealth, Power and Instability," 61.

38 Bruce Blair of the Brookings Institution sent me a Pentagon document, based on a 1993 consultants' report on developing a new SIOP (standard integrated operations plan) for 1994, in which the section entitled "SIOP Echo" suggested the necessity for a "nuclear expeditionary force" on call twenty-four hours a day and directed at "China and other third world states."

39 John Reilly, ed., *American Foreign Policy and Public Opinion, 1995* (Chicago: Chicago Council on Foreign Relations, 1995).

40 See Takashi Inoguchi, "Four Japanese Scenarios for the Future," *International Affairs,* 65, no. 1 (winter 1988–1989): 27.

41 Takashi Inoguchi, "Developments on the Korean Peninsula and Japan's Korea Policy," *The Korean Journal of Defense Analysis,* 5, no. 1 (summer 1993): 34.

42 Bruce Cumings, "The Seventy Years' Crisis and the Logic of Trilateralism in the New World Order," *World Policy Journal* (spring 1991), and "Comment," *World Policy Journal* (spring 1994).

43 Readers may wonder why Russia is not listed here. The reasons are given in Vladislav M. Zubok, "Russia: Between Peace and Conflict," in *Whose World Order? Uneven Globalization and the End of the Cold War,* ed. George Sorenson and Hans-Henrik Holm (Boulder, Colo.: Westview Press, 1996), 164. Zubok argues that Russia has probably already sunk into the semiperiphery of the world economy.

44 Mary Kaldor argued that people's movements in Western and Eastern Europe were essential in demolishing the Iron Curtain and ending the cold war. See "After the Cold War," *New Left Review* no. 180 (March–April 1990): 25–40.

45 U.S. Central Intelligence Agency, *World Factbook* (Washington, D.C.: 1997).

46 Polanyi, *Great Transformation,* 133.

47 See Perry Anderson, "Modernity and Revolution," *New Left Review,* no. 144 (March–April 1984): 96–113.

48 Above all John Mearsheimer, in his widely cited "Back to the Future: Instability in Europe after the Cold War," *International Security,* 15, no. 1 (summer 1990): 5–36.

49 Preeminently Karel van Wolferen, whose *Enigma of Japanese Power* not only revives prewar stereotypes about Japan and sees no watershed changes after World War II, but uses the words "German" and "Nazi" interchangeably. The best scholarship on Germany, however, argues that Germans have learned the lessons of the European civil war, and wish not only to live comfortably within a plural and diverse Europe, but have a political system structured to yield that outcome. Peter Katzenstein terms the Federal Republic a "semisovereign state," penetrated by NATO security mechanisms, "deeply enmeshed" in multilateral economic institutions like the European Community, and unyielding to reactionary attempts to rekindle a strong nationalism. It is "semisovereign" at home as well, through a political system that is remarkably decentralized and thoroughly democratized. See Peter J. Katzenstein, *Policy and Politics in West Germany: The Growth of a Semisovereign State* (Philadelphia: Temple University Press, 1987), 9–10, 15–23, 371–85.

50 For a recent book that supports many of the points I make but from a different perspective, see Latham, *Liberal Moment.*

51 Aaron Friedberg began his 1994 article with the assertion that "the dominant trend in world politics today is toward regionalization rather than globalization," somehow for-

getting to offer evidence supporting his assertion in the rest of the article. See Friedberg, "Ripe for Rivalry," 5.

52 The *Far Eastern Economic Review* has estimated this Pacific community of consumers at around 330 million, and that does not include the 150 to 200 million consumers capable of consumer-durable purchases in coastal and urban China.

53 Quoted in Drinnon, *Facing West*, 241, 315–18.

INDEX

Colonialism: in Korea, 70, 72, 73–77; legacy of, 70–71; in northeast Asia, 86–92; in Taiwan, 70, 77–82; versus U.S. imperialism, 41–42; in Vietnam, 70–71, 73, 82–86
Colonies, definition of, 70
Columbia University, 181, 183–86
Comfort women (*ianfu*), 44
Communism: impact on academic integrity, 174, 179, 257 n.48; impact on area studies, 177–78; reasons for success of North Korean, 242 n.62; role in division of Asia by United States, 63
Communist Party (China), 162, 163. *See also* Mao Zedong
Communist Party (USA), 183, 185
Communitarianism, 99
Conant, James B., 181
Conference on Soviet and Slavic Area Studies, 184–85
Containment policy: dual United States, 130; of Kennan, 3, 213–14; philosophy of, 167–68, 211–12; toward China, 169
Copeland, William, 229 n.17
"Cultural Construction of Human Rights and Democracy," 201
Cultural Revolution, 156

Dahl, Robert, 98, 110, 117–18
Datsu-a ("away from Asia"), 7
Datsun motorcar, 26, 232 n.70
Davies, John Paton, 180, 181, 189, 254 n.17
Davis, Forrest, 47
Davis, Mike, 7, 9, 10
Defense spending, in Asia, 252 n.18
Democracy: capitalist development and, 118–19; China and, 167; definition of, 117–20; in Hong Kong, 165; in Italy, 98; in Japan, 111, 118, 119, 211; Japanese model of, 168–69; in Korea, 112–17, 246 n.47; procedural, 117–18; public opinion in, 110; in South Korea, 111, 112–13; substantive justice and, 119; Taisho, 7, 25; in Taiwan, 111, 165; U.S. model of, 119–20, 168
Democratic Liberal Party (DLP) (Korea), 114, 115
Deng Xiaoping, 163; books about, 252 n.7; Ford visit with, 156–57; foreign policy of, 166–67; on multiparty systems, 162;

reform patterns of, 152, 156; reforms of, 158, 159, 161, 216; symbolism of, 157
Dennett, Tyler, 233 n.84
Depression, 1930s global: Germany and, 40–41; Japan and, 25–26, 30–31, 40–41; Korea and, 75–76; Vietnam and, 85
Derian, Jean-Claude, 218–19
Development, East Asian model of, 71, 82, 88–92, 163, 206, 252 n.16. *See also* China: economic development models for; Modernization
DeVoto, Bernard A., 204
Dews, Peter, 101
Diamond, Sigmund: on area studies development, 181; on Carnegie's anti-Left policies, 256 n.36; criticism of academics and covert intelligence, 254 n.18; on FBI investigations of academics, 182; on Russian Research Center, 258 n.61
Donovan, William "Wild Bill," 176, 180–81, 187. *See also* Office of Strategic Services (OSS)
Dower, John, 7, 44
Drinnon, Richard, 42
DuBois, Cora, 175, 180
Duke, James B., 231 n.57
Dulles, Allen, 184, 185, 190
Dulles, John Foster, 128, 129, 210
Dyads, 19

E. H. Harriman Trust, 28
Eagleberger, Lawrence, 251 n.86
Eichmann, Adolph, 258 n.57
Eisenhower, Dwight D., 128, 261 n.18
Eisenhower administration, 128–29, 213
Elshtain, Jean Bethke, 48
England, 137, 223; in China, 153; as first hegemonic power of nineteenth century, 104; Japanese alliance with (*see* Japan: alliance with England); Nietzsche on, 248 n.43; reaction to Korean War armistice, 128; U.S. replacement of hegemony of, 209. *See also* Germany: England and
Enigma of Japanese Power (Wolferen), 32, 96, 263 n.49
Enlightenment, 32, 33, 100
Enola Gay (airplane), 52, 57
Epstein, Israel, 182

Eulau, Heinz, 257 n.45
Euro, 224
European Community, 224
Exceptionalism, American, 8
Export Association Law (1925), 30
Exportation Compensation Act (1930), 233
n.94
Export-led development, 71; in China, 159–
61; in Korea, 113; Taiwan as model of, 78
Export zones, 78, 165–66

Fainsod, Merle, 184
Fairbank, John King, 175, 195–96
Fallows, James, 2–3, 110
Far Eastern Economic Review, 139–40, 264
n.52
Farley, Miriam, 30
Fat Man (bomb), 53
Federal Bureau of Investigation (FBI), 199;
investigations of academics by, 181–82,
187–88, 255 nn.21, 25, 257–58 n.52; Rus-
sian Research Center and, 181; Taylor
denunciation of academics to, 188–89,
257 n.49
Fenton, William Nelson, 180
Feuerwerker, Albert, 182
Fiske, John, 226
Fitzgerald, C. P., 153, 167, 169
Flanagan, Thomas, 146, 250 n.81
Foght, Alice, 69
Foght, Harold, 69
Ford, Betty, 156–57
Ford, Gerald R., 131, 156–57
Ford Foundation: area studies and CIA
involvement of, 186; Conference on
Soviet and Slavic Area Studies of, 184–85;
funding for area studies, 180, 196; funding
for JCCC, 195; government work of, 181
Foreign Areas Research Coordinating
Group (FAR), 195–96
Formal theory, 197, 203
Foucault, Michel: colonialism in critique of
modernity and, 72; Gutting on, 228 n.11,
229 n.20; on knowledge and power, 228
n.11; metaphor of culture of, 151, 152; on
morality, 20–21; use of Panopticon as
metaphor, 137–38
Foundation for Ethics and Meaning, 97–98

Foundations, area studies and. *See* Ford
Foundation; Rockefeller Foundation
Four Cardinal Principles, 161
Framework Agreement (1994), 123, 147–48
France: Asian industrialization plans of, 86;
economy of, 223; Germany and, 105;
intellectuals and civil society in, 106;
Japan and, 24; Vietnam and (*see* Vietnam)
Franck, Harry A., 81
Frankfurt School, 245 n.36
Free export zones, 78, 165–66
French Imperial Conference (1934–1935),
85–86
Friedberg, Aaron, 220–21, 263–64 n.51
Fused state, 106; definition of, 111; Ger-
many as, 245 n.39; Korea as, 112, 113–14;
in Taiwan and South Korea, 112

Gaddis, John, 213
Gallucci, Robert, 144
Garrison Decree, 113
Gary (Indiana), 12, 15
Gelb, Leslie, 126, 141, 247 n.9
Genealogy, 20–21
General Electric, 23, 229 n.17
General Order Number One, 63, 214
Genocide, 44–45
George III, 153, 166, 169
Gergen, David, 249 n.53
Germany, 24, 198; civil society in, 103,
104–5; East, 213; economic depression
and, 40–41; economy of, 223; England
and, 25, 94, 104, 105, 211; Enlightenment
project and, 32, 33; France and, 105; as
fused state, 245 n.39; hegemonic impact
on, 94, 209; as industrialization model,
206; as late industrializer, 18, 242–43
n.71; Marx on, 111; scholarship on, 263
n.49; *Staatswissenschaften* and, 94, 111;
West, 243–44 n.16
Gerschenkron, Alexander, 206
Gingrich, Newt, 96, 191
Gold, Thomas, 82
Gō Seinosuke, 233 n.94
Gosling, L. A. Peter, 192, 194
Gotō Shimpei, 81
Government General's Industrial Commission (1921), 64

Korea, 112–13. *See also* Intelligence-university nexus

Intelligence Authorization Act (1992), 193

Intelligence-university nexus: academics and, 257 n.45, 259 n.66; area studies creation and, 176–79 (*see also* Area studies); "black budget" for, 139; communism and, 174, 179, 257 n.48; effect on academic integrity, 199, 258 n.52, 259 n.79; FBI and (*see* FBI); firing of tenured professors and, 186–87, 257 n.48; impact of global economics on, 200, 202; liberal academics and, 185; NSEA and, 191–92; projects funded by, 256–57 n.44, 256 n.34; rationale for, 175–76; Russian Institute, 180, 181, 183–86; Russian Research Center, 180, 181. *See also names of specific universities and centers*

International Atomic Energy Agency (IAEA), 136, 139–40, 142, 249 nn.57, 67

International Monetary Fund (IMF), 216, 217, 262 n.32

International studies, during cold war, 189–91

Iriye, Akira, 7, 261 n.12; on American hegemony, 30; discursive treatment of Japan by, 27–29, 232 n.78; on Japanese and U.S. expansion, 232 n.76; on Japanese development in northeast Asia, 261 n.9; on militarist period of Japanese history, 31; on role of oil in Pearl Harbor attack, 46; "Washington system" of, 209

Ishihara, Shintaro, 6, 19, 262 n.26

Ishikawa, Father, 66–67

Isolationism, 5–7, 41

Italy: civil society in, 98, 102, 243 nn.4, 5; democracy in, 98; economy of, 223

Itō, Hirobumi, 92

Jameson, Fredric, 8, 66

Janowitz, Morris, 257 n.45

Japan, 96–97; alliance with England, 23, 24–25, 28, 30, 232 n.79; American assumptions about, 7, 207; area studies and, 178; atrocities of, 44; "big bang" development in, 86, 261–62 n.21; colonialism legacy of, 72–73; democracy in, 111, 118, 119, 168–69, 211; differences between United States and, 36–37, 207; dyad of, 19; economic depression and, 25–26, 30–31, 40–41; educational system in, 89; Enlightenment and, 32; export planning and, 233 n.94; feudalism in, 244 n.19; France and, 24; General Order Number One and, 63, 214; hegemony and, 26–32, 94, 205, 206, 209, 229 n.21, 260 n.6, 262 n.27; individualism in, 32; industrialization in, 14, 31, 210; industrialization phases of, 23–26, 242–43 n.71; investments of, 216–17; isolationism of, 6–7; Korean expansion of, 29, 41, 70, 72, 73–77; Korean War impact on, 213, 214; labor habits in, 24; labor movement in, 119; late development theory in, 242–43 n.71; liberal view of, 2–3; Manchurian expansion of, 25, 29, 41; mining and, 13–14; national ideology in prewar, 90; normalization of relations with North Korea, 144; normalization of relations with South Korea, 216; normalization of relations with United States, 215–16; in northeast Asia, 119, 215–20, 232 n.78, 261 n.9; North Korea–U.S. NPT conflict and, 146; as number two, 16; Pacific War and (*see* Pacific War); police surveillance system in, 89; political economy in prewar, 90–91; political parties in, 114, 115; postwar industrial revival of, 31–32, 210–11; quotations about, 16–19; regional political economy and, 92; reparations, 261 n.13; Russia and, 24; societal universals and, 93–94; as subimperial power, 15; technological supremacy of, 218–19, 229 n.14; textile industry and, 14; trade and, 30–31; trilateral partnerships and, 27, 207–8; U.S. investments in, 23; war crimes of, 64; Western images of, 22. *See also* Hiroshima; Iriye, Akira; Korea; Nagasaki; Pearl Harbor; Racism: against Japanese; Taiwan; United States

Jefferson, Thomas, 99, 102

Jenner, W. J. F., 162, 251 n.3

Jiang Qing, 157, 158

Jiang Zemin, 159, 161, 163

John Reed Club, 182

Johns Hopkins University, 195

Johnson, Chalmers, 110, 213

Wittfogel, Karl, 188, 189
Wo-Lap Lam, Willy, 251 n.5
Wolff, Robert Lee, 255 n.25
Wŏnsan Oil Refinery, 13
Working Committee on Attitudes Toward
    Unconventional Weapons, 257 n.44
World Bank, 160, 216
World system, basic, 11, 202, 222–23
World War I, impact on understanding of
    war, 39–40
Wouk, Herman, 35
Wright, Quincy, 39
Wu, Rong-I, 80
WuDunn, Sheryl, 251 n.1

Yale University, 254 n.18
Yamamoto, Isoroku: on *bushido* and war,
    236 n.46; on Pearl Harbor, 46, 235 n.36;
    on *Time* cover, 26, 31

Yeltsin, Boris, 223
Yi, Prince, 85
Yin, K. Y., 80
Yŏngbyŏn, 135; energy and, 133–36; impact
    on foreign policy, 139; Kim Il Sung freez-
    ing of, 250 n.74, 251 n.86; Korean purpose
    for, 249 n.61. *See also* Nonproliferation
    treaty (NPT)
Yongjo, King, 153
Yoshida Shigeru, 213
Yukichi, Fukuzawa, 6
Yusin system, 113

Zagoria, Donald, 186, 256 n.43
Zhangjiagang, 163
Zhao Ziyang, 158–59, 164
Zhu Rongji, 164

Bruce Cumings is Norman and Edna Freehling Professor
of History at the University of Chicago. He has won
numerous awards and is the author of the acclaimed books
Korea's Place in the Sun, War and Television, and *The
Origins of the Korean War.*

Library of Congress Cataloging-in-Publication Data
Cumings, Bruce.
Parallax visions : making sense of American-East Asian
relations at the end of the century / Bruce Cumings.
p.   cm. — (Asia-Pacific, culture, politics, and society)
Includes index.
ISBN 0-8223-2276-5 (cloth : alk. paper)
1. East Asia—Relations—United States. 2. United States—
Relations—East Asia. I. Title. II. Title: Making sense of
American-East Asian relations at the end of the century.
III. Series: Asia-Pacific.
DS518.8.C76 1999   303.18'27305—dc21   98-32017 CIP